THE PATH TO GENEVA

THE PATH TO GENEVA

THE QUEST FOR A PERMANENT AGREEMENT, 1996–2004

BY YOSSI BEILIN

Contributing Editor: David Silver

RDV Books
New York

Published by RDV Books/Akashic Books
©2004 Yossi Beilin

Layout by Johnny Temple
Israel map by Alexis Fleisig
Cover photo ©Joel Robine/Getty Images

ISBN: 0-9719206-3-X
Library of Congress Control Number: 2003116635
Printed in Canada
First printing

RDV Books/Akashic Books
PO Box 1456
New York, NY 10009
Akashic7@aol.com
www.akashicbooks.com

For Daniela

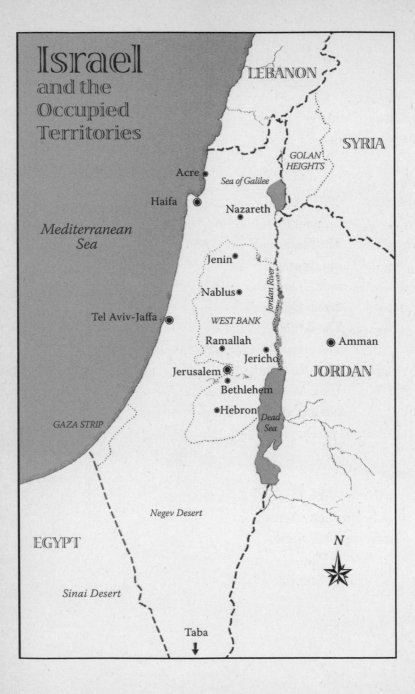

Israel
and the Occupied Territories

LEBANON

SYRIA

GOLAN
HEIGHTS

Acre

Sea of Galilee

Haifa

Nazareth

*Mediterranean
Sea*

Jenin

Nablus

Jordan River

Tel Aviv-Jaffa

WEST BANK

Ramallah

Amman

Jericho

Jerusalem

JORDAN

Bethlehem

Hebron

*Dead
Sea*

GAZA STRIP

Negev Desert

EGYPT

N

Sinai Desert

Taba

TABLE OF CONTENTS

TIMELINE OF EVENTS

October 30, 1991: The Madrid Conference, sponsored by the United States and the Soviet Union in the wake of the Gulf War, initiates official talks between Israel and a Jordanian-Palestinian delegation.

June 23, 1992: The Labor Party wins general elections and Yitzhak Rabin becomes Prime Minister.

September 13, 1993: The Oslo Declaration of Principles is signed on the White House lawn. The two sides formally recognize one another for the first time, and an interim period of Palestinian self-rule is proposed.

May 4, 1994: The Cairo Agreement, also known as Oslo I or the Gaza-Jericho Agreement, is signed in Egypt. It formally establishes limited Palestinian autonomy in Gaza and Jericho, and sets up the Palestinian Authority.

July 1, 1994: Yasser Arafat returns to Gaza from Tunis.

October 26, 1994: A peace treaty between Israel and Jordan is signed in the Arava Desert.

September 28, 1995: The Interim Agreement on the West Bank and Gaza Strip, known as Oslo II, is signed at the White House. Defines length of interim period of Palestinian self-rule and sets a deadline for the signing of a permanent agreement five years after the Cairo agreement (i.e., May 4, 1999). Sets out timetable of Israeli withdrawals from the West Bank, which is divided into three zones: Area A (full Palestinian control), Area B (Palestinian administrative and Israeli security control), and Area C (full Israeli control).

October 31, 1995: The Beilin–Abu Mazen Understandings, which establish the principles for a permanent agreement, are completed.

November 4, 1995: Rabin assassinated by Yigal Amir in Tel Aviv; Shimon Peres becomes Prime Minister.

May 29, 1996: Likud leader Benjamin Netanyahu is elected Prime Minister by a narrow margin over Peres.

September 24, 1996: Violence and unrest erupt in the territories after Netanyahu decides to open a tunnel along the Western Wall, adjacent to the foundation of the al-Aqsa Mosque.

January 15, 1997: The Hebron Protocol is signed by Netanyahu and Arafat; it stipulates Israeli withdrawal from most of Hebron, which will be divided into two zones, and revises the timetable of redeployments from the rest of the West Bank originally specified by the interim agreement.

October 15, 1998: The Wye River Memorandum is signed by Netanyahu and Arafat, under the auspices of President Clinton, near Washington. It modifies for a second time the redeployment schedule first laid out in the interim agreement.

May 4, 1999: The deadline specified in the 1995 interim agreement for the conclusion of permanent status negotiations.

May 17, 1999: Ehud Barak is elected Prime Minister and forms a government led by the Labor Party.

September 4, 1999: The Sharm el-Sheikh Memorandum is signed in Egypt by Arafat and Barak. It sets out the third revision of the redeployment plan originally described in the interim agreement of September 1995, and sets a new deadline of September 2000 for the conclusion of final status talks.

January 3–10, 2000: Peace talks between Israel and Syria take place in Shepherdstown, West Virginia.

May 24, 2000: Barak withdraws the Israel Defense Forces (IDF) from Lebanon unilaterally, ending the two-decades long Israeli military presence in south Lebanon.

July 11–25, 2000: Lengthy talks are held at Camp David between Barak and Arafat, under the auspices of President Clinton, but no agreement is reached.

September 28, 2000: Ariel Sharon, accompanied by members of the Likud Knesset faction and policemen, visits the Temple Mount in Jerusalem.

September 29, 2000: Violence erupts in Israel and the territories following Sharon's visit to the Temple Mount, and four Palestinians are killed, marking the beginning of the second Intifada.

October 16–17, 2000: A summit is held at Sharm el-Sheikh between Barak and Arafat, with the participation of Clinton, Egyptian President Hosni Mubarak, and Kofi Annan, calling for an end to the violence and a return to negotiations.

January 21–27, 2001: Intensive talks take place between Palestinian and Israeli negotiators at the Egyptian Red Sea resort of Taba.

February 26, 2001: Ariel Sharon beats Barak handily in a special election for Prime Minister, and forms a national unity government with the Labor Party.

March 29, 2002: Israel launches Operation Defensive Shield in the West Bank, moving armed units into major Palestinian cities.

January 28, 2003: The Likud coalition wins an overwhelming Knesset majority in general elections; Sharon organizes a new right-wing government.

April 30, 2003: The United States unveils its own plan for resuming the peace process, known as the "Road Map."

October 12, 2003: The Geneva Draft Permanent Agreement is signed in Jordan.

Acknowledgments

I would like to thank the friends who have assisted me in recent years who are referred to in this book, and those who have helped with the preparation of the book itself: my partners at the ECF, particularly Dr. Yair Hirschfeld, Dr. Ron Pundak, Dr. Nimrod Novick, and Boaz Karni; those people who have served as my advisors in recent years—Shlomo Gur, Daniel Levi Chaim Weizmann, and Amir Abramowitz; Orit Shani, the head of my bureau; Hagit Ofran, the first person to read this book, who also helped me with the research; Shira Herzog for her extensive assistance; Danny Goldberg, Victor Goldberg, and Robert Greenwald from RDV Books; and Jonathan Shainin and Johnny Temple from Akashic Books for their valuable editorial contributions.

The story told here is incomplete, of course. I have naturally dealt with events in which I participated in greater detail (and not everything I participated in can yet be shared with the reader), while I have tried to fill in the missing pieces with the aid of those who were present at the time. Anyone wishing to understand the complete picture will have to read other books written about these years from the Palestinian side, the American side, and the Israeli side. There is no doubt that the same events will be seen in a different light by different observers. In the final analysis, what is important is the "bottom line"—the agreements and their implementation. Nevertheless, the story of events, as all those connected with the work see it, could in the future serve the decision-makers both in the Middle East and in other regions. Human nature is, after all, much the same all over. Our partial success, the mistakes we made, could, perhaps, contribute something to those who will never relinquish hope.

INTRODUCTION

I GREW UP IN A HOME IMBUED with the national spirit of Israel. My grand-father on my mother's side was a delegate to a number of Zionist Congresses and was very close to Chaim Weizmann, the first President of the state of Israel. My father was a member of the Haganah for decades, and participated in the War of Independence as a soldier of the Israel Defense Forces (IDF). When my parents bought each other books for their birthdays, they used to write above the dedication, next to the date, the number of years since our "redemption"—that is, since the founding of the state.

I was on the David Ben-Gurion side of the political spectrum—Ben-Gurion, the progenitor of all future Labor Party politicians—as distinguished from the Irgun side, led by Menachem Begin, who eventually became the first Likud Prime Minister. The arguments at school were less about the question of Israel's character in the future than about questions concerning the past. These discussions mostly revolved around the disputes between the Haganah and the Etzel (a Hebrew acronym for "national military organization," commonly known as the "Irgun"). Several decades later, these old arguments continue to influence Israeli politics.

In 1967, I fought in the Six-Day War, less than a year after being conscripted into the army. I was a Morse Code Radio Operator, and my job was to recruit aviation operations to assist the armored brigade to which I was attached. I was extremely proud to be participating in the capture of both the Sinai Peninsula and the Golan Heights within those six short days. In the War of Attrition, which commenced immediately after the Six-Day War, I was north of the Suez Canal. I had no second thoughts whatsoever at that time about our mission. I held the Prime Minister, Levi Eshkol, in great esteem and I admired the charismatic Minister of Defense, Moshe Dayan. I was convinced that it was impossible to prevent the war, and that the right thing to do was to wait for the "telephone call" from the Arab leaders to reach an agreement with them, as Dayan had advised.

The 1973 Yom Kippur War was the decisive event in the formation of my ideological beliefs. I served in this war as a member of the reserve forces for about six months in the General Headquarters, and even though I was not part of the combat forces, I was nevertheless witness to a traumatic picture. I listened to the main radio networks, I watched the Chief of Staff, David Elazar, and the other generals, and I saw that we were on the brink of collapse. I understood how senseless the whole discussion about "security borders" had been, the futility of the 1967 occupation of territories in terms of offering us any real protection, and how different things would have been had we withdrawn from those territories, or most of them, unilaterally, in the event that no peace agreements could be reached. I was transformed from a fairly typical representative of the moderate establishment into an active "dove."

My political activities ever since have been devoted, for the most part, to convincing others of my opinions, to searching for possible partners for dialogue, and to examining ways to reach an agreement, primarily with the Palestinians.

David Ben-Gurion was a man whom I greatly admired as a child. Even during my military service, when I learned not just about his achievements but also about his serious errors, I continued to view him as the most significant political figure in Israel, a true leader. After the Six-Day War, he recommended giving back the territories we had captured, apart from Jerusalem (there were other proposals, in which he added Hebron and the Golan Heights in Syria to his exceptions), and I understood how right he had been in suggesting this. Other people who were ahead of their times, and with whom I came to identify after the Yom Kippur War, were Yitzhak Ben-Aharon (a former government minister and the former Secretary of the Histadrut, the labor union founded in the 1920s), who as early as 1971 referred to the territories which we had occupied as "burning coals" and proposed that we give them back; and Lova Eliav, Secretary-General of the Labor Party in the early '70s, who expressed resolute positions against Israel's continuing hold over the territories, in opposition to the opinion of Prime Minister Golda Meir, and was forced to resign from his office. In 1972, Eliav wrote *Eretz Hazvi* ("The Deer Country"), a book that became a guide for many doves in Israel who saw themselves as part of the Zionist peace camp.

We doves believe it is essential that Israel take a persistent and proactive approach toward making peace with our neighbors.

Since the Yom Kippur War in 1973, there has been no significant change in my beliefs. In 1975, I became an active member of the Young Guard of the Labor Party; in 1977, I became the spokesman for the Labor Party; and in 1979, I was elected, in addition to my position as spokesman, to be the International Secretary of the Young Guard and the chairman of its political committee. In the course of these positions, I met many of my peers in sister parties around the world; I was also exposed to the events taking place in Spain and Portugal, and to the events in South America which was then ruled by dictators and officers; I became aware of the developments in East Timor; etc. Such exposure enabled me to compare the conflict in the Middle East with other conflicts, and it made my attempts to propose solutions easier. (I had learned, for example, of the solution provided in the Aland Islands, an area once bitterly contested by Sweden and Finland; and of the solution to the problem of Trieste between Italy and Yugoslavia.)

It is my belief that serious reconciliation between Israelis and Palestinians is essential; whatever actions can work toward stemming the hostilities must be taken, in order to create a fair and livable solution for the Palestinians within the inarguable need for complete Israeli security. It is clear to me that a permanent peace has to be sought for Israel to grow and prosper, as well as for the amelioration of the living conditions of Palestinians.

For a period of seven years (1977–1984), I accompanied Shimon Peres, then the Chairman of the Labor Party, on his travels around the world. I met with many world leaders in both public and private meetings; I was exposed to their opinions and beliefs, and this enabled me to understand the international dimensions of the conflict in the Middle East—and the degree of willingness of others to assist in achieving a solution. There is no doubt that this experience played a significant role in the formation of my approach to final status agreements and in finding possible partners for these agreements.

My status in the Labor Party was somewhat strange. On the one hand, I was the official spokesman for the party, and the person closest to the party's leader; on the other hand, as one of the heads of the Young Guard in the Labor Party, I expressed minority opinions with respect to withdrawing from the occupied territories in the West Bank and Gaza, and with respect to conceding the Golan Heights. I was part of a group that included Haim Ramon (who later served as the Chairman of the Histadrut and as Minister of the Interior) and Avraham Burg (who became Chairman of the Jewish Agency and the Speaker of the Knesset). This group formulated unequivocal opinions on the issues of separation between religion and state, reform in the Histadrut, and full equality for Arabs and Jews in Israel. Within ten years, our minority opinions were to become the official positions of the Labor Party, and in the 1990s this perspective came to dominate the Labor Party and, consequently, Israeli politics.

In 1981, I set up a group called Feedback in the Labor Party. This group was dovish in nature and met frequently with Palestinians—often with the East Jerusalem leadership headed by Faisal Husseini, Hanan Ashrawi, and others. I continued with these meetings when I served as Government Secretary, Director-General of the Ministry of Foreign Affairs, member of the Knesset, and Deputy Finance Minister. In 1988, after the PLO Council passed a resolution in favor of adopting UN Security Council Resolution 242—passed in the wake of the 1967 Six-Day War and providing the basis for a two-state settlement—I called upon the government of Israel to recognize the PLO and to open negotiations with it. The Prime Minister, Likud's Yitzhak Shamir, asked Shimon Peres, the Foreign Minister, to fire me, but Peres refused to do so. (As a consequence, the Likud initiated a draft law according to which the Prime Minister would be able to dismiss deputy ministers without the permission of the ministers who are their direct superiors.) As a Knesset member, I made efforts to repeal a law that prohibited talks with members of the PLO; my attempts came to no avail, however, until 1992, when Rabin's government adopted this measure.

In the second half of the '80s and the first half of the '90s, I was one of the most prominent political spokesmen in Israeli politics. I wrote and gave interviews frequently, both inside the country and abroad. When Terje Roed-Larsen, a member of the Norwegian research institute FAFO, visited Israel in April 1992, he asked to meet with me, and he proposed Oslo as a possible venue for holding quiet, informal negotiations. When I was appointed Deputy Foreign Minister, and when I realized that the talks in Washington were going nowhere, I took advantage of the proposal made by Larsen, and I initiated what was to become known as the "Oslo process."

In 1997, I set up the Movement for Withdrawal from Lebanon, which was instrumental in shifting public opinion in Israel in advance of our government's decision to make a unilateral withdrawal from Lebanon. I had written and spoken about it since the beginning of the war in 1982 and I believed that the formation of the government led by Peres in 1984 would be conducive to a total withdrawal from Lebanon. The decision in January 1985—to withdraw from Lebanon, but to keep the security zone—was a big achievement. I was the one, as the cabinet secretary, who broke the news to the nation. We read the decision of the cabinet and Peres explained it later—a very exciting moment in my career. Then, when it became quite clear that remaining in the security zone would not help us, I expressed my view from time to time that we should withdraw totally from Lebanon and not be afraid of the consequences. That if we left then we would not have to confront Hezbollah directly—because I believed that Hezbollah was a local Lebanese force, and if we withdrew, they would not continue to fight us in the Galilee.

Between 1985 and 1990 the death toll in Lebanon had been relatively low. It grew worse after 1990, however, and when I became a minister in the Rabin cabinet in 1995, I again suggested we have a debate in the cabinet about a total withdrawal from Lebanon. This was rejected by Rabin. During Operation Grapes of Wrath under Peres in April 1996—when Israel launched a massive bombardment of Southern Lebanon in retaliation for Hezbollah's Katyusha rocket attacks on Northern Israel—I suggested Peres use this opportunity and conclude the operation by leaving Lebanon. I must say that he was momentarily quite tempted to do so, and then he said firmly, "No, no, no. I am not doing that"—especially when the army was so much against it.

When Likud came into power in May 1996 and Labor became the opposition party, I convened a transparty meeting in my room in the Knesset with people from Likud and other political parties, suggesting the formation of a public movement for unilateral withdrawal from Lebanon. Soon after, tragically, there was a two-helicopter collision in which seventy-three soldiers were killed on their way to Lebanon. That added immediate momentum to our movement. I supported the group "The Four Mothers," made up primarily of women, who demonstrated to get out of Lebanon. I built a political lobby out of various groups and raised the issue time after time in the plenary of the Knesset. It was not long after this, in 1997, that I created the Movement for Withdrawal from Lebanon. We organized many demonstrations and media events, and public support for withdrawal jumped from under twenty percent to over seventy percent in less than two years. Barak was convinced to make the withdrawal his most important commitment during the elections.

The Oslo Agreement was an interim settlement, which was due to have ended on May 4, 1999, exactly five years after the agreement for the transfer of the Gaza Strip and the Jericho area to the Palestinians. It was a phased agreement, with a time frame that became altered by force of circumstances, and even by means of an agreement (it was decided, for example, in the Wye Agreement of October 1998, to defer Israel's further redeployments). Even so, these changes were still within the five-year framework of the interim agreement. When the five years came to an end, Benjamin Netanyahu was the Prime Minister of Israel. Netanyahu, a Likud leader, had opposed every peace initiative from Rabin and Peres. He undoubtedly perceived it as an achievement that in the three years he was in office, nothing had been agreed upon, and the negotiations for the final status settlement had not even commenced.

Ehud Barak, ex-General and the Labor Prime Minister following Netanyahu's tenure, intended to iron things out, to prevent a situation in which the interim period would come to its end with no final status settlement and no deadline for such a settlement. In the only agreement that he signed as Prime Minister, the Sharm el-Sheikh Agreement, it was determined that by September 2000 (exactly seven years after the signing of the Oslo Agreement on the White House lawn) the final status settlement would be signed.

The subsequent failure of the Camp David talks and the outbreak of an Intifada once again created a situation in which there was no target date for the final status settlement. All the attempts made in 2001 and 2002 to offer the parties a respectable way out of the cycle of violence came to naught.

The current "Road Map"—proposed by the Quartet (U.S., Russia, the European Union, and the UN) in late 2002, and submitted to the parties in the spring of 2003—extends the Oslo process to the end of 2005, and adds another interim stage to it: a Palestinian state with temporary borders. This proposal is particularly suitable for current Israeli Prime Minister Ariel Sharon, who for many years seems to have believed that the solution to the Palestinian problem is a Bantustan-style state—in other words, a state whose sovereignty is severely limited, surrounded on all sides by another country, which is geographically divided. Sharon understands that no Palestinian partner will be found for a final status settlement of this nature, and he hopes that if this state is indeed set up, it will then be possible to transform the Israeli-Palestinian conflict from a national conflict into a run-of-the-mill border conflict, which could go on for decades. He does not understand that this type of Palestinian state would not only be a problem for the Palestinians themselves, but would also pose a grave danger to Israel, since it would be unable to last, in the long term; accordingly, the perpetuation of the state's existence would be tantamount to the perpetuation of the conflict with Israel.

The Palestinians are afraid to enter into this trap, as they see it, of the temporary state, and for this reason, efforts will be made on their part not to reach it. This situation, whereby Ariel Sharon's Israel does not want to reach a final status settlement and the Palestinian leadership does not want to reach an interim agreement, could very well be the demise of the Road Map. The way to turn the Road Map into a realistic option is to agree *in advance* on a framework for the permanent solution. The Geneva Agreement, unveiled on October 12, 2003, may now be the only way to keep the possibility of a lasting peace on track.

THE POLITICAL PROCESSES IN THE MIDDLE EAST have always been closely intertwined with political processes in Washington. Not only did President Jimmy Carter's actions make peace between Israel and Egypt possible, the Oslo process—which took place without any direct American involvement—could not have been realized without the efforts of President Bill Clinton, much like the peace agreement signed by Israel and Jordan in 1994. Presidential attention, the President's time, his willingness to invest in the Middle East, his sympathy or dislike toward leadership in the area—all these are key factors in determining the future of the Middle East.

President Clinton became very involved in Middle East politics. He had an emotional connection to the subject, and throughout his years in the White House, his administration was highly driven to resolve the Israeli-Arab conflict. Efforts by Russia and other European countries to mediate or become otherwise involved in the situation were (usually) politely declined by the Clinton administration. Thus, any void formed as a result of other White House priorities was left unfilled, and the process was slowed down.

This book deals largely with the political process during Clinton's last four years in the White House, while in Israel Benjamin Netanyahu and Ehud Barak presided as Prime Ministers. My narrative is not presented in a strict chronological sequence; rather, each chapter explores either a major event (i.e., the 2001 Taba talks, Camp David) or the impact of specific individuals (i.e., Clinton, Netanyahu, Barak) on the peace process. I have also addressed the implications that the events of September 11, 2001 have had on the U.S. government's attitude toward the Middle East, as well as on the war Israel has declared on the Palestinian Authority. This story concludes with the achievement of the Geneva Draft Agreement on October 12, 2003. The book was written primarily for myself. It is the soul-searching of someone who helped to instigate the Oslo process, the Beilin–Abu Mazen Understandings, and participated in innumerable negotiations over the past two decades.

There is an inherent ambivalence in this project. On the one hand, I am very sure that I have been doing the right thing, because I believe that there is still an opportunity to have two states in the land of Israel—and that this opportunity may disappear. Perhaps at a certain point, because of the demographics, there will be further opposition by the Palestinian side which will negate the idea of a Palestinian state. For some of the Jews on the right, this might yield a sigh of relief. For me, it could be the end of the process. This is why I am so sure of what I'm doing. On the other hand, there is no question that the eruption of violence on the Palestinian side in September 2000—with or without Ariel Sharon's provocation—was a very problematic development. Not totally unexpected, but for sure, intolerable. I could not ignore the critics who said we believed that if we signed an agreement, and even if we later breached it, the Palestinians would not retaliate with violence. Violence should not have been an option, but it was.

This book attempts to reach a better understanding of what went wrong, to see how we can try to overcome the very different readings of reality by each of the two sides, and mainly, to explore how to strengthen this thin layer of ice called the *peace process*. This is my personal breakdown of the actual origins of the current Middle East peace process, in which I was intimately involved for well over a decade. I want to clarify how we progressively tried to create the right conditions for a true rapprochement between the two sides and a formula for a long-lasting peace.

CHAPTER 1
2001: A LITTLE TOO LATE

ACROSS THE TABLE SAT Abu Ala, Yasser Abed Rabbo, Dr. Saeb Erekat, Mohammed Dahlan, Dr. Nabil Sha'ath, and Hassan Asfour. On our side were Shlomo Ben-Ami, Yossi Sarid, Amnon Lipkin-Shahak, Gilead Sher, and myself. We were discussing Jerusalem and the refugees, borders and settlements, security arrangements and water, but with a slightly strange feeling. It was January 2001 in Taba, the Egyptian Red Sea resort. The election contest between Ehud Barak and Ariel Sharon was only a few weeks away, and Sharon was ahead in the polls.

We were sitting in the Taba Hilton, which had come to life after a few months of desolation, discussing the core issues of the Israeli-Palestinian dispute. Reporters waited in the foyer below with their cameras and tape recorders, attempting to wrest from us any snippet of information—news of some progress or crisis. To the chagrin of the media, most of us rushed past with stern expressions on our faces, saying that we had nothing to announce at this stage. Outside an end-of-January cold, which did not prevent a few brave tourists from swimming in the hotel pool, gripped this usually hot spot.

Inside that room, there was unquestionably the capability to make peace. But this was very much in contrast to the situation outside the room, across Israel, the West Bank, and much of the Arab world. The surreal sensation that prevailed in the conference room stemmed from the disparity between the progress in the discussions—the feeling shared by both sides that we were closer than ever to a permanent agreement—and a sense of foreboding that all this could not yet be realized.

On one side sat an authorized Israeli team, ministers who represented the most moderate line in Barak's government. Yossi Sarid had resigned from his post as Minister of Education, but was asked to join the delegation. A veteran dove used to minority positions, he was firm but skeptical about reaching a permanent agreement at this juncture. Shlomo Ben-Ami had risen like a meteor from academia in 1996, won wide public acclaim, and became the Barak government's Foreign Minister following David Levy's resignation. He often proposed creative policies in the political discussions in which he participated. Amnon Lipkin-Shahak, Minister of Tourism and Transport, was one of the pleasant surprises of Barak's government—judicious, responsible, moderate, and well-liked by the Palestinians. Throughout his tenure he behaved like a guest stuck in our house, unsure whether to remain for long; but while he was with us he dispensed doses of sanity. Gilead Sher played a central and vital role in the peace process; he participated in the negotiations on the interim agreement and had become very close to Barak, eventually serving as his Chief of Staff.

The Palestinian delegation at Taba was headed by Abu Ala, the Chairman of the Palestinian Legislative Council, and was composed of veterans from several earlier rounds of negotiation. Abu Ala had conducted the Oslo talks with us, and in 2003 would become the second Palestinian Prime Minister. He was the most experienced Palestinian negotiator, but had been restrained and reserved at Camp David. Saeb Erekat, Minister of Local Government, jokingly described himself as an "Indian"—the man who gets the work done. He was the translator, the spokesman, the writer of perfect English, and the walking memory of the political process. His debut in the international arena came when he participated in the 1991 Madrid Conference—and took the controversial step of draping a kaffiyeh around his shoulders to demonstrate his support for Arafat. In the early '90s he was considered an extremist, but over the years has come to be regarded by Israel as among those Palestinian leaders most committed to peace. His daughter joined the "Seeds of Peace" project, which brings together Israeli and Palestinian teenagers. Dr. Erekat lives in Jericho, in the home where he was raised. He is one of the few leaders in the Palestinian Authority who did not come from Tunis. In effect, he is the unchallenged leader of Jericho and one of the most prominent negotiators on the Palestinian side. He is a true intellectual, with an M.A. in Political Science from the University of San Francisco and a Ph.D. from Bradford University in Britain. He lectured at Al-Najah University in Nablus, and he has told me that he misses teaching and research.

Nabil Sha'ath, Minister of Planning and International Cooperation, was considered Arafat's chief spokesman on external affairs; a moderate man, a permanent participant at negotiations with the Israelis, and very committed to peace. Dr. Sha'ath is sometimes called "the Palestinian Abba Eban." He is considered the most eloquent Palestinian spokesman, and has maintained relations with various Israelis since the '80s. Sha'ath, born in Safed in 1938, moved as a child to Jaffa, and spent his youth in Egypt. He has a Ph.D. in Economics and was a lecturer at the American University in Beirut. He grew up in an upper-middle-class family and is affluent in his own right, as the manager of an Egyptian technology firm.

Sha'ath was not involved in the military activities of the PLO. He was elected to the Palestinian Parliament with a large majority in his constituency in the Gaza Strip, but derived most of his power from his closeness to Arafat—although he is not considered to be among those who might succeed Arafat. Undoubtedly one of the most western PLO leaders, Sha'ath lived for several years in the U.S., where some of his family still resides. He has an excellent sense of humor and is a sensitive person, scarred by the trauma of his wife's death in a road accident. In 1995 he remarried, and I was one of the Israelis who attended his East Jerusalem wedding.

Sha'ath is a great believer in a political solution to the conflict, and was committed to it long before many of his colleagues in the PLO. I have spent dozens of hours talking with him in various places around the world, particularly in his Gaza office and at his home on the beach. Sha'ath was responsible for the refugee issue in the negotiations, though he represents a totally different type of refugee: He nostalgically recalls his childhood in Jaffa, but has no harsh memories of the 1948 war since by that time he was already living in Egypt. This unusual position allows him tremendous commitment to the issue without being constrained by an emotional involvement which could impede his handling of the negotiations.

Hassan Asfour, a former member of the Palestinian cabinet, participated in the Oslo talks and those that led to the 1995 Beilin–Abu Mazen Understandings, and headed the Palestinian Authority's negotiations department.

Mohammed Dahlan was the only one of the circle in Taba who had come from within the security apparatus. At the Camp David talks he was considered one of the people pushing hardest for a permanent settlement. During the first Palestinian Intifada in the late 1980s, he made some harsh statements and was thought to be linked indirectly with actions against Israel. Younger than his colleagues, and with a forceful personality, he presented himself at one time as disillusioned with peace, but has since "returned to the fold." He was very close to Abu Mazen until 1998, when they fell out over the details of a proposed prisoner release in the Wye Agreement. They later reconciled, and Dahlan was put in charge of internal security when Abu Mazen became Prime Minister.

I SERVED AS MINISTER OF JUSTICE in Ehud Barak's government, and considered myself to be one of the peace camp's longest-serving soldiers. After the Yom Kippur War in 1973, I believed the only possible solution to the ongoing conflict was to establish a Palestinian state next to Israel, based on the 1967 borders. In all the positions I held from 1977 onwards I did everything within my power to promote a political settlement. In 1992, as I have mentioned, I launched the Oslo process—the secret talks between representatives of Israel and the PLO which led to the signing of the Declaration of Principles on the White House lawn on September 13, 1993. In 1995, Abu Mazen and I completed the draft framework agreement intended to serve as the basis for a final status settlement between Israel and the Palestinians.

Abu Mazen, whose brief turn as the first Palestinian Prime Minister in 2003 was thwarted by Arafat, was my counterpart in the Oslo process. He was always considered "Number Two" to Arafat, though never officially. He was behind their negotiators, as I was behind ours; he gave guidelines to

Abu Ala, and I directed Yair Hirschfeld and Ron Pundak; that is, until the negotiations became a more official project. Abu Mazen and I did not actually meet until September 13, 1993, when we came face-to-face in Washington after the signing ceremony. It was a very pleasant meeting. He came to see Peres and myself and we exchanged words.

A month later, I met with Yasser Arafat in Tunisia and suggested that we create and employ a kind of back channel to continue the work of Oslo. The idea was to do something parallel to the official work on the interim solution—just to see whether it was possible to work with Arafat's people toward a permanent solution. We thought it might be possible to bypass the interim stages and have a permanent settlement well ahead of the existing schedule. Arafat said that he wanted Abu Mazen to serve as my counterpart. It was his decision, and I had no reservations about it. In the following two years, Abu Mazen asked two Palestinians living in London, Hussein Agha and Ahmad Khalidi, to negotiate an agreement with my people, Hirschfeld and Pundak.

Abu Mazen didn't have to be elected. He was never in the government nor the Parliament. Even this early in the game, it was quite clear that he was not enthusiastic about working under Arafat. There was respect on both sides, though to the best of my understanding they were never close friends. But because Abu Mazen was one of the founding fathers he always had an advantage that others didn't.

In late October 1995, a meeting was held at my office in Tel Aviv to conclude the negotiations on the draft framework agreement. Along with Abu Mazen were Agha and Khalidi. Hirschfeld and Pundak were also present, as well as Hassan Asfour and Nimrod Novick. It was a very emotional moment when we could finally declare: "We have finished the job, including the maps and the text." We raised a toast, hugged, and kissed. But we did not sign anything. Since it was not an official agreement, we had to present it to Arafat and Rabin before signing.

Five days later, Rabin was assassinated.

AT TABA IN JANUARY 2001, I asked myself how much more time would pass before two delegations like these would be sitting together again, discussing the permanent settlement, if we didn't reach an agreement within a few days. But the two delegations had arrived with their hands tied. In order to reach a framework agreement, each side had to go a step further. For us, the elections loomed, and we predicted that a concession was liable to exact an electoral toll. The Palestinians, for their part, feared that even if an agreement was reached, Ariel Sharon would nevertheless defeat Barak and, as he had already announced, disavow the agreement, considering Palestinian concessions made at Taba to be merely an opening position for future talks.

Nonetheless, we held serious negotiations. We did not waste time—we talked, argued, and made agreements even during meals and breaks. On weekdays, we Israelis would cross the border at Taba, traveling from the Princess Hotel in Eilat, where we were staying, to the Taba Hilton; while on Saturdays, the Palestinians came to visit us at our hotel.

Troubled by optimistic reports that appeared in the press, right-wing Israeli demonstrators, carrying placards demanding we cease negotiations with the Palestinians, gathered at the entrance to our hotel. One day, members of the Israeli left came to Taba in a Peace Now ship, and we all went out to greet it. Peace Now ("Shalom Achshav") was founded in 1978 by 348 reserve officers of the Israel Defense Forces who believed that only a negotiated end to the conflict in the Middle East could bring true security to Israel and her people. The picture that was published in the newspapers the next day of Israeli and Palestinian ministers waving together was one of the last positive glimmers of the peace process at that time.

For many years, at least since 1967, Israel's left has been defined by a willingness to compromise on the issue of land and agree to a Palestinian state. The right—the hawks—will never acknowledge the existence of a Palestinian people, and they are not ready to share the land of Israel, the land between the Jordan River and the Mediterranean Sea. Through the years, of course, many changes have taken place. There have been some rightists ready for a compromise, but they are still outnumbered. Generally speaking, this has been the main political divide for four decades: readiness (or lack thereof) to compromise with the Palestinians, to accept their right to self-determination, to share the country.

On Tuesday afternoon, January 23, 2001, we were notified of the murder of two Israelis who had gone to Tulkarm to buy pots for their restaurant on Sheinkin Street in Tel Aviv. In accordance with written procedure, the talks ceased and we returned to Jerusalem. The talks were renewed only two days later, after the funerals, but some of the momentum had been lost.

On Saturday night, January 27, we decided to make a joint announcement which did not reflect the full extent of what we had actually achieved. Although no agreement was ultimately signed at Taba, the talks had brought us very close to reaching one; they neither failed nor broke down. In a conversation in April 2001, Nabil Sha'ath lamented: "If the Taba talks had been held immediately after the Camp David summit, a permanent agreement would already have been signed."

It had been a little too late. After the end of Clinton's tenure, and a few days before the elections in Israel, when many people on the right, and even the left, were questioning the legitimacy of negotiations at so late a stage, it was apparent that time had run out. Clinton had said that his plan would be off the table once he left office. After losing the election, Barak announced that everything agreed upon at Camp David and Taba would be null and void. But history cannot be wiped out even by those who made it, and everything remains relevant: Camp David, the Clinton Plan, and Taba. The right says: "We told you it wasn't possible to make peace with the Palestinians," while the peace camp is licking its wounds and looking for explanations. Since the outbreak of the second Intifada on September 29, 2000, the most pressing question in Israel has been: *What went wrong?*

Was it really the case, as the right claims, that the Oslo process was merely a means for Arafat to control land Israel had justly conquered in 1967, to establish armed forces there, and to exploit the area transferred to him to fight against Israel? Or was the Oslo process an Israeli ploy to exploit the initial Declaration of Principles in order to make a peace agreement with Jordan, to make contacts in North Africa and the Gulf, to improve Israel's international standing and economic situation, leaving Yasser Arafat as "Mayor of Gaza"—as the late professor Edward Said believed? Or was it perhaps an Israeli plan to secure the occupation without bearing the demographic costs, as the Israeli journalist Amira Hass suggests?

Perhaps, as surmised by my friend Yoel Singer—a former legal advisor to the Foreign Ministry and a key figure in the Oslo negotiations—there is no chance of peace with the Palestinians until they have had their own war of independence. Perhaps without blood, fire, and brimstone they will not be able to compromise and sign an agreement.

Perhaps Barak did force Arafat into a corner at Camp David, and in order to extricate himself, Arafat had to ride a wave of violence. Perhaps Arafat intended to advance toward peace, but when he got to the moment of truth he did not have sufficient support for the necessary concessions, and then it suited him to return to his position as the leader of a national liberation movement. Perhaps it was the sense of distress and frustration among residents of the Palestinian Authority at the failure to fully implement the interim agreements—while a permanent settlement appeared more remote than ever—that led to an explosion when Sharon visited the Temple Mount in September 2000.

Barak had taken an "all or nothing" approach: While he had been ready to concede, he was also prepared to "expose the true face" of the other side; he believed such an outcome was nearly as valuable as an agreement. So it was all or nothing, and this dichotomy with Barak was very dangerous from the start. There was also, on the Palestinian side, the undercurrent of a threat to resort to violence if there were no results by the end of the year, since Barak had promised a final agreement by that point. It was a situation boiling over with frustration, set to worsen with a failure to fulfill the promise to conclude negotiations, especially since the earlier deadline of May 1999 had already passed.

THERE ARE AS MANY ANSWERS AS EXPERTS. Therefore, with the wisdom of hindsight, there will be more than one answer to this question: Why does prolonged frustration break into violence at a particular moment in history?

The late Faisal Husseini, who was responsible for the Jerusalem portfolio in the Palestinian Authority, said that many revolutions occur when an enlightened king replaces a tyrannical one. Husseini was one of the most important leaders in East Jerusalem, the unelected mayor. He was the scion of a very aristocratic family, and his father, Abdul Qader al-Husseini, was a leader of the Palestinian factions that fought harshly against Israel in the War of Independence. His father was killed in the famous battle for the Castel, near Latrun, in 1948, and Faisal Husseini grew up in Jerusalem in the shadow of his fallen father. But unlike his father, a fighter, Faisal Husseini was a political leader, who was committed to the peace process and believed that relations with Israel would eventually strengthen the Palestinian cause. At one point, when we spoke about the possibility of a future confederation between the Palestinian state and Jordan, he said, "Why not a confederation between Israel and the Palestinian state? Actually, we can gain much more from your experience and your democracy than from Jordan." This did not prevent him, however, from regarding Zionism as the invasion of a land which did not belong to the Jews; he was ready for an agreement only because he was pragmatic and believed that it would help the Palestinians.

It is precisely when people realize the contrast between what *can* be achieved and what they are actually achieving that they resort to violence. Yasser Abed Rabbo, my Palestinian partner in the 2003 Geneva Draft Agreement, says that making the Temple Mount the central issue in earlier talks was a serious error. It would have been more effective, he claims, to deal with all the other issues first, and only then try to solve the question of the Temple Mount. Once the Temple Mount became the focal point, Ariel Sharon's visit there lit a fuse leading to a barrel of gunpowder.

CHAPTER 2
CLINTON: PRO-ISRAEL, PRO-PALESTINE

WILLIAM JEFFERSON CLINTON did not enter the Oval Office with confidence that he could resolve the Israeli-Arab conflict. He knew this was a hot potato that nobody had yet managed to handle, and that his own glory would not be based on a remote peace. He remembered the work of Jimmy Carter, who had succeeded in concluding an historic peace between Israel and Egypt, only to be defeated later by Ronald Reagan.

After twelve years with conservative Republicans in the White House, the issues on Clinton's agenda were largely domestic: health care, for instance, and the issue of homosexuals in the military. On the international scene, post-Soviet Russia took up much of his attention, with the concern the country might collapse in the transition from a planned to a free-market economy. The dismemberment of Yugoslavia was also a high priority on the young President's desk, given the possible risk to the stability of Europe. The fear of nuclear proliferation in Iran and Iraq was also on Clinton's mind, alongside other problematic issues in Southeast Asia, Africa, and South America.

Clinton was the anti–status quo president. He wanted to effect change and felt that he had tremendous freedom of action, particularly in foreign affairs. Though he held no illusions about the nature of the conflicts in the region, he was not afraid to set foot in the sickbed allegedly awaiting any president who showed an interest in the Middle East. He devoted countless hours to the conflict, met with many people, got to know them well, came to the region on a number of occasions, and frequently invited leaders to the United States. He became so well-acquainted with the issues that he was able to argue intelligently over details with Israelis and Palestinians who had devoted many years of their lives to finding a solution to the conflict. He traveled to Damascus to meet with President Hafez al-Assad, despite his consultants' advice against visiting a country that appeared on the list of sponsors of terrorism. He took an active part in the Wye Summit, together with Netanyahu and Arafat; in the Shepherdstown Peace Talks with Barak and Syrian Foreign Minister Farouk al-Shara; and in the Camp David Summit with Arafat and Barak. He believed that his intensive participation could bring about agreement. Sometimes he was wrong, sometimes he was right.

His victory in 1992 had seemed almost a miracle for liberals around the whole world. People such as myself saw it as their own triumph, after twelve years of conservative rule. His optimism, until his very last day in office, was contagious. He possessed a rare combination of personal charisma, deep understanding of human relations, high intelligence, and extensive knowledge and diligence—though he was also impaired by human weaknesses which caused him, in effect, to discontinue much of his work in office and concentrate on defending himself. His friendships with Rabin and Barak enabled them both to make brave political decisions with the knowledge that he was there, at the White House, giving them all the support they needed.

Clinton's eight years as President presented a tremendous opportunity to advance the peace process in the Middle East, but this opportunity was not fully seized. In the Middle East he found a structure bequeathed to him by George Bush Sr. and James Baker: talks in progress in Washington between Israel and delegations from Syria, Lebanon, and a joint Jordanian-Palestinian delegation. These talks had been moving in slow motion since the Madrid Conference in October 1991, when the level of violence in the region was not particularly high. This was considered a "managed conflict" that did not require any special creative effort; one needed only to wait until the negotiations produced some kind of an agreement.

Clinton made no waves in the negotiating team, and surprised many when he retained Dennis Ross—who had helped Baker manage Bush's election campaign—at the State Department, to head the team dealing with the peace process in the Middle East. Ross, who had been involved in the peace process for many years, had an unusual career; the peak of his activities came when James Baker, to whom he was very close, became Secretary of State. Oddly enough, given his connection with Baker, Ross had been a supporter of Senator George McGovern, the liberal Democratic presidential candidate in 1972. He joined the State Department during the Republican era, and was so close to Baker that he followed him to the White House when Baker resigned as Secretary of State to serve as George Bush's campaign manager in the 1992 election. In a conversation we had on the eve of that vote, when it looked as though Bush had little chance to win, Ross told me that the likelihood of reaching an agreement with Syria under another Secretary of State would be significantly reduced, since it was only the trust between Hafez al-Assad and Baker that had enabled any genuine progress.

With Clinton's victory, Ross's diplomatic career was thought to be over. But Clinton then proposed that Ross work with the new Secretary of State, Warren Christopher, as the chief negotiator for the United States in the Middle East peace talks. In this capacity, he would be the main player in this political process for the next eight years.

Initially, Ross preferred the Israeli-Syrian track, and he told me on a number of occasions that, from a strategic perspective, this was the most important American interest. Nevertheless, once he became aware of the Oslo process, he understood the huge opportunity that had arisen, and did everything within his power to promote its success. President Clinton and both Secretaries of State, Warren Christopher and Madeleine Albright, considered Ross to be a professional of the highest caliber and accepted his assessments.

Ross, a proud Jew, was viewed by the Israeli right as a person who pressured Israel into reaching peace against its best interests, and by the Palestinians as too pro-Israel. For a while, Arafat considered him a real enemy and refused to meet with him. In Syria, too, Ross lost his sway with

President Assad. Until Clinton's very last day in office, Ross wanted to believe that it was possible to reach an agreement. The failure of the negotiations with the Syrians and with the Palestinians was the failure of Dennis Ross.

Other pivotal people in this field were Ross's deputy, Aaron Miller, as well as Assistant Secretary of State Edward Djerijian and his deputy, Dan Kurtzer. Warren Christopher, who had served as Deputy Secretary of State under Cyrus Vance in the Carter administration, surely did not expect that he would be crossing the ocean to land at Ben-Gurion Airport so many times during his tenure.

IN A MEETING BETWEEN CLINTON and Prime Minister Yitzhak Rabin just before Clinton took office in January 1993, the two developed an excellent rapport. Rabin presented his political intentions to Clinton, as well as his commitment to reach an autonomy agreement with the Palestinians within nine months of taking office. Rabin had become Prime Minister in July 1992, and the deadline was approaching.

There were two outstanding issues for Rabin regarding the separate Syrian and Palestinian negotiations. First, with the Palestinians, there was no clear partner. We had a joint Jordanian-Palestinian delegation, with which we had been negotiating in Washington since the Madrid Conference in 1991. Rabin did not challenge the legitimacy of this delegation after becoming Prime Minister; he did not say, excuse my language, "Cut the bullshit. Let us talk directly with the Palestinians, or directly with the PLO." He continued to acknowledge this artificial creature made up of Jordanians and Palestinians, though in his heart he knew this was not a good approach, and that there would probably be no positive developments. There were impediments and obstacles on the way to any understanding between the Israeli delegation and this joint delegation. On the other hand, Rabin also knew that Assad was trustworthy, and Rabin believed that if an agreement was reached with him, Assad would implement it, exactly as he had implemented all the previous agreements between Syria and Israel: the tacit agreements, the half-official agreements, and the official agreements.

The second outstanding issue for Rabin was that the Americans did not hide their preference for the Syrian track; they had stressed repeatedly that, in their view, peace with Syria would alter the basic threat in the Middle East, while peace between Israel and the Palestinians was a local negotiation that would not transform the whole region. So, being close to the Americans, especially to Clinton, Rabin believed that the Syrian track might have to be the top priority. Rabin had promised in his campaign that he would never fully withdraw from the Golan Heights, but he also understood that there could not be peace with Syria without that total withdrawal; being a man of his word, he felt quite uncomfortable with the idea of withdrawal.

From the American point of view, the Palestinian conflict seemed to be a painful, difficult issue that deserved a resolution but had a risk of combustion. There was still no official Palestinian delegation, and the Palestinians in Washington insisted on consulting with the PLO leadership in Tunis after every round of talks. Rabin was inclined to work with Assad, who was careful to maintain quiet on the northern border between Syria and Israel, and radiated great power as the sole ruler. An agreement between Israel and Syria would also signify peace between Lebanon and Israel and diminish the possibility of a regional conflict. There was an understanding between Rabin and Clinton, despite the former's discomfort on the issue, that if there were to be an Israeli withdrawal from the Golan Heights, Clinton was prepared to position American troops there in order to maintain the demilitarized zone.

DURING THE NEXT NINE MONTHS there was a covert rivalry between the Syrian and Palestinian tracks, while the Washington talks continued on their slow-moving course. In Norway, the secret talks between Israeli and senior Palestinian figures—the "Oslo route"—were becoming more and more intensive, while Warren Christopher conducted shuttle diplomacy between Damascus and Jerusalem, with the sense that the gaps between the two capitals were closing.

Since I was very, very close to Shimon Peres and he trusted me, I was in a unique position of independence, both as Deputy Minister of Finance and as Deputy Minister of Foreign Affairs. There was never any friction between us, which is not usually the case between a minister and a deputy minister.

I appreciated Peres and knew him from my work as a journalist; I had interviewed him several times. I supported Peres when he replaced Rabin as Prime Minister in 1977, before I began to work with him, though I cannot say that I admired his policies. I supported him mainly because I thought he could win the elections, and I felt that Rabin had failed in his first term as Prime Minister. But ideologically, Peres was a hawk. He was opposed to a territorial compromise. He supported the settlement projects. I did not become the party spokesman because I identified with his policies, but because the Labor Party was in a shambles, and I believed it was my mission to help whoever was the leader of the party. Then things changed; I became much closer to him, and our ideologies became much closer as well.

Peres was and remains the most important statesman in Israel, and one of the most important in the world. He has rare strategic vision, the curiosity of a young boy, the diligence of someone who knows that time is never on his side, and a charisma resulting from media exposure, extensive experience, and a lengthy political career. Once considered to be one of Ben-Gurion's boys, a young technocrat devoid of ideology, a capitalist in a party which had lost its socialist values, and a hawk who encouraged the construction of settlements and vehemently objected to a territorial compromise in the West Bank, Peres has been transformed into a brave and independent politician, one of the heads of the Socialist International, and the leader of the peace camp in Israel.

Peres is the phoenix of Israeli politics—in the Knesset since 1959, a minister in almost every possible ministry, and twice Prime Minister. He has been saddled with the epithet of "loser," despite the fact that objectively he is perhaps the most successful person in Israeli politics. He has made his mark on the political scene, leading it to unexpected places, and has retained a surprising level of public popularity—even when his policies are no longer supported. Peres himself is a man who has never given up, who has never despaired. He constantly sets new goals for himself. He sees himself, first and foremost, as Mr. Security: the man who, in his youth, headed the Ministry of Defense delegation in New York, became Director-General of the Ministry of Defense at age twenty-nine, served as Deputy Minister of Defense and Minister of Defense, and whose social circle consists mainly of people who were his friends in the defense establishment. The fact that he has in recent years been labeled a man of peace, while his defense background has been forgotten, troubles him greatly. This defense expert, who sought to make peace only after concluding that it was the best way to guarantee Israel's security, is sometimes perceived as having the Arab interest at heart.

THE OSLO PROCESS, WHICH I HAD BEGUN INFORMALLY before I became Deputy Foreign Minister, and was conducted in Norway by two academics close to me, Dr. Yair Hirschfeld and Dr. Ron Pundak, became much more official when I told Shimon Peres of its existence and he then informed Prime Minister Rabin. In the spring of 1993, it was decided that the Israeli team to Oslo would be headed by the Director-General of the Foreign Ministry, Uri Savir, and this decision turned the talks with the PLO into an official process. For the first time in history there was a relationship between Israel and the Palestinian national movement.

During the talks, which were designed at first to be a back channel for those in Washington, not only did creative solutions emerge for difficult problems that were deadlocked in Washington, but the two sides discovered a willingness for mutual recognition. This made it possible for the secret route to be revealed to the world, because as soon as the talks were being held between two parties who recognized each other, there was no longer any reason to keep them secret. This was a far-reaching change, and the Oslo process would in the future become much more significant than it had originally appeared.

In August 1993, the American peace team in the Middle East, after discussing the matter and even holding a kind of vote, decided to take a vacation; Christopher and Ross returned to California, while the others went to the East Coast. There was no break in the Oslo talks, however, and on August 20, the agreement was initialed by Abu Ala and Shimon Peres, who was visiting Scandinavia.

At that point, only a few people in the American peace team were aware of the Oslo process, and this information was also very fragmented and informal; Rabin had responded earlier with ridicule to a question from Warren Christopher about secret talks being held between Israel and the PLO in Scandinavia. As a result, we feared that Christopher would not welcome the news of an agreement in Oslo.

On August 27, Peres, Norwegian Foreign Minister John Holst, and their assistants arrived in Southern California. They met with Christopher and Ross and told them the sensational news. Christopher was concerned about the implications of mutual recognition on American policy toward the PLO, and Peres said that Arafat would send a letter to Rabin denouncing terror, which would enable the U.S. to revoke its boycott of the PLO (under the Mack-Lieberman Act).

It was now clear that these developments in Oslo were reducing the chances of making further progress with Syria. From the American perspective, a problem had thus been created, but Christopher made no hint of this to Peres.

At first it looked as if there would be a ceremony in Washington, at which the agreement would be signed with Faisal Husseini as the leader of the Palestinian group in the joint delegation with Jordan. On September 9, there was an exchange of letters between Arafat and Rabin, ratifying mutual recognition. The next day, Clinton announced the resumption of contact with the PLO after a four-year hiatus.

It was Clinton who turned the signing of the Oslo Declaration of Principles into the most prominent media event of the 1990s. The signatures of Peres and Abu Mazen on a five-year interim agreement with many question marks would definitely have been interesting and unusual, but it would not have amazed the world. Part of Clinton's unique quality was his talent for perceiving the greatness of the hour. It was an opportunity for him to position himself as a statesman who had transformed the Middle East. Although he had not been at all involved with the Oslo process, the fact that he was there now could make him a winner. I think that in the beginning of his term he needed successes, and Oslo was a success which had been prepared for him, without any effort. So why not? The same happened with Shepherdstown, and with Camp David. Clinton took risks in diplomacy, and this was one of them. I think that it stemmed mainly from his self-confidence: He said to himself, "If I am part of this summit, it will succeed," and sometimes he was right, as at the Wye Summit. But with the Middle East, it was not so easy every time. Visiting Syria, to take one example, was very, very questionable, because of its designation as a state sponsor of terrorism. Merely meeting with Assad was momentous, not to mention going to Damascus, to Assad's home. Such a meeting should have taken place only if one could envisage tangible success as a result. But there was no agreement beforehand; nothing happened, and in many ways, Clinton was humiliated by Assad's behavior. It did not help anybody.

During a flight to Cleveland on September 10, Clinton phoned Rabin and proposed that he come to Washington to sign the agreement himself. Clinton suggested that the opposite party should be Arafat. Rabin was very hesitant, but Arafat was not. Ultimately, the world will remember for many years the picture of a tall young man joining two leaders a generation older and much less tall. America had refused to make the Oslo Accords into an American proposal (as Peres had suggested to Christopher), but it was no longer important after that photograph. The Oslo Accords, signed at the White House on September 13, 1993, became Clinton's agreement within a few hours.

Clinton's decision to bring Arafat and Rabin to Washington had broad implications. Arafat's status was not mentioned in the Oslo Accords, nor in the lengthy talks that had led to the agreement. We naïvely believed that the issue of Arafat's role would arise only when we reached the permanent agreement, not as part of the interim agreement and the elections to the independent Palestinian government. At the end of August, I was interviewed on *Nightline* by Ted Koppel, who asked if Arafat would come to Jericho to sign the agreement transferring Gaza and Jericho to the Palestinians. I said that this was not on the agenda; it sounded like a diplomatic answer, but it was the whole truth.

Clinton brought forward the meeting between the Israeli and Palestinian leaders, and bypassed a great many hesitations and dilemmas. All at once Arafat became legitimate, a natural candidate to lead the Palestinian Authority during the interim phases who would come on the scene not only for the permanent settlement, but in a few months' time, for the signature of the Gaza-Jericho agreement.

NINE MONTHS AFTER CLINTON ENTERED THE OVAL OFFICE, he had found himself doing the impossible, accomplishing a political feat that none of his predecessors had dreamed of—watching Rabin and Arafat shake hands in his presence. The highly problematic Middle East had become an arena in which major achievements were seemingly attained with ease.

On the day the Oslo Declaration was signed, I met Clinton for the first time. The Israeli team entered the Oval Office alongside Christopher and the National Security Advisor, Anthony Lake. Clinton expressed his appreciation of the initiative to commence the Oslo process "against all odds," and asked what I would have done in his place.

"I would have closed the circle," I said. "It is possible to make peace with the other neighbors in the Middle East."

"I agree," Clinton replied. "I would like the next target to be Syria."

But in October 1994, Rabin surprised Clinton by presenting him the Israel-Jordan agreement on a silver platter. The agreement, the preparation of which had begun one day after signing the Oslo Accord, was then signed in the Arava Valley on the Israel-Jordan border by Yitzhak Rabin and King Hussein, with the participation of President Clinton. Again, it was a very moving ceremony, although less sensational than the agreement between Israel and the PLO. But this time it was a full peace agreement.

Clinton's trip to Damascus after the ceremony to meet with President Assad wasn't another success, and it seemed that Assad enjoyed not giving Clinton any leeway. Nevertheless, it appeared that the Middle East was changing. Clinton invested a great deal of time in the region, offered financial aid to both the Palestinian Authority and Jordan, and made the region one of the most important issues on his agenda. The Palestinian attacks that began forty days after the massacre of twenty-nine Palestinians by Baruch Goldstein at the Cave of Machpelah in Hebron, were very difficult for him, but he felt that the process was in high gear and that there was no return.

At the U.S. Congressional elections in 1994, the Democratic party lost its majority in the Senate and the House of Representatives. The elections weakened the President, but this concerned mainly domestic affairs. On foreign policy issues, he seemed to have the same relatively free hand. In any event, it is certain that his involvement in the peace process was not atrophied. He monitored from afar the Israeli-Palestinian negotiations on the interim agreement—popularly known as Oslo II—that was signed by Rabin and Arafat at the White House on September 28, 1995. Clinton made sure that the parties to the Oslo Declaration of Principles continued toward the permanent agreement without bothering the U.S. too much. He followed with concern Yitzhak Rabin's political distress, and the increasing threats on his life, but he believed that this mature and experienced man, who had become a personal friend, would overcome them.

It must be said that following the Oslo Accords, there were frequent demonstrations in Israel in which Rabin was portrayed as a Nazi. Rabbis issued pronouncements that Rabin had betrayed his country and should be punished. Many banners appeared along the main roads, including the high-way from Tel Aviv to Jerusalem, listing the names of five "traitors." Rabin was first. The second was Peres. I was the third. Uri Savir was the fourth. And Yoel Singer, the Foreign Ministry's legal advisor, was the fifth. We were all threatened, though nobody was threatened like Rabin. It was all very public, yet there were also many phone calls and letters which were not exposed.

I saw it as something that came with the job, part and parcel of such a huge controversy; I did not think for one moment that it might end with a real murder. I saw it as part of a very tough opposition to the very significant revolution we had introduced.

Rabin's assassination, on November 4, 1995, was a terrible blow for Clinton. A true personal loss accompanied his concern that it would now be impossible to maintain the political momentum. His immediate response to the murder was very moving, and his statement in Hebrew, *"Shalom, haver"*—Goodbye, friend—is now the phrase used in Israel to remember Rabin, seen on hundreds of thousands of bumper stickers as a symbol of mourning and identification with the murdered leader.

CLINTON CAME TO THE FUNERAL. Before it began, he met with Rabin's replacement, Shimon Peres, to discuss the Syrian route. Clinton wanted to make sure that Peres was aware of Rabin's commitment to Clinton on the Israeli-Syrian border: Rabin had "deposited" with the Americans his willingness to withdraw to the June 4, 1967 lines if Syria met certain conditions. Peres was not aware of Rabin's promise, which was no surprise, considering the distant relations between Peres and Rabin, as well as the secrecy with which Rabin conducted the Oslo process. Details were shared only with the four of us involved in negotiations; nobody else in Rabin's office, not even his personal secretary, knew about it. Rabin, essentially a loner, was quite concerned about leaks; he was afraid Peres would leak or oppose the commitment, so he kept it between him and Clinton. Peres was embarrassed and assured Clinton that he would adhere to Rabin's commitments. Peres attempted to locate documentation in the Prime Minister's office to confirm the "deposit," but it turned out that the negotiations had only been verbal.

TALKS BETWEEN ISRAEL AND SYRIA RESUMED in December at the Wye Plantation near Washington. But following the assassination of Hamas bomb-maker Yahya Ayyash, known as "the Engineer," the principal explosives expert among the Palestinian terrorist organizations, Israel was struck by a wave of bombings in February 1996. After four very brutal attacks which killed sixty-three Israelis, an international anti-terrorist summit was held at Sharm el-Sheikh in Egypt. Clinton arrived in Israel on March 13 and participated with us in a government session. The next day he took a central position at the convention alongside Arab and world leaders. He considered it his mission to prevent the collapse of the peace process, despite criticism that a visit to Israel a few months before elections was an attempt to intervene in Israel's internal affairs.

The hope that Clinton aimed to engender with the summit was no match for the deepening Israeli fear of violence. On May 29, Netanyahu beat Peres by a margin of 0.8 percent, and it was clear that the peace process would suffer.

Opposite Netanyahu stood a new American team: Madeleine Albright was now the Secretary of State, while Sandy Berger had become National Security Advisor. The Americans were determined not to make any concessions to Netanyahu. They demanded that he uphold the Oslo Accords as promised, including the agreed timetable, which required that a permanent agreement with the Palestinians be concluded by May 4, 1999.

It was important for Netanyahu to create the impression of closeness with Clinton, and it should not have been very difficult. They were of the same generation, with the same background—American-educated, photogenic, media-savvy. But to Clinton, it was clear that Netanyahu intended to drag his feet. Clinton's principal concern was that progress would halt under Netanyahu—and that after five years of the Oslo process, the President of the United States, who had hosted the signing of the accords, would be forced to face Arafat with empty hands.

After Netanyahu, counter to the advice of his Defense Minister and Security Chief, ordered the opening of an archeological passage along the Western Wall of the Temple Mount—the retaining wall of the Haram al-Sharif, one of Islam's holiest sites—on September 24, 1996, three days of protest and rioting ensued in the territories, leaving fifteen Israeli soldiers and eighty Palestinians dead. Clinton seized on the violence to summon Arafat and Netanyahu to Washington for a meeting. These three-sided talks led to an even deeper American involvement than before. The President was convinced that without a significant push by the United States, there would be no negotiations between the parties, and perhaps even a replay of the "tunnel uprising."

Clinton had no illusions about Netanyahu. He saw Netanyahu as a very ambitious man who was talented, right-wing, and determined to keep his government in place without making an agreement with the Palestinians to relinquish the West Bank. The relationship between them became very cold, and worsened with each problem that arose under Netanyahu: opening the tunnel, the construction of new neighborhoods in East Jerusalem (Har Homa and Ras al-Amud), and Netanyahu's insistence on "reciprocity," a new term with which he justified his failure to implement the agreed-upon timetable, contending (occasionally with justification, but sometimes without it) that the Palestinian side was not yet ready to fulfill its obligations.

BY CLINTON'S SECOND TERM, many difficulties had arisen. Madeleine Albright had little experience with the Middle East, save for her stint as ambassador to the United Nations during Clinton's first term. She vowed upon taking office not to repeat the frequent Middle East trips made by her predecessor, Warren Christopher, who had logged twenty-three visits to the region in four years. But she too was drawn inexorably into the process: The clock was ticking, and there was no telling what might happen should the five-year deadline arrive without even the skeleton of a permanent agreement.

Albright worked with the peace team, headed by Dennis Ross, and stuck to the previous policy. She played a particularly important role before the Shepherdstown peace talks in January 2000, where she succeeded in creating an atmosphere that was both comfortable and focused. The peace process became a more personal issue for Albright as time passed: The outbreak of the second Intifada was a tragedy for her, and her intensive efforts to save the process in Paris in October 2000 reflected her feeling that such a precious endeavor was slipping out of her hands.

But there was no "Albright Plan"—she did not present any original proposals to resolve the conflict. Rumors persisted throughout her term that she would be replaced, and she was said to have less authority within the administration than Berger. When Clinton had to leave the Camp David talks in August 2000 to attend the G-8 summit in Japan, Albright stepped in as chief mediator, but she failed to salvage the talks despite her tremendous desire to do so.

Berger himself had never properly visited Israel before he became the Deputy National Security Advisor, and during his eight years in the White House he had come only on brief trips to accompany the President, until his independent visit in the spring of 2000. Berger was a liberal Jew and a supporter of Peace Now in the United States, but the Israeli-Arab conflict had never been a central concern to him, neither as an individual nor as a senior official in the Clinton administration. However, the new situation—which combined a process with stages defined in a set timetable with a right-wing Israeli government determined to shake off those commitments—obligated Berger to see more and more guests from the Middle East, and to become deeply involved in the matter.

The Monica Lewinsky affair had a decisive impact on the administration's efforts in the Middle East. Though business seemed, at first glance, to proceed as usual, in practice the changes were marked. When the President hosted regional leaders in the White House, reporters only wanted to discuss Monica's dress and other scandal minutiae. With such a heavy cloud hanging over the administration and the President threatened with impeachment, all other issues began to fade and it became impossible for Clinton to devote the necessary time for discussion or the required creativity to the peace process.

The majority of work was therefore handed over to Dennis Ross and his team: Aaron Miller, Gamal Hilal, Toni Verstandig, Robert Malley, and a few others, alongside the American embassy in Israel and the Consulate in Jerusalem. The American emphasis had shifted from pushing for peace with Syria to pressuring Israel to comply with commitments in the agreement with the Palestinians.

When the Hebron Agreement—which transferred most of the city of Hebron to the Palestinians—had been signed in January 1997 at the home of the American ambassador, it was reflective of the great change in the U.S. role since the early days of Oslo, when the two negotiators on the interim agreement, Uri Savir and Abu Ala, had hidden their papers from Dennis Ross when he came to visit them in Eilat. Now the parties could not hold negotiations without American involvement. But just at the stage when it was most critical, circumstances had severely hindered the American role.

During the second half of 1997 and throughout the following year, the Americans argued about how to deal with Netanyahu; whether to declare him recalcitrant, or attempt to persuade him to conclude an additional interim agreement with the Palestinians. Clinton was among those who supported an effort at persuasion. He was probably concerned about alienating his Jewish supporters, in whose eyes a deterioration in relations with Netanyahu represented a neglect of the relationship with Israel.

Clinton had opened his administration to Jews, many of whom had worked alongside him on the liberal McGovern campaign in 1972. There was clearly no "affirmative action" for Jews in the administration, but by his second term, Clinton had surrounded himself by colleagues who were Jews or of Jewish extraction: Secretary of State Albright; Secretary of Defense Richard Cohen; National Security Advisor Sandy Berger; CIA Director John Deutch; UN Ambassador Richard Holbrooke; the first Jewish ambassador to Israel, Martin Indyk; ambassador to Egypt Daniel Kurtzer; Dennis Ross; and many others. Palestinians, and Arabs in general, found this hard to understand, and while many held Clinton personally in high esteem, they considered the large number of Jews in his administration as a sign that he had to accept Israel's dictates. Clinton himself—according to all the evidence—believed the opposite: The general sense was that he couldn't care less about anyone's religion—whether they were Jewish or Buddhist, they were his friends and colleagues.

Nobody could suspect Clinton of hating Jews or Israel, and he could afford to stand against what he considered to be bad Israeli policy. But such confrontations were better avoided, and Clinton preferred to host further negotiations, which appeared at first glance to be a success.

Clinton devoted long days in October 1998 at the Wye Summit to obtain the parties' consent to a new timetable—the third one—for the implementation of the interim agreement and the details of Israel's further withdrawal; the President invested a great deal of energy on a technical issue that should have been resolved at the sub-ministerial level. At the time, he had cause for great concern: The five-year interim agreement was set to expire seven months after the summit. The Palestinians refused to begin talks on a permanent settlement—where agreement with Netanyahu seemed unlikely—without first securing a new interim arrangement. They pressed for consent on the interim agreement as a condition for opening permanent status negotiations. Clinton wanted to resolve the interim arrangement so that permanent negotiations could commence.

His intensive involvement in the Wye Summit—both formally and informally—was critical to its success. Israel refused to agree to a further withdrawal unless the Palestinians would ratify the revocation of the PLO covenant, even though the Palestine National Council had already adopted a resolution to do so in April 1996. To convince the Palestinians to convene another forum to ratify the resolution, Clinton himself promised to attend the gathering in Gaza. His commitment sealed the agreement for

the Palestinians, and the Israelis agreed to withdraw to the extent demanded by the Americans. The President had come to feel that maintaining the
peace process was his personal responsibility. The regional engine that
existed in the past, which had led to agreements that had surprised him,
was no longer functioning. He held both leaders in low esteem, so *he* had
to act instead. When he appeared as promised in Gaza in December 1998,
he had the privilege of seeing his picture favorably distributed in the streets
for the first time; meanwhile, Israeli officials criticized him for granting the
status of statehood to the Palestinian Authority by the mere fact of his visit.

In the end, the Wye Agreement—save for its first modest phase—was
never implemented. As the Israeli elections, set for May 17, 1999,
approached, and the five-year interim agreement expired, neither side
made an attempt to negotiate. Those close to Netanyahu suggested that he
might welcome a Palestinian decision to cancel the Oslo Agreement and
unilaterally declare a Palestinian state—relieving him from having to persuade the electorate to accept a permanent agreement, and from adhering
to the other aspects of Oslo.

Arafat, for his part, passed the buck to the world, as if to say: "I have
waited patiently for five years for this great moment. Surely nobody expects
me, after all this time, without any agreement on the horizon, to give up my
right to declare a Palestinian state!" Clinton felt that the responsibility was
his: He asked Arafat to refrain from a unilateral declaration of statehood,
and promised that a permanent arrangement would be reached within a
year, by May 2000. Actually, without being asked to do so, Clinton stepped
into Israel's shoes and reached an understanding with Arafat extending the
five-year agreement to six years, estimating that by then Barak would be
Prime Minister, and a permanent agreement could be signed.

THERE IS NO DOUBT THAT CLINTON was looking forward to the replacement
of Netanyahu with a Labor Prime Minister; the day before Barak's first visit
to Washington as Prime Minister in July 1999, Clinton went so far as to say
that he was waiting for Barak like a child waiting for a new toy. However,
the "toy" did not fulfill all of Clinton's expectations: Barak wanted to
reconsider the Syrian track; he proposed another stage in the political

process with the Palestinians, a "framework agreement," which would have to be concluded before the start of negotiations on the permanent agreement; and he insisted that during the next fifteen months, he would be able to determine for himself whether or not it was possible to make peace.

Clinton saw Barak's ideas as an additional complication. He wanted Barak to implement the Wye Agreement immediately, to commence intensive negotiations on the permanent agreement with the Palestinians, and only then to go to Syria. But when Barak insisted on following his own route, the President accepted it, and even mobilized to convince Arafat not to reject Barak's plan outright. Clinton made the same mistake as all of us in the peace camp: After three years under Netanyahu, who nearly destroyed the political process, we gave Barak unconditional support because of his commitment to the process; we did not attempt to convince him to abandon these new stages, which we thought were superfluous, and perhaps even harmful.

The original idea of an interim agreement preceding the permanent settlement was hatched by Menachem Begin and Anwar Sadat in 1978. They had suggested a framework for agreement between Israel and the Palestinians, though it was conceived without any Palestinian partner at the table. Begin and Sadat proposed five years of Palestinian autonomy in the West Bank and Gaza, during which time Israel and an unspecified Palestinian party would negotiate a permanent solution; after five years, a permanent government would be installed. The Palestinians rejected this idea, because they did not want an open-ended interim agreement; they were ready to discuss an interim agreement only in the context of a permanent settlement whose terms were known in advance.

At the Madrid Conference in 1991, the invitation to which included mention of Begin and Sadat's plan for interim autonomy, the Palestinians—as part of a Jordanian-Palestinian delegation—accepted, for the first time, an interim arrangement: five years of autonomy, with a permanent agreement at the end. When we negotiated in Oslo, our guidelines from Rabin were to follow this path, to *refer* to the outstanding issues that the permanent agreement would solve, but not to actually try to resolve them just yet. I came to believe this was a mistake, and tried to convince Rabin and Peres to aim directly for the permanent solution. They thought—and perhaps rightly so—that this was too ambitious; in order to retain the support of the electorate, it was necessary to follow the path of Begin and Shamir and not attempt to invent a new one.

BASHFULNESS WAS NEVER BARAK'S STRONG POINT, and he constantly called Clinton to comment, criticize, and argue. He met with the President frequently, never forgetting to be late. A number of Clinton's close aides thought that he treated Clinton like his clerk, and urged Clinton to reject some of his proposals. But Clinton saw in Barak the only chance of reaching a permanent agreement with the Palestinians before the end of 2000, and he was prepared to pay a high price for it, not only out of a desire to see the completion of the process he had helped initiate in 1993, but also because he was concerned that the failure to reach an agreement in 2000 would lead to a breakdown in the process and inevitable violence.

Although Clinton had his reservations on returning to the Syrian route, he agreed to Barak's request for Israeli-Syrian negotiations. Barak preferred talks at the highest level, and assured Clinton in a December 1999 meeting in Washington that he, like Rabin, was prepared to commit to a withdrawal to the 1967 borders. On the basis of that commitment, the Shepherdstown Summit was held in January 2000, with the participation of the most senior personnel ever involved in Israel-Syria negotiations, the Prime Minister of Israel and the Foreign Minister of Syria, Farouk al-Shara.

At the conference hardly a word passed between Barak and al-Shara. During the first week there was no progress at all, and only near the end, when Clinton asked Barak to moderate his behavior, did Barak explain to Clinton, according to the Americans, that he had never intended to make any real concessions due to the strong Israeli opposition to returning any part of the Golan. Clinton, who participated intensively in the conference, found this difficult to accept, and the talks collapsed. Clinton's meeting with Assad at the beginning of 2000 in Geneva, according to American sources, was also unsuccessful because of Barak's reversal of course, after Clinton had already told the ailing Syrian leader that he had obtained a breakthrough proposal from Israel.

Clinton told Barak he would only be able to participate effectively in the political process for a few more months; as soon as the 2000 presidential election got underway, his influence would be very limited. He encouraged Barak to hold talks at the ministerial level before any summit with the Palestinians, and Barak did try to set up such talks in Stockholm between Shlomo Ben-Ami and Abu Ala. But Barak's clear preference was for a summit between top leaders, where it would be possible to persuade and be persuaded, and to achieve the difficult concessions critical to any final agreement.

Barak's pressure won out in the end: He insisted on a summit in July, and Clinton obliged, convincing Arafat—who felt a premature summit would end in failure, and wanted to hold lower-level talks as a preliminary step—to attend.

ROB MALLEY, CLINTON'S ADVISOR on Middle Eastern affairs, and a member of the National Security Council, in a public appearance shortly after leaving the administration, said that President Clinton was the friendliest president to the Palestinians *and* the friendliest to the Israelis. He was right. It was Clinton who opened the gates of the United States to Arafat, and Arafat made more visits to the White House than any other foreign leader—thirteen—during Clinton's presidency. At the same time, Clinton felt a great affinity with Israel and many of its leaders, and wanted very much to help it become a safe haven after so many stormy years. I do not think he was a neutral player. I think that he strongly supported the Israeli state—its character, its democracy, and its history—and he was much closer to Israel than to the Palestinians. But he was not blind to Palestinian needs, and he understood, unlike many others, that being a supporter of Israel did not contradict being a supporter of the Palestinians; sometimes, in fact, being too supportive of Israel meant opposing a solution to the conflict, which would be the worst thing for Israel in the long run. Clinton was very wise, and had a creative mind; he saw himself as the most important leader in the world—the head of the lone superpower—and wanted very much to use this leverage to make peace. He wanted peace for its own sake, but also for posterity, for it to be his legacy.

At the Camp David Summit in July 2000, the President felt that a great deal rested on his shoulders; his time in office was dwindling, but he might still be able to bring to an end the longest-running international dispute since World War II. His relationship with both Arafat and Barak was excellent, and he was as well-versed in the material as if he had been in charge of the Israeli-Palestinian desk at the State Department.

But all of this could not ensure the success of the summit. A detailed account follows later on, but it is clear that Clinton did whatever he could: promised, asked, threatened, raised his voice, and became angry. He made no written proposals of his own, and at the end of the summit he accused Arafat of not going the extra mile toward Barak, although beforehand he had promised that he would place no blame for its failure.

Clinton refrained from presenting a "Clinton Plan" at the opening of the conference and from pushing Arafat into a corner at its end, and these were his two contributions to the crisis that exploded in the fall of 2000. But there is no comparison between those two small mistakes and the enormous effort he invested in the course of fifteen long days at Camp David to save the Middle East. His correct perception of the solution, his profound familiarity with the people and the issues, and his true desire to resolve the problem could have made him the ideal intermediary leading to an historic peace agreement—but it was all in vain.

Clinton did not give up. He still hoped that Barak and Arafat would continue to talk, and that after some progress they would return for a two-day summit in Washington to sign an agreement. In the months after the Camp David talks he almost despaired of this. He hoped that he could get Barak and Arafat to meet at the UN Millennium Assembly, on September 6, 2000, but was forced to settle for separate meetings with them. There was a moment of hope on September 25; at the advice of his friend Danny Abraham, Clinton called Barak's home and found him there with Arafat. But it was only a glimmer, and it turned out to be the sole meeting of the two leaders between Camp David and the start of the second Intifada.

On October 16 and 17, about twenty days after the Intifada had begun, and a few days after the failure of the meeting between Madeleine Albright, Barak, and Arafat in Paris, the Sharm el-Sheikh Summit was held, with the participation of Clinton, Kofi Annan, Hosni Mubarak, King Abdullah of Jordan, and Javier Solana, the European Union Foreign Policy Chief. The summit was supposed to establish a fact-finding committee on the outbreak of violence, and to conclude a full cease-fire between the two sides.

This summit was very different from Camp David. Barak and Arafat did not exchange words and did not shake hands. There were already many new casualties and both sides felt betrayed: Israel, by the very fact of the Palestinians' use of violence, in contravention of the Oslo Accords; and the Palestinians, by the intensity of the Israeli response. Clinton was again at his best: He neither rested nor relaxed. He pleaded, pressed, demanded, and eventually read out a summary which both sides accepted, although they did not sign it.

In time, the Sharm el-Sheikh talks may turn out to have been of great importance; they produced the committee headed by former Senator George Mitchell, which later presented an outline to return quiet to the region and resume negotiations. But at the time, in October 2000, the summary to which both sides had agreed upon was a dead letter; there was a brief attempt at implementing the requirements, but within a short time the violence had surged, becoming ever more brutal, and the fire was impossible to extinguish. Like the Shepherdstown talks and the summit at Camp David, Sharm el-Sheikh was a failure.

IN THE COURSE OF A VISIT TO WASHINGTON in December 2000, I went to meet Sandy Berger. America was still counting votes in Florida and did not know who would be the next president. One day it looked as if things were going in the direction of George W. Bush, and the next, toward Al Gore. The Intifada in the territories was already two months old and did not especially interest the American public. But in the White House, the issue of the Middle East had become a personal one. When I arrived at Berger's office, President Clinton was waiting for me at the door. I raced in and there he stood. At first I was confused. I had visited Berger's office many times, and he had become a close friend, so I knew his staff and no one made a fuss when I arrived. Clinton's office was on the other side of the building, and I was surprised to see him. He smiled because he knew I was not expecting him, and said, "Yossi, I'm waiting for you!"

It was a race against time, because we knew Clinton's participation was crucial to finish the job. The remaining month or so of Clinton's term was our last hope, and it was difficult for me to understand why Barak was not taking advantage of Clinton's offer to help. Clinton said that he had come to see me out of appreciation for my work toward peace, from the initation of the Oslo process to the Beilin–Abu Mazen Understandings and up to the present. He told me not to give up, and to continue to believe that something could be achieved. The Israeli-Palestinian dispute, he promised, remained his highest priority. He told me he had just had a very good conversation with Barak, and that he believed there was a serious chance to solve the outstanding issues in the coming weeks, despite the recent setbacks.

"I have another fifty days left in the White House," Clinton said in all seriousness, "and only one international commitment—a three-day visit to Ireland. Except for that engagement, I am ready to devote this period to assist in ending the dispute in your region. I am all yours: Use me!"

I thanked him for the enormous effort he had made in the Middle East and for his patience in meeting so often with the leaders of the region, and expressed the hope that he could complete this important project by the time he left the White House. From my point of view, I told him, it would have been better for the world if he had served a third term—if it were up to Israeli law, I said, perhaps I could do something as the Minister of Justice. But my jurisdiction, alas, lay across the Atlantic.

I returned to Barak with my report from Washington, but the Prime Minister told me that he preferred to exhaust the bilateral process, and only then to explore the possibility of American involvement. I told him that Clinton's offer was unique and rare: If "exhausting the bilateral process" dragged on for too long, he would be unable to obtain Clinton's assistance even if he wanted it. We would simply miss the train.

On December 23, 2000, a few weeks before leaving office, Clinton did what had long been expected of him: He presented a plan of his own. This was done very carefully, and without a formal commitment. The plan did not provide solutions to all the issues, but it laid out the boundaries for negotiations and the room on each side for flexibility, based on Clinton's assessment of the situation. Clinton summoned the Israeli and Palestinian delegations, read to them all the points at dictation speed, asked for responses within a few days, and threatened that if he did not receive affirmative replies the plan would be off the table. Both parties responded positively, but each attached a list of reservations which called into question the extent of their agreement.

By January 19, 2001, Clinton's last day in office, there had been no breakthrough based on the Clinton Plan, but two days later, when talks between Israel and the Palestinians began at Taba, the Clinton Plan was the basis for all discussions, even if this was not formally acknowledged. These talks saw the greatest progress between the two sides since the beginning of Oslo, and President Clinton's contribution proved decisive. But the Taba talks, like the Clinton Plan itself, came at a time when it was impossible to achieve a breakthrough, with elections in Israel just weeks away.

THE FIRST TIME I SAW CLINTON after Sharon's election was in New York, at an evening in honor of the "Seeds of Peace" project at Carnegie Hall on June 11, 2001, at which we both spoke. After the event, he and I discussed what could still be done in the Middle East, under the new circumstances. His interest in peace between Israel and the Palestinians had not dissipated; on the contrary, this was a man who had been hurt by the failure to conclude an agreement, and who was still willing to do everything in his now-limited power to lend a hand. I told him that I felt the Clinton Plan had been his greatest contribution; he had withdrawn the plan after leaving office, and it was not binding on the new administration, but no entity in the world could ignore it. When sanity returns to the region, I assured Clinton, both parties would resume talks, and his plan would be the only basis for further negotiations. He was glad to hear this, and glad to hear that Yasser Abed Rabbo and I were involved in informal negotiations for a draft permanent agreement, based, of course, on his plan.

CHAPTER 3
THE NETANYAHU YEARS: KILLING THE PEACE, SOFTLY

M R. PRIME MINISTER, *there have been examples, in this century, when heads of state have gone crazy . . . Chamberlain acted with blatant stupidity when he believed the liar Hitler and that is exactly what you are doing . . . You are far worse than Chamberlain. You are endangering the security and freedom of your own people. In this case you are giving credence to the liar Arafat, as if his promises, his words, his agreements have some value. You cannot believe a word the man says . . . We will use all legitimate means at the disposal of a democratic opposition to stop this foolish process, which endangers the very future of the country."* This was Benjamin Netanyahu's statement in the Knesset on August 30, 1993, when word arrived of the agreements reached at Oslo; since then, and throughout all his years in opposition, Netanyahu has continued to attack the Oslo process from every possible platform.

AT THE END OF THE BEWILDERING NIGHT of May 29, 1996, after the tense counting of the votes, and the apparent reversal of fortune, from the anguish of defeat to the joy of victory, I awoke to a traumatic surprise. The polls and the early returns the night before had suggested a Peres victory, and I had been interviewed very late on all of the networks—CNN, CBS, ABC, and the BBC—as if Peres had won. But by morning, the situation had changed dramatically, and Netanyahu was the winner.

Until Rabin's assassination in November 1995, the two parties had been very close in the polls, and a victory by Netanyahu at the next elections was not out of the question. But following the assassination, the polls gave a huge advantage—nearly twenty-five percent—to Peres, and while such a vast margin was sure to diminish over time, a Labor victory seemed a sure thing.

Netanyahu's position in the wake of Rabin's murder was made even more difficult because he had been accused of incitement against Rabin; it was suggested that he was, however indirectly, one of those who had caused the murder. When I was interviewed on Israeli television, I said, "Be careful with such accusations, because Netanyahu is not behind such a murder. I'm sure that he is shocked, exactly as I am, and even if he said some harsh things, he did not incite to kill Rabin."

After this TV appearance, I got two phone calls. The first was from Leah Rabin, who was furious with me. "Why are you saying these things?" she asked. "He did incite. We all saw him. And he should take part of the blame for the murder of my husband." The second call was from Netanyahu, who said, "Yossi, you are a true friend, and I appreciate it. There is a kind of lynching against me, and you are the only voice saying otherwise."

At this point, Netanyahu was no competition for Peres; the very legitimacy of his candidacy was in question. Had Peres believed he had even a slim chance of losing, he would never have called for early elections, as he did in January 1996. But the four major terrorist attacks in February played a critical role in shifting the electorate toward the Likud; there was a heavy death toll, and people said "enough is enough." The public felt that the government had not done enough to prevent the attacks, and this, more than anything else, turned the election against Peres. Netanyahu claimed he would support Oslo, but would not tolerate any violence from the Palestinians.

But Netanyahu's victory was not part of the plan. I was worried that the progress that had begun at Oslo would slow down, if not cease entirely. These were critical years, when the timetable called for negotiations on a permanent settlement, and a victory by the right-wing, with Netanyahu at its head, was almost certain to prevent this from happening. Before Rabin's death, I had hoped the Beilin–Abu Mazen Understandings could be the basis for a permanent settlement before the next elections in Israel, but after the terrible blow of the murder, Peres insisted that the permanent settlement would be discussed only after elections. That morning, May 30, 1996, I feared that everything would be destroyed.

Netanyahu himself was surprised by his narrow victory over Peres. He entered office with a hawkish ideology that strongly opposed the creation of a Palestinian state and any negotiations with the PLO, but he did not propose any practical alternative path. Netanyahu had been an excellent spokesman for the right for several years; he was great on television, where he could attack his opponents with great skill and passion and eloquently defend his own side. But as Prime Minister, he had to abandon rhetoric for political action, and this proved quite a challenge.

According to the interim agreement known as Oslo II, signed September 28, 1995, three redeployments were set to take place during Netanyahu's tenure, and a permanent agreement was to be signed by May 4, 1999. Netanyahu regarded the Oslo Agreement as a mere component in what he suspected was a "stage by stage" PLO plan to destroy Israel; he saw it as his mission to bring about the dismantling of the Oslo process—and he succeeded. In those critical years, the government of Israel prevented the implementation of the interim agreement and ruined any hope of collaboration with the Palestinian Authority. In my view, Netanyahu is the person most responsible for the persistence of the Israeli-Palestinian crisis, though the Palestinians, of course, should not be exonerated for their part in the matter.

The PLO, as Netanyahu tells it in his 1993 book, *A Place Among the Nations*, has only one aim, which he calls *policide*—to destroy the Jewish state. "A PLO state implanted ten miles from the beaches of Tel Aviv," he writes, "would be a mortal danger to the Jewish state."

"At Oslo," he says in another book, *Fighting Terror*, "Israel in effect accepted the first stage of the PLO's Phased Plan: a gradual withdrawal to the pre-1967 border and the creation of the conditions for an independent PLO state on its borders." By the time Netanyahu was elected Prime

Minister, a considerable portion of the leadership of the right in Israel had come to terms with the inevitable establishment of a Palestinian state; their principal concerns were to keep it demilitarized and to prevent a return to the 1967 borders. On the eve of the elections, Netanyahu had announced that he too would abide by the Oslo Agreement, but if he still believed what he had written in his books, this was a promise that he had no intention of keeping.

Netanyahu, who had not voted for Oslo and had agitated for years against it, could nevertheless see in opinion polls that the public still backed the peace process. His vow to support it appeared to be a gambit deployed when he thought he had no chance of winning. But it paid off: The four terrorist attacks in February and March of 1996 severely damaged Peres, and Netanyahu's eventual narrow victory was almost certainly a result of this ploy.

IN ANY AGREEMENT, RECIPROCITY IS TAKEN FOR GRANTED; no party wants to fulfill its side of a contract without the compliance of the other side. However, in a political agreement, you are both a party to the agreement and its judge; it is necessary to sometimes turn a blind eye to a minor breach in order to sustain the agreement itself. For example, the Egyptians and Jordanians withdrew their ambassadors to Israel following the outbreak of the second Intifada in 2000. This is counter to the original agreement, and we could have said, "If you are recalling your ambassadors, we will do the same"—that would have been reciprocity. But no one even suggested it, not even the far right, because in such a delicate situation, both sides were invested in the success of the agreement.

It might be acceptable, in private life, to insist on complete reciprocity in every interaction. But the truth is that nobody will appreciate this, and you will be seen as an unrealistic person. The question becomes, what are the red lines? If you allow the other side to breach an agreement in a way that goes against your national interest, then you are not a responsible leader. But if you turn a blind eye to something which is marginal because you know that down the road there are more important things, then you are a realistic leader.

With Netanyahu, the truth was very clear: He had no use for the Oslo Agreement, and he manipulated the situation to his benefit. He didn't have to lie; the other side did the breaching. When he said, "I will not tolerate any breach of the agreement," it was not out of fidelity to the Oslo Accords or a desire to hold the Palestinians to their word, but rather because he was eager to be free of the agreement itself. The other side delivered just the right pretext. Netanyahu wasn't disturbed by the Palestinian violations; in fact, they gave him license to violate the agreement himself. If the implementation of the Oslo Accords were to go before a neutral adjudicator, he or she would presumably rule that both sides made significant violations. Israel's violations can be measured; withdrawals were scheduled for specific dates, none of which Israel managed to fulfill on time. The Palestinian violations—in the realms of security cooperation, prevention of incitement, and so on—cannot be quantified as precisely, but the evidence is ample. Netanyahu was fond of quoting Rabin—who had said, "There are no holy dates"—to defend his delays on the Palestinian track; this surprisingly injudicious statement by Rabin allowed Netanyahu to justify to many people his failure to fulfill the agreement.

Netanyahu did not carry out the interim agreement of September 1995, and reciprocity was the device he used to justify his actions. Beyond the problem of his own ideology, he was flanked by a rightist government that had no desire to pay a price for peace. Netanyahu had been appointed to drive a train that was traveling along a fixed track according to a predetermined timetable, which was a rare and unique opportunity. All of his predecessors as Prime Minister had taken up their posts, announced their commitment to Israel's security, and then attempted—each according to his predisposition and ability—to hold political talks with the neighbors while "offering his hand in peace." Netanyahu had already vowed to do the opposite, declaring in 1994 that he would not honor the Oslo Agreement when the Likud returned to power because "the PLO had already violated it by not preventing terror." He had changed his tone to get elected, but now he was in office, and was faced with the real decision.

The train was on the Oslo track: peace with the PLO under Yasser Arafat's leadership; the transfer of territories on the West Bank to the

Palestinian Authority; and a permanent settlement by May 1999. Most of Gaza and the area around Jericho had been transferred to the Palestinians following the 1994 Cairo Agreement; the other Palestinian cities (except Hebron) came under the control of the Palestinian Authority in December 1995, following the Oslo II interim agreement. A separate arrangement had been reached in September 1995 for the IDF's departure from Hebron, with the Jewish quarter remaining in Israel's hands, but this had been postponed—with Palestinian consent—until June because of the terrorist attacks at the start of 1996. The timetable called for Netanyahu to carry out three withdrawals at six-month intervals beginning in September 1996, and to complete the talks on a permanent settlement that had officially begun at Taba on May 4, 1996, by the required date.

Wary of negotiating with the Palestinians, Netanyahu tried to shift the discussion to other channels; he declared early in his tenure that he would put Lebanon first, and tried to examine possibilities for an agreement with Syria, with the IDF's evacuation of southern Lebanon as a proposed first stage. But Netanyahu was caught; the peace talks with Syria, begun under Peres's direction in December 1995, were not going well. It was clear to everybody that in principle, as the late Prime Minister Yitzhak Rabin had stated, Israel was willing—in return for peace—to withdraw to the lines of June 4, 1967 and to evacuate the Golan settlements. The IDF continued to control southern Lebanon, and each day on which no soldiers were injured and no Katyusha rockets were fired into Israel was regarded as a lucky one.

It quickly became clear to Netanyahu that the last thing Hafez al-Assad wanted was to relinquish his Lebanese card. Assad wanted complete Israeli withdrawal from the Golan Heights, "in return" for which he was prepared to allow Netanyahu to finally leave Lebanon. Netanyahu's term began with his "Lebanon first" announcement, and ended with the highest number of casualties there in a single year since the start of the war in 1982.

NETANYAHU IS UNMISTAKABLY A MAN OF FIRST IMPRESSIONS. Many world leaders, upon meeting him, were very impressed by his knowledge, his demonstrable humanity, his self-confidence, and particularly his deep commitment to peace. He impressed his listeners with his plans to make peace with the

Palestinians, with Syria, and with Lebanon during his tenure, as if he knew precisely how this was to be done. He would assure each of his interlocutors that, by their next meeting, he would have a full update of the progress made on a given initiative. A European head of state once told me that one should arrange to talk directly to Netanyahu only at a second meeting with him. "Only then," he continued, "will it be apparent that nothing said at the first meeting has been delivered."

The credit Netanyahu gained from his first meetings with Arab leaders, especially with President Mubarak and King Hussein, enabled him to delay the execution of his first task—the Hebron Agreement—by six months, and then to boast that his rightist government had (ostensibly) accomplished what Peres had not done. The ice between Netanyahu and Arafat was broken in their first meeting at the Erez crossing at the northern end of the Gaza Strip at the beginning of September 1996. The cameras caught every flicker of body language, focused on the handshake of the two leaders who had never met before, and tried to capture their discomfort, their artificial smiles, and the "It almost didn't hurt!" expressions on both of their faces. A short while later, however, Netanyahu made his worst blunder. This was the rash decision on September 24 to open the Western Wall Tunnel, a Hasmonean passage leading from the Temple Mount to the Muslim quarter. Excavation work on the tunnel had already been completed in the summer of 1995 but security officials had made it clear that opening the tunnel would be an explosive decision that would undoubtedly be perceived as a provocation by the Palestinians. Netanyahu did not heed their advice and, much to the surprise of the security service, gave instructions to open the tunnel on the evening after Yom Kippur. The reaction from the Arab world and the international community was extremely severe. Arafat said, "For their nation, Palestinians will kill and be killed," and the occupied areas were indeed ablaze the next day. There were serious clashes at Kfar Darom in the Gaza Strip and at Joseph's Tomb near Nablus. For the first time, Palestinian police shot at IDF soldiers; Israel moved tanks into West Bank towns. Fifteen IDF soldiers and eighty Palestinians were killed, and another 1,290 Palestinians were wounded.

During Netanyahu's three years in power, more than 4,000 housing units were built in settlements in the territories, and tension and hostility grew. The multilateral talks on issues of water, arms control, the environment, economic cooperation, and refugees drew to a halt. A veritable peace industry had been born at the 1991 Madrid Conference, incorporating thirteen Arab states and professionals from all over the world—Arabs, Israelis, Americans, Russians, Europeans, and others—who saw themselves as part of the new chapter opening in the Middle East. Joint ventures were established; real problems began to be solved. But now nothing remained of all this. The annual Middle Eastern and North African economic conferences that began in Morocco in 1994, and had become a real success story, also ceased. The Arab world was not prepared to continue with steps toward normalization because they were not accompanied by the implementation of the peace agreement. Netanyahu refused to abide by the timetable because there was no reciprocity: The Palestinians had not collected arms, turned over a list of Palestinian police, or moved to combat incitement. Each side prepared its own details of the other's violations. The Palestinians offered the dossier of Israeli violations to anyone who requested them; Israel publicized the Palestinian violations. And the sides returned to their usual way of working, each one presenting the other to the world as an empty vessel and expecting applause.

The United States quickly entered the picture, and arranged for representatives to meet in Washington under the auspices of President Clinton, a week after the tunnel riots. From that moment on, American involvement became a fact, and the two sides were virtually unable to talk without the United States. No longer were principle documents prepared in Oslo to the surprise of the American Secretary of State; no more peace treaties, like the one with Jordan, through secret talks. All the work was now trilateral.

On January 15, 1997, after a night meeting at the Erez crossing between Netanyahu and Arafat, the Hebron Agreement was signed. Hebron is a very important place for several reasons. The Tomb of the Patriarchs—one of two Jewish holy sites in the West Bank—is located there, and Hebron is the first important city in Jewish history; in the Bible, Abraham lives in Hebron, and he is buried there. The Hebron protocol divided the town into a Palestinian zone (H-1) and an Israeli one (H-2). It specified patrol activities, established a temporary international presence in the town (a force of 200 observers), assigned responsibility for the holy places, and attempted to ensure the unity of the town despite the division. The Palestinians imposed limitations themselves on planning and building in their zone.

On the day the protocol was signed, Dennis Ross, the American special envoy to the Middle East, prepared "a note for the record" at Netanyahu and Arafat's request, as an alternative to a signed agreement between them. The "note" contains an explicit commitment to continue the Oslo process and to implement the previous requirements. Netanyahu committed himself to carry out the next stage of the planned redeployment in the first week of March 1997 (in other words, six months after the original date), deal with the release of political prisoners, and renew negotiations on all disputed subjects. The Palestinians committed themselves to complete the alterations to the Palestinian covenant, to combat terror and incitement, and to confiscate illegal arms. After the Hebron protocol was signed, Secretary of State Warren Christopher sent a letter to Netanyahu; he congratulated Netanyahu on the signing, promised that the United States was committed to Israel's security, and asserted that, in the view of the United States, all redeployments had to be completed by the middle of 1998.

After the Hebron Agreement, it seemed that Netanyahu would be forced to stay on the Oslo path. There was speculation that he would be another Charles de Gaulle or, at least, a new Begin. Netanyahu often told the media that he would surprise everybody, and when a Prime Minister says something like that, it must be taken seriously. As he acquired more esteem in the Arab world, the United States, and Europe, his parliamentary support from the left in Israel grew (the Hebron Agreement was approved in the Knesset by an overwhelming 87-to-17 margin), so the right made life more difficult for him.

The cabinet meeting to approve the same agreement, by contrast, lasted more than fifteen hours, and became a forum for the most right-wing ministers—particularly the so-called Likud "Princes"—to express their distaste for the peace process. The Princes were all sons and daughters of former Likud Knesset members. The Likud had been a very small group when it originally formed, but a very tight one; they called themselves—seriously at first, and later on with a smile—the "fighting family." They saw themselves as a persecuted minority in the era of Mapai, the ruling Socialist-Zionist party of Ben-Gurion and the forerunner of today's Labor Party. Israeli social democracy in the 1950s and 1960s was anathema to the Likudniks, who saw it as a replica of Soviet Russia; the Likud even fought the kibbutzim, seen by many as Israel's greatest success, because of their supposedly "communist" collective structure. Before 1977, there had been a clear division between the parties regarding the peace process; the Likud had always opposed territorial compromise and been uninterested in peace talks. During the negotiations between Sadat and Begin, however, Likud took the lead and Labor supported them; similarly, the 1991 Madrid Conference took place during the Likud premiership of Yitzhak Shamir. So while it would be incorrect to say that the Likud were always hawks and Labor always doves, most of the time it was the case.

The meeting to approve the Hebron Agreement dragged on into the night, and after nine o'clock, the father of Limor Livnat, then the Communications Minister, called his daughter. He told her that Israel's Channel 1 was reporting that a U.S. State Department spokesman had announced that the Israeli interpretation of the agreement, according to which Israel would determine the size of each redeployment, was not acceptable to the United States. This, however, had been the principal argument Netanyahu used to placate his ministers, insisting Israel alone would have the authority to decide on withdrawals. When Livnat told the others what her father had said, Netanyahu stopped the meeting. "If there is no American clarification," Netanyahu insisted, "there will be no vote tonight." Some thought that this put an end to the matter, and Ariel Sharon quickly approached Livnat to ask her to congratulate her father on his behalf. Only a few minutes had passed when frantic telephone calls began to come in from Dennis Ross and Martin Indyk, who explained that the announcement did not reflect the American position, and that the actual position was expressed in Warren Christopher's letter, which made clear that such withdrawals were Israel's sole decision. These telephone conversations enabled a vote to occur, in which eleven ministers voted in favor and seven against, but they also allowed Netanyahu to propose a meager withdrawal on March 6 that was intended merely to discharge his duties, since it was clear in advance that the Palestinians would not accept such a minor redeployment.

The September 1995 interim agreement had divided the West Bank into three zones: In Area A, about four percent of the West Bank, including the largest cities, the Palestinian Authority had administrative and security control; in Area B, roughly twenty-five percent of the territory, Israel controlled security while the Palestinians retained administrative authority; and Area C, the rest of the West Bank, remained under Israeli control, with incremental redeployments to follow according to the timetable. Netanyahu's post-Hebron proposal, rejected by the Palestinians, was to transfer 0.13 percent of the West Bank from Israeli-controlled Area C to Area A, and 1.87 percent from Area C to Area B. The right fiercely criticized the Hebron protocol. Some members of Netanyahu's family spoke out against him in interviews, and Benny Begin, the Science Minister, resigned from the government. As expected, the Palestinians claimed that this withdrawal was a mockery, and refused to accept the territory.

Less than two months later, the government made a decision that led to the total cessation of talks with the Palestinians on the implementation of the Hebron Agreement. This was the decision to build a Jewish neighborhood at Har Homa, in the southern part of East Jerusalem, and to establish another neighborhood next to it for young Arab couples. Land in the area had already been expropriated by the Shamir government in 1991, but previous governments had not approved any construction. After the decision was made, Arafat refused any attempt by Netanyahu to meet, contending that if bulldozers appeared at Har Homa after their meeting, it would appear that he had lent his support to the construction. President Clinton approached Netanyahu three times to request that he not build at Har Homa, but Netanyahu repeatedly refused. Abu Mazen said to his Israeli interlocutors: "You are turning a diminishing dispute, an Israeli-Palestinian dispute that was about to be resolved, into a hopeless Jewish-Muslim dispute. Do you have any idea of the effect of the television images on millions of Muslims who view Har Homa as a provocation? Have you any idea how many of them will decide to do something about it? The tension and the strained atmosphere are liable to lead a few lunatics to carry out terrorist actions, against the wishes of Arafat's government!"

At the end of March 1997 the bulldozers moved onto the Har Homa site, and a short while later approval was given for the building of 231 housing units at Ras al-Amud in East Jerusalem to meet the needs of an ultra-orthodox community. The Palestinians put a stop to negotiations on both an interim agreement and a permanent agreement. The United States used its veto to block a United Nations Security Council resolution denouncing the settlement construction, further deepening the Palestinian disillusionment with the peace process. Israel and the Palestinians, it seemed, were determined to continue the conflict. Over the course of the next few months, many proposals to break the deadlock, both American and Palestinian, were rejected by the Netanyahu government, chiefly because of the demand to freeze the settlements.

The situation was undermined further on October 1 with the botched Mossad attempt to assassinate a Hamas leader, Khaled Mashal, in Amman, by injecting poison into his ear. The Israeli agents were arrested by Jordanian security officials during the failed operation; in order to secure their release, Israel had to deliver an antidote for Mashal, who had been poisoned but was not yet dead, and release Sheikh Ahmed Yassin, the founder and spiritual leader of Hamas. Yassin was flown to Amman in the middle of the night in King Hussein's own helicopter.

This was a fatal operational and political failure. Relations with Jordan, which were particularly important to Netanyahu, suffered a severe blow, and Danny Yatom, the head of the Mossad, became persona non grata there. Netanyahu found himself in the position that he had long derided, surrendering to terror. Netanyahu, Mr. Anti-terrorism—who had been a fierce critic of the 1985 deal with Ahmed Jibril's Popular Front for the Liberation of Palestine–General Command, which freed 1,150 terrorists in exchange for three Israeli prisoners—had released from an Israeli prison the man who more than anyone personified Palestinian terror, to free two Israelis. From the seat of the Prime Minister, no doubt, things are more complicated, but the price we paid was very high; not just an increase in terror and damage to relations with Jordan, but another strain in relations with Arafat.

On the Palestinian street, Hamas is the PLO's greatest rival. The Oslo Agreement had strengthened the PLO against Hamas because it proved their ability to offer the Palestinians a genuine change in their lives, beyond eternal war with Israel. Arafat had requested the release of Sheikh Yassin even before he returned to Gaza. At our first meeting in October 1993 in Tunis, Arafat suggested that if Yassin was released as a result of his request, he could guarantee that Yassin would not conduct a policy of terror. Arafat asked Rabin a few times for Yassin to be released into his hands, but his request was refused because security officials believed Yassin would not take any notice of Arafat and would increase terrorist activity. The release of Yassin into the hands of King Hussein was a tough political blow for Arafat. Arafat's supporters were content to blame Netanyahu—"While you demand that we arrest Hamas members, you release their leader!"— but Arafat himself was forced to visit Amman to pay homage to Yassin and kiss him. The sickly Sheikh discovered new physical strength, undertook a long trip to great acclaim around the Muslim world, and collected funds for Hamas, with Netanyahu helpless to stop him. This strengthening of Hamas at the PLO's expense further clouded the already turbid relationship between Netanyahu and Arafat.

EVEN AFTER NETANYAHU'S VICTORY I maintained my network of Palestinian contacts, and we met regularly. We felt it was important to continue working together to keep the process alive for the future, though it quickly became apparent that these meetings were producing results in the present as well. One of these channels was the talks that Haim Ramon, Nimrod Novick, and I had with Abu Mazen and Saeb Erekat at the residence of Mohammed Bassiouni, the Egyptian ambassador. We tried to advance toward the final status agreement by suggesting proposals to bridge the Palestinian demand to implement the Hebron Agreement with what seemed to us to be Netanyahu's practical room for maneuver. The Prime Minister was talking about a withdrawal of approximately ten percent and about reciprocity; Arafat spoke about forty percent and reciprocity. We formulated a multi-stage proposal that balanced Israeli and Palestinian actions and included the transfer of thirteen percent of the West Bank from Area C, full Israeli control, to Area B, partial Palestinian control, and the transfer of fourteen percent of the West Bank from Area B to Area A, full Palestinian control. The aim of the Israelis in the group, including myself, was mainly to persuade the Palestinians, who had despaired of ever reaching an agreement with Netanyahu, that despite everything, he was a reasonable man of the world who would not lead Israel into an impasse and damage relations with the United States. If Netanyahu was offered a package he could live with, the interim agreement would be signed in the end.

We exchanged drafts for three or four months with the United States government—the State Department and occasionally the National Security Council—and the State Department presented the package to the Israelis and Palestinians in March 1998. Egypt pressed both sides to accept the American proposal, and on March 20, the Palestinians conveyed to the Americans their willingness to agree. The following day, Netanyahu called Clinton to say that his government would not last five minutes if he agreed to the American plan; one day later, the cabinet formally rejected the proposed thirteen-percent withdrawal.

At the time of Rabin's funeral in 1995, I accompanied Prince Charles, and then Tony Blair, throughout the proceedings. I had never met Blair before, but he and I had a chance to talk extensively at the King David Hotel in Jerusalem. He knew about my work on the Oslo process and I told him about the understandings that had been reached with Abu Mazen; he suggested that we have a kind of joint seminar with Clinton, about whom he spoke very highly. Blair was very friendly and informal in all our meetings; he believed throughout that a clear plan was possible, and that it was imperative to move as fast as possible.

On March 13, 1998, I met in London with Blair and his Foreign Secretary, Robin Cook, and they described a long telephone conversation between Blair and Clinton that had taken place a few days earlier, in which Blair had urged Clinton to present an American plan to implement the interim agreement. According to my hosts, European pressure was building, and an anti-Israel declaration had been narrowly averted at a recent meeting of European foreign ministers. But the call for a European initiative—or to convene another Madrid Conference—would grow stronger if an American plan was not submitted by the end of the month.

In order to prevent further delays, the Americans concocted an artificial target date, May 4, 1998—a year before the deadline for the permanent agreement—and announced a summit on that day in London, to be attended by Albright, Netanyahu, and Arafat. On April 20, the Americans declared: "If the sides do not make tough decisions this time, we are pulling out of the process."

I met Albright on April 26 during a visit to the United States. I had known her for a few years and we had met many times, but I had never seen her so angry. The procrastination had become a personal insult to her. "Netanyahu's playing for time will not be endless," she insisted. "Within a few days, this whole embarrassing process will stop, one way or another."

That same day, Dennis Ross met with Arafat. Relations between the two had been very strained. Arafat had described Ross, unfairly, as an arrogant person who was too close to the Israelis; at one point, Arafat had gone so far as to refuse to meet with him. It fell to me, somewhat awkwardly, to explain to Arafat what a mistake it was to shun Ross. After that, Arafat displayed a readiness to meet Ross, at least as a personal gesture toward me.

At this meeting with Ross, Arafat heaped scorn on Netanyahu. He complained that he had reached the limit of his capabilities—that Netanyahu was pressing ahead with the settlements, continuing the land expropriations, and failing to abide by the timetable to which he had committed himself. The situation had become so bad, Arafat told Ross, that he was incapable of explaining to his advisors why he remained committed to the process and was still making an effort to prevent a violent eruption. Ross promised Arafat that on May 4 in London, the die would be cast. If the American proposal was not agreed to, Clinton would announce who had accepted it and who had rejected it in an upcoming speech on the Middle East.

On the eve of the summit, the Palestinians made it clear that the American proposal for a redeployment of thirteen percent was acceptable to them, but Netanyahu declared he would not agree to it. On May 4, there was no trilateral summit and the meetings took place separately. Netanyahu pressed the fuming Albright not to release the American proposal, while Arafat demanded its publication as a condition for the trilateral talks with Netanyahu and Albright.

Albright and Netanyahu sat for five hours, and the Prime Minister insisted he could not withdraw more than eleven percent. After meeting with Arafat and again with Netanyahu, Albright asked for Clinton's permission to make a speech that would place the blame on Israel, but the President asked her to wait for a few days. The meeting between Albright and Netanyahu the next day, May 5, lasted exactly ten minutes. Netanyahu protested that he had to present the American proposal to his ministers before reaching a decision. She said to him: "You are the Prime Minister and you are the leader. You understand the significance of the situation and you need to lead the way." After a short meeting with Arafat, she invited the two leaders to another summit the following Monday in Washington. She made it clear to Netanyahu that if by then an understanding had not been achieved and "a clear Israeli answer" to the American initiative had not been delivered, the summit would not take place, and the United States would "reexamine its approach to the peace process." She would say later, of her discussions with Netanyahu, that it was like "negotiating in hell."

"A senior source" in Netanyahu's office was quoted in the press to the effect that "the Prime Minister's strategic goal was achieved: The Oslo process was halted." Netanyahu said it was not certain that he would attend the proposed summit and told Dennis Ross a few days later in Jerusalem that the Americans "want to humiliate me." Clinton cancelled the summit and asked Albright to meet with Netanyahu, who was visiting the United States. On May 12, before her meeting with the Prime Minister, Albright appeared at the National Press Club in Washington to deliver an address on the peace process, in which she expressed her disappointment unequivocally. She had hoped, she said, to launch the permanent agreement talks in Washington by this date, but the disparities between the sides were preventing it. The past year, she lamented, had been the most disappointing one since Oslo, and a crisis of confidence between the two sides was turning a situation in which each problem seemed solvable into one where there was endless dispute over every small detail. For more than a year, Albright noted, the United States had tried to bridge the gaps. Netanyahu had asked for her help in the transition to negotiations on the permanent settlement, and President Clinton had enlisted in the cause. The Palestinians and Israelis had already agreed, in September 1997, on a four-point agenda, which included accelerated negotiations toward a permanent agreement and an effort at security collaboration, but Israel was reassessing its position, and there had been no further steps. Since then, of course, negotiations had not gone well.

With the process at an impasse, Albright explained, the United States decided to submit a proposal of its own to bridge the four issues, aiming to take the interests of both sides into consideration, ensure reciprocity, and progress in stages. These were just proposals, not an ultimatum or an attempt to enforce a settlement. The two sides were given lots of time to consider the American proposal, though Israel requested even more time to examine them, while Arafat agreed in principle to accept—in spite of the fact, as Albright pointed out, that the area the Americans had proposed for Israel's withdrawal had been much closer to the Israeli position than to the Palestinian one. Even though the principles were not agreed upon, the Palestinian Authority was entitled to commendation for its activities against terrorist elements. The negotiations on the permanent settlement had to be completed by May 4, 1999, Albright said, and "those who believe they can declare unilateral positions or take unilateral acts when the interim period ends are courting disaster." In response to questions, Albright said that the current process could not continue forever, and that the present stage was rapidly nearing its end; she reiterated that if the American proposal was not accepted, the United States would reconsider its approach to the conflict.

This was the most Albright could do. Anybody reading her remarks carefully will find in them a severe criticism of Netanyahu, while those who actually heard her speaking may have perceived a cautious, diplomatic speech. This was the most far-reaching alternative to what she really wanted to do: present the American proposal publicly, point an accusing finger at Netanyahu, and announce that the United States was taking time for reassessment.

THE AMERICAN ISRAEL PUBLIC AFFAIRS COMMITTEE (AIPAC) held its annual conference in Washington three days later, on May 15. A few words about AIPAC, the powerful American lobby, are in order. It has been around since 1953, but it has not always taken such a hard line; for many years, in fact, this was not the case. AIPAC has helped Israel to get serious financial and security support from the United States, and it has always been very efficient. So AIPAC is undoubtedly a success story, and it has helped Israel in many ways, but it has moved further and further to the right in the last few decades, especially after Tom Dine ended his term as Director in 1993. It was a confrontational organization even during the years of the Labor-Likud unity government, from 1984 to 1990, and always found a pretext on which to take the more hawkish line. Today, however, AIPAC is not a player in Israeli politics or media; it is rarely discussed or referred to except by insiders.

The 1998 AIPAC conference was a clear demonstration of the power of the organization, which had earned a reputation as the most important and daunting lobby in the United States. Dozens of senators and hundreds of congressmen were due to attend the event, and Prime Minister Netanyahu was scheduled to appear in the evening. The atmosphere in Washington at the time was one of bitter confrontation between the American administration and the Likud government; Clinton and his team felt they had made every effort to assist with the implementation of the Oslo Agreements, while Netanyahu had done everything he could to crush the process and play for time. The Israeli right, and the Jewish right in the United States, went so far as to accuse the Clinton administration of bias toward the Palestinians. Such acrimony between Israel and the administration was practically cause for rejoice within AIPAC, which had no trouble raising money and recruiting new volunteers in such an atmosphere—the days of Rabin and Peres, by contrast, had been a time of frustration for them. The expectation was that Netanyahu would be delighted at the prospect of battle and that he would deliver a fiery speech at the event, explaining why he had not implemented the agreement he signed with the Palestinians, thereby winning the enthusiastic support of the AIPAC members.

I wanted to draw the attention of the members of AIPAC to the mistake they were making by automatically supporting Netanyahu's stance, which was liable to endanger Israel as May 4, 1999 approached and could lead to a confrontation with Clinton's friendly administration. I decided to do something I had never done before: On the day Netanyahu was due to talk, with the aid of a friend from Atlanta, Steve Berman, I placed a full-page advertisement in the *Washington Times*. In the ad, I expressed appreciation for all AIPAC's work to secure assistance for Israel, but I stressed that the implementation of the Oslo process had become a salient Israeli interest, and that Netanyahu had signed the Hebron Agreement in which he changed the timetable for Israeli withdrawals. This commitment had not materialized, the Clinton administration had suggested a new timetable, and acceptance of the American proposal was now the only way to continue the peace process—which had brought Israel peace with Jordan and led to relations with a large part of the Arab world. If the process was abandoned and we did not reach an agreement by May 4, 1999, the five years of the interim agreement would end, and we could expect a very severe crisis that no true supporter of Israel wanted. The advertisement read as follows:

> One of our main strategic assets alongside a strong IDF is our relationship with the United States, and for this reason I turn to you. AIPAC's very raison d'être, as defined by yourselves, is "to further deepen and strengthen the U.S.'s relationship with Israel." And this cause has been served over the years by a responsible policy of consensus and seeking common interests. Recently there have been signs of a dangerous deviation from this path— exemplified by the Senators' letter.
>
> AIPAC must never be open to the accusation that it is serving the interests of the extreme right in Israel; it should never be open to the accusation that it has become an obstacle to peace; and it must never be open to the accusation that it is championing confrontation rather than cooperation with the United States government.

When you applaud Prime Minister Netanyahu on Sunday night, remember that you are applauding Israel, her relationship with the United States, her closeness to American Jewry, and that we will applaud you as long as you remain true to your founding principles and to our shared Israeli-American agenda.

I suspect that the leaders of AIPAC did not really like this ad, but the general public in attendance at the annual conference could not ignore it. It became the subject of arguments in the corridors, and contributed to the fact that opposition to the American initiative was not taken for granted. However, at that time it was clear that the Jewish-American establishment, including the Conference of Presidents of Major American Jewish Organizations and the American Jewish Committee, supported Netanyahu's policy of foot-dragging.

"WE HAVE GONE FROM *SHALOM TO SHLEP*," said Thomas Pickering, Under-Secretary of State for Political Affairs, when we met in Washington on June 19, 1998. The feeling was that each time new hope had been raised for an Israeli-Palestinian agreement, it was dashed again. Precious time was passing, and the end of the interim agreement was imminent. Dennis Ross reckoned that Netanyahu would agree to the American proposal in the end. Although it was important, Ross said, to create a moment of truth for the two sides, the danger of an American proposal that was not followed by a positive Israeli answer was great, and it would be liable to lead to a setback in the situation. In his opinion, it was judicious to operate on the assumption that a positive answer would be forthcoming. The United States wanted an agreement and not declarations, but if there was no choice, a declaration would be released, its main aim being to prevent a tragedy in May 1999. Aaron Miller, Dennis Ross's deputy, told me that Arafat's agreement to the thirteen-percent withdrawal had been a pleasant surprise, and it was the task of the United States to get Israel to agree to it, but the waiting could not go on forever. The Palestinians and the Egyptians, who had initially expected a positive Israeli answer, were becoming impatient and now preferred the American proposal to be revealed and the blame placed on

Netanyahu. But the United States would not do this in a hurry.

Over the next few months the relationship between Netanyahu and Clinton deteriorated, to the point where Clinton simply avoided talking to him on the phone. However, the matter dragged out for a few more months, because the massively obtrusive Monica Lewinsky affair shifted the Middle East from the top of the American agenda. At this point it seemed that two schools of thought were emerging in the American administration—one seeking to force a quick decision in order to advance the political process and prevent its collapse, and the other lobbying for more time so that Netanyahu could stabilize his coalition. Madeleine Albright led the first school and the President was inclined toward her approach. Her argument was that further delays in the implementation of the interim agreement would jeopardize the standing of the United States in the Middle East. Dennis Ross, representing the second, believed that by forcing the issue, the Americans would bring about a situation in which the United States could be held responsible for the violence that was liable to ensue as a result.

The next key date was June 5. State Department officials hinted to Arafat that by then they would present the detailed plan publicly. The plan now included convening the Palestine National Council to approve the specific alterations to the Palestinian covenant, and the immediate renewal of negotiations on the permanent settlement. Clinton wanted to have Arafat's answer to the plan before his impending visit to China, and he believed that these adjustments to the agreement would bring about Netanyahu's assent. Back in the Middle East, however, a competition appeared to be underway to declare the patient dead.

June 5 passed, but the Americans did not "tell the tale" and publicize the document and Israel's refusal to sign. Instead they explained to the Palestinians that they believed Netanyahu would eventually agree to a withdrawal of thirteen percent, and that they would do all they could to persuade him because his assent was more important than the most con-vincing speech by any representative of the administration might be. On July 7 a meeting took place at the White House that was attended by the peace team. Those present accepted President Clinton's decision: The administration would come out with its initiative within a week, giving details of the steps to be taken and placing the blame for the deadlock on both sides. Henceforth, if Israel and the Palestinians wanted American involvement, it had to be at their initiative. The administration would announce that the Palestinians had accepted the American proposal and that Israel was not willing to give a positive answer.

In a briefing on July 13, State Department spokesman James Rubin explained that the United States had been asked to be involved in "prolonged and exhaustive" mediation between the two sides because of their inability to talk to one another. However, it was clear to the United States that a solution to the problem would not be found if the Israelis and Palestinians did not sit down together to determine the future steps that would enable the implementation of the Oslo Agreement. The ball, Rubin stated, was now in Israel's court; the Palestinians had replied positively to the American proposal, and if this did not satisfy Israel, she had to persuade the Palestinians to accept changes to the package. According to Rubin, the initiative was based on the positions of the two sides on dozens of issues, and Arafat had compromised in accepting a much smaller withdrawal than his original claim. The fact that the two sides were not talking to one another made a solution far more difficult, and the Americans were now being forced to deal with the tiniest details. They were at the final stage of the game. If it became apparent that there was no agreement between Israel and the Palestinians, the United States would end its involvement.

After a few weeks the atmosphere changed. In August, Arafat visited Oslo and said that he would not refuse a proposal in which three percent of the thirteen-percent withdrawal would be defined as a nature reserve. On September 28, Clinton, Netanyahu, and Arafat met in Washington, and a decision was made to hold a prolonged summit beginning on October 15. In a speech shortly afterwards at the United Nations, Arafat, at the request of the Americans, refrained from announcing his intention to declare a state unilaterally if there was no agreement by the May 4, 1999 deadline.

On October 7, Netanyahu and Albright were guests of Arafat's at a relaxed meeting prior to the summit. Two days later Netanyahu appointed

Ariel Sharon as his Foreign Minister, and on October 14, the government unanimously approved. Netanyahu and Sharon embarked on a joint visit to Jordan to meet Crown Prince Hassan, and that same evening they left for Wye Plantation, outside Washington. In an interview on the eve of the summit, Sharon declared, "I will make every effort to achieve peace, but I will not shake Arafat's hand"—and he would keep his word. But many people thought that Sharon's inclusion in the proceedings increased the chances of agreement, despite the fact that it seemed the gap between the sides could not be bridged.

THE SUMMIT AT WYE PLANTATION began on October 15, 1998, and lasted for eight days. The President's advisors were strongly against his decision to participate in the talks; an American president simply does not take part in intensive technical discussion of this type. President Carter's involvement at Camp David had been extremely limited, and Clinton himself had not participated in the Oslo process or the peace talks with Jordan, nor in the 1996 Wye talks between Israel and Syria. The summit was not meant to lay down any new principles or break new ground, nor to deal with any issues connected to the permanent agreement. The issues raised were technical and were supposed to be dealt with at the level of the American peace team and no higher. The Wye Summit was, in fact, superfluous. The 1995 interim agreement set out a timetable for Israeli withdrawals. When it was not implemented, it was replaced by the Hebron Agreement in 1997; when the Hebron Agreement was not carried out, an additional Israeli-Palestinian agreement was supposed to replace it, providing a third timetable for redeployment. But Clinton was invested in the process and he saw it collapsing in front of his eyes, so he decided that only his personal intervention could save it, even if his participation seemed out of place. He was right.

It was a summit in both letter and spirit: sweaters instead of ties, informal meals, and the negotiators giving one another rides on golf carts; raised voices, crises, and continuing terror in Israel; the Israelis packing their bags to return home, only to unpack and remain at Wye; and finally, on October 23, the signing of an agreement that was almost identical to the original

American proposal. In the last moments before the Sabbath eve, Clinton, Netanyahu, Arafat, and a dying King Hussein gathered, made speeches, and signed. Netanyahu gave up his insistence that only Israel could determine the scope of its withdrawals, Sharon came to the conclusion that a withdrawal of thirteen percent would not imperil the state, and Arafat sent flowers for Netanyahu's forty-ninth birthday.

The Wye Memorandum is a detailed paper. Its essential components set new dates for—and determined the size of—the redeployments. The first two phases of redeployment that had been planned were replaced with three smaller redeployments, to be carried out concurrently with Palestinian actions, principally with regard to security. Only then would the third phase of redeployment take place. These three phases, which together made up the thirteen-percent withdrawal, were steps intended, according to the Wye Agreement's introduction, "to facilitate the implementation of the interim agreement with respect to the West Bank and the Gaza Strip signed September 28, 1995." Of the thirteen-percent withdrawal from the West Bank, three percent was defined as a nature reserve, where primary security responsibility was to remain in Israeli hands.

The Palestinians committed themselves in the Wye Agreement to a policy of "zero tolerance of terror and violence toward both sides," and they were required to present to the United States a plan for combating the terrorist organizations. They would prevent the entry of arms into the areas under the jurisdiction of the Palestinian Authority, issue a special decree to prohibit incitement, and hand over to Israel a list of people serving in the police. Another part of the Wye Agreement, its most ambiguous, addressed alterations to the Palestinian covenant. Likud attached enormous importance to the PLO covenant, which made an explicit claim to the whole of Palestine. On the eve of the elections back in 1996, the leaders of Likud had pronounced that the Palestinians would never agree to renounce it. But at a session of the Palestine National Council in 1996, it had been decided by a large majority to revoke the clauses in the Palestinian covenant that were inconsistent with the Oslo Accords. Shimon Peres, who was then Prime Minister, and President Clinton welcomed the decision, regarding it as Arafat's fulfillment of his written commitment to amend the charter. Netanyahu, however, proclaimed that the covenant had not been altered by this decision at all. Even after Arafat sent a detailed letter to President Clinton in January 1998 indicating which clauses had been revoked, Netanyahu claimed that this did not constitute a legal change to the covenant. At Wye, he demanded a special session of the Palestine National Council to revoke the specific clauses, but finally accepted a compromise, which stipulated that the Executive Committee of the PLO and the Central Palestinian Council (a smaller version of the Palestine National Council) would ratify Arafat's January 1998 letter to Clinton describing the revoked clauses. Arafat, the Chairman of the PLO, along with the Chairman of the Palestine National Council, and the Chairman of the Palestinian Council (the Palestinian Authority parliament), would invite the members of the PNC, members of the Central Council, the Council, and the cabinet ministers to a conference at which President Clinton would speak, for the purpose of reaffirming their endorsement of the peace process and of the above-mentioned decisions of the Executive Committee and the Central Council.

The incorrigible Netanyahu made two miscalculations here. First, he abandoned his insistence on a resolution by the Palestine National Council, while conceding that the principal decision had actually been taken by the Palestinians in 1996. Second, he inadvertently brought about Clinton's appearance in Gaza before the Palestinian institutions within the PLO, thus lending an impetus to the establishment and recognition of a Palestinian state, which he regarded as a tragedy.

The Wye Memorandum ends with a mutual commitment to hold negotiations on the permanent status on an accelerated basis, to "make a determined effort to achieve the mutual goal of reaching an agreement by May 4, 1999," and for both sides to refrain from "unilateral activities," code for halting settlement construction. Six months remained until the end of the five-year interim agreement period, and no decision to postpone the date was made. It is hard to tell if Netanyahu really believed that he would get closer to the permanent settlement within six months. The timetable for Israeli withdrawal and for concurrent Palestinian activities lay at the heart of the document, but it was presented as its appendix. It contained a number of reciprocal steps that would all be completed within three months. Among the documents prepared along with the Wye Agreement was a letter from Albright to Netanyahu dated October 29, 1998, according to which the United States promised not to take a stance with regard to the size of the third phase. Another letter, prepared the following day, promised that the United States would act to oppose any unilateral steps, including a Palestinian declaration of statehood. In a third letter, this one from Dennis Ross to Israeli Cabinet Secretary Danny Naveh, the United States confirmed that the number of Palestinian police would not exceed thirty thousand. Yet another letter, also from Ross, assured Naveh that Israel would determine its own security needs. All these letters were on the Israeli government's desk on November 11, 1998, when it decided to approve the Wye Memorandum and the map of the first withdrawal. The cabinet resolved that the implementation of Israel's withdrawals would be dependent on the execution of parallel activities by the Palestinians, and that each stage would be submitted for the government's prior approval.

At the time of the Wye Summit I was in the opposition. I watched the proceedings in a TV studio, where I was interviewed for my reaction—I represented one side, and Rehavam "Gandhi" Zeevi, a member of the Knesset from the right-wing Moledet party, the other. It was Friday, the eve of Shabbat, and in Washington they were in a hurry to conclude everything and to prevent desecrating Saturday. As always, there was a rushed feeling at the last moment, the hurry to deliver the speeches, to listen to others, and to leave the scene. I spoke very positively about the results; when people sit together, I said, they can almost always find solutions. I praised the contribution of Clinton, and especially that of King Hussein. And I said that the Wye Agreement would hopefully accelerate the process, so that it would be possible to conclude the negotiations on the permanent solution by the deadline, a sentiment that turned out to be far too optimistic. Zeevi criticized Netanyahu for having betrayed his supporters; Netanyahu had vowed that he would not go beyond nine percent, and then he agreed to more than thirteen percent. "How is it that someone like Netanyahu," Zeevi complained, "who should understand that you cannot count on the

Palestinians, is ready to give them so much land? You can never agree with them, and Netanyahu should abandon the Oslo process."

Other stipulations, however, were made along with the government's approval of the Wye Agreement. One was that if the Palestinian Authority unilaterally declared an independent state, the government would consider itself entitled "to take all the necessary and appropriate steps, including applying Israeli law and administration in the settlement and security areas of Judea and Samaria [the West Bank]." Another stated that "the government will continue strengthening and developing settlement in Judea, Samaria, and the Gaza Strip according to a long-term plan." The most ridiculous stipulation established that the third phase would not be greater than one percent. And Foreign Minister Sharon used the opportunity to call upon the settlers to build on every hill before it was too late.

All these stipulations rendered the decision to approve the Wye Agreement meaningless. When the proposals were put to the vote in the cabinet, eight ministers voted in favor, four against, and five abstained. In the Knesset, Netanyahu had an easier time due to the support of the left. In a vote that took place on November 17 and became essentially a vote of confidence in the government, he had the support of seventy-five members against nineteen who opposed and nine who abstained. The next day, Sharon and Abu Mazen met in Jerusalem to begin negotiations on the permanent settlement. Abu Mazen was hardly enthusiastic: For him it was the second official opening within three years of the same negotiations. This meeting would also lead nowhere. On November 20, the first phase of the Wye Agreement was implemented—two percent of the West Bank in Area C was transferred to Area B in the vicinity of Jenin, and seven percent was transferred from Area B to Area A. The airport in the Gaza Strip began to operate and 250 Palestinian prisoners were released. This was the only part of the Wye Agreement carried out by Netanyahu, who avoided the implementation of the other clauses by accusing the Palestinians of failing to fulfill their end of the agreement.

IN ACCORDANCE WITH HIS COMMITMENT AT WYE, Clinton prepared for his visit to the Middle East at a time when the Palestinians were due to ratify the decision to alter the Palestinian covenant. In Israel there was much criticism of Clinton's visit to Gaza: The Palestinians had still not fulfilled their obligations, and the visit was a slap in the face to Israel. The right called for Netanyahu to boycott Clinton's visit.

On December 7, Sharon notified Albright that Israel would not continue the withdrawal unless the Palestinians revoked the covenant. The next day Netanyahu told Dennis Ross that he would not participate in the trilateral summit with Clinton and Arafat if the covenant were not revoked. On the eve of the visit of the President of the United States, the situation on the ground was turbulent. There were riots in the occupied territories on December 9, in which ten Israelis were injured, one Palestinian killed, and 192 Palestinians injured. Arafat issued one of his inflammatory declarations: "We will free our land centimeter by centimeter until [we reach] Jerusalem." Netanyahu threatened that if such declarations continued there would be no political process, and announced that he was not afraid of a confrontation with Clinton.

The next day the Central Palestinian Council decided to change the Palestinian covenant, and this removed the final obstacle in Clinton's way.

Gaza prepared excitedly for President Clinton's visit. Gaza City, in which so many American flags had been burnt before the visit—and after it—went on a spree of pro-American celebration. American flags were raised, photographs of Clinton adorned the shops, and large crowds gathered to see this man, who was so familiar from the television, in the flesh. On Saturday night, December 12, Clinton arrived in a seething Jerusalem, beginning his visit at the residence of the President of Israel. To the surprise and displeasure of President Ezer Weizman, Netanyahu, who was not supposed to speak at the ceremony, took the floor and declared that "an agreement that is violated is worthless." Clinton promised that "the United States will march alongside Israel on the path to peace," and added, "There are people who think that peace is impossible. That is why I am here." Albright demanded that Israel carry out the second phase as agreed at Wye. But in order for that to happen, another government was needed in Israel.

On Monday, President Clinton and his wife arrived at Dahaniyeh in the

Gaza Strip to inaugurate the airport. Afterwards, a conference of Palestinian institutions was held at the Shawwa Center in Gaza. Nobody checked the voting rights of the participants. Among those present were representatives of the Palestinian Authority, the Palestine National Council, the Central Council, and many "VIPs"; a number of Jewish- and Arab-Americans were there as well. The atmosphere was particularly festive, and an array of television networks made every effort to transmit the event live. Clinton delivered his speech after an open vote was taken in which a sea of hands was raised in favor of altering the covenant.

Clinton began by saying that he was the first American president addressing the Palestinian people in a city governed by Palestinians. Only a decade ago, the President said, it was inconceivable to think about a Palestinian Authority, elections in Gaza and the West Bank, relations between the United States and Palestinians, Israeli troop redeployments from the West Bank and Gaza, and Palestinian control of Gaza, Ramallah, Bethlehem, Hebron, Tulkarm, Jenin, Nablus, Jericho, and so many other places. Nobody expected an international airport in Gaza. "There is still so much mistrust and misunderstanding," Clinton said, but "you did a good thing today in raising your hands. You know why? It has nothing to do with the government in Israel. You will touch the people of Israel." The audience applauded. Clinton expressed empathy with Palestinian suffering, economic hardship, and frustration, and said that the great progress was made possible only because five years earlier the Oslo Accords had been signed, and because, in spite of the difficulties, Palestinian commitment to support the Oslo process had continued.

Clinton moved his audience when he spoke about children whose fathers were imprisoned, children whose parents had been killed during the conflict, and the need to see the other side as people and not as enemies. "Neither side," he said, "has a monopoly on pain . . . There has been a lot of hurt and harm." The need of the Palestinians to fulfill their identity and the need of the Israelis for security formed a second thread in Clinton's speech. He stressed that these two needs did not have to come at each other's expense. He spoke about the Israelis, their fears, and the younger generation, and expressed his hope that today a new page had been turned in relations between the two peoples, against the backdrop of the rejection of the relevant passages in the covenant. He devoted an important passage of the speech to incitement: "The time has come," he said, "to sanctify your holy ground with genuine forgiveness and reconciliation. Every influential Palestinian, from teacher to journalist, from politician to community leader, must make this a mission to banish from the minds of children glorifying suicide bombers; to end the practice of speaking peace in one place and preaching hatred in another; to teach school children the value of peace and the waste of war; to break the cycle of violence."

It was a speech full of hope and emotion that accentuated the achievements of recent years, did not paint the present too rosily, and anticipated groundbreaking events in advance of the permanent settlement—although it also referred to expected crises. These were words about people's ability to shake off hatred and solve long-standing international disputes. He made reference to the common past of the sons of Abraham, the chance that they would now understand one another and move forward together toward a common future.

The day after Clinton's visit to Gaza, a summit between Clinton, Netanyahu, and Arafat took place at the Erez crossing. Its aim was to ensure continued implementation of the Wye Memorandum, but its failure was indisputable. Clinton left the region on a discordant note and with hard feelings toward Netanyahu. Netanyahu was angry about what Clinton had said in his speech in Gaza, when he compared the children of murderers to the children of victims. After the Erez meeting, Netanyahu told the media that the meeting had not broken down: "The Palestinians have to fulfill the rest of their commitments." At this point, however, it became apparent that Israel was determined not to continue the implementation of the Wye Agreement. That same day, Yaakov Neeman, the Minister of Finance, resigned his post. There was a sense that the government was fragmenting; it had lost its best ministers and was left without room to maneuver. When a motion to dissolve the Knesset was brought to a vote on December 21, Likud joined the supporters for dissolution and Netanyahu did not have a majority to prevent it. In the vote, eighty-one members voted in favor and only thirty against. Israel entered a six-month campaign, with the elections set for May 17, 1999, exactly thirteen days after the permanent agreement between Israel and the Palestinians should have been signed.

ON A VISIT TO CAIRO FOUR DAYS BEFORE the end of the year, I found that expectations had been lowered substantially. Amr Moussa, the Egyptian Foreign Minister, told me that Middle Eastern leaders had "lost their faith in Netanyahu a long time ago." At the start of his tenure, they had given him credit as a young man who seemed to know the world and showed promise, but he lost it very quickly. The non-implementation of the Wye Agreement, said Moussa, had a negative impact on the region as a whole and was liable to undermine the relative stability that existed at the time. He promised that Egypt would propose an agreement to prevent the unilateral declaration of a Palestinian state, because "if this were to happen," Moussa said, "the political process could well be destroyed." He asked me to give my word that Ehud Barak would immediately make clear pronouncements, if elected, of his intention to continue with peace negotiations and the implementation of what had already been agreed. That, Moussa suggested, would make it easier to prevent the Palestinians from acting unilaterally.

My next meeting was with Dr. Osama al-Baz, President Mubarak's political advisor. He had participated in the Israeli-Egyptian peace process from its outset, and was held in high regard by both the Palestinians and the Israelis. He is an open, sincere man who hates posturing. He is very knowledgeable, and has a western education and a keen sense of humor. An exceptional person, he is a genuine believer in peace. We have had many meetings, both clandestine and open, since the '70s, and I have always appreciated his analytic ability, along with his restrained optimism. He told me about an attempt to initiate an American-Egyptian proposal that would postpone the deadline for the permanent settlement another six months. It was his view that Netanyahu had no interest in an effort of this sort, and might well try to force the issue with Arafat in an attempt to demonstrate, before the elections, that Arafat never really intended to reach an agreement with Israel. However, Egypt regarded itself as responsible for the success of the process, and would make every effort to prevent its collapse at the end of the five-year interim settlement period. He also expressed his hope that if Barak was elected, he would not continue delaying the political process.

May 4 was still being cited as the official deadline, and as late as the end of December, people were still asking if there was a chance to reach a permanent agreement by May. But after the start of the new year, the main question concerned the intentions of the Palestinians: Will they unilaterally declare a Palestinian state, or will they resort to violence? Among the Palestinians there were those, like Nabil Sha'ath, who believed that in the absence of an agreement the Palestinians had to do something, and that violence and frustration would be averted by the unilateral declaration of a Palestinian state. In contrast, Saeb Erekat believed such a declaration would display both the weakness of the Palestinians and the disparity between the actual area under their control and the area that would be declared by them to be under their sovereignty. On March 19, Arafat made another of his reckless statements: "The PLO," he boldly asserted, "is always ready for the battle of Karameh"—a reference to a 1968 raid against the PLO in Jordan, in which the Palestinians suffered heavy losses but turned back the Israeli forces—"if anybody attempts to make a mockery of us and our declarations about the establishment of a state with Jerusalem as its capital." In a speech to three thousand Fatah activists in Ramallah he said: "We are capable of starting another Intifada. The state will be founded with Jerusalem as its capital, whether they want it or not. It they don't want it, they can drink from the Dead Sea." A Palestinian official told the press afterwards that Arafat was determined to declare the Palestinian state in May.

The next day, the Foreign Ministers of Jordan and Egypt released a joint statement supporting the Palestinians' right to declare a state on May 4, and blaming Israel for undermining the peace negotiations. I was concerned that a unilateral declaration by the Palestinians would force Israel to announce that the Oslo process had been halted, and that if Barak was then elected, he would be unable to resume the negotiations. It seemed to me that some sort of "bridging loan" was the only solution for the vacuum that was liable to be formed after the deadline. We discussed this issue intensively during the meetings that Abu Mazen and I continued to hold at the residence of the Egyptian ambassador; the only question was, who could give us the "loan"?

The Americans had misgivings, but the Europeans were more concerned. During a visit to Israel by Gerhard Schroeder in May 1998, before he became the German chancellor, I hosted a breakfast for him in Jerusalem. I told him that one of the challenges he would face after his election was the May 4 deadline, which would occur during Germany's six-month tenure in the rotating European Union presidency. He was not aware of the problem, and he asked his office to remain in contact with me to examine the various ways to disarm this "mine" if, as we expected, no permanent settlement was reached. We remained in close contact, and after Schroeder's election, he dispatched an official from the German Foreign Ministry to Israel to discuss what Europe could do to prevent the Palestinians from taking any irreversible steps. The intention was to produce a European call for the Palestinians to refrain from making a unilateral declaration of statehood, and to promise them backing for their state at a later stage.

The pressure of time provoked particularly urgent European activity, although Netanyahu displayed no concern whatsoever over the impending date, and perhaps even thought that it would be a fitting opportunity to proclaim the abrogation of the Oslo Agreement on the eve of the elections. On March 25, 1999, the heads of state of the European Union accepted the Berlin Declaration. In this important document, Europe welcomed the change in the Palestinian covenant but expressed concern at the deadlock in the peace process. It called on the parties to resume final status negotiations and set a new date for ending the interim agreement, and estimated that the negotiations could be concluded within a year of starting. The Europeans urged the parties to refrain from unilateral activities and supported the Palestinian right to self-determination including an independent state. In Berlin, the European Union declared its readiness to consider the recognition of a Palestinian state if it was established in accordance with the principles of the declaration.

This was a ladder for Netanyahu to climb down, but his hysterical response hinted that his preference was for a unilateral Palestinian declaration that would kill off the process and prove—before the elections—that even Barak would not be able to negotiate with the Palestinians. On March 26, he said: "It is sad that Europe, where a third of our people perished, is attempting to impose a solution that endangers Israel." Only a month later, on April 26, the United States joined the "ladder" initiative when the administration announced its intention to conclude the Israeli-Palestinian negotiations on a final settlement within a year. This was followed by a letter from Clinton to Arafat, in which the President declared America's commitment to the peace process and its opposition to any negotiation not limited by time. At this point, Netanyahu decided to change direction, and to credit himself with the fact that Arafat had not made a unilateral declaration of statehood. At a press conference arranged by the new troika—Netanyahu, Foreign Minister Sharon, and the new Minister of Defense, Moshe Arens— the Prime Minister claimed that "the fact that Arafat did not declare a state is an important achievement for the state of Israel."

"For a whole year," Netanyahu went on, "Arafat promised dozens of times that he would declare a state and split Jerusalem. For a whole year we warned him not to do so. Arafat is a wise man. He understood that we are adamant in our responses."

Madeleine Albright, in one of her speeches most critical of the Netanyahu government, told the American Jewish Committee on May 7: "America's commitment to Israel and to the Middle East peace process is unwavering . . . On the Palestinian side, we have seen serious efforts to prevent terrorist strikes, to renounce the Palestinian Covenant, and to avoid a unilateral declaration of statehood. On the Israeli side, implementation has stalled and, unfortunately, unilateral settlement activity has persisted. This is a source of real concern to us, because of its destructive impact on the ability to pursue peace . . . America is on the side of those who are committed to peace, who uphold the law, and who judge others not on the basis of who they are, but on how they act, and whether they respect the rights of others."

CHAPTER 4
IN OPPOSITION

A FTER LOSING THE 1996 ELECTIONS, Shimon Peres resigned as head of the Labor Party. Rabin and Peres, from the generation of the 1920s, had been in and out of the government as the heads of Labor over a period spanning twenty-three years; now, at least for a while, the leadership was passed to the generation of the 1940s. There were four candidates: Ehud Barak, Shlomo Ben-Ami, Ephraim Sneh, and myself. In 1997, I was one of the most experienced politicians in the Labor Party. As a member of the party for twenty-five years, who had been elected to all of its institutions and who had served, on its behalf, in the Knesset for nine years as a deputy minister and a minister, I felt that it would not be unreasonably presumptuous to run for the party leadership. The two highest priorities, in my opinion, were to withdraw the Israel Defense Forces from Lebanon and to reach a final status agreement with the Palestinians, based on my 1995 understandings with Abu Mazen. Ehud Barak, the favored candidate, was opposed to both of these initiatives, and this was why I declared my candidacy, even though I had not been planning to do so at that point in my life.

Barak was an army Chief of Staff who had come into politics. He arrived with no political baggage and no ideology, but with the hope of introducing pragmatic policies and rehabilitating the defeated party. He represented the hawkish group in the Labor Party, while the other three of us were regarded as doves. Barak stringently opposed the acknowledgment of a

Palestinian right to statehood, which he saw as a critical bargaining card to be deployed only later in negotiations. Eventually, at the Labor Party congress that took place a short while before the primaries for the party leadership, he was prepared to compromise on a resolution that recognized the right of the Palestinian people to self-determination, which did not rule out a state as one possible manifestation of this self-determination. Barak, who as Chief of Staff had not concealed his reservations about the Oslo Agreement, and had abstained from the vote on the 1995 interim agreement when he served as a minister in Rabin's government, also opposed the idea of a withdrawal from Lebanon without an agreement with Syria. He favored a withdrawal in stages accompanied by close monitoring of each stage, to be conducted with Syria's agreement.

The race for the party leadership was a long one; it took nearly six months, during which I had to be almost everywhere in the country. There were members of the Labor Party all across Israel: I went from moshav to kibbutz, to small places and big places, and I talked endlessly. I campaigned around the clock and spoke about ten times a day. It was a fascinating and ultimately educational experience for me. I came to know so many places and people, and to learn the issues that other people truly care about. I was struck by the support that I received, and I felt I owed something in return—that I had to succeed because of my supporters, so as not to let them down. A strong collective show of support is a truly moving phenomenon, and therefore your commitment has to be very real. One could never, for example, decide to quit the race—not that I considered it. But I couldn't imagine retiring after having seen all these people applauding, with my bumper sticker on their cars and posters with my picture displayed all over the place. The campaign becomes bigger than you, and it's a truly inspiring thing.

In the primaries, Barak won a little more than half of the votes, I won over twenty-eight percent, Ben-Ami about fourteen percent, and Sneh less than seven. That day, June 3, 1997, marked the beginning of Barak's tenure as leader of the opposition. Barak did not set up a shadow cabinet, nor did he create a framework for orderly consultation. He held lots of forums at which he met with senior and junior Knesset members. Some people were insulted because they were not invited, others because they were invited but felt irrelevant. Barak's method of working quickly became clear. He would usually convene a given forum after devising a plan of action for himself. The function of the forum would not be to seek counsel, but rather to present Barak's decision—his analysis, conclusions, and recommendations—and to assign the tasks required to implement his own recommendations. Members of the Knesset who were accustomed to having their opinions considered at discussions of this sort—and affecting the conclusions—never quite got used to Barak's method, but they had no choice.

Three tactical paths were open to the Labor Party: to become a fighting opposition to Netanyahu and his government on the basis of its economic and political failures, and to try and shorten the government's life; to set up a national unity government with the Likud; or to serve as a safety net for Netanyahu, in order to encourage him to continue with the peace process. Barak weighed the alternatives by himself, and in fact tried them all. He managed the opposition diligently and with considerable success. The Netanyahu government started to show signs of weakness and became progressively weaker. Coalition discipline crumbled, and on many issues the government could be defeated. In no-confidence votes we did not manage to obtain the necessary sixty-one votes, but the opposition otherwise almost always won a majority. Gradually Netanyahu's magic vanished: He lost his popularity and his government, constantly denigrated by its own ministers, and was perceived as a failure.

There were regular arguments within the Labor Party regarding the "safety net" approach. Providing a safety net, in this context, meant supporting the government in no-confidence votes brought by the right, which were attempts to scuttle the peace process by toppling the government. We felt this was a viable way of pressuring Netanyahu to continue the peace process, but some Labor members, like Haim Ramon, vehemently opposed the safety net. I thought it might be necessary; otherwise, it would be too easy for Netanyahu to avoid any political settlement. We would get to May 4, 1999 empty-handed, and the Palestinians might declare their state, provoking the use of force by Netanyahu, making it nearly impossible for us to resume the peace process when we returned to the government. Barak tended toward the approach of Ramon, but was not set on it.

The idea of a national unity government was in the air from the moment the results of the 1996 elections became known. There was, as it happens, a willingness to discuss the possibility within Labor, but Netanyahu did not propose it. Later on, near the end of 1996, the idea was discussed by associates of Netanyahu and Peres, but nothing came of it. In the summer of 1998, further discussions were held on the topic by Netanyahu and Barak at the Mossad compound. At the beginning of August 1998, the four former candidates for the party leadership—Barak, Ben-Ami, Sneh, and I—along with Alon Pinkas, Barak's political advisor, traveled to the United States for talks with the administration, Congress, and American Jewish organizations. Barak and I stayed on after the others had left, and one evening in New York we went to a restaurant for a nice long dinner. Barak asked me a lot of questions about the nature of the national unity government that had lasted from 1984 to 1990. He made no mention of his discussions with Netanyahu, but it was clear to me from his questions that he was at an advanced stage of negotiation. I told him that he was liable to pay a high price for helping to establish a national unity government, because he would be granting it a life expectancy until November 2000, and pushing the Likud into an even more hawkish approach, since that party would seek to distinguish itself from Labor. I told Barak he would damage the slight chance that still remained of reaching a political settlement during Netanyahu's tenure. Furthermore, it would be very hard, perhaps impossible, to prove his uniqueness to the voters after collaborating with the Likud for over two years, just as Peres had failed to do so in 1988. I do not think my counsel convinced Barak not to join the unity government. What really convinced him, it seems, was his own sense that the junior party in the unity government would have no effective veto, and that he would be at the mercy of the whims of Netanyahu, over whom he would have no influence.

THE VISIT TO THE UNITED STATES was critical for the Labor Party, both to present our political program and to forge relationships between the new party leadership and the American administration. Barak was perceived by many in America as Rabin's successor, a military man, down-to-earth, confident, and pragmatic; a person who had concluded that peace was essential to Israel's national interests. We met National Security Advisor Sandy Berger and Secretary of State Madeleine Albright, who were keen to hear Barak's parliamentary intentions in the near future and his thoughts on how best to advance the peace process under Netanyahu, assuming the Prime Minister actually had an interest in doing so.

But our most emotional meeting in the United States was not with an American. It was with King Hussein, who was suffering from cancer and undergoing chemotherapy at the Mayo Clinic in Minnesota.

Hussein became king of Jordan at the age of seventeen, and he was nicknamed "the Baby." Israeli leaders would refer to him that way, saying things like, "There was a message from the Baby." He was overshadowed by his grandfather, King Abdullah, and was at first not taken very seriously, a reputation that was not helped by the defeat of the Jordanian army in 1967, when Hussein made a terrible decision to participate in the war and was tremendously weakened by his mistake. But over the years, he became one of the oldest and most experienced leaders in the Middle East; nobody had served through as many years as he had. During his lifetime he had a chance to meet almost everybody in Israel, Egypt, Syria, and Lebanon, and he became the wise man of the Middle East. His network of contacts with European and American leaders, especially before the first Gulf War, were invaluable. Even his support for Iraq during that war was forgiven, because everybody understood he had no choice. Hussein could pick up the phone and talk to everybody, including Arafat, who had been his nemesis in the '60s and '70s and then became a kind of friend. His influence extended the importance of Jordan as a state, while he became a veritable institution. Of course, peace with Israel helped his cause considerably, especially in the United States. He became a real VIP, and a fascinating one, because he was a king. People like to talk to kings, and they felt flattered when they met him and the queen. He had fine facilities, despite the poverty of Jordan. He would invite people and host them, using his private airplane to get them around. Everyone, of course, likes to be hosted in a palace. Hussein spoke

English beautifully, his knowledge was wide and unique, and he was a delight to talk to. This was part of the special charm he had in the last decades of his life.

The Hashemite royal family was never anti-Israel or anti-Semitic. I think, in fact, that it was the other way around; historically, they have been the closest to Israel. Since the beginning, King Abdullah had been inclined toward cooperation with Israel. King Hussein himself was seen as a good neighbor until 1967, and then later on again as well. In 1967, he found himself in a coalition at the last moment with Nasser, and he felt committed to move against his own will, but he was very young and inexperienced at the time.

In August 1998 we kept in touch with the King's office throughout our visit to the U.S., and the Court Minister sent word that Hussein wanted to meet us. We changed our schedule and flew straight to Minnesota in a plane belonging to Danny Abraham, an American businessman and the chairman of the Center for Middle East Peace and Economic Cooperation, along with the late Wayne Owens, a former congressman and a friend of King Hussein. Over the years I had heard wonderful things about the Mayo Clinic, and I imagined a pastoral place with small buildings set amidst vast lawns. Upon our arrival, under a torrential August rain, this was hardly the scene. Instead there was a large, ordinary hospital, with all the familiar scents in the hallways and elevators. We were sent into a spacious room where a carpet had been spread to hide the hospital's tiled floor. We sat in armchairs and after a few minutes, the King entered. Because I had seen him on television recently, I was not so taken aback, but he was nevertheless a different King Hussein. He was extremely thin and totally bald, and his facial bones had become very pronounced, but his eyes really sparkled. He entered in his usual way, smiling and with confident steps. First he embraced Barak, who he knew from previous meetings, both clandestine and open, and he embraced me too; we had met often, in various places and in various guises, and after the peace agreement was signed with Jordan I had visited him at his palace. He had never met Shlomo or Ephraim, but had heard about them and was pleased to see them.

He spoke about his disease with optimism. He said he had to undergo another series of treatments and that his doctors believed that by November he would be able to return to Jordan. He promised to assist with the peace process in any way he could, along with President Mubarak and President Clinton, but he asked if it would be possible to make progress under Netanyahu's leadership. We told Hussein that the public supported the peace process and understood that time was against us. And just as Netanyahu understood that without guaranteeing the continuation of the Oslo process he could not have been elected, he should now understand that halting the peace process would only harm him and jeopardize his future prospects. Before the discussion ended, the King asked if there was still a chance of returning to November 3, meaning the day before Rabin's murder, and we said, enthusiastically, that it was possible. We took our leave feeling that we might well see him again, and we wanted to have faith in his optimism. When we returned to our car we asked each other if we had not perhaps been too hasty in saying resolutely that it was possible to return to November 3.

Today, after the death of Hussein, who helped a few months later to achieve the Wye Memorandum, and after Barak's stunning victory and later his devastating defeat, I do not have the same resolve. It remains a prayer, but it is no statement of certainty.

A SHORT WHILE AFTER THE EXISTENCE of the Beilin–Abu Mazen Understandings was leaked to *Ha'aretz* in March 1996, Michael "Miki" Eitan, a member of the Knesset, asked to meet me. At the time I was serving as Minister Without Portfolio, and Miki was one of the Knesset members for whom I had the highest regard. I did not know at the time why he wanted to meet, and it would not have occurred to me that Miki, one of the most hawkish Likud Knesset members, would actually be interested in the understandings I had reached with Abu Mazen. He began by saying that reality had changed, and that from his point of view it was clear that the dream of the whole land of Israel under our sovereignty was no longer realistic. After the signing of the Oslo Agreement he realized that the map of the future would be different from the dreams of the Greater Israel movement. At the same time, he had the impression, from published accounts of the Beilin–Abu Mazen document, that there was no talk of uprooting settlements, and that assurance had been given that most of the settlers would be able to live under Israeli sovereignty without having to move their homes. I was pleased to hear what he had to say and described to him the components of the understandings I had reached with Abu Mazen. He said that it was worth exploring further and would be happy to deal with the matter in the future.

Following our defeat in the May 1996 elections and the establishment of the Netanyahu government, Miki Eitan was elected Chairman of the Knesset coalition. One day he appeared at my office in the Knesset eager to continue our earlier conversation. I remarked that a few months beforehand he had sought to "limit damage," whereas now there was no need to do so; the government in power apparently had no commitment to reach a permanent settlement whereby we would relinquish the territories. He said, however, that the die was cast, and that no matter what government was in power, the outlines of the solution would not be very different from the understanding I had reached with Abu Mazen in October 1995. Miki suggested setting up a special project—a series of meetings between a few Likud and Labor members of Knesset to produce a joint paper that would have both an educational and a political purpose. It would need to incorporate a significant territorial concession, but there would be no return to the 1967 borders and no Israeli recognition of the right of return for Palestinian refugees. We discussed the project with Dr. Arye Carmon, President of the Israel Democracy Institute, who was happy to put the Institute at our disposal for a long biweekly meeting, and provided a research assistant, Eran Shalev, who accompanied our work and helped with the preparation of materials. The Likud members of the Knesset who joined the project with Miki were Meir Sheetrit, Yehuda Lankari, Modi Zanberg, Michael Kleiner, and Naomi Blumenthal. I was joined on the Labor side by Shlomo Ben-Ami, Haim Ramon, Avraham "Beiga" Shochat, Uzi Baram, Ephraim Sneh, and Yona Yahav.

Our first meeting was held on November 4, 1996, and dealt mainly with general principles. Each of the subsequent meetings was devoted to a specific issue among the subjects included in the permanent settlement, and outside experts were occasionally invited. The following topics were covered: the nature of the Palestinian state, solutions to the problem of water, the borders of the state, the status of settlements, security arrangements, the solution to the refugee problem, and various proposals for Jerusalem. After ten meetings and thirty hours of discussion, we were ready to sign a joint paper, with only two outstanding points: the inclusion of the Jordan Valley under Israeli sovereignty, and the definition of the "Palestinian entity" as a state. It is no misrepresentation to say that even on those points, there was broad agreement. With regard to the first, there would be temporary security control rather than Palestinian sovereignty in the Jordan Valley. As for the second, everyone had already become reconciled to the idea of a Palestinian state; even so, for various reasons, some people felt most comfortable giving the public impression that these controversial matters remained unresolved.

I initiated a meeting with Prince Hassan in Amman on January 2, 1997. Present with me at the meeting were Knesset members Haim Ramon, Haggai Merom, Nawaf Mazalha, and Yona Yahav. After we told him about our meetings with members of the Likud faction, the Prince wanted to know what we were expecting to achieve from these discussions. We explained that the opposition in Israel that we represented was not just a parliamentary party, but an ideological movement that had paved the way to peace, that wanted to make a supreme effort to reach a permanent settlement with the Palestinians by May 4, 1999. These discussions, in which the Likud recognized the need to transfer most of the West Bank to Palestinian sovereignty, while Labor recognized the need to leave most of the settlers in their homes and grant Israeli sovereignty to their land, might make it easier for Netanyahu to reach a permanent settlement that was also acceptable to the Palestinian side. Haim Ramon stressed the historic change that these talks represented, while Prince Hassan expressed his appreciation of the effort to reach a political understanding between the Likud and Labor and his hope for an expeditious signing of the Hebron Agreement.

The Prince regarded Netanyahu's recent pronouncements, in which states like Andorra and Puerto Rico were cited as models for the Palestinians, as progress toward understanding the need to establish a Palestinian state. As usual in discussions with him, Prince Hassan emphasized the need to include Jordan in any discussion of the refugees in the permanent settlement, because the future of the refugees was bound up with the future of Jordan, the only Arab state to have granted them citizenship and work permits. He felt that Jordan should also be party to the negotiations over Jerusalem, so that he would not be presented with a *fait accompli*, to be contended with after the fact, as had been the case with the Oslo Accords.

Not all the participants in the Democracy Institute discussions stayed to sign the document: Michael Kleiner, for instance, parted ways with us because the document did not limit the number of refugees who could return to the Palestinian state; Ephraim Sneh insisted that the Israeli settlements in the territories should be under Israeli sovereignty, but that the borders should be withdrawn to the 1967 lines. Most of the participants remained, however, and the document was signed on January 22, 1997. I was very happy to have formulated such an agreement, between a key group in the Likud and a key group in Labor, that was not counter to the Beilin–Abu Mazen paper on any point, despite minor variants in terminology. The Israeli document, for example, mentioned a "Palestinian entity," whereas the Israeli-Palestinian document referred to the "state"; the former referred to the "principal city," the latter to the "capital"; but the basic precepts of each document were in agreement.

The more garrulous Netanyahu became about the importance of a permanent settlement, the more we felt we had to hurry to complete the document. It became a matter of urgency to present him with principles that the Likud Party, or at least parts of it, could support, and that would stand a good chance of not being dismissed by the Palestinian side. As the signing of our document approached, the media became more and more curious, and when it was finally published, it generated a great deal of interest as well as some criticism. The Palestinian press was disappointed, claiming it was merely an agreement between Israelis that would not be able to secure a Palestinian partner because it distanced itself from issues that were taken for granted by many Palestinians and Israelis. The right-wing of the Likud accused Eitan of abandoning his ideological positions and accepting the political outlook of the left. Ehud Barak went even further, and said that it was because of Beilin–Abu Mazen that Labor lost the 1996 elections, and that the Beilin-Eitan document was liable to lose us the next elections as well. On the left, the head of the dovish Meretz Party, Yossi Sarid, claimed that the Beilin-Eitan document was a far-reaching Israeli annexation plan, that the map of the West Bank resembled a zebra rather than a state.

In contrast, Abu Mazen welcomed the document. He said, in an interview with a BBC magazine published in Arabic: "I believe that this document is very important, and what is important in it is not what was agreed between the sides, but the topics discussed, which relate to the permanent settlement. They addressed Israeli public opinion and spoke about matters that are normally considered by the Israelis—the leaders and the masses alike—as red lines that cannot be dealt with or talked about. Along comes this document, and Jerusalem and the discussion surrounding it, as well as the settlements, the refugee problem, borders, and so forth, have become a matter worthy of debate."

Eitan and I wanted to present the document to Prime Minister Netanyahu and to the head of the opposition, Shimon Peres. Peres met us immediately and expressed great appreciation of our combined effort and his hope that it would be able to advance the peace process. Netanyahu did not respond. In private talks, Palestinians expressed their support for the move; they regarded it as another step in the effort to shift the political situation in Israel toward the support of Oslo. Ambassadors hastened to obtain an English translation of the paper, and the world press described the project and its results in detail.

It is impossible to say, in retrospect, whether the joint Labor-Likud document advanced the peace process at the time, but it was, in many respects, a breakthrough. Beyond the great significance of a dialogue between the right and left on very sensitive political matters, in which there was the ability to find common ground and refrain from unnecessary wrangling, the joint document was an important step in making the wider public familiar with the nature of any eventual permanent settlement. There would be a concession of territories conquered in 1967, but a majority of the settlers could stay in their homes, and Israel would not recognize the right of return for Palestinian refugees.

IN TANDEM TO THIS POLITICAL EFFORT to render the future permanent settlement more realistic, we worked to produce more detailed papers and maps to submit to the decision-makers. This is where the Economic Cooperation Foundation (ECF) came into the picture. The Foundation's aim was to prepare economic and political programs with the Palestinians that would accompany the peace process, together with programs to bring together Israeli and Palestinian professionals. The Foundation backed the launching of the Oslo process, the Beilin–Abu Mazen Understandings, and many other initiatives.

There was a great deal of effort invested in the preparation of a draft Israeli-Palestinian economic agreement, which proposed a combination of a free-trade zone and a customs union. The matter was dealt with on both sides by very senior economists: The Israeli team was headed by David Brodet, the former Director-General of the Finance Ministry; and the Palestinian team by Dr. Maher al-Kurd, the Deputy Economy and Trade Minister and an advisor to Arafat. The two sides finally signed the draft agreement in 1998, and the detailed document, essentially an extension of the 1994 Paris protocols on economic cooperation, was given to the Netanyahu government and presented to senior figures in the Finance Ministry, as well as to economists at the U.S. State Department. Eventually, a number of the Israelis who had participated in the preparation of the document, like Professor Avi Ben Bassat, joined Barak's government, and the draft agreement became the principal basis for economic negotiations under Barak.

The multilateral peace industry that was frozen during the Netanyahu era continued to operate, at least partly, through the ECF. Doctors from Khan Yunis in Gaza were trained at Ichilov Hospital in Tel Aviv; there was cross-border cooperation between the governor of Jenin, the Haifa municipality, the Gilboa regional council, and the Bet She'an Valley regional council; and a study was conducted to determine the applicability of the Benelux model to Jordan, Israel, and the future Palestinian state. We dealt with a long list of practical issues, in order to keep the process moving in the present, and to prepare for the more congenial political atmosphere we anticipated in the near future. Though I did not personally have much contact with the Netanyahu government, save for official matters in the Knesset and its committees, I tried to ensure continuing government support for initiatives and economic projects vis-à-vis the Palestinians. To that end, I met with Finance Minister Dan Meridor and Trade and Industry Minister Natan Sharansky, and with Eitan Ben-Tzur, Director-General of the Foreign Ministry, who approached me to obtain details of the Beilin–Abu Mazen Understandings. We met for breakfast at the YMCA building in Jerusalem on January 14, 1997, and I sat at a side table and read him the understandings while he copied down every word. I have no idea what became of his papers, but I felt that it would be irresponsible of me to wait four years until a Labor government might return to power, and I told him so. My duty was to do whatever I could to promote the Oslo process in order to arrive at a final settlement before the approaching deadline.

I worked hard to maintain contact between Israelis and Palestinians, arranging seminars, meetings at home and overseas, and establishing joint projects like the regional framework on the environment, which was headed by Prime Minister Rabin's widow, Leah. Her appointment to that post on September 13, 1997, four years after the signing of the Oslo Agreement, was marked by a large gathering in Ramallah, at which both she and Yasser Arafat confirmed their commitment to continue the peace process out of a sense of obligation to Rabin's legacy. We held meetings through the so-called Mashov ("Feedback") Circle, which I ran in the Labor Party, with members of the Palestine Legislative Council like Marwan Barghouti and Qadoura Fares, two former prisoners who spent many years in Israeli jails and had studied their Hebrew and Israeli history. They managed to somehow combine hostility toward Israelis with respect for them, and to support the Oslo process. At the first meeting between representatives of the Circle and former prisoners, the members of the Palestinian delegation had between them spent 150 years in Israeli prisons. They saw those lost years in much the same way Israelis view basic training and compulsory army service, and, much to our surprise, we learned that in jail, of all places, the Palestinians had discovered the existence of "good Israelis."

In April 1997, under the auspices of the ECF, Yair Hirschfeld, Ron Pundak, and I met with Barghouti, Fares, and two of their Fatah colleagues. Barghouti and his colleagues were concerned about the deterioration in the peace process; they feared that Fatah, the largest Palestinian party, which was headed by Arafat himself, was losing support among the Palestinian people as the peace process dragged on. "Yesterday's revolutionaries and fighters," they said, "are today wearing suits and have drivers. They justify the compromises, the agreements, the readiness to wait, and the coopera- tion with Israel, but even the youth can no longer get enthusiastic about these things. Over the last four years they have suffered a decline in their standard of living and rising unemployment on the one hand, and the non- implementation of the Oslo Agreement by Netanyahu—who is violating his obligations—on the other. Fatah's role is to prevent mass outbursts but also to continue to compete for the support of young people, who view the extreme organizations opposed to the Oslo Agreement as a real focus of identification."

The Fatah members hoped that they could win back the attention of young Palestinians by holding public meetings between the Israeli and Palestinian peace camps, so we agreed to have a broader session in a few weeks. An opportunity for this arose on May 15, 1997, when—at the joint initiative of myself and my old friend Pierre Schori, who served as Sweden's International Cooperation Minister—a European-Israeli-Palestinian meet- ing took place, with the participation of the international secretaries of the British Labor Party and the German Social Democrats, in addition to Yair Hirschfeld, Marwan Barghouti, and Fatah veteran Hani al-Hassan. Fatah aimed to transform itself from a militant organization into a legitimate socialist party, and we all shared a stake in this process of "naturalization." At the meeting, al-Hassan described the importance of both peoples work- ing together to supplant their mutual animosity, while Barghouti spoke in favor of continued dialogue between Israelis and Palestinians, with the assistance of those outside the region for whom Middle East peace was a priority. We were very ambitious and agreed to establish a joint Israeli-Palestinian committee for long-term planning on the environment, communication, transport, and the job market, as well as a trilateral committee with Jordan for political planning. We decided to create various joint frameworks for party activists to work together on common issues, and the Europeans promised to take part in these activities and to assist with funding. This event took place a few days before the Labor Party primaries in Israel; after Barak's election as party chairman, the European representative sought his approval for the continuation of these initiatives, but it was apparently not forthcoming. The attempt to formalize inter-party contact failed, but the personal contacts continued.

At another meeting with Barghouti and Fares, in December 1998 at their office in Ramallah, they told us that Fatah's standing in the West Bank had finally begun to rise after the Wye Agreement, following a long period of decline. But the delays in the implementation of the Wye Memorandum, and the bitter disappointment over the small number of political prisoners who had been released, they said, had brought frustration back to the Palestinian street after there had been a spark of hope that progress could be made, even with Netanyahu. This frustration, they argued, was liable to lead to violence unless some hope emerged. And the only hope was the return of a peace government in Israel. Such a government, they expected, would freeze the settlements and reach a permanent settlement quickly. At the time I had no idea that my two interlocutors would become the heroes of a new Intifada within less than three years.

CHAPTER 5
BARAK DAYS

BARAK'S LANDSLIDE VICTORY OVER NETANYAHU kindled new hope in the Israeli peace camp and around the region. But the new Prime Minister was faced with a frozen peace process and a spate of commitments he had made both before and after the elections. On the Syrian track, Rabin's vague commitment to return to the 1967 lines on the Golan Heights if all Israel's security demands were met was still outstanding. Furthermore, indirect negotiations had been conducted between Netanyahu and Assad, at which it was also understood that Israel was willing to relinquish the Golan Heights in return for peace. However, like the negotiations Peres had conducted as Prime Minister, and Rabin before him, this negotiation was left incomplete, though it appeared a settlement was at hand. On the Lebanese track, Barak changed his approach. He had in the past vehemently opposed unilateral withdrawal without an agreement, going so far as to argue in print that such a withdrawal embodied great danger to the towns and villages in the north of the country. His plan was to withdraw the IDF from South Lebanon in stages, with Syria's agreement. On the eve of the elections Barak announced that he would pull out of Lebanon once his government was in power; he added that this would be accomplished with Syrian cooperation. After forming his government, Barak repeated this promise, but it had taken on a practical significance: Israel was now due to depart, by agreement, from the Lebanese quagmire before July 7, 2000. Senior IDF officers and the Chief of Staff himself protested any unilateral withdrawal—they were concerned that even without an agreement with the Syrians, Barak had obligated himself to withdraw. Because of this promise, and his desire to withdraw within the framework of an agreement, he was forced to make a special effort on the Syrian track from the outset.

Expectations for Barak were sky-high. When he was elected, the news-paper headlines in France read, *"The Three-Year Footnote Has Ended."* The day after the elections Clinton said, "I look forward to working closely with Ehud Barak and his new government as they strive to reach that goal with their Palestinian and Arab partners." A Palestinian source was quoted as saying, "We want to erase and forget the three years of the Netanyahu gov-ernment, and to renew relations with Ehud Barak from the point at which they were broken off because of the murder of Rabin . . . We will not per-mit Hamas and its associates to destroy this opportunity to make progress in the negotiations." In a speech he delivered in New York five days after the elections, King Abdullah, the new ruler of Jordan, said, "I have high regard for Ehud Barak, and we intend to be at his side through thick and thin . . . Barak's election constitutes a golden opportunity to achieve set-tlements with the Palestinians and with the Syrians."

On June 24, while Barak was still trying to form his government, it was reported in *Al-Hayat* that Hafez Assad had told his regular interviewer, Patrick Seale, "I have followed [Barak's] career and his statements. He seems to be a strong and honest man. As the election results show, he evi-dently has wide support. It is clear that he wants to achieve peace with Syria. He is moving forward at a well-studied pace." Assad had never said anything of this sort about any Israeli Prime Minister.

Barak pursued open diplomacy as well, and told Seale in an interview, "[Assad's] legacy is a strong, independent, self-confident Syria—a Syria which, I believe, is very important for the stability of the Middle East . . . I am truly excited to see if there is a possibility of concluding a 'peace of the brave' with Syria . . . The only way to build a stable, comprehensive peace in the Middle East is through an agreement with Syria. That is the keystone of peace." A day after the establishment of the Barak government,

President Mubarak said to *Le Figaro*, "I think that Ehud Barak is a man with promise, and with his election things will begin to move."

It was important to Barak to do things in his own way. In various interviews he intimated that he would not be making peace by way of "academics going astray in the forests of Scandinavia," an allusion to the start of the Oslo process. Quite naturally, he did not want people who had been involved in the peace process to continue dealing with it, both because he wanted to try a different approach and because it was important for him to reach the decisive juncture with the support of at least some people from the right of the political spectrum. In this respect his appointment of David Levy, from the Likud, as Foreign Minister was meant to help him reach the moment of truth from the right, not from the left. Levy, though often characterized as a hawk, was considered a moderate within the Likud, and had fought the party line to fiercely oppose Ariel Sharon's conduct of the bloody Lebanon war.

Barak was also eager to release the United States from the role it had assumed as an intensive mediator. He detested the fact that the peace negotiations had become indirect because of the alienation between the Netanyahu government and the Palestinians, and consequently announced that the United States would revert to the role it originally held, as a facilitator rather than a mediator. He declared that within fifteen months—by September 2000—he would know if it was possible to reach a permanent settlement with the Palestinians. Barak's attitude about time was undoubtedly unusual, as reflected in his famed love for taking watches apart and reassembling them. Setting precise target dates became a standard component of his approach, and he persisted with it despite the fact that they were generally not met.

AFTER THE TREMENDOUS DISAPPOINTMENT with Netanyahu, the world expected Barak to return Israel to November 3, 1995, and he took up the challenge by presenting himself as Yitzhak Rabin's political heir, for which he received a great deal of leeway. The peace camp, myself included, said to Barak, "Because you are prepared to make peace, because you have your own way of doing things, and because for this purpose it suits you to have a very low-profile peace camp, do what you regard as right, so long as you make peace. Syria first, Lebanon first, fifteen months, framework agreement, permanent settlement—whatever allows you to make peace, so be it."

Barak, who was unquestionably one of the most intelligent people to enter Israeli politics, a quick-witted, learned man, with a deductive mind, reached the pinnacle of his influence at a time when his political and parliamentary experience was extremely limited. He presented assertions that often raised doubts in the minds of his audiences, but did so with such confidence that they began to think he was right, and certainly to hope he was. He would often say, "What has to happen will happen," reflecting his inner conviction that even if the other side did not accept his view at first, they were certain to come around in time because he was surely correct. At the same time, he was convinced that if it proved impossible to realize his plans for peace, "Honest people in Europe will understand we have done all we need to, and that it is not because of us that there is no settlement." Frequently, when he presented the two outcomes in this manner, it seemed to the listener that Barak had no preference between them: either there would be a settlement, or we would not be blamed for not achieving it!

A new leader had come to the Middle East and presented the established players with his own plan: the Israeli-Syrian track and the Israeli-Palestinian track would operate in parallel; the IDF would withdraw from Lebanon by July 7, 2000; negotiations with the Palestinians would be direct and would not require American help; and new dates for implementing the Wye Memorandum and a date for a framework agreement that would lead to a permanent agreement a few months later would be set at the negotiations. Within fifteen months everybody would know if the Middle East was heading toward peace or not.

The government was formed on July 6, and immediately afterwards Barak met with the leaders relevant to the peace process. On July 9 he met President Mubarak in Alexandria; on July 11 he met Chairman Arafat at the Erez crossing; on July 13 he met King Abdullah in Aqaba; and on the fifteenth of the month he met President Clinton in Washington. He enthusiastically and convincingly explained his new approach to the various leaders, but they were less rapturous. That is, except for Clinton, who was very enthusiastic, having already made the announcement to the media about seeing Barak as "a new toy." Their meeting lasted about five hours, and afterwards Clinton said, "I could have listened to him all night."

"Rabin would have been proud to see you here," Clinton continued, and he went on to promise Barak that "America will march with you."

Barak laid out his plans for peace with Syria and the Palestinians, stressing the Syrian track, the new idea of a framework agreement, and the implementation of a third phase of redeployments only with the enactment of the permanent agreement. "The decisive moment has arrived," Barak said, "and I am prepared to make difficult decisions. I have no fear. I have great hope." Clinton told Barak that changing a signed agreement—to incorporate the framework step and the delayed implementation of the third redeployment—would prove very problematic. Netanyahu, after all, had tried to change the Oslo Agreement, at great and needless cost to both sides. Clinton told Barak that Arafat saw the implementation of the Wye Memorandum by the new Prime Minister as an obvious move, which would serve as a kind of litmus test of Barak's intentions. This would require the release of prisoners and additional redeployments by Israel, and close security collaboration to combat incitement on the Palestinian side, but without these steps it would be very difficult to make further progress.

Clinton had grave reservations about two points raised by Barak. First, the fifteen-month target, which in the opinion of the Americans was quite unnecessary; and second, the decision that the Americans would not mediate between the two sides. The Americans warmly welcomed the proposed changes, but they were very offended by the manner of Barak's presentation, which suggested that they were no longer needed. Barak's evident preference for the Syrian track was received with less enthusiasm than the Americans might have demonstrated a few years earlier, when they felt that, in strategic terms, peace with Syria was more important to the Middle East than peace with the Palestinians. Now, however, the Clinton administration strongly favored "closure of the Palestinian file." Nevertheless, right after meeting with Barak, Clinton contacted Arafat and suggested that Arafat listen carefully to Barak's proposals before rejecting them. Clinton told him that Barak's ideas had taken account of the interests of both sides, and should meet the demands of both. However, the President stressed that the decision to accept Barak's proposals was Arafat's; the Wye Accord was a signed agreement which Clinton himself had made a great effort to achieve, and if Arafat insisted that Barak implement the agreement, Clinton would not withdraw his support from it.

A second meeting between Barak and Arafat took place at the Erez crossing on July 27, where Barak presented his outline plan. He proposed exchanging the withdrawal from the nature reserves for better areas, releasing prisoners, immediately implementing the second part of the second phase, and explained his wish to delay the implementation of the third part until after the framework agreement had been signed. In the meantime, he suggested that his negotiator, Gilead Sher, and Saeb Erekat should begin to discuss the implementation of the Wye Agreement. He urged Arafat to decide within two weeks whether he was amenable to the outline plan. Thus began the "Barak method" of negotiation. Taking heed of Clinton's advice, Arafat did not reject Barak's initiative outright. Instead, he chose to delay his rejection of the plan for two weeks, and proposed in the meantime to establish a joint Israeli-Palestinian committee to discuss the proposal "out of courtesy," as he explained his decision to the Americans.

August was devoted to intensive negotiations that attempted to adapt the Wye Agreement to Barak's new parameters. Reluctantly, the Palestinians found themselves negotiating issues that had already been settled with another Israeli government less than a year earlier. "The Likud violated Rabin's agreements," they complained at the outset of the talks. "Barak, Rabin's successor, does not have the right to violate the Likud's agreements." But they nonetheless came to terms with the new circumstances.

In a frenzied speech delivered in Ramallah on August 4, Arafat promised, "We shall continue the struggle until our little children wave the flag atop Jerusalem." But on the eighth of the month he agreed to Barak's outline plan to delay the implementation of the Wye Memorandum until September. Albright wanted to visit the region and Barak, faithful to his principle of keeping the Americans away, asked her not to come so that the two sides could exhaust the solutions alone.

The fiercest argument raged over Barak's demand for a framework agreement to be signed before completing the negotiations on a permanent settlement. The Palestinians believed that this was an unnecessary stage that would complicate the negotiations and argued that it was not part of the Oslo Agreement. The Egyptians and the Americans played a key role in convincing the Palestinians to come to terms with the framework agreement. Barak wanted to sign the framework agreement by November 4, 2000, the fifth anniversary of Rabin's murder, near the end of Clinton's tenure, and spoke of fulfilling the terms of the permanent agreement within five years. Arafat pressed for the permanent agreement to be signed no later than May 4, 2000, within the one-year extension set out in the Berlin Declaration. When it appeared that the Palestinians were persisting with their opposition to the Israeli proposals, the Israeli representatives said that Barak was proposing a new package—the Palestinians were entitled not to accept it, but then the Wye Agreement would be implemented "according to the book," as Netanyahu had signed it, including a third-phase redeployment of only one percent. Finally, agreement was achieved.

Thus the Sharm el-Sheikh Memorandum was signed on September 4, 1999. It too would have been superfluous were it not for the fact that previous agreements had been sabotaged: The Hebron Agreement was signed because the interim agreement had not been implemented; the Wye Memorandum was signed because the Hebron Agreement had not been implemented; the Sharm el-Sheikh Memorandum was now signed because the Wye Memorandum had not been implemented, and the target date for the permanent agreement had passed without any decision on a new deadline. Sharon, the head of the opposition, was furious not only about the agreement but also about its location. In a radio interview on August 31, he said the following: "Egypt is Israel's greatest enemy. Egypt cannot be granted the right of patronage at a time when not far from Cairo, Azam Azam, an innocent Israeli citizen, is rotting in jail . . . And does anybody imagine that the Egyptian President, Hosni Mubarak, or his advisor Osama al-Baz, or any other personality in the Egyptian administration are our friends? They are our enemies and are plotting against us all the time."

Present at the ceremony, which was held in Sharm el-Sheikh on a Saturday evening, besides Barak and Arafat, were President Mubarak, King Abdullah, and Secretary of State Albright. In the memorandum the two sides committed themselves to implementing the interim agreement on the way to a permanent agreement, and to reaching a framework agreement—and this was Barak's achievement—within five months from the start of the discussions on the permanent settlement, by February 2000, and a permanent agreement within a year, by September 2001. A new target date was finally set for the permanent settlement, sixteen months later than the original deadline. The agreement provided details on the dates when eleven percent of Area C would be transferred to the Palestinians and just over eight percent of Area B would be upgraded to Area A, with these phases completing the second redeployment by January 20. Security prisoners would be released in two groups, with their names agreed on by both sides. The first group would be released the day after the signing of the agreement, and the second a month later, so that additional prisoners would be released before Ramadan. Negotiations on the third redeployment—the one Barak desperately wanted to avoid—were set to begin within nine days, and the southern safe passage between Gaza and the West Bank was supposed to be opened on October 6, 1999, while the northern transit route would open four months after its course was agreed. The building of Gaza harbor was due to begin in October 1999, and the Palestinians were supposed to transfer the list of their policemen to the Israeli side within a week.

The atmosphere at Sharm el-Sheikh was reminiscent of ceremonies in the days of Rabin and Peres: embraces, brave handshakes, and familiar faces. Barak and Arafat signed for the two parties; Mubarak, Abdullah, and Albright were the witnesses. Barak announced, "Today we have embarked on a new road. We are paving the way for settling the hundred-year dispute between us and the Palestinians. We hope that within a year we will reach a permanent settlement." Arafat, for his part, said, "We extend our hand to Barak, our new partner to the peace of the brave, and say to you: We are ready to cooperate for peace, in order to turn the peace of the brave into a reality, to turn peace into a central component of our lives."

The following day the cabinet approved the agreement by a majority of twenty-one against two—Yitzhak Levy of the National Religious Party and Natan Sharansky of Yisrael Ba'aliyah, two right-wing ministers. In the Knesset itself the margin was smaller: fifty-four against twenty-three. Among the parties in the goverment, Shas, a Mizrahi Orthodox party, was absent, while four of the five NRP members and two from Yisrael Ba'aliyah voted no; it was clear that we had a very limited coalition. A day after Knesset approval was given, 199 prisoners were released; some had wounded Jews and others had killed Arabs. On September 13, precisely six years after the signing of the Oslo Agreements, a (third) ceremony was held at Erez to mark the opening of talks on the permanent settlement.

It was the first and last agreement signed by Barak and Arafat. It is reasonable to assume that at Sharm el-Sheikh neither of them had any idea that this would be the case. The feeling was that after a delay of two months, the Israeli-Palestinian peace process had finally gotten back under way. The path, however, was not free of obstacles; this time they were personal. The Attorney General, Elyakim Rubinstein, was unhappy that the head of the Israeli negotiating team, Gilead Sher, was not a civil servant; Sher refused to leave his law practice and join the civil service and was forced to resign as head of the delegation on September 8. Six precious weeks passed before Barak appointed Dr. Oded Eran, the Deputy Director-General of the Foreign Ministry, in Sher's place, and much to the chagrin of the Palestinians, no significant discussions took place during the course of September and October.

ON SATURDAY EVENING, OCTOBER 2, 1999, Barak invited me for a personal talk. It was the most candid political discussion we had ever had. I understood from his behavior that he was in the middle of a campaign to familiarize himself with the objective before "conquering it." The two of us sat alone for two hours at his home in Kochav Ya'ir, with him taking notes in a little notebook. During the first part of the discussion Barak asked a lot of questions: What room for flexibility do the Palestinians have in negotiations on a permanent settlement? Was it better to conduct talks secretly or openly? What influence would Arab leaders have on the Palestinian negotiators? What was the right role for the United States in the negotiations?

I told him that like us, the Palestinians were apprehensive about conducting in-depth discussions among themselves on the core issues of a permanent settlement, for fear of leaks and because of an unwillingness to reveal the differences between them; it is easier for everyone to present traditional stances and to say that the decision rests with Arafat. To me, the only way of knowing what they would accept as a basis for negotiation was to return to the understandings I had reached with Abu Mazen, yet these positions were likely outdated after four years, and unsigned as well. In spite of this caveat, it was possible to make a rough assessment of the room for maneuver along the following lines: First, the borders were the most important issue; the best way to reach an agreement was for us to prepare for a minimal annexation of settlement blocs, and agreement on an exchange of territories without reference to percentages (in 1995 we had drawn a map in which 250 square kilometers were annexed to Israel while the Palestinians received 200 square kilometers in the region of the Halutza dunes to extend the Gaza Strip). On the question of Jerusalem, a decision could be postponed if an interim solution were found and if the next stage was defined. In the understandings with Abu Mazen, a postponement was made possible by our agreement to Palestinian ex-territorial sovereignty—on the model of a foreign embassy—over the Temple Mount; Palestinian recognition of Israeli sovereignty over only West Jerusalem; Israeli recognition of a neighborhood in the region of Jerusalem but outside its territorial area (like Abu Dis) as al-Quds; and a decision that the whole area Israel had annexed in Jerusalem after the Six-Day War would remain in dispute, the administration of which would be determined without setting a date in advance. If we wanted recognition of our sovereignty over eleven Israeli neighborhoods in Jerusalem that were conquered in 1967, we would have to recognize Palestinian sovereignty over their neighborhoods in the city.

With regard to the refugees, a detailed agreement dealing with the various aspects of compensation and rehabilitation would be necessary. Unlimited right of return would apply only to the Palestinian state. As far as the right of return to Israel, the wording would have to artfully allow the

Palestinians not to relinquish this right—they have no room for maneuver on this point—but also allow Israel to not recognize the right of return, as such recognition would likely be interpreted as an implicit commitment to absorb all who wish to return. The result, at any rate, would have to be a genuine and appropriate solution to the problem with preference for the Lebanese refugees, and create a scenario in which the Palestinian leadership could face its public and say that it has not neglected the refugee problem.

I estimated that the Palestinians would not oppose the existence of those settlements that were not annexed to Israel within the bounds of the Palestinian state, with agreement on special security arrangements, and without any special status for that land. The Palestinians expect that the majority of settlers would prefer to leave their homes and receive compensation, but anybody who wished to stay and abided by Palestinian law—as an Israeli citizen—would be able to do so, in order to facilitate Israel's implementation of the agreement, and so as not to provoke a physical confrontation with the settlers. This did not apply to the Gaza Strip, where the settlements would have to be evacuated completely.

Finally, with regard to the military status of the Palestinian state, the Palestinians were not demanding an armed state, though they would prefer, probably, to reach a detailed agreement permitting some types of small arms, and to use a word other than "demilitarized," but here we could expect a great degree of agreement. Other security arrangements, such as IDF control of the Jordan Valley, would have to be limited by time. The negotiations would deal with how long the arrangement would last. My sense was that this would be a relatively easy issue to resolve.

I suggested that Barak open a secret channel, by which it would be possible to convey informal messages alongside the public channel that was to be launched. With a secret channel in place he would also not be subject to pressure from his surroundings, from violence, or from belligerent statements, which would sometimes force closure of the formal talks. The advantage here lay in it being out of sight. I stressed to him the importance of updating Mubarak and Abdullah regularly, so that they could assist when necessary and also try to curb Arab criticism, principally from Syria, of Palestinian concessions. With regard to American involvement—this would be important at moments of crisis, but whatever could be achieved bilaterally with the Palestinians, as we did between 1993 and 1996, was preferable. I gave Barak a copy of the Beilin–Abu Mazen Understandings, and at his request, promised to prepare a paper detailing the predicted room for maneuver the Palestinians would have in every sphere.

In anticipation of negotiations on a permanent settlement, he revealed to me his view of what the principal features of the agreement should be. The aim of the agreement should be separation between Israel and the Palestinians, requiring a 400-kilometer security fence that would replace the present 700-kilometer border. There would be seven or eight crossings along the border, where it would be easy to cross with a handprint check. The Jerusalem area would remain open, but it could be closed if necessary. No settlements would remain on the Palestinian side of the fence, and there would be an elevated bridge between the Gaza Strip and the West Bank. Barak preferred economic separation as well, and believed that it would be better for the Palestinians to develop their own economy—while retaining good contacts with Israel—than to perpetuate their dependence on Israel. He felt that the area of the Palestinian state did not have to be as large as that proposed in the Beilin–Abu Mazen Understandings. When looking at the map, he said he saw "that even fifty percent of the West Bank looks like a state. A few bridges and a few tunnels, and you have total contiguity." He wanted to have the IDF stationed in the Jordan Valley and in the settlements, "until the peace was assimilated into people's hearts."

His goal was to conclude the negotiations with the Palestinians within a relatively short time, the chief deadline being the end of Clinton's tenure. The president had told him at their last meeting that by his reckoning he could be active and available until the middle of the year 2000. Hence, for Barak this was a target date. He very much wanted to be able to talk intimately with Arafat, despite the attendant problems. He expected Arafat to understand the magnitude of the moment, like Ben-Gurion in his time, and to take a step that involved relinquishing part of his dream. He also wanted to try to talk to Assad, to convince him of the possible coincidence of interests if an agreement could be reached. His main worry was the out-break of terror. "That would be liable to end everything," he said.

I went out into the cold night of Kochav Ya'ir realizing that Barak was a person who very much wanted to make peace, but I was concerned that the expectation of Ben-Gurion–like behavior from our Palestinian partner was too optimistic, particularly given the intransigent opening postures on our part. Furthermore, I had little predilection for barbed-wire fences. However, Barak's enthusiasm and his belief that he was capable of accomplishing things in his own way boosted my hope that this time we would get to the finish line.

ON NOVEMBER 8 THE TWO "VETERAN SOCIALISTS," Barak and Arafat, attended the International Socialist conference in Paris. At a news conference he held with Lionel Jospin, the French Prime Minister, Barak dropped a bombshell when he announced that, in his interpretation, Security Council Resolutions 242 and 338, which call for Israel to withdraw from territory conquered in the 1967 and 1973 wars, respectively, did not apply to the Israeli-Palestinian negotiations. As Barak explained, "In the case of Jordan, Egypt, Syria, and Lebanon, we are talking about states that have recognized, agreed borders with us. In the past, on that same border there was belligerent action, the results of which led to Israel holding onto territory. Resolution 242 refers to these territories. There is no such border on the West Bank." There were irate responses to Barak's statement, and not only from the Palestinians, since the Oslo Agreement was built on Resolution 242 and made no suggestion of a different interpretation of this resolution for the West Bank and Gaza. That evening Barak's office in Jerusalem published a clarification: "The Prime Minister maintains that Resolution 242 is applicable to the negotiations with the Palestinians, and clearly it is mentioned in the agreements. However, its context with regard to negotiations with the Palestinians is different from the context with regard to the other fronts."

Barak's statement was totally unnecessary, which was highlighted by the half-hearted attempt to retract it. Even if he was right, and there was no agreed international border on the West Bank, while a border of this sort did exist between Israel and its other neighbors, merely raising the subject at the outset of the negotiations on a permanent settlement created misgivings about Israel's intentions. Arafat and Barak met the next day for twenty minutes and engaged in mainly polite talk. On stage at the Socialist International their exchange was more fierce. Arafat insisted that Resolutions 242 and 338 did apply to the border between Israel and the Palestinians. His wife made her own contribution to aggravating the situation when, two days later, while Hillary Clinton was visiting Gaza, she said without batting an eyelid that Israel had poisoned Palestinian water and air. Nevertheless, the Israeli government approved (with the opposition of Yitzhak Levy and abstention of Natan Sharansky) the transfer of another five percent to the Palestinians within the framework of the second-phase redeployment of the Sharm el-Sheikh Agreement.

On November 14 a meeting took place between Barak and Arafat; the media reported that it was held at the Mossad headquarters. With Barak were Danny Yatom, his National Security Advisor, Oded Eran, and Yossi Ginosar, a former General Security Services official. Arafat was accompanied by Abu Ala, Saeb Erekat, and Yasser Abed Rabbo. Afterwards both sides felt it had been a wasted meeting. Arafat grumbled a lot, despite the fact that the government had decided to implement the Sharm el-Sheikh Memorandum. He asked for alterations to be made to the withdrawal map, and for Arab villages adjoining Jerusalem to be included in it. Barak rebuffed him. Arafat again raised the issue of the settlements, and said he expected Barak to check the Israeli proposals in this context against the Oslo Agreement and get back to him. There was no sense of progress even in the most limited sense.

The Palestinian side did not understand the significance of these meetings, concluding that a permanent agreement was dependent on the potential of the Clinton-Barak combination, and that if this did not happen it would be difficult, perhaps impossible, to reach a settlement later. In discussions with me the Palestinians expressed their amazement at the lack of focus in the talks, claiming that they dealt mostly with marginal issues instead of the substantial ones, that they were always arranged at the last minute and were not properly planned. The fact that a number of these meetings were held at security facilities only increased their sense of discomfort. They did not understand the system of target dates that Barak had constructed, which led to suspicion that the Prime Minister's efforts were directed at Syria rather than the Palestinians.

Of all people, Abu Mazen, my partner in the 1995 understandings and one of the great believers in the possibility of peace, became frustrated. He decided at the end of 1999 that the disparity between the parties was too great to lead to an agreement. In Clinton's time, he thought, there would be neither a framework agreement nor a permanent agreement. All we could hope for in the next year were additional interim agreements.

PALESTINIAN CONCERNS ABOUT THE PRIORITY of the Israeli-Syrian track were confirmed in December. Following Albright's visit to Syria and Israel on December 8, President Clinton announced at a news conference that Barak and the Syrian Foreign Minister, Farouk al-Shara, would meet within a few days in Washington to renew the talks from the point at which they had been halted in 1996. Before the President's announcement, Barak called to inform me, and I reminded him of what the late King Hussein had said about returning to November 3, 1995. That was the feeling we had—the chance to erase Netanyahu's years of darkness and return to the path of dialogue.

Clinton, speaking in messianic terms, declared, "We have a truly historic opportunity now. With a comprehensive peace, Israel will live in a safe, secure, and recognized border for the first time in its history. The Palestinian people will be able to forge their own destiny, on their own land. Syrians and Lebanese will fulfill their aspirations, and enjoy the full fruits of peace. And throughout the region, people will be able to build more peaceful and, clearly, more prosperous lives . . . Israelis and Syrians still need to make courageous decisions in order to reach a just and lasting peace. But today's step is a significant breakthrough, for it will allow them to deal with each other face-to-face, and that is the only way to get there."

A week later at the White House, the atmosphere was less optimistic. Barak spoke within the time limit set for him. He avoided trying to settle past accounts with Syria, describing his hopes for the future. Al-Shara, however, refused to shake Barak's hand and spoke at length in a stony tone. He said that peace with Syria meant the return of all conquered land and that only the end of the occupation would eliminate the barrier of fear and anxiety among Israelis. He stressed that it was Israel that had initiated the incidents that led to the conquest of the Golan Heights in the Six-Day War, and he paid no heed to President Clinton, who twice whispered to him during his speech, "It's not the time." At a meeting between the parties, the beginning of intensive negotiations was set for January 3, 2000.

From talks which took place at Blair House between Barak and the American peace team, the Americans understood that Barak was prepared to withdraw to the lines of June 4, 1967, and believed that the intensive negotiations could be short. The world was convinced that the Israeli-Syrian agreement had already been concluded and that the two sides were just seeking to create the appearance of negotiations. In Israel, debate focused on the question of a referendum on the withdrawal from the Golan, and whether a special majority was required in order to discount the Arab vote, as the Likud demanded. The stock market rose, and the Golan settlers demonstrated. President Weizman hastily announced that if the referendum failed, he would resign.

In the meantime, the progress on the Palestinian track was principally administrative. A Peace Directorate was established in the Prime Minister's office, which included a large apparatus, headed by Oded Eran, to prepare the framework agreement for the negotiating team. Another division, also headed by Eran, formed a steering and monitoring team for the interim agreement. It consisted of economic, legal, and security committees, as well as a committee on prisoner affairs. Another division was supposed to prepare the negotiations for a permanent agreement. The talks between the Israeli and Palestinian teams avoided touching on sensitive topics like Jerusalem and refugees. They focused primarily on the security perceptions and needs of each side, and their territorial context. They were interesting, detailed discussions but they lacked real authority. The prolonged talks provided the Palestinians with a framework in which they could complain and threaten to break off further discussion. When it became known that tenders had been issued for the building of 1,800 housing units in the West Bank settlement of Ofra, for example, the Palestinians announced they would be halting the negotiations. Against this backdrop, at the beginning of December 1999, Barak announced that the government would not issue additional tenders for building settlements until the middle of February (the intended date for the signing of the framework agreement). Another serious Palestinian complaint concerned the committee that was supposed to begin discussions in September about the third and final Israeli withdrawal before the implementation of the permanent agreement, but did not convene at all.

On Monday, January 3, 2000 at 12:30 p.m., talks began between Israel, Syria, and the United States in the small town of Shepherdstown, West Virginia. The world was forced to make do with a few color photographs—Clinton, Barak, and al-Shara striding out together on a bridge, against a green pastoral background; Nava Barak, the Prime Minister's wife, drinking coffee with President Clinton at a local café, and so on. The negotiations themselves were much less colorful. From Clinton's first private discussion with Barak, he could see that there had been a change of heart; the Prime Minister was no longer ready for the same concessions he had hinted about at Blair House a few weeks earlier, citing recent demonstrations in Israel and his fear that the public might not accept concessions of this sort.

The Shepherdstown conference was a failure. No real progress was made and contact between the parties was marginal. The first meeting between Barak and al-Shara without an American presence only took place two days before the end of the talks, in a gym, and the two men devoted the time to mundane talk. Clinton came to Shepherdstown every two days for an extended sortie. On Friday, January 7, the Americans presented a working paper that was supposed to reflect the agreements reached by the two sides. The seven-page paper contained a summary of the issues discussed at each of the four committees: borders, security arrangements, water, and normalization. The resolution with regard to borders was very general: The paper stated that Israel was ready for an agreement based on Security Council Resolutions 242 and 338, and that she would agree to withdraw to borders that reflected her security interests. Syria insisted on withdrawal to the June 4 lines. On the question of the settlements on the Golan Heights,

Syria pressed for their removal, whereas Israel lobbied to allow those Israelis who wished to do so to remain on the Golan even after the withdrawal. On security issues the Syrians proposed that the United States and France would man the early-warning stations on the Hermon, with the possibility of an Israeli presence, while Israel insisted on an effective Israeli presence. The Syrians insisted on an equal area and degree of demilitarization on the two sides of the border, while Israel pressed for a full demilitarization of the Golan Heights, and was only willing to have a buffer strip beyond this border. With regard to water, the Syrians proposed a joint council that would ensure the quantity and quality of water in the two countries, whereas Israel wanted a guarantee of its continued use of all the reservoirs in advance.

These proposals, as described in the American paper, were essentially opening positions that still required extensive negotiation. Consequently, the talks ended on January 10 and were due to be renewed within nine days. But they were never renewed. The Syrians fumed when the American document was leaked to the Israeli press and began to reassess the results of the talks, at the end of which they issued an ultimatum: the promise of a different Israeli position with regard to borders, before the delegation left for the United States. Barak rejected the ultimatum and the second round of the talks in Shepherdstown was cancelled with hardly a murmur from either side.

THREE PARALLEL INFORMAL TRACKS between Israel and the Palestinians began to operate after the end of December 1999. On one, Abu Mazen and Amnon Lipkin-Shahak discussed principal issues in advance of the permanent agreement. On another, Abu Ala and Shlomo Ben-Ami began to formulate a framework agreement. On the third, Oded Eran and Yasser Abed Rabbo conducted secret talks alongside the open talks they were already holding. The approach of the intended date for the signing of the framework agreement, February 13, 2000, and the sense that the actual agreement was not taking shape, caused considerable concern for those of us committed to the Sharm el-Sheikh Agreement. President Mubarak urged Arafat to speed things up, suggesting a marathon discussion by February 1, followed by negotiations between then and February 13 in Washington, until an agreement could be signed.

On January 17 a meeting was held at the home of Yossi Ginosar in Kochav Ya'ir between Barak, accompanied by David Levy and Danny Yatom, and Arafat, accompanied by Abu Mazen, Abu Ala, and Nabil Abu Rudaineh, an advisor to Arafat. The overall feeling was one of gloom. The Palestinians felt like a lesser priority than the Syrian track, Barak felt that the Syrian option was slipping through his fingers, and everyone understood that it would take a miracle to produce a signed agreement by the middle of February. Barak told Arafat that negotiations with the Syrians were stuck, and that the main track was now the Israeli-Palestinian one. His intention had been and remained to reach a signed framework agreement by February 13, Barak said, and to that end marathon talks were needed. The Palestinians raised the issue of the third redeployment, and complained that the committee dealing with the issue had met only once, which indicated the Israelis were merely going through the motions and had no intention of fulfilling obligations. In reply, Barak virtually confirmed their feeling on the matter by suggesting that they drop the issue of the withdrawal until it became clear whether a framework agreement would be achieved or not. If indeed it appeared that it was impossible to reach a framework agreement, then the two sides would work seriously to reach agreement on the third withdrawal. At the end of the discussion, however, Barak agreed to resume the work of the committee, but this never happened. Needless to say, after the failure to reach a framework agreement by the middle of February, no attempt at all was made to implement the third redeployment.

In anticipation of Arafat's January meeting with President Clinton in Washington, President Mubarak pressed the Palestinian leader to present his stance on the framework agreement to the American President, and Arafat readied himself for the task. When he arrived in Washington for his visit he had three documents ready: the first, a draft of the framework agreement; the second, a paper describing the state of negotiations at that time, including relatively flexible Palestinian stances; and the third, Palestinian concessions that were to remain in the hands of the President until such time as, in his opinion, they should be given to the Israelis. But in the end none of these papers were presented to Clinton. The draft of the framework agreement was shown to Aaron Miller prior to Arafat's meeting with the President, and he recommended that the Palestinians stash it away so as not to annoy Clinton unnecessarily. Arafat, who was not interested in presenting any sort of paper, and had prepared it in order to placate Mubarak, immediately complied with Miller's recommendation and decided to stash away the two other papers as well. When Mubarak found out later, he did not conceal his anger from Arafat. The meeting between Arafat and Clinton on January 22 was singularly unsuccessful. The Palestinian leader did say the "right" things. He displayed determination to reach a permanent settlement; he said he understood the settlement would involve real compromises for both sides; and he spoke about the annexation of settlement blocs to Israel, an exchange of territories, a creative solution for Jerusalem. But at the same time, he pressed the Americans to force Barak to implement the interim agreement, and expressed his concern that the Syrian track would push the Palestinian issue aside. Clinton concluded from the meeting that the two parties were still not ready for real progress, and that it would be impossible to reach a framework agreement by the February deadline, despite Barak's and Arafat's repeated commitment to abide by the timetable.

MANY PEOPLE THOUGHT ARAFAT would have been unable to make peace without Abu Mazen and Abu Ala behind him. Abu Mazen, one of the most fascinating Palestinian figures, is a refugee who was born in Safed in 1933 and later moved to Qatar to work. He was one of the founders of the PLO, responsible for its funds and its informal ties with Israel. Although he was never a PLO fighter, Abu Mazen had always been considered one of the organization's leaders, even before he was appointed Secretary of the PLO's Executive Committee in the '90s, making him number two in the organization. As such, he was Abu Ala's mentor during the Oslo talks. Abu Mazen is a soft-spoken person who keeps a low profile: He gives few interviews, does not stir the crowds, and prefers parlor meetings, where he knows how to charm the participants. He is aware of his importance and feels no need to prove it. From all appearances, he does not play the power game. Even though he is often suggested as a possible successor to Arafat—when the idea was put forward of appointing a Palestinian Prime Minister, he was the obvious candidate—it is not by chance that he has never run for a seat in the Palestinian Parliament and has never been appointed a minister in Arafat's government. Abu Mazen did not accompany Arafat on his arrival in Gaza in 1994, and over the years he has been careful to preserve his independent status, keeping his distance from Arafat while at the same time accepting his authority.

Abu Mazen is pragmatic but not moderate. His willingness to compromise with Israel does not derive from a belief in the validity of Israeli claims, but rather from a realistic assessment of the situation. When he thought that it was wrong to reach an agreement at Camp David, he had a different perspective than the Abu Mazen who, together with me, had reached the draft final status agreement five years earlier. In a conversation I had with Madeleine Albright and her team after the Camp David talks, they did not conceal their fury with Abu Mazen and their anger about the diffidence he had displayed during the summit. The truth is that he is diffident in most political dealings. He is quick to take offense and get hurt, and once offended, he prefers to disappear for protracted periods of time. He is capable of disappearing to Qatar, where he has spent many years; or to Moscow, where he was a student; or to Jordan; or to North Africa. His political strength derives from the fact that politics needs him far more than he needs politics. For this reason, it is easy for him to lay down conditions to friends—they know that if they do not accept his conditions, he will simply walk away or disappear, as he did when he terminated his brief four-month term as Prime Minister in 2003.

Abu Mazen found himself in a difficult situation after the Wye talks in 1998. A number of his associates, including Hassan Asfour and Mohammed Dahlan, pointed an accusing finger at him (and perhaps something more than a finger) because the delegation had not insisted on the distinction between political prisoners and prisoners who were criminals. This had allowed Netanyahu to embarrass the Palestinians by releasing hundreds of thieves and drug dealers, which he said was part of the agreement reached at Wye. Abu Mazen was not connected in any way with this matter, but no one from the Palestinian leadership was prepared to defend him, and he felt cornered. This was a watershed moment, which included violence and threats against people close to him, and he cut his ties with Dahlan and Asfour. It was a serious blow to the peace process, a clear example of an internal struggle directly affecting foreign policy. Toward the end of January 2000, Abu Mazen prepared his own outline plan for peace. It was a conservative plan and the main points were Israeli agreement to certain Palestinian principles and Palestinian willingness to take account of Israeli needs. Israel was unable to accept the new plan, but Abu Mazen's approach facilitated the building of a new, more pragmatic Palestinian axis—which later manifested itself at Camp David—that included Dahlan and Asfour, who by then had reconciled with Abu Mazen, along with Mohammed Rashid, Arafat's advisor and secret financial consultant.

On Saturday, February 5, 2000, I met Abu Ala at a private apartment in Jerusalem. As it was a secret meeting, I was not surprised to see him appear wearing sunglasses and a peaked cap. At the beginning of the discussion I told him that in contrast to other meetings between us, this time the Prime Minister had requested that I present his views to Abu Ala, and then to listen to Abu Ala's frank opinion on them and relay it back to the Prime Minister. We discussed the crisis of the third stage of the second redeployment (over a withdrawal of 6.1 percent), the need to set up a secret channel, and the link between the Syrian and Palestinian tracks.

Abu Ala had been our first contact with the PLO. He was our interlocutor, on the recommendation of Dr. Hanan Ashrawi, and throughout the period of the Oslo negotiations he acted as head of the Palestinian group that negotiated with Yair Hirschfeld, and later, with Uri Savir. We had not heard of him before that, and it was only in anticipation of the talks that we found out some information about him. He was one of the Fatah veterans, regarded as the PLO Finance Minister and considered a confidant of Abu Mazen. Abu Ala was responsible for the multilateral talks that followed the 1991 Madrid Conference, and remained in a hotel in Madrid, working behind the scenes during all the committee sessions. The law prohibiting Israeli contact with the PLO was not revoked until 1993, so in the talks in the wake of Madrid, Abu Ala did not participate, but gave direction to the Palestinian delegation, composed of residents of the territories and Palestinians living abroad, none of whom were members of the Palestine National Council. In our telephone calls home from Oslo we referred to him in code as "the son" (Arafat was "the grandfather" and Abu Mazen "the father"). There, his affectionate nickname was "Pantoffel," after the famous slippers he wore at informal talks. He was a tough negotiator, a man with a big, sensitive heart who shed tears without much effort and passionately believed in the need to make peace. He had a close and special relationship with Uri Savir that led to a real friendship between their families. For us, he was the first human representative of the PLO.

I presented Abu Ala with what I understood to be Barak's outlook: the wish to create a total political revolution within a year; to get out of Lebanon; to work with the Palestinians and the Syrians; and to move from the framework agreement to intensive negotiations on the final settlement. This was all to be achieved while observing our red lines, which the other side also needed to understand and respect, as we would respect their red lines. Abu Ala listened with great patience to my presentation, and then replied point by point, as was his habit. In his opinion there would be an historic change in Israel's situation after the permanent settlement. Only an agreement of this sort would open doors in the Arab world to Israel and free it from the siege it was still under, because the Arab world was waiting for a resolution of the Palestinian issue irrespective of its feelings about the Palestinians themselves. An agreement of this sort would need to solve all the problems on the agenda, and negotiators should not be tempted to leave any issues for the future. According to him there would be no end to the dispute without a comprehensive solution to all the problems, including Jerusalem.

He welcomed our apparent progress with the Syrians but was afraid that this might prevent real progress on the Palestinian track. "Some people hold the view," he said, without specifying if he was among them, "that Israel wants to solve its problems with Syria and Lebanon by leaving the Palestinians 'on the back burner,' taken for granted." In his view, if there was a genuine desire to get the Palestinian track moving, the second-phase crisis had to be resolved, perhaps through an immediate withdrawal of six percent and the remaining one-tenth percent in the near future, and with an attempt to include the villages adjoining Jerusalem (including Abu Dis, Abu Ala's village). The delay in discussing the third phase, Abu Ala insisted, also had to end; Barak's evasion here was transparent and only a serious discussion of this issue could provide a safety net for a situation in which we do not adhere to the timetable for the permanent settlement. He added that the discussion of the permanent settlement could only be held in the framework of a secret channel. The clumsy open talks, at which one had to always demonstrate progress in front of the cameras, would never lead to an agreement. Only Israeli agreement to secret talks would prove that Barak was serious about his intentions. His behavior at the last Erez meeting—his unilateral stances and disregard for the Palestinian side and Arafat—proved the opposite. "Even if it is not his intention," Abu Ala pointed out, "Barak exudes contempt and arrogance, and to be sure, attitude plays an important part in negotiations."

This issue of public exposure is critical. There is a certain advantage to the media's awareness of the existence of talks, in that it acts to put pressure on the negotiators to reach agreements. The fear of the talks breaking down is much greater than in circumstances where nobody knows about them, so that the public awareness may, on occasion, actually be instrumental to their success. On the other hand, the public exposure makes things awkward for the negotiators, tying them down to artificial deadlines (such as the evening news), and precluding them from holding a genuine marathon of substantial talks unaffected by external circumstances. It is no coincidence that the Washington talks were suspended over the deportation of 415 Hamas members from Gaza to Lebanon by Rabin's government, while the Oslo talks did not experience a single interruption. The Washington talks were held under the watchful eyes of the media, while the Oslo talks proceeded behind the media's back.

At the end of the discussion Abu Ala surprised me with a question about Barak's opinion of the Beilin–Abu Mazen Understandings. At all of our meetings since 1995, Abu Ala had chosen to ignore the paper or to treat it with scorn. Now he was very serious, perhaps because the moment of truth was approaching. I told him that in public pronouncements Barak had discounted the paper.

ON FEBRUARY 7 THE PALESTINIANS FROZE NEGOTIATIONS with Israel until further notice, or until an agreement was reached, with American mediation, on the implementation of the second redeployment and a date for the implementation of the third. The framework agreement was due to be signed on Sunday, February 13, but it was nowhere near completion. Barak announced that he did not intend to meet Arafat; the Palestinians claimed that Israel had reneged on all its obligations. Arafat called on the world to put pressure on Israel. At a news conference on February 19 with Johannes Rau, the German president, Arafat vowed to declare a state on September 13, while Barak was reported to have said in closed talks that the new target date for a framework agreement was May.

I met in Jerusalem on February 7 with the American peace team of Dennis Ross, Aaron Miller, Rob Malley, Nick Rasmussen, and Gamal Hilal. Ross surveyed the problems in the negotiations with Syria and the Palestinian concern over Barak's preference for the Syrian track. In his estimation, if there was no real progress Arafat would not be able to avoid declaring a state in September 2000. By the end of February, the inability to reach a framework agreement had become an indisputable fact. With this in mind, Osama al-Baz, Mubarak's veteran political advisor, invited me to a meeting. After arranging the meeting, he informed me that President Mubarak wanted to meet me on Sunday morning, February 27. Since there was no commercial flight departing at that early hour, the President offered to send his plane to fetch me, though I preferred to travel by car. My political advisor Shlomo Gur and I left after the end of Shabbat, drove via the Rafah crossing in Gaza, and reached our hotel in Cairo six hours later.

At the July 1978 meeting between Anwar Sadat and Shimon Peres in Vienna, in which I participated, Sadat mentioned to Peres that he intended to appoint a deputy for himself, and that man was Hosni Mubarak. A few months later, Peres and I met Mubarak, newly installed in his position, in Cairo. He surprised us with the simplicity of his conduct, his direct speech, and his strong sense of humor. Truly a man of the people, Mubarak did not

hesitate to speak his mind: As a pilot, he underwent a long period of training in the Soviet Union, and a large part of our first conversation with him
was devoted to jokes at the expense of the Soviets. Mubarak made us
laugh, and he laughed with us. The years have not changed him. We have
met on many occasions, in various circumstances, and he has remained the
same man of the people, the wise and pragmatic Egyptian, albeit more
experienced and more confident, but without pomp and ceremony, and
with a pronounced sense of humor, deep voice, and emotive hand gestures.
His entire conduct exudes a certain no-nonsense approach: "Why do we
need to argue all the time? It's clear to everyone that peace is the best way,
and that it is possible to make peace. We all know what the final status
solution will be, so what are we waiting for?"

My meeting with Mubarak in Feburary 2000 took place only days after
he returned from a rare visit to Lebanon, during which he had expressed
his feelings about Hezbollah. Some in Israel interpreted his statements as
support for Hezbollah, but I could relate to the misgivings he had voiced
about any extreme Muslim organization capable of threatening the stability
of the Arab states. He expressed appreciation for what I had said, suggesting that only someone who does not understand what is going on in the
Arab world could think that a person like him would support Hezbollah.

After more than an hour of private discussion, the talks were extended
for another hour, with the participation of Osama al-Baz, Israeli ambassador Tzvi Mazal, and Shlomo Gur. The President analyzed the situation in
the region—the changing of the guard in Jordan and Morocco, the decline
in President Assad's health, and principally, Arafat's standing. He spoke at
length about the Palestinian leader, saying that only Arafat could reach an
agreement with Israel and win the support of the Palestinian people, and
that this was the moment, perhaps the last such moment, to reach an historic agreement. Mubarak spoke positively about Barak. He saw Barak as
the new kid in the neighborhood, full of good intentions, lacking experience, and with no real knowledge of how to realize his plans. He said he
had not yet been able to fathom why Barak was so insistent on a framework
agreement which was not mentioned at Oslo. However, because it was
clear that for Barak this was a crucial link in the process, Mubarak had per-

suaded the Palestinians to come to terms with the idea. As always, he was prepared to assist wherever necessary and would be happy to place Taba or Sharm el-Sheikh at the disposal of the parties as a place for the two sides to hold talks. Mubarak exuded optimism but also concern. He believed that the Clinton-Barak-Arafat triangle could manage to reach an agreement, but he also feared what might happen if the agreement was not achieved. He described to me at length the growing alienation from Israel taking hold in certain circles of Egyptian society, and expressed his worries that this dynamic, which had started during the Netanyahu era, would intensify if there was no settlement. This would have far-reaching implications for the regimes in the region.

Our meeting took place only a few days after an unforgettable Knesset speech by Foreign Minister David Levy, in which he cited statements made by Hezbollah in Lebanon and threatened that if children in Israel were hurt by attacks from Lebanese territory, Israel would hurt Lebanese children in return. "Blood for blood! A child for a child!" Levy roared, shaking the rafters with an inflammatory speech in the style of Gamel Abdel Nasser. Mubarak asked me about the significance of the speech. In Israel I had criticized Levy, but in Egypt I was forced to defend him; not the speech, but the Foreign Minister. I explained that Levy was an important constituent of the coalition Barak had assembled; Barak's strategy was to reach the moment of truth with the widest possible public support, and Levy had been one of two Likud ministers who supported the IDF evacuation of Lebanon in 1985. I explained that Levy regarded himself as a person of the center: In the Likud government headed by Netanyahu he had resigned because of the lack of political progress, whereas in the leftist government he constituted a sort of right marker. "If this is the case," Mubarak asked, "why was Levy a 'rimmer' in Shamir's extreme right-wing government?" In 1989, along with his fellow ministers Ariel Sharon and Yitzhak Moda'i, Levy had tried to set "rims" to limit the peace plan then being formulated by Shamir and his Defense Minister, Yitzhak Rabin; Mubarak's sharp question made my defense of Levy seem rather specious.

My next meeting was with the Foreign Minister. Throughout his ten-year tenure, Amr Moussa was thought to have serious reservations about

Israel. He was sharp, very cynical, perceptive, and critical. During the Rabin government he turned the issue of the proliferation of nuclear weapons into a central one in relations between Egypt and Israel, and frequently made things difficult for us in international forums. Israel's reply— that she would be prepared to establish a nuclear-free zone in the Middle East with mutual inspections once there was peace between all the peoples in the region—never satisfied him. He and I began to meet when he was Egypt's ambassador to the UN, and have maintained our contact since then. He never hesitated to say no, but was also able to answer in the affirmative, a rare quality.

As I expected, this meeting was not an easy one. According to Moussa, Egypt's main hope was to achieve Israeli-Palestinian peace by the end of the year 2000. By their estimation, once Clinton left office the window of opportunity would close and there was no telling when it would open again. During the Netanyahu government, Egypt's principal effort was to limit damage. With Barak, Egypt had been prepared to be much more active. Barak had convinced Mubarak and Amr Moussa of his commitment to peace, and they had accordingly persuaded Arafat to agree to Barak's strange stipulation to reach a framework agreement first. But Barak was not adhering to the timetable he himself had imposed on all the other players! The middle of February had passed with no trace of a framework agreement. There was growing concern in the Arab world that they were facing a repeat of the Netanyahu syndrome: impressive commitment one day and then foot-dragging the next, avoiding the moment of truth. According to Moussa, influential Arab elements were beginning to suspect that Barak's goal was to draw out talks for as long as possible, until he reached a point where, because of the political timetable in the United States and in the region, it would be too late to conduct serious negotiations. This may have been a groundless suspicion, but Barak was undoubtedly losing credibility every day, in the Arab world and beyond. There was a sense that if in the time of Netanyahu there had been a freeze, in Barak's a crisis was looming.

I described to the Egyptian Foreign Minister the difficulties Barak faced at home; the tremendous effort being made by the government; and the

difficulty of ensuring that the referendum following the permanent settlement would be successful because of the tight links between the right and
the religious parties, both within the government and outside of it. I told
him that this was the real test of the peace camp in Israel and in the Arab
world. What was important now was not to criticize the Barak government,
but to support its efforts to reach an agreement with the Palestinians while
Clinton was still in office.

The next day I met Abu Mazen in his office in Ramallah. His remarks
were similar to Abu Ala's: Barak is trustworthy and seeks peace, but he is
creating an impression of contempt for the Palestinians; he wasted valuable
time before settling on a chairman for the negotiating team, and afterwards
refrained from granting Oded Eran a real mandate; now he was wasting
more time in a futile attempt to sign a framework agreement. Abu Mazen
doubted it would be possible to hold two referenda in Israel in one year—
on the question of the Golan Heights and on the West Bank and Gaza. In
his opinion, the only way to conduct serious negotiations between Israel
and the Palestinians was to establish a secret channel between the sides
immediately.

Two days after our talks in Cairo, Osama al-Baz arrived in Jerusalem.
Following a meeting with Barak, he asked to hold a trilateral discussion
with Saeb Erekat and myself. The discussion, which was held at the Larom
Hotel, was opened by al-Baz, who said that the parallel negotiations Israel
was conducting with the Palestinians and the Syrians should continue. If
peace could be reached with Syria, this was the time. With regard to the
Palestinians, the challenge was to complete parts of the second withdrawal
and agree on the third; to reach the framework agreement as soon as possible and then the permanent agreement; and to freeze the settlements. All
this needed to be achieved by the deadline set by the Sharm el-Sheikh
Memorandum—September 13, 2000. This was a tougher task than it
appeared at the time of the signing of the memorandum, but it was—and
had to be—possible, for even September 2000 would push Clinton's availability to the limit.

Saeb Erekat changed the atmosphere in the room with the first sentence
he uttered. He seethed with anger at Barak's handling of the negotiations,

and did not believe that it was possible to meet any target date at all. In his estimation, the Israelis, myself included, did not understand the atmosphere in the territories. According to his analysis, in March and April Barak himself would only be dealing with the Syrian track and would freeze the Palestinian track. He compared Barak's approach to the Palestinian leadership to monkey hunters in Africa who lure the animals into the traps by offering them watermelons coated in oil. With a bitterness that I do not ever recall having heard from him, Erekat insisted Barak had impugned the honor of the Palestinian leadership, and all that was left for it to do was to defend its honor. He proposed that we prepare a plan that could dispel the tension if a full permanent agreement could not be reached within the year, to ensure that the Palestinians did not fall between two stools. The plan's main points would be completion of the second redeployment and implementation of the third, finalization of the opening of the northern safe passage, and the release of another group of low-risk political prisoners. The Palestinians, Erekat stressed, felt they were in a pressure cooker which was liable to explode as a result of their frustration. Al-Baz stopped Erekat's momentum by asking why he had to portray the worst possible scenario. Erekat answered, "Osama, you too do not understand what is happening on the ground and the extent of the despair in the face of the continued building of settlements and the foot-dragging. For three years we were able to say that everything would change when the Israeli peace camp returned to power. Today we have nothing to say, not to ourselves and not to our people. Arafat needs strategic assets in order to withstand the pressure being applied to him. You do not understand what it means when the members of the Central Council call for Arafat to act like Assad."

ON MARCH 1 BARAK SUFFERED HIS WORST PARLIAMENTARY defeat since the formation of his government. Twenty-six members of the coalition voted in favor of a law put forth by Silvan Shalom, which would require a supermajority in any referendum on relinquishing territory, in order to prevent Israel's Arab citizens from casting the deciding votes. This was only the bill's first reading, but the results reverberated through Israel and around the world.

The Americans now had fresh concerns that we would get to September without an agreement with Syria or the Palestinians. On March 2, against the backdrop of the Knesset vote, I met Ambassador Martin Indyk, who was more worried than usual. "There has to be an intensive negotiation with Arafat," Indyk advised, "and he has to understand that the target date remains September 13. By then, there has to be completion of the withdrawal, implementation in stages of the third phase of the redeployment, agreement on the framework agreement, and marathon negotiations on the permanent settlement."

The final communiqué from the Palestinian cabinet meeting in Ramallah on March 3 stated that "September 13 is the definite date for ending negotiations on the permanent settlement of Palestinian lands." A Palestinian source close to Arafat said to the media, "There is great disappointment with Ehud Barak, even more than with Netanyahu, since after the elections in Israel there were very high hopes for Barak, who continues to disappoint."

In March 2000 a meeting took place at the home of MK Collette Avital between six members of the Knesset and six members of the Palestinian Legislative Council, headed by Marwan Barghouti; all of them were members of Fatah, former prisoners, and connected to the Tanzim. For the majority of the Knesset members, this was their first acquaintance with the Tanzim, the organization founded by the Fatah youth in 1983 and rehabilitated following the Western Wall Tunnel riots in 1996. At that point the members of the Tanzim took up arms; Arafat tried to disarm them in 1998 but abandoned his efforts after a number of incidents. The Tanzim was active in elections for Fatah's Central Council and its Revolutionary Council, and it played an important role in the PLO leadership. Barghouti was the chief speaker at the meeting, and he conveyed a message of despair. According to him, the Palestinian street had lost its hope for peace, and Fatah had lost its trust in the Barak government. Israel continued to build settlements and was laying bypass roads in the West Bank, while the Palestinian Authority kept quiet and was accused of collaboration. The supporters of peace and the members of Fatah found it difficult to defend both the corruption in the Authority and its silence in the face of Israel's actions. There was also no way to explain why they, the leaders, had been released, while their charges, many of whom were supporters of the Oslo process, remained in Israeli prisons. Barghouti told those present that it might be possible to ensure calm for another six months, until September 2000. But if a permanent settlement had not been reached by then, it would be hard for Arafat not to declare a state unilaterally. "The quiet," he said, "is a result of attacks being foiled by the Authority." The continued settlement construction, along with the lack of progress in the peace process, was sure to intensify criticism among Palestinians and across the Arab world, in which the Authority is seen as a collection of traitors and collaborators.

The United States and Egypt were forced to propose a new timetable in order to defuse the crisis: A framework agreement would be achieved by May, after which a third redeployment, much larger than the Netanyahu government had proposed, would be completed; and the permanent settlement would be signed by September 13. After hesitation by both sides, the proposal was accepted and a few cordial meetings took place between Arafat and Barak. On March 19, the government approved the last phase of the second redeployment, and the withdrawal took place two days later. When the Clinton-Assad summit in Geneva failed on March 26, and the Americans declared that the gaps between Israel and Syria were too wide, the Israeli-Palestinian track naturally gained momentum. But the atmosphere on the Palestinian street was still grim. I heard an echo of this when Yuli Tamir and I met with Arafat, Saeb Erekat, and Nabil Abu Rudaineh in Ramallah on April 4. Arafat argued that too much time had been wasted on negotiations and that pressure was mounting among the Palestinian public for real change. He attached enormous importance to the September deadline, and said, "Three years of the Netanyahu government have gone to waste, and since the Sharm el-Sheikh meeting another eight months have been wasted. Very little time is left until September 2000. There is a narrow door of opportunity, and we have to march through it. This requires very hard work, but it will be a calamity if we don't do it." He added that the mood of Palestinian public was like sizzling coals, and the danger of fire existed at all times. It was very hard to placate the public without progress, especially when the frustration and the pressures were so great. Erekat complained that Oded Eran—whom he praised highly—did not have a mandate to discuss the central components of a permanent settlement or even to exchange nonbinding drafts: "If we want to achieve this by September it is no use holding such preliminary negotiations. We have to get to the main points and discuss them honestly."

The general assessment that Israeli-Syrian negotiations had ceased caused a sigh of relief among the Palestinians, but they did not admit it. Now that Barak was ready to present his position on a permanent settlement to the American administration he suggested that Arafat do the same, after which the Americans could make mediation proposals. Barak met Clinton in Washington on April 11, and nine days later, on April 20, Clinton met Arafat, who for the first time presented an outline of his plan for a permanent solution.

Three days later marathon talks began in Eilat to draft a framework agreement. The Israeli and the Palestinian delegations were headed by Oded Eran and Yasser Abed Rabbo, respectively. Informal talks were conducted at the same time between Shlomo Ben-Ami, Amnon Lipkin-Shahak, Abu Mazen, and Abu Ala, with Barak and Arafat available to make decisions. Dennis Ross took part in the talks, with the intention that at a later stage Albright would also participate, and in anticipation of September 13, everybody hoped a trilateral summit would take place to bridge the unsolved issues if any still remained. Although Eran headed a large negotiating apparatus, Barak barred him from conducting negotiations on sensitive issues such as Jerusalem and refugees, and the Palestinians, as mentioned, were aware of this limitation. At the end of April, in Eilat, the Israeli side presented a map to the Palestinians. It showed a Palestinian state on sixty-six percent of the West Bank, with fourteen percent annexed to Israel, and twenty percent held in Israeli custody until there was an agreement about the future; there would be no exchange of territories. The Palestinians were shocked, or at least they looked as though they were. From their point of view, they argued, they had already made a prodigious compromise in coming to terms with the 1967 borders, which meant accepting twenty-three percent of historic Palestine and less than half of what was allocated to an Arab state in the 1947 United Nations Partition Plan. Any consent to alter the 1967 borders would require territorial compensation from sovereign Israeli territory. They felt that the Israeli proposal was "ridiculing the poor," and that the distance between the Israeli and Palestinian perceptions obliged them to terminate the talks. This was a crisis.

There was a surprisingly large discrepancy between this Israeli proposal and the understandings I had reached with Abu Mazen in 1995. In discussions I held with Dennis Ross, Aaron Miller and Martin Indyk, they asked me to present to them the understandings I had reached with Abu Mazen, which had been leaked to *Ha'aretz* in 1996 but were never published in detail, since Abu Mazen and I had agreed that a mutual decision was required to make the documents public, and he would not allow it. I was happy to present the understandings to Ross and his team, and they asked Abu Mazen to send representatives who were conversant with the document and the maps attached to it to Washington on his behalf. He obliged and sent Ahmad Khalidi and Hussein Agha to Washington; after they presented the material to senior officials at the State Department, Ross and Abu Mazen agreed that Khalidi and Agha would meet Gilead Sher, who was no longer the chairman of the negotiating team but remained Barak's unofficial representative.

In due course the meeting took place in London. Gilead Sher had worked with me at ECF as a legal advisor before Barak's election, and was very familiar with the Beilin–Abu Mazen document. Meeting Khalidi and Agha, who drafted the document, reinforced his belief that a reasonable permanent settlement could still be reached. On May 11, my associates Yair Hirschfeld and Ron Pundak were invited to Washington to present their view of the Beilin–Abu Mazen Understandings to a joint team from the National Security Council and the State Department. They did this in great detail and answered a barrage of questions; the full document had by this point reached the State Department, so the questions were focused on the interpretation of particular clauses, not just the general concepts. This detailed examination of the document was intended to prepare National Security Advisor Sandy Berger for his visit to Israel, where he was scheduled to hear the details of the document directly from the people who lent their names to it. Berger came to Israel in May to receive an honorary doctorate from Tel Aviv University, and Ambassador Indyk contacted me to find out if I would participate in a dinner at his residence with Berger and Abu Mazen, at which we could present our paper. I agreed, but I said I was not sure Abu Mazen would, as over the years he had avoided any discussion of the document, insisting that its ideas were not binding.

But Abu Mazen did agree, and the dinner was held on May 19. Initially only a few couples took part, and other guests joined in later. The atmosphere was social and informal, but for the American administration the meeting was an important test of the feasibility of the permanent agreement. Without wasting time, Berger asked us who would begin. Abu Mazen, perhaps out of politeness, smiled and pointed to me. I told Berger that it was clear he was familiar with the document, so I would present the principles we were most concerned about. I discussed the background of the paper's preparation, and its goal to meet each side's essential needs without either party forcing its ideas on the other. Afterwards I presented the various remaining issues, disputes, and points of agreement, and Abu Mazen added some comments of his own. It was the only time Abu Mazen and I ever appeared together to present the paper.

A few years earlier my friend Ruby Rivlin, a Likud member of the Knesset, confessed to me that he questioned the existence of the document. He found it hard to believe that the Palestinians would agree to Israel's annexation of the settlement blocs. One day, he happened to meet Abu Mazen and asked him if this was really the case. Contrary to his habit of shirking questions about the document, Abu Mazen confirmed the facts. The next day, Rivlin came to me all excited and said, "Not that I agree with your paper, but as you know, I found it difficult to believe some of the extracts from it that were published. Now I know it exists." To his credit, Rivlin took the trouble afterwards to acknowledge in the press that the document did exist, despite the fact that its political outlook was very different from his own. Now Abu Mazen had taken a much more far-reaching step by presenting the paper with me to Clinton's advisor. It was clear that the Americans viewed this paper as an important component in the groundwork for negotiations on a permanent agreement.

BY THIS POINT THE TALKS IN EILAT HAD FAILED. Dennis Ross met Barak and then Arafat in an attempt to break the deadlock. On May 7 Barak, Ben-Ami, and David Levy met Arafat, Abu Mazen, and Abu Ala at Abu Mazen's home in Ramallah. Barak proposed a "package deal" in which three villages in the vicinity of Jerusalem—Abu Dis, Azariyeh, and Sawahra—would be transferred to full Palestinian control, and in return the Palestinians would be more flexible on a number of points in dispute in the framework agreement. The two sides did not agree. The framework agreement that had been postponed from February 13 was due to be signed on May 13, but now seemed further away than ever. At his meeting in Cairo with Mubarak, Arafat reiterated that the talks were in deep crisis. The territorial issue was overshadowing everything else.

A few of my colleagues and I met a number of senior members of Fatah from the West Bank at the Larom Hotel in Jerusalem on May 14. By chance the meeting took place the day before Nakba Day—commemorating the 1948 war, which the Palestinians call al-Nakba ("the Catastrophe")—and it proved to be a day of violence in the territories. The Palestinian group included Marwan Barghouti, Qadoura Fares, a member of the Palestinian Legislative Council and one of the leaders of the Tanzim who had been party to many meetings between Israelis and Palestinians over the years, and Mamduh Nofel, a member of the Democratic Front who had written a book on the secret negotiations in Oslo from the PLO perspective. I presented the picture as I saw it at that stage. We had never been so close to an agreement. Arafat was not getting any younger, but he was the only leader capable of leading the way to peace. In Israel, a leader like Barak who had the courage to leave Lebanon should also have the courage to pay the price of peace with the Palestinians. The aim at that moment was to complete the negotiations without either side feeling it had been the loser. Barak was very keen to reach an agreement with Arafat before the end of Clinton's tenure, and he was prepared to risk his government and his coalition to achieve this. He thought that the target date for ending negotiations on the permanent settlement, September 13, was realistic, and he estimated that if the agreement was brought to a referendum, the people would support it because Barak himself would testify that it fulfilled Israel's security requirements. Barak also understood the question of the political prisoners very well and had made two substantial changes in this sphere—for the first time prisoners "with blood on their hands" were released, although not people who had murdered Jews, and for the first time prisoners from East Jerusalem were released as part of a package.

Referring to the unrest underway in the territories, I said that if the established groups resorted to violence, trust between the sides would be lost, and we would lose the support of the Israeli public for a possible agreement. The duty of the leadership was to channel public frustration into other directions, and not to ride the wave of violence. If it became too easy to move from talking to throwing stones, from throwing stones to throwing Molotov cocktails, and from there to the use of conventional weapons, the public in Israel would fear that violence would continue even after an agreement was signed. When Sadat said, "No more war," there really was no more war, and this had enabled the wide support for peace with Egypt.

Marwan Barghouti replied that although there were people in Barak's government who believed in peace, the prevailing spirit was still that of Netanyahu. Thousands had participated in demonstrations in Ramallah and Nablus, some with weapons, and Barghouti feared escalation. The failure to release prisoners and the expansion of settlements were inflaming the street. Something had to be done to turn things around. The Palestinian Authority had destroyed Palestinian terror and it had not been easy. Israel had not rewarded her for it. The public in Israel failed to appreciate at what cost Arafat destroyed the Hamas infrastructure and mobilized the Palestinian people against terror.

"In Netanyahu's time," Barghouti continued, "we could say: this rightist government opposes peace and when a Labor government comes to power it will resume the process. Today we have nothing to say to the street. Everything is stuck, and it is because of your government. Barak has made you a laughing stock. He dressed you up in a jurist's robe, made a policeman out of Shlomo Ben-Ami, invented a nonexistent ministry for Peres, did not even find a ministry for Ramon, and he manages defense and foreign affairs with David Levy. There is no framework agreement, no third phase, and no deadline is sufficiently important to adhere to. Arafat genuinely wants to reach an agreement by September 13. If only it were possible. I am not sure it is. But if prisoners are released, the settlements frozen, and the interim agreement implemented, the situation on the ground could calm down even if there is no permanent settlement. If that does not happen, and a permanent agreement is not signed, the disappointment and the frustration are liable to lead to an explosion. We are not proud of what happened today on the West Bank. It embarrasses us more than it hurts you. But we have an obligation to the Fatah prisoners—we were in jail with them only a few short years ago. We are the Fatah leaders in the territories and these demonstrations are the minimum we can do to show solidarity, to avoid losing power to extreme groups, with whom you will not be able to talk even if you are willing to do so. We understand Barak's difficulties, but we do not understand his behavior: How can we reach a permanent settlement if you are not implementing the interim settlements and Barak is not even prepared to transfer Anata [a small village outside Jerusalem] to us?"

Qadoura Fares admitted that the disappointment in the Palestinian camp was not just because of the stalled peace process, but internal problems as well. Extreme Islamic elements had been greatly weakened by the Palestinian Authority's fight against their terrorist attempts, but an issue like the prisoners' strike was liable to strengthen them again. If there was no progress on the release of the prisoners, he contended, all the confrontations and frustrations might coalesce and present Fatah and Israel with a new and difficult situation. "It is necessary," he said "to create a sense of hope stemming from real development."

Mamduh Nofel said this was an historic moment, which could lead to the longed-for peace agreement, or, God forbid, the opposite. The Palestinian people and the leadership are disappointed with Barak, he said, because he does not keep agreements, is continuing with the settlements, and is not releasing prisoners. The fact that he has not transferred Abu Dis, Azariyeh, and Anata is seen as an admission of his inability to carry out what he has promised. "Rabin was a man of honor," Nofel went on. "He signed and did. Arafat trusted him. He does not trust Barak to the same extent. The present Palestinian leadership can make historic decisions only if Arafat is not pushed into a corner. The matter of the prisoners is most important. I sent people to perform deeds for which they are sitting in an Israeli prison, while I walk around free and meet you in an elegant hotel in Jerusalem, in front of your calm-eyed bodyguard. We are talking about approximately fifteen hundred prisoners, their families, and friends who were with them in prison. If we deal correctly with this matter, we can reach September peacefully, and an explosion triggered by the extreme forces will be averted."

At exactly quarter past ten the bodyguard with the calm eyes asked me to come out to take an urgent telephone call. The Prime Minister was on the other end of the line, and he said: "I have decided to bring the matter of the transfer of Abu Dis to the Palestinians before the Knesset tomorrow. We need to ensure that there is a majority for it in the plenum. I have reached the conclusion that this could ease the tension, and security-wise it is preferable for Abu Dis to be in Area A rather than Area B." I told him about the meeting I was in, saying that based on what I had just heard from the Palestinians, this could be a real turn. I congratulated Barak on his decision, and promised to do all I could to make sure hands would be raised in the Knesset in favor of his proposal. Barak asked me not to publicize his decision in the meantime.

I returned to the room and summed up my feelings: "It is very hard for me to visualize the people with whom I am sitting around a table today in such a relaxed fashion, tomorrow participating in violent demonstrations and revealing a different face in front of the television cameras. It seems you feel the need to conduct activities of a violent nature, despite knowing that your ability to control and curb them is very limited. There are ways to demonstrate anger besides throwing Molotov cocktails, shooting an effigy of Ehud Barak, and burning Israeli flags. I understand the difficulty you face, but if violence breaks out now, no peace agreement will be signed by September.

"What do you expect from Barak?" I asked. "Just as you are interested in reaching a peace agreement with the support of the widest possible Palestinian front, he too cannot make peace with Yossi Beilin alone. He needs the immigrants from Russia and the religious groups. If he has no choice he will get there alone, but if he has the choice, he will come with a broad political front, and that has a price. Once there is a permanent agreement, the remaining prisoners will almost certainly be released, but before we reach an agreement of this sort, we must not burn the bridges between us and set fire to all our hard work. The Prime Minister just called, and I told him we were meeting. He informed me of an important political step he is going to take tomorrow in the framework of his peace efforts. I cannot tell you exactly what it is, but if the violence increases tomorrow, you will make a mockery of him. It is liable to cause terrible damage to the process."

Barghouti stretched his arms into the air like someone unable to deliver, and said, "The instructions for tomorrow have already been given. But in the future it will be possible to steer things in a different direction."

The next day, Nakba Day, was even bloodier: A confrontation took place between IDF soldiers and hundreds of Palestinians. The Tanzim used firearms, and the Palestinian police were slow to respond; twelve Israeli soldiers were wounded, one seriously. Five Palestinians were killed and 188 injured. There had not been such a violent day in the territories since the tunnel riots in September 1996. In the evening, Barak succeeded in getting his proposal to transfer Abu Dis from Area B to Area A through the Knesset. There was a majority for the motion (fifty-six in favor, forty-eight against, one abstention) because of the absence of the Shas and Yisrael Ba'aliyah ministers and deputy ministers. The rest of the members of these two factions—both part of our coalition—voted against the motion. Ironically, the violence in the territories reached its peak exactly when the Knesset made its decision. Right-wing groups had asked Barak not to bring the matter to a vote, but he insisted. In the end, however, the decision was not implemented before Barak left office.

Arafat needed three days to restore calm. The Israeli-Palestinian Monitoring Committee, which supervised the implementation of the interim agreement, convened on May 17 to discuss the events of Nakba Day. Oded Eran referred to the gravity of these recent developments, and urged the Authority to operate in a totally different fashion. Saeb Erekat said that the Palestinian Authority did indeed have a duty to prevent violence, but the deep reasons for the violence could not be ignored. He gave an assurance that Arafat had given instructions to prevent activities of this sort in the future. But the real job of the two sides was to eliminate the causes of such disturbances.

AT PRECISELY THE SAME TIME, Shlomo Ben-Ami and Abu Ala were trying to root out these causes in a secret channel in Stockholm—Ehud Barak's promise not to hold secret talks in the Scandinavian woods had been broken. Gilead Sher, who had become the official negotiator, also participated on the Israeli side, and Hassan Asfour participated on the Palestinian side. John Hogarth, who had served as the Swedish ambassador to Israel, took part in the talks as well. The Stockholm channel was short-lived, but it generated a sense of real progress on the core issues: borders and refugees. The subject of Jerusalem was ostensibly not to be raised, but in fact it too was discussed in an unofficial and non-obligatory manner. Barak was very involved throughout the talks, reading the various proposals and making alterations to them. The aim was to reach maximum agreement on a series of issues to enable a summit meeting to be held in the United States in the middle of June. The Israeli side presented a map in which the Jordan Valley was, for the first time, under Israeli security control rather than Israeli sovereignty. The Palestinians announced that without an exchange of territories Israel would not be able to annex parts of the West Bank. On the subject of refugees, a joint attempt was made to construct a range of situations that would nullify "return" in practice without negating it by right.

According to reports in the media, the Stockholm talks were suspended only two days before an agreement was complete; this was on May 21, after two more "days of rage" in the territories. As senior political figure said to the press, "The Prime Minister simply decided that if the territories are ablaze and a two-year-old girl set on fire [by a Molotov cocktail in Jericho], then he actually does not feel any urgent need to speed up the talks with the Palestinians." At Camp David, two months later, each party claimed that the other side had backtracked from its position in Stockholm.

Because only informal minutes were kept of all these meetings, from the time they started until the end of 2001, these claims are difficult to verify. The central reason, however, for the termination of the Stockholm talks, was Abu Mazen: He was angry that Arafat had opened the channel without his knowledge, that Hassan Asfour was participating, and that Abu Ala was dealing with a long list of details without preceding this with a substantial discussion of principles.

IN THE MEANTIME, THE LEBANESE FRONT WAS HEATING UP. The July 7 deadline was approaching, an agreement with Syria was not on the horizon, and the South Lebanese Army (SLA)—the Israeli-supported militia in the southern security zone—was showing signs of tension and weakness. Barak had promised to leave Lebanon within a year by agreement, and like every case where a target date is attached to a mutual decision, there was an inconsistency between them. In interviews and responses to the media, IDF commanders frequently stressed that "as the Prime Minister and Defense Minister said," everybody wants to leave Lebanon, but it is clear the departure will be only by agreement. It seemed they were primarily addressing Barak, to remind him that there would be no withdrawal without an agreement. The Prime Minister himself was much more cautious and refused to commit to a particular course of action if there was no agreement by the date. It was not hard to see that the date he had set—a year from the swearing in of his government—was more important to him than the agreement itself. However, there was no doubt he very much wanted to reach this agreement, and thought that setting a date would make this easier, because Syria had no interest in relinquishing the card of Israel's presence in Lebanon without deriving some benefit from it.

Having drawn the conclusion that it was not possible to reach peace with Syria (unless he agreed to Syrian territory reaching the northeast shore of Lake Kinneret), and discerning the rapid disintegration of the SLA, Barak decided on a unilateral withdrawal from Lebanon on the night of May 24. At dawn I received one of the most moving telephone calls of my life. The Prime Minister's office was on the line to tell me that the IDF had withdrawn from south Lebanon to the international border. Not one soldier had been wounded in the course of the withdrawal. If I were a very religious person, I would certainly have said the *Shehehiyanu* prayer, giving thanks to God for enabling us to reach this day.

The withdrawal from Lebanon was not carried out quite as I had expected. In a book I published in 1998, *A Guide to Leaving Lebanon*, I discussed the possibility of building an electronic fence before the withdrawal, and a list of points to coordinate "back to back" with the United Nations. In the end the fence was built only after the withdrawal, while the Syrians prevented the Lebanese army from fulfilling Lebanon's part of Security Council Resolution 425 from 1978 and exercising sovereignty over the southern area of the country. Hezbollah spread out along the border and the 1989 Taif Agreement, which addressed the disarming of the militias, was not carried out. After eighteen years of needless sojourn in Lebanon, the defense of our northern settlements proved to be far more effective from within the international border, even without an agreement. It was undeniable that the Katyusha rockets that fell on Kiryat Shmona and other settlements had been the result of the unnecessary friction between the IDF forces and Hezbollah in the security zone. Nevertheless, Hezbollah's nonrecognition of the border drawn by the United Nations, which was fully accepted by Israel, led to a series of clashes in the region of Shebaa Farms.

Barak had come a long way to get to the point of unilateral withdrawal. When I had suggested it in 1997, Barak said it was a reckless gamble that would endanger the northern settlements. Only when he appeared on Israeli television on January 3, 1999, the day after Brigadier-General Erez Gerstein, journalist Ilan Ro'eh, and two soldiers were killed by an explosive charge in Lebanon, did he for the first time—and without any prior warning—advocate withdrawal from Lebanon within a year. By that stage the idea had public backing and his announcement contributed to his electoral victory in no small measure.

The majority of the public was happy about the departure from Lebanon but uneasy about the hasty retreat, with thousands of SLA soldiers thronging around the fence and the attendant difficulties dealing with their arrival in Israel. Of course, a unilateral withdrawal of this sort could not have been anything other than hasty: If Israel had withdrawn slowly, the

Hezbollah would have known in advance when the IDF forces were leaving southern Lebanon, and could have contrived to attack them. Some in Israel later argued that the unilateral withdrawal from southern Lebanon encouraged the Palestinians to employ violence against Israel, in the hope that Israel would also withdraw unilaterally from the territories; but this is like saying that Israel should not have participated in the 1991 Madrid Conference, because it would lead the Palestinians to feel that the first Intifada had forced us to do so, and that violence bears fruit. The real question is whether it was necessary to continue to bleed in Lebanon. It is hard to believe there is any significant person or group today who would prefer to return to Lebanon. It also seems clear that the IDF's departure has led more and more Lebanese to publicly question the justifications for Syria's continued presence in Lebanon. The withdrawal lent credibility to Barak in the eyes of his negotiating partners, and demonstrated his ability to carry out his decisions.

Looking back on Barak's short tenure, this was his principal accomplishment. Considering the four years in which I struggled by demonstrating, writing, and establishing a public movement for withdrawal from Lebanon, I consider myself fortunate to have played a part in effecting a radical change in the public's attitude and an alteration of policy.

CHAPTER 6
CAMP DAVID

AFTER THE WITHDRAWAL FROM LEBANON, debate persisted over various related issues, including the future of the fighters of the South Lebanese Army and their families, thousands of whom had sought refuge in Israel. But the Israeli-Palestinian clock did not stop ticking toward September 13, and Barak sensed that the time had come to hold the permanent settlement summit in Washington. He gave very little leeway to the people negotiating on his behalf, certainly not on the issue of Jerusalem, not with regard to the extent of territory that would be annexed, and not with regard to the refugees. He believed that the real decision would be taken by the leaders, and that only once he was sitting with Arafat and Clinton could they reach the moment of truth and decide on the price and the dividend. He very much wanted to convene a summit meeting and wanted to do it in the summer of 2000, to reach a signed agreement—a permanent agreement or at least a framework agreement—by the deadline.

The Palestinian side did almost everything it could to avert the summit, short of refusing to participate. Arafat was afraid that the summit would take place without him knowing in advance what Barak really intended to offer. He did not want to be caught off guard, and did not want to face the Clinton-Barak axis and be blamed at the end of the summit for not compromising enough. At my meetings with Palestinians they conveyed these concerns, and tried to dissuade us from foisting the summit on them. However, it was clear they would not be able to refuse Clinton. On June 15, after a meeting with Arafat in Washington, Clinton said, "Conditions are not yet ripe for a summit." Arafat was insisting on the implementation of agreements already signed, particularly the release of prisoners and the third redeployment, but in their talks Clinton had not concealed his preference for dealing with the permanent agreement. "I want to complete the work, and I want to see it finished in time," Clinton said. For Barak, the delay on the third-phase redeployment was a matter of principle: He was not prepared to complete it or even discuss it until he could be sure he had a partner for the framework agreement.

On June 19 I went to Ramallah to visit Abu Mazen, who had recently met with Barak. Abu Mazen spoke highly of the Prime Minister as a person, but sharply criticized Barak's recent statements, including, "There is no Palestinian nation or people," and, "There has never been an international border on the West Bank."

"Why does he make rightist statements," Abu Mazen asked, "and undermine our trust?" According to Abu Mazen, Arafat felt deceived: There had been no progress in negotiations on the third phase, and he believed Barak had no real intention of implementing it. Arafat was also angry that during his last trip to the United States, Israel had released only three Palestinian political prisoners, after there had been talk about a few dozen. The release of the three had humiliated Arafat and displayed his weakness to his people. Abu Mazen heaped praise on Abu Ala, referring to him as "the bravest and the most suitable person of all of us to conduct negotiations." The tension between them after the Stockholm talks had dissipated to such an extent that Abu Ala had accepted Abu Mazen's authority over him. My host expressed his wish for Abu Ala to continue conducting the negotiation with Israel, but he believed the disparities were still great and, unlike the Palestinian group, the Israeli delegation did not have permission to conclude matters. The right thing to do was to continue the negotiations intensively only after basic principles were agreed upon, and to appear at the summit with Clinton only as a closing ceremony to the negotiations. "Arafat does not negotiate," Abu Mazen said, "and he is not thrilled about being drawn into a Wye-like framework for a second time. He prefers that other people negotiate, with him giving final approval." He felt that if serious talks were held it would be possible to hold the summit in another month, but he did not want Barak to apply pressure.

But Barak was applying a lot of it. On Saturday evening, June 25, he asked me to get ready for a mission to Egypt the next day, to meet Mubarak and persuade him to convince Arafat to participate in the summit. After my own talk with Abu Mazen, I was not quite convinced that this was the correct approach, but Barak insisted, and I appreciated his determination. I cancelled everything in my schedule for the next day, including the "Holy of Holies"—the committee for selecting judges. After a cabinet meeting I met with Barak briefly and he presented me with an updated rough outline of the settlement. He felt he could only allow himself to make concessions at a summit of this sort, and additional delay was liable to drag on to the end of Clinton's tenure. If we succeeded in reaching an agreement, he would personally bring it to a referendum, and he believed it would win a majority even if his coalition became shaky. If he failed, he would consider going for an interim agreement and co-opting Ariel Sharon. I asked him what I could say to Mubarak regarding territory. Without hesitation he said: "We need to annex thirteen percent. The rest will be for a Palestinian state."

A special plane was waiting for me, and I made use of the flight to organize my papers following my talk with Barak. As soon as we landed I was taken directly to President Mubarak, to the same palace and the same room in which we had met about four months earlier. The meeting, between just the two of us, lasted about two and a half hours. On this occasion too, considerable time was devoted to a discussion of the general situation in the Middle East, but this time it included Mubarak's analysis of the recent death of Hafez al-Assad and the inauguration of his son Bashar. Mubarak reminisced about the Arab League conference, and was full of humor and good intentions. He asked how he could help, and I told him that he carried a heavy burden. Barak saw him as a friend and partner in the peace process, and hoped that he would be able to play a central part in the preparations for the summit and perhaps also the summit itself. I told him that it seemed we were approaching the final leg of the peace process. In a few months we would be losing Clinton and his knowledge and willingness to deal with the Middle East. It seemed that the final concessions would only be possible in the framework of a meeting of leaders. I asked him to use his influence on Arafat so that the summit could be held forthwith.

Mubarak told me that he was personally prepared to support the idea of a summit, but Arafat had grave reservations. Arafat was afraid that holding a summit while the discrepancies between the sides were so great would inevitably lead to failure, for which he would pay a heavy price. He had no interest in a three-way meeting with Clinton and Barak, at which, he was convinced, they would pressure him together. A whole series of clarifications was required for Arafat before he would attend.

Toward the end of our meeting Mubarak asked me who would participate on the Israeli side if a summit was held—if both politicians and experts were included, he explained, that would make it easier for Arafat to attend. If only politicians were invited, it would be a harder sell. Osama al-Baz, the President's senior advisor, accompanied me to the airport. On the way, I drafted a list of potential participants, including both ministers and senior officials, and passed it on to him. This should have made things easier for Arafat, who felt time at the summit should be devoted to work at the technical level before decisions were made by the leaders. That same night, Shlomo Ben-Ami visited Arafat's office. While they were talking, Mubarak called Arafat and relayed to him the list of summit attendees I had given al-Baz. Ben-Ami felt Mubarak's call had done the job.

On June 28 at a White House press conference, Clinton announced, "I do not believe that they can resolve the final, most difficult issues without having the leaders get together in some isolated setting and make the last tough decisions." Barak considered ending all contact with the Palestinians until the summit, to make it clear to Arafat that all other possibilities had been exhausted and an agreement could only be reached at a summit. The Palestinians said, officially and unofficially, that it was essential to hold another serious round of talks before the summit, but if Clinton invited Arafat he would go. In an interview with Israeli television Channel 2 on

July 1, Mohammed Dahlan described the grave situation of frustration in the territories: "Nobody can prevent a national conflagration. Nobody can promise that the situation will not explode. The guarantee that there will be no explosion is carrying out the agreements."

The July summit soon became a fact. On July 4 invitations to a summit at Camp David seven days later went out to the two sides. In his announcement of the summit, Clinton explained that it was necessary because the Israeli and Palestinian negotiating teams "can take the talks no further at their level. Significant differences remain, and they involve the most complex and most sensitive of questions. The negotiators have reached an impasse. Movement now depends on historic decisions that only the two leaders can make . . . But to delay this gathering, to remain stalled, is simply no longer an option. For the Israeli-Palestinian conflict, as all of us has seen, knows no status quo. It can move forward toward real peace, or it can slide back into turmoil. It will not stand still. If the parties do not seize this moment, if they cannot make progress now, there will be more hostility and more bitterness, perhaps even more violence. And to what end? Eventually, after more bloodshed and tears, they will have to come back to the negotiating table."

THIS WAS A VICTORY FOR BARAK THAT, in hindsight, was the fateful turning point on the way to his devastating political defeat. He presented it as an extraordinary effort to either reach peace with the Palestinians or expose their real face. He repeated this so many times, both in closed talks and to the media, that people began to think that he attached equal historical importance to the two results. Afterwards, Palestinians claimed that his whole intention was to prove there was nobody to talk to. This was definitely an unfair accusation.

On the eve of the summit, the Palestinian side felt under great pressure. Their main fear was that the summit would end without an agreement and that the frustration on the ground, in the face of the high expectations, would cause a conflagration. Some Israelis argued afterwards that Camp David failed because the Palestinians wanted to prove they were right— that the matter was not ripe for resolution and that the negotiations should continue at a low level in order to prepare the foundation for the leaders' final decisions.

On July 3 in Jerusalem, during the last week before the Camp David conference, I met one of the central figures in the evolving Palestinian delegation. I did not know whether he had come in Arafat's name or in his own, but his message was both clear and disturbing: "We have to do something more before the summit." In his view, the summit was destined to become a dramatic failure, and because not enough had been done in practical areas, it was important to at least improve the atmosphere. He suggested a private meeting between Barak and Arafat to build up mutual trust between them. "A year has passed since Barak's government was established," he said. "Until now, contrary to the expectations of those who believe in peace on the Palestinian side, all that has been done is the implementation of agreements signed by Netanyahu, without adding a single thing to them. Barak has even boasted about it occasionally. A supreme effort has to be made to avoid the failure of the summit, because nobody knows what it can lead to. Confidence-building steps could be taken prior to the summit: Israel could release a few dozen Palestinian prisoners, make a commitment to transfer the three villages adjoining Jerusalem to Area A at a later stage, and promise the United States partial implementation of the third redeployment after the summit. For his part, Arafat would publish a list of the weapons collected by the Authority—including those held by the Tanzim, which had been exposed during the Nakba Day violence—renew the work of the committee against incitement, and tighten security cooperation with Israel."

I passed this proposal on to Barak, but he and Arafat did not meet before the summit.

On July 8, a few days after my special meeting with the senior Palestinian figure, I met the Prime Minister at his residence in Jerusalem. We had a private talk in the late morning, and he expressed his hopes for the summit. It did not seem right, he felt, to take confidence-building steps, which would mean unnecessary arguments within the government, before the big showdown. The overall solution, the end of the dispute, seemed so revolutionary to him, that any marginal concession beforehand would be difficult to make and would be superfluous once there was a definite agreement. Barak graphically described to me the difficult decisions Arafat had to make and the benefits awaiting him if he did so. I felt torn in half, or, more accurately, into one-quarter and three-quarters. Three-quarters of me was happy: I was very grateful to Barak for the departure from Lebanon and respected his courage in withdrawing without an agreement, over the disapproval of most of his security chiefs. I wanted to believe in his optimism but I was afraid that the summit would fail. I told him that in interviews with the media, I had said the summit had a fifty-one-percent chance of succeeding, since summits of this sort are not convened for nothing. I really believe that summits have a dynamic of their own, since neither side, supposedly, has an interest in their failure. It was likely that even with insufficient preparation, an atmosphere of collaboration and trust would be formed between the huts at Camp David which could make it possible to bridge the gaps. But there were fears that the summit would break down, and that had to be prevented at all costs.

I believed this was the exact moment to put the Beilin–Abu Mazen Understandings on the table as a basis for negotiation. I told Barak that if Clinton had submitted the understandings to the parties, time and squabbles could have been saved and real decisions might have been reached. Barak was thinking in different terms, and it was almost time for his next meeting. Before leaving I took a large, sealed envelope out of my case and I presented it to him like somebody giving a charm to a soldier heading off to battle. I told him that the paper had been prepared by the ECF—the "peace factory" now directed by Yair Hirschfeld, Ron Pundak, and Nimrod Novick—and was in tune with my thinking. It was a detailed proposal, written like an agreement in every respect, and constituted an alternative to a framework agreement, in case it turned out that the preferred agreement could not be concluded. Barak seemed delighted to take the envelope, or at least he had what looked like a benevolent expression on his face.

A few months later I learned that on that very Saturday, a few hours later, the unsigned paper containing the Beilin–Abu Mazen Understandings was placed on President Clinton's desk. Clinton read them studiously from beginning to end, jotted down a number of comments, and when he had finished reading, told members of the peace team who were with him in the room, "This is it. This is simply the whole framework agreement. It is exactly this paper that has to be signed." However, the United States did not submit any paper to both sides, not even this one. Throughout the Camp David summit it was in the air, as all three sides were conversant with it, but it was not explicitly discussed. Barak had announced that if the Americans submitted a paper, he would pack his bags and return to Israel. When I later met Madeleine Albright after the Camp David failure, she said to me, "Although you were not physically at the summit, you were in fact there the whole time. We touched and we didn't touch your paper." It was like salt in my wounds . . .

BACK TO JULY 8. That evening, I returned to the Prime Minister's residence. With a grave expression on his face, he asked if anybody other than myself had seen the draft agreement I had given him earlier. No, I replied, only those who had drafted the document. "Very good," he said. "It must not exist. If I come out with a partial alternative, the Palestinians will prefer it to the painful permanent settlement. I do not need it; you can take it back."

Barak had never been forthright in relations between us, and that moment was extremely difficult. The draft agreement in the white envelope included the general principles of a permanent agreement, including a commitment to end the negotiations on the permanent settlement within a year. In the meantime, the third withdrawal would be carried out; and on January 1, 2001, Israel would recognize the Palestinian state on all the territories (comprising Area A and B) then in Palestinian hands; from that point the negotiations would continue between the two states. A multinational force would supervise the border crossings and operate alongside the IDF, which would remain in Area C, still under Israeli control. The Palestinian side would commit to combat terror and violence, and the Israeli side would commit to freezing the settlements, in accordance with Rabin's negotiations with Arafat. A joint planning committee would be set up to prepare the separation of the infrastructures and coordination between the two states. Various other committees would be established to deal with everyday matters related to the city of Jerusalem, while negotiations on the city's future would begin as soon as the interim agreement was signed, to determine a special status for the Holy Basin—the half-square-mile area that contains sites holy to Jews, Muslims, and Christians.

The paper detailed the principles that dictate the resolution on the refugee issue, and proposed an international council to deal with rehabilitation and absorption in various countries that have expressed their willingness to participate, and to address personal compensations. It contained an economic agreement based on the principles of the World Trade Organization, and a section dealing with cultural links and various other civilian topics, based on the Barcelona framework established by the European Union.

Everything was left in the sealed envelope. That evening I informed my colleagues who had written the paper that Ehud Barak was about to swing on the trapeze without a safety net, because I was still holding his safety net in my hand. They had difficulty understanding Barak's decision. I did too.

THE NEXT DAY I TRAVELED TO GAZA to address a group of Israeli and Palestinian legal practitioners who were participating in a seminar on road accidents and insurance. By this stage, joint activity had become intensive and quite natural. From my point of view, this was one of the important aims of the Justice Ministry, along with a goal I had not managed to achieve: the establishment of two liaison offices of lawyers in the Gaza Strip and the West Bank to assist with legal-civil problems between Israelis and Palestinians and to jointly coordinate legislation for the European directives. This seminar was one of the last pictures of peace engraved in my memory. The Israeli judges and the lawyers stayed with their Palestinian colleagues at the Al-Andalus Guest House in Gaza, where the discussions took place. It is an elegant hotel with old-style furniture, looking out onto the sea. Most of the Israelis had never visited Gaza before, and almost no one had been there since the Palestinian Authority was set up. They told me they expected to find an enormous refugee camp, and could not believe that the city boasted skyscrapers, gardens, fancy hotels, ornate restaurants, and a country club. On both evenings in Gaza they walked the city streets without any special security, and many decided they would return on Saturdays with their families for a full tour of the city. Links between the participants tightened. When I arrived at lunchtime, Israeli and Palestinian lawyers were sitting next to one another exchanging legal opinions in English. I sat next to Dr. Friekh Abu-Medein, who was in charge of the Palestinian Authority's Justice Ministry. He looked at me viewing the show and said, "A vision of the End of Days!"

The United States funded the seminar, and Ambassador Martin Indyk came to Gaza to welcome the participants. Indyk took advantage of the meeting to have a private talk with me. He expressed his deep concern over what might happen at the Camp David summit, where he was to be part of the American delegation. According to him, Barak would have to agree to three things in order to avoid the failure of the summit: exchange of territory; advance clarification that if there is a gray area not annexed to Israel but not given to the Palestinian state, it will eventually be transferred to the Palestinians; and transfer of part of the sovereign section of the municipal area of Jerusalem to the Palestinians. He stressed that he was saying this as a private individual and not as a representative of the United States. As somebody who, through his various posts, knew the Middle East well, he was very apprehensive about the coming days, because all the parties, including the United States, were marching toward the unknown without adequate preparation.

Barak managed to drag the faltering coalition carriage he headed almost to the moment of truth, but not quite. The dream of reaching the historic junction together with the right, compromising with the Palestinians, initialing the permanent agreement, separating from the right, moving to a referendum, and winning it with a huge majority, ended when Barak accepted the invitation to participate in Camp David. The National Religious Party faction in the Knesset left the coalition; the Yisrael Ba'aliyah Party headed by Natan Sharansky also left, and when the talks started, Sharansky joined the protest tent in front of the Prime Minister's office. David Levy, who had felt for a long time that the management of foreign policy was out of his hands, decided, just as he had on the eve of the Madrid Conference in 1991, not to take part in Camp David. Finally, on the eve of the summit, after the

NRP and Yisrael Ba'aliyah had announced their resignations, the Shas ministers informed Barak that they too were abandoning the government ship unless he presented his "red lines" to their spiritual leader, Rabbi Ovadia Yosef. Barak informed them that it was impossible to make a commitment to red lines beyond what he had already said in public—and he lost Shas.

Barak's formal coalition now numbered only forty-two—twenty-six members of the "One Israel" faction led by Labor, six members of the Center Party, and ten members of Meretz, who had left the government but remained in the coalition. The ten members of various Arab parties were a possible but uncommitted source of support. In a no-confidence vote on the eve of Barak's departure for Camp David, fifty-two members supported him and fifty-four voted no-confidence. The government did not fall because the measure required sixty-one votes (a majority of the Knesset), but it was a very inauspicious send-off. Barak announced, "I will continue with the negotiations even if I am left with nine ministers and a quarter of the Knesset."

Barak arrived at Camp David after losing his parliamentary majority, after compelling the Palestinian side to take part in the summit, without adequate preparation and with no escape plan. The ministers who joined him were Amnon Lipkin-Shahak and Shlomo Ben-Ami. Later, Dan Meridor, a Likud moderate, also yielded to his entreaties and became part of the delegation.

THE SUMMIT LASTED FIFTEEN DAYS and was apparently the longest of its kind in American history. All the participants—the Americans, the Israelis, and the Palestinians—later admitted that there had been progress relative to the positions the parties had previously held, that a lot of time had been wasted, that no party had arrived sufficiently well-prepared, and that its failure was inherent from the outset, or at least from the first week of discussions.

To a large extent the negotiations were conducted between experts, with the political leaders close at hand. The leaders did not conduct negotiations, and proposals made by their representatives did not commit them. The other participants divided into three committees—refugees, borders, and Jerusalem—in which daily wrangling took place. There was some creativity in the Jerusalem committee and the sides got closer; it became apparent in the borders committee that the disparities were not bridgeable; and in the refugee committee there was almost no progress at all.

President Clinton, together with his peace team—members of the National Security Council and the State Department—appeared to be the most interested party. Clinton turned night into day, met frequently with the committee heads, and tried to mediate between the positions. Arafat and Barak received daily reports on what had happened in the committees, but three-way meetings were rare. The Palestinians claimed that the frostiness toward Arafat which emanated from Barak was one of the reasons for the failure of the talks. Only once did Barak go into Arafat's living quarters, and even at this forced meeting, no political discussion took place—it was a social chat. During the course of the summit both sides claimed that the other had reneged on the proposals made at Stockholm, and both claimed the other side had not come with any new proposals. The delegations themselves, it turned out, were not all of one piece. On the Israeli side a dovish axis emerged, led by Shlomo Ben-Ami and Amnon Lipkin-Shahak, facing a hawkish one headed by Dan Meridor and the Attorney General, Elyakim Rubinstein. The division on the Palestinian side was less predictable. Abu Mazen and Abu Ala were the diffident ones—they simply neutralized themselves by insisting in advance that "nothing good can come out of this summit." On the other side, members of the younger generation—Mohammed Dahlan, Hassan Asfour, and Mohammed Rashid—took pragmatic positions, and wished to use Clinton's last days in power to create a situation which would ultimately allow an agreement to be signed. The Palestinians would later claim that the Americans tried to split them by exploiting the generation gap.

Clinton took advantage of the proximity of Camp David to the White House and divided his time between the summit and his ongoing work. Arafat and Barak were confined to the camp, and neither of them utilized his time in an optimal manner. Because Barak chose not to employ an existing paper as a starting point, the negotiations had no agreed basis. Instead, they were conducted according to the method of the bazaar, whereby each side adopts an unrealistic initial bargaining stance, and after an argument, "concedes" and compromises on the price. As Shlomo Ben-Ami testified in an interview with *Ma'ariv* in April 2001, "Our working assumption was that the maps we presented to them before Camp David were not acceptable, but certainly a basis for negotiation." It was hard for the one side to know when the other had really reached its red line. For instance, the Israeli delegation presented opening positions that referred to the annexation of thirteen percent of the West Bank and proposed a functional division in Jerusalem while opposing a division of sovereignty. The Israelis retreated from all these positions to more moderate stances, particularly on borders and Jerusalem, but the Palestinians had no way of knowing if the new positions were final or not. Consequently, this was an Israeli invitation to be pressured.

The Palestinians arrived with a different approach. They sought Israeli agreement to their principles, promising to be generous on pragmatic matters once this was achieved. They wanted Israel, to take one example, to agree that the future border between Israel and the Palestinian state would run along the Green Line (i.e., the 1967 border). After this was agreed, the Palestinians would be willing to discuss Israeli needs on the settlement blocs, and if Israel annexed areas limited in size on the West Bank, they would insist on an exchange of territory on the same scale. With regard to the refugees, the Palestinians demanded Israeli recognition of the right of return, but with the creation of a framework for rehabilitation and absorption of refugees that would make the actual return to Israel a negligible issue. On security arrangements, they demanded recognition of the fact that they should not jeopardize Palestinian sovereignty, and for Jerusalem, they wanted the 1967 line as a starting point which, if accepted by Israel, would make finding pragmatic arrangements possible.

The talks revolved around these competing methods: the bazaar on one hand, and principles before particulars on the other. Arafat felt like he was facing an American-Israeli axis, and had to fight bravely for his national interests. He claimed he heard no innovations from the Israeli side and that he had been brought to Camp David so that he could be made to submit. Barak believed Arafat was not prepared to move one iota from his rigid positions, and that the Americans were not doing enough to convince him that this was an opportunity that would not return. The truth was different. Both sides became more flexible during this prolonged summit. Israel agreed to make do with annexation of about nine percent of the West Bank, and to relinquish its sovereignty in parts of the Arab neighborhoods of Jerusalem. The Palestinians agreed for the first time to recognize that the Israeli neighborhoods built in East Jerusalem would be part of Israel. This was significant progress—the Israeli concession was especially remarkable—but considering these changes were the outcome of a summit on which so many hopes had been pinned, one can understand why there was a sense was that this was not a real turnaround.

On July 16 there was a demonstration by one hundred and fifty thousand right-wing Israelis against the negotiations at Camp David in Rabin Square in Tel Aviv. The next day Clinton gave his first interview since the talks started, telling the editor of the *New York Daily News:* "God, it's hard. It's like nothing I've ever dealt with. All the negotiations with the Irish, all the stuff I've done with the Palestinians before this and with the Israelis, the Balkans at Dayton . . . I would be totally misleading if I said I had an inkling that a deal is at hand. That's just not true. But we're slogging . . . [Barak and Arafat] know if they make a peace agreement, half of their constituencies will have to be angry at them for a while. They're trying. It's so hard. My heart goes out to them. It's really hard. It's the hardest thing I've ever seen. It's raining like hell at Camp David . . . I hope it's not a metaphor."

A change occurred in the course of the summit on July 17, when Clinton presented some nonbinding, unwritten ideas of his own after prolonged talks with the two sides. He proposed that nine percent of the West Bank would be annexed to Israel and one percent adjoining Gaza would be transferred from Israeli to Palestinian sovereignty. In the Old City of Jerusalem, the Muslim Quarter and the Christian Quarter would be transferred to Palestinian sovereignty, whereas the Jewish Quarter, the Western Wall, and the Armenian Quarter would be under Israeli sovereignty. On the Temple Mount, the Palestinians would be given administrative control, while residual sovereignty would be in Israeli hands. The outer neighborhoods in East

Jerusalem would be under Palestinian sovereignty, and the inner neighborhoods, like Ras al-Amud, Silwan, Wadi Juz, and Sheikh Jarrah, would be under autonomous Palestinian management but Israeli sovereignty.

Barak was prepared to accept these principles, but Arafat viewed the proposal as an American-Israeli plot, and expressed his opposition in writing. On July 19 he sent a letter to the President rejecting the proposal as a basis for negotiation. In a conversation with Clinton he said that he was not willing to be the first Palestinian leader to grant legitimacy to Israeli sovereignty over the Haram al-Sharif—the Temple Mount. Clinton was annoyed by Arafat's rejection. He began a round of phone calls to Arab leaders, but they refused to ask Arafat to change his mind. None of them were prepared to take the risk of pressuring Arafat to be more moderate on the Jerusalem issue; after all, each of them was threatened at home by an Islamic opposition. The President spoke bluntly to Arafat, and told him Barak had gone a long way and that he was not contributing to the settlement. If there was no agreement, Barak would form a unity government or lose the elections, neither of which would bring a settlement closer. Clinton also suggested that Palestinian relations with the United States would be jeopardized if indeed a negative reply was given to all the American ideas.

The tension at Camp David forced Clinton to delay his trip to the G-8 conference in Japan for as long as he could. He was about to fly off on Thursday, July 20, when he received a letter from Barak at noon lamenting the end of the talks and blaming Arafat for their failure. A short while later, the President met Arafat and tried to bridge the disparities on the question of East Jerusalem. Arafat said to him: "It is not me, it is the whole Arab world. It's not me you have to deal with. You have to deal with the Saudis, the Egyptians, the Moroccans, the Syrians, and the Jordanians. A billion Muslims will not forgive me. I do not have a mandate to make concessions on Jerusalem."

"There are things that are impossible to achieve," Clinton replied. "You have to display flexibility. You will lead your people and the whole region to disaster."

Barak informed Clinton that the Israelis were leaving. The members of the Israeli delegation met and held a prolonged internal discussion. They were joined at seven p.m. by Clinton and Albright, who had some stern words to say. Barak had already finished packing and so had the Palestinians, but at forty minutes past midnight, Clinton reached the communications center and announced that Barak and Arafat were not leaving, and that Albright would stay with the teams until his return from Japan.

Clinton offered a number of alternatives with regard to Jerusalem: joint sovereignty over part of the city, postponing the whole issue of Jerusalem and removing it from the agreement equation, and so on. The Israeli team announced it would not negotiate with the Palestinians while Clinton was away until Arafat announced his answer to Clinton's proposals.

On his return, Clinton poured all his energy into the negotiations, holding marathon talks with the sides separately and together. His talks with Arafat were particularly candid. Clinton told the head of the Palestinian Authority that he was not presenting anything in response to compromises Barak was willing to make. "You missed an opportunity in 1947, and you are now repeating the same mistake," Clinton said. "If you stop your people from having what I am suggesting, they will judge you accordingly. You will be the reason for the Temple Mount remaining under Israeli sovereignty." Arafat answered him angrily: "Even if you offer me Haifa and Jaffa without sovereignty over the Haram al-Sharif, I will not take it."

The calls I received at night from Barak while he was at Camp David testified to his severe distress. His reports were generally pessimistic. He said there was no real communication between him and the Palestinians, that Arafat was not moving forward. At a certain stage he feared the Americans would surprise him with a paper of their own, and even said the Israeli delegation would have to leave Camp David if that happened. The most difficult and anxious call came on July 21. Barak said it was clear to him that this was an historic moment, but it was also exceptionally difficult. He had talked at length with King Abdullah and President Mubarak, in the hope that they could induce Arafat to compromise on a number of topics, but they backed Arafat automatically. Arafat's behavior seemed strange to Barak, and the Americans were not pressuring Arafat to give answers to their questions. He finished the conversation by saying, "Returning home will be a mental relief for me."

ECHOES OF THE NEGOTIATION ON JERUSALEM reached Israel, and the question of the unity of Jerusalem reappeared on the public agenda. There is more hypocrisy surrounding this issue than any other in Israeli politics. No government has managed to unite the city since 1967, when dozens of Arab villages covering seventy square kilometers were annexed to it following the Six-Day War. This move, which enlarged East Jerusalem tenfold, made about two hundred thousand Palestinians holders of Israeli identity cards, without the character of the eastern city changing one iota. Any tourist visiting Jerusalem knows exactly where the Jewish city ends and the Arab city begins, a division reinforced by disparities in infrastructure, education, and even electricity.

The political pledge not to divide the city may be consequential in speeches at fundraising events in the United States, but in Israel everyone knows the city is simply divided. In the '70s, Israel built eleven Jewish neighborhoods on land conquered during the Six-Day War. The Palestinians considered them settlements, as did the rest of the world. Recognition of Israeli sovereignty over these neighborhoods, and a special arrangement in the Old City, which is less than one square kilometer in size, will make the Jewish city of Jerusalem larger than it has ever been in its long history, and the recognized capital of the state of Israel, after more than fifty years in which the world has refused to acknowledge it as such.

In order to bring home the fact that Jerusalem is divided and that, besides the Old City, Israel has no real interest in East Jerusalem, I organized a tour of the eastern neighborhoods for Knesset members and some public figures. The tour took place on July 23, and I was joined by Knesset members Elie Goldschmidt, Zahava Gal-On, Avshalom Vilan, and Mossi Raz, as well as David Grossman, Haim Oron, Dr. Menachem Klein, retired Deputy Police Commissioner Aryeh Amit, former Security Chief Carmi Gillon, and others. There was great media interest in the event from Israel and the rest of the world. The truth is that until our tour, even I did not realize just how absurd and futile the common statement, "Undivided Jerusalem shall remain forever under our sovereignty," really was. First of all, no Israeli transportation company was prepared to take us through the streets of the eastern city. In the end, the group traveled on a bus from an

Arab East Jerusalem company. The passengers, some of whom were long-time Jerusalemites, admitted they had never been to most of the places we visited. In the north of the city we reached a security checkpoint four kilometers *inside* the city's municipal boundaries. The police and security personnel did not allow us to enter the Qalandia refugee camp, which is formally under Israeli sovereignty.

The tour served its purpose. It proved—to ourselves and the reporters who accompanied us—that this was a case of an agreed lie, with local and national politicians uttering slogans for applause, despite the knowledge that Israel has no real sovereignty over a considerable part of East Jerusalem. It also has no need for sovereignty of this sort, except to facilitate travel between the Jewish neighborhoods, which could be arranged in other ways without Israel annexing hundreds of thousands of Palestinians. In formulating the understandings with Abu Mazen, we were afraid of breaking the taboo about Jerusalem too soon. The taboo was broken at Camp David.

The common lie about Jerusalem was encouraged by moderate people, like Teddy Kollek, who served as mayor for almost three decades. The call for this city to never be divided again, the memories of the wall inside the city that should never be rebuilt: All these myths were so powerful that to say, "Okay, let us divide Jerusalem," during any negotiation seemed next to impossible. Even in my talks with Abu Mazen in 1995, Jerusalem was postponed for a later stage, with the suggestion of an interim solution for the city—kind of a municipal solution, rather than one connected to each state and its respective sovereignty. My reasoning for this approach was very clear: I was sure that if at that time I had suggested to Rabin that we divide Jerusalem, he would have rejected the whole package. Abu Mazen understood this as well, so we agreed that the two states would have their municipal rights in Jerusalem, and that both parties would negotiate a permanent solution with no deadline.

At Camp David, Barak displayed real courage on this point, because for the first time there was an Israeli suggestion to divide Jerusalem. Not in the way which Clinton eventually suggested, in which any Arab areas would join the Palestinian state while the Jewish neighborhoods would become part of Israel. But Barak did agree that some of the neighborhoods in East Jerusalem which Israel annexed would be part of the Palestinian state. And this was the way in which he broke the taboo—you can say, in that respect at least, that he went further even than Abu Mazen and I in 1995.

Perhaps the reason why Barak pushed so hard for the summit is that he believed that he had the winning card. But because he was so guarded, he did not consult anyone, and he did not prepare his plan in a detailed or practical way. When Barak returned from Camp David, Ehud Olmert, the right-wing mayor of Jerusalem, seized on this lack of preparation to criticize Barak: "You will see that you cannot divide it," he insisted, "because people will have to go through four sovereignties in order to get from one place to another, from your workplace to your home, and this is crazy." Olmert was against the division of Jerusalem, but as he told Barak, "Even if I agreed with you, it could have never been possible." Barak had indeed not prepared a plan of the contiguity of Jerusalem.

The idea that had been hovering throughout was the one eventually made explicit in the Clinton Plan: Jerusalem would be divided by a new border, not necessarily a physical one, so that all the Arab neighborhoods in East Jerusalem would be part of the Palestinian capital, al-Quds; while on the Israeli side there would be a combination which would include West Jerusalem, meaning the Israeli city as it existed before 1967, the Israeli neighborhoods which have been built in East Jerusalem since then, and part of the Old City, which would include the Wailing Wall and the Jewish Quarter.

This was actually in line with the Palestinian demand. Since Oslo, they spoke constantly about their capital in East Jerusalem. They didn't say, "We want al-Quds, the whole of al-Quds," but rather, "We want East Jerusalem." So it was clear that if a solution referred to East Jerusalem as their capital, it would be a fair solution and they would accept it. The Jerusalemites, at least, know that they cannot cross the street and go to East Jerusalem. They don't do that, actually; it is not theirs, and they don't see it as part of their city. Consequently, it is perhaps easier for them to accept a division of the city than for people in New York or in Tel Aviv. In New York, it's easy to think, "Oh, Jerusalem. It was conquered by Israel. It is fundamentally Jewish, and it should remain under Israeli sovereignty forever." But then when you come to Jerusalem, you see how divided it really is, and it becomes clear that it was never actually united. This is the greatest illusion—that it is a united city. There are areas which you cannot visit. You cannot collect taxes. You never send the police there—it is simply beyond the horizon. And this is under both Likud and Labor municipalities. It is an illusion that has been put past the Jewish people for decades. They are paying lip service to a united city which has never actually been united.

Barak's moves were, in the end, characterized most of all by his suspicion. He never believed anyone, from either side. So he was not ready to work with someone and to say, "I'm going to divide Jerusalem. Give me a plan for the division."

UPON CLINTON'S RETURN FROM JAPAN the negotiations returned to their earlier pace. The teams began to devise drafts for a framework agreement; there were four members in each team, two from each side, and the four drafting teams dealt with security arrangements, borders, Jerusalem, and refugees. A few hours past midnight on Tuesday, July 25, precisely when it seemed that real progress was beginning, Saeb Erekat conveyed Arafat's negative answer to all of the President's creative ideas on Jerusalem. That was the signal of the end of the talks.

A day earlier, Cinton had summoned Shlomo Ben-Ami, Gilead Sher, Saeb Erekat, and Hassan Asfour to a discussion that lasted four hours. Erekat urged everybody not to quit. He suggested preparing a three-way paper presenting a progress report, asserting that certain disparities remained and that all sides would make an effort to reach an agreement by the date agreed at Sharm el-Sheikh, September 13, 2000. Ben-Ami said that if the summit ended without any agreement at all, it meant that the process had collapsed, the peace camp in Israel would disintegrate, the Barak government would fall, and a national unity government would be formed in which Sharon would have the veto on all political steps.

That night Barak called me. He sounded very pessimistic. He was worried that the Palestinian side was not preparing its public for the expected compromises, and worried about the political consequences in Israel if there was no agreement. He was not convinced that the American proposal—to summarize what had been achieved and return for a similar summit within a few weeks—was realistic. If there were no agreements here and now, he said to me, it would lose momentum. He was full of praise for our tour of East Jerusalem: "That is part of the education work our side is doing," he said. "The problem is that the other side is not arranging tours like that."

On July 25 the summit drew to a close amidst great disappointment. Clinton and Sandy Berger invited Barak, Danny Yatom, Arafat, and Saeb Erekat to come and see them. Clinton began by saying it was sad that it had not been possible to reach an agreement, but there had been a lot of development in the positions of the sides, and he was asking them to do their utmost to reach an agreement by mid-September. Arafat promised to make every effort to stick to the timetable. Barak joined Arafat by saying that the process must not be allowed to collapse. Some people thought this was another "suitcase crisis," like the one that had occurred a few days previously, which ended with the two sides complying with Clinton's request to make an extra effort, remain at Camp David, and reach an agreement. But this time the Americans believed the discussions could not be continued because no solution for the disputed issues had emerged, and the date for the Democratic and Republican Party conventions was drawing near. The President's time was not unlimited; at a certain point the Americans had to terminate the prolonged talks and admit that the summit had failed.

ONE OF THE MEMBERS OF THE AMERICAN delegation made a comparison between the progress made at Camp David and the terms of the Beilin–Abu Mazen Understandings. A Palestinian state is established in both cases. In the 1995 understandings, Israel annexes 250 square kilometers of the West Bank (representing 4.5 percent) for the purposes of retaining three settlement blocs (Gush Etzion, the Jerusalem region, and Ariel), and makes some small border modifications. Israel transfers 200 square kilometers in the region of the Halutza dunes near Gaza to the Palestinians. At Camp David, Barak agreed to annex no less than nine percent and the transfer of no more than one percent to the Palestinians. And no agreement emerged.

The solution to the problem of Jerusalem is temporary in the 1995 understandings. Jerusalem remains an open, undivided city. Its municipal boundaries are expanded, and include, among other places, Abu Dis, Azariyeh, A-Ram, A-Zaim, Ma'ale Adumim, Givon, and Givat Ze'ev. The Israeli neighborhoods in Jerusalem are defined as "Israeli boroughs" and a sub-municipality will be established in them. The neighborhoods populated by Palestinians are defined as "Palestinian boroughs" and a sub-municipality will be established in them. The ratio between the quarters is two-to-one in Israel's favor. The expanded city will elect a mayor from among the members of the expanded council. West Jerusalem will be recognized as the capital of Israel; East Jerusalem, outside the present municipal boundaries, will be declared al-Quds and will be recognized as the capital of the Palestinian state. All areas conquered in the Six-Day War will be declared an "area in dispute." A joint Israeli-Palestinian committee, with no target date set, will determine sovereignty over this area, and then the status quo will remain. The Palestinian state shall be granted extraterritorial sovereignty (like that granted to states at their embassies abroad) over the Haram al-Sharif, under the administration of the Waqf, the Islamic trust that runs the site. The present status quo, regarding the right of access and prayer for all, will be secured.

At Camp David, there was no agreement on Jerusalem. The American proposal, which was rejected by both sides, was for the remote Arab neighborhoods in Jerusalem to be transferred to the sovereignty of the Palestinian state, with the neighborhoods adjoining the Old City administered by the Palestinians under temporary Israeli sovereignty. In the Old City, the Christian and Muslim Quarters would be given over to the Palestinian state; the Jewish Quarter and the Armenian Quarter would be transferred to Israeli sovereignty. The Temple Mount would be transferred to Palestinian sovereignty, and the area underneath it given to Israel.

On the subject of refugees, the 1995 document states that the Palestinians understand that they will not be able to implement what they consider their right to return to their homes; that the Israeli side recognizes the material and mental suffering caused to the Palestinian refugees; and that both sides seek to establish an international organization, led by the government of Sweden, to deal with the subject of compensation. Israel will participate in financing the international fund that will compensate the refugees and will continue to absorb refugees in the framework of family unification and in special humanitarian cases. In 2000, there was no agreement with respect to the origins of the refugee problem, with respect to compensation or the number of refugees who would be absorbed by Israel.

With regard to security arrangements, in 1995 it was agreed that the IDF would withdraw from the territories in three stages within five years, after which three reinforced battalions and two emergency stores would remain on the ground. Three early-warning stations and three air defense units would be maintained for twelve years, or until peace agreements or bilateral security arrangements were secured between Israel and the Arab states, whichever comes last. It was agreed that the state of Palestine would be demilitarized, that joint Israeli-Palestinian patrols would be held along the Jordan River, and that a permanent international observer force would be established to ensure the implementation of the agreed security arrangements.

At Camp David the sides got closer on security issues, but there was no agreement. The Palestinians agreed that their state would be "non-militarized." Israel agreed that the military force remaining in the territories would not be Israeli but international. A disparity remained with regard to the period of time in which the IDF would withdraw from the territories (eighteen or thirty-six months). The Palestinians agreed to IDF early-warning stations but insisted there should be Palestinian communications officers for these stations. Israel insisted on maintaining axes within the Palestinian territory that would permit rapid deployment eastward in an emergency. The Palestinians opposed this. Israel demanded use of the skies above the Palestinian state for Air Force exercises, and the Palestinians refused this as well.

Many months later, after the outbreak of the Intifada, after Bush's victory, Barak's defeat, and the election of Sharon to the premiership, that same senior American said to me that Barak's renunciation of the 1995 understandings was his biggest mistake at Camp David.

ON THAT SAME DAY, JULY 25, 2000, the White House published the trilateral announcement by Clinton, Barak, and Arafat. The announcement pointed out that although the parties had not reached agreement on a final settlement, the negotiation was unprecedented in scope and attention to detail. The two sides to the dispute agreed to the following: the aim of the negotiation is to reach a final settlement, they will continue their efforts as soon as possible, and they will base their discussions on Security Council Resolutions 242 and 338. Both sides understood the importance of avoiding unilateral steps which are liable to predetermine the results of the negotiations, and both of them regard the United States as a partner for achieving peace. Apparently, everybody had "won." Barak had achieved his secondary goal: Clinton's final announcement presented him as having been prepared to go a long way, without receiving a commensurate response from the Palestinians. Clinton explained that because the sides had not made sufficient progress and because the September deadline for achieving an agreement was fast approaching, a summit had been, in his opinion, the only way in which they could strive for overall peace. The talks at Camp David were comprehensive, he said, and had touched on the most sensitive and complex issues.

Prime Minister Barak, Clinton continued, showed particular courage, vision, and an understanding of the historical importance of this moment. In referring to Arafat, the President was less complimentary: "Chairman Arafat made it clear that he, too, remains committed to the path of peace." The two sides, Clinton said, are supposed to complete the negotiations by mid-September and it is essential they do not lose hope. Israelis and Palestinians are destined to live side by side, destined to have a common future, and they made real headway in the last two weeks. The negotiation should be renewed in the coming weeks, and the United States will assist the sides in their goal to adhere to their deadline—September 13.

In reply to a journalist who asked if Barak had been more prepared to make compromises than Arafat, President Clinton was explicit: "The

Palestinian teams worked hard on a lot of these areas. But I think it is fair to say that at this moment in time, maybe because they had been preparing for it longer, maybe because they had thought it through more, that the Prime Minister moved forward more from his initial position than Chairman Arafat, particularly surrounding the questions of Jerusalem."

Praise for Barak, Clinton said, however, was not condemnation of Arafat. "This is agonizing for them—both of them . . . This is like going to the dentist without having your gums deadened . . . I mean, this is not easy." In reply to a question about Barak's ability to convince the Israeli public to agree to far-reaching concessions despite his weakness, Clinton said that Barak "is not a weak man . . . He didn't come over here to play safe with his political future; he came over here to do what he thought was right for the people of Israel . . . So I think the people of Israel should be very proud of him. He did nothing to compromise Israel's security, and he did everything he possibly could within the limits that he thought he had . . . to reach a just peace. So I would hope the people of Israel will support him."

A few days later Clinton was interviewed on Israeli television and he presented Barak as a courageous man of peace who did not get Palestinian cooperation. He also spoke about American willingness to assist Israel, and the assistance that was supposed to be given to the Jewish refugees from Arab countries as well as to the Palestinian refugees. For Barak, at least one honest person in America knew he had right on his side. In Europe and in other places around the world, the perception rapidly took root that "Barak conceded and Arafat rejected."

In his remarks directly after the close of the summit, Barak said:

I understand the disappointment of many in Israel, who believe in coexistence and extending a hand in peace to our Palestinian neighbors. I even join them in their disappointment. However, we will not cease our effort to achieve peace and will continue to work to bring it about—yet not at any price. Arafat was afraid to make the historic decisions necessary at this time in order to bring about an end to the conflict. Arafat's positions on Jerusalem are those which prevented the achievement of the agreement. We in the delegation worked day and night in order to reach an agreement . . . I bear supreme responsibility for the results of this summit, and for the fact that we don't yet have an agreement in hand and that we will have to go on working toward achieving one . . . The Israeli positions were accorded full legitimacy by the U.S. government, and there is no dispute that Israel was prepared to go all the way to achieve that peace. Ideas, views, and even positions which were raised in the course of the summit are invalid as opening positions in the resumption of negotiations, when they resume. They are null and void.

Arafat returned to the territories a hero. He had not "conceded" on the Haram al-Sharif and was able to make a rousing speech about returning to Jerusalem and all the territory conquered in 1967. On his arrival home in Gaza he was given a warm reception, the likes of which he had not received since he first got there in 1994. A television announcer declared, "You are the Palestinian national hero, guardian of the rights of the Palestinian people. You are the victor." Arafat just repeated his vain mantra: "On September 13 we will declare an independent state with Jerusalem as its capital. Whoever wants to accept it, will accept it and whoever does not can drink the sea at Gaza."

Akram Haniyeh, a member of the Palestinian delegation, published his diary of the talks at Camp David in the daily *al-Ayyam*, which he edits. In the last section, he wrote: "The negotiators took a deep sigh of relief at leaving the place where they had spent fifteen difficult days. As they looked out to the retreat from the windows of their cars, they left behind hours of tension, wait, and exhausting negotiations. They were carrying with them memories of the place, the people, and the events. But in their hearts they had treasured moments. They had said a clear 'no' to the United States while on the land of the United States. It was not for the sake of heroics. It was a 'no' that was politically, nationally, and historically positive and correct."

Within hours, a number of Palestinian delegates were en route from their hotel in Virginia to Reagan International Airport, on their way home. They struck up a conversation with their cab driver whose features seemed to indicate he was Pakistani or Indian. When he realized that his passengers were Palestinian and were at Camp David, Niyazi, the Pakistani driver said,

"You were excellent, Jerusalem is ours. We should not give up any part of it. Arafat's position is great. Jerusalem is ours!" When these delegates got out of the cab and carried their luggage toward the airport's entrance, Niyazi closed the cab's trunk and returned to his seat, waving at them and shouting, "Brothers, don't surrender Jerusalem! Don't surrender Jerusalem!" A Jewish cab driver in Jerusalem would have been, at the time, likely to say the exact same thing. On the Jewish side of the barricade, too, many people heaved a sigh of relief and were glad that nothing happened. Long live the virtual world: The Jews did not relinquish the Temple Mount at Camp David, even though they had, in fact, relinquished control over it back in June 1967; the Palestinians did not give up Jerusalem, despite having never held it.

Clinton, too, did not suffer any harm. His efforts were impressive, and the feeling among the delegates at the end was that the two sides would continue discussions and return to the United States within two to three months to sign. Camp David was not an important topic on the American nightly news, and its lack of success did not embarrass him. Even after the Monica Lewinsky scandal, Clinton remained a very popular American president. The citizens of the United States would have elected him for a third term, had it been possible, both before and after Camp David. The principal loss from the failure of the summit was the chance of reaching peace, and the losers were all the citizens of the Middle East.

CHAPTER 7
THE WRITING ON THE WALL

AFTER THE FAILURE OF CAMP DAVID, the two sides were chiefly preoccupied with retrospective analysis and mutual recriminations, but they also attempted to plan the next summit. The Israeli side claimed that the Palestinians had arrived at Camp David determined not to reach an agreement, to prove they had been right when they asked the Americans to wait and not to foist the meeting upon them. The Israelis also claimed that the first week had been completely wasted because of inactivity, and that the dispute between the old guard and the young guard eventually led to the paralysis of the Palestinian side. The Arab states, in the Israeli contention, had proven to be a disappointment; despite their great wish for the talks to succeed, they did nothing to advance them. Mubarak saw his contribution as convincing Arafat to participate in the summit, but he was not prepared to pressure him into being more flexible once there. On Revolution Day in Egypt, July 23, he flew to Saudi Arabia to meet some senior Palestinian figures, and thereby gave the impression of having backed Arafat's unyielding stance on the question of the Haram al-Sharif.

The Palestinians admitted that some of these accusations were correct. They really did not want a summit and its failure was something of a self-fulfilling prophecy. The first week had indeed been an appalling waste. According to them, their experience at the conference confirmed their great fear of being confronted by an American-Israeli axis, and they felt they had to defend themselves. But sometimes they defended themselves unnecessarily against proposals that might have answered their needs. To them, the summit confirmed the Palestinian lack of trust in Barak because the Israeli side reneged on a number of positions it had put forward at Stockholm, because it presented negotiating stances and not guiding principles, and because it did not understand that ultimately the agreement would be made with Arafat, Abu Mazen, and Abu Ala, even if other members of the delegation sometimes expressed a more moderate stance.

At the same time, the Palestinians did acknowledge that a number of taboos were broken at Camp David by both sides, particularly on the question of Jerusalem. They also conceded that there was a chance of reaching an agreement during the course of Clinton's tenure if attempts were made to change the situation by releasing political prisoners and by agreeing on the third phase of the redeployment. In return the Palestinians would take steps in the spheres of policing and incitement.

ON MONDAY, JULY 31, IN A BOLT OUT OF THE BLUE, Shimon Peres lost the election for the post of president, which he had been expected to win handily. In the second round of a secret ballot among Knesset members, he won only fifty-seven votes, while Moshe Katsav took sixty-three. This was a further reminder of our diminished coalition: The parties that had supported Silvan Shalom's law requiring a supermajority in any territorial referendum now all backed Katsav. There were far too many disappointments in July.

On August 2 the Knesset passed a bill to hold early elections by a majority of sixty-one to fifty-one. Although it was only a preliminary reading, history has shown that such a motion, if it has a majority in the first reading, will certainly succeed. Faced with early elections, a permanent settlement due September 13, and elections in the United States on November 7, we were forced to act quickly or fade away. In another indicator of the looming end of the government, David Levy resigned from his post as Foreign

Minister on that same day and accused Barak of poor conduct in the negotiations.

I participated in an unusual meeting on August 4 in Jerusalem with two members of the more pragmatic wing at Camp David, Mohammed Rashid and Mohammed Dahlan. My previous meetings with them had always taken place in a broad forum where they were the quiet ones in the group. Dahlan is considered among the second generation of Fatah leaders. He was born in the Gaza Strip in 1961 and was active in Shabiba, the Fatah youth movement, eventually becoming its leader. He was one of the central activists in Fatah and its representative in the Palestinian Students Association, for which he was imprisoned by Israel in 1983–84. In January 1987, he was expelled by Israel to Egypt and then ejected by the Egyptians as well, so he moved to Tunis, where he lived for five years and grew close to Arafat. Dahlan was allowed to return to the Gaza Strip in December 1993, and moved to Khan Yunis, where he was appointed head of the Palestinian Authority's preventative security apparatus for Gaza. Dahlan speaks Hebrew better than English, and when political discussions are held in English, someone usually translates the proceedings into Hebrew for him. He loves joking around, is very cynical, easily angered, but frequently quick to bury the hatchet. He is endowed with natural leadership ability, and has closer ties to Israelis than most of his colleagues. Dahlan's friend Rashid is not part of the Palestinian Authority's political or security hierarchy. He is Arafat's economic advisor, of Kurdish and not Palestinian extraction, and for some years has been regarded as the person closest to Arafat. He is considered a very pragmatic man, intimately connected to the world of Israeli economics. We had barely exchanged a word before this meeting.

I did not know why they wanted to meet, but they insisted, so we met at a hotel in West Jerusalem (neither Palestinians nor most of the ambassadors ever visited my office at the Ministry of Justice, on Salah al-Din Street in East Jersualem). Shlomo Gur, the Director-General of the Ministry of Justice, was with me. At the start of the meeting I expressed my appreciation of their pragmatic stance at the summit, and my regret that this approach had not been taken by the whole Palestinian side. They had plenty of allegations toward the Israeli side and Barak himself. According to them, his near-complete disregard for Arafat caused great damage, because in situations of this sort personal relations are very important. It was, they said, as if Barak was flaunting the lack of importance he attached to the subject.

During the two weeks at Camp David, the Palestinians believed that the Americans and the Israelis had agreed between them to offer Arafat extended autonomy while annexing a substantial area of the West Bank to Israel, and then were very surprised when Arafat rejected the proposal. Another allegation of theirs was that the Israeli position was never "final," particularly with regard to territory, and this made it difficult for the moderate Palestinians to try to sell any Israeli position to their camp. "The map that Israel presented at Camp David," they said, "was the primary cause of the undoing of the talks, because it meant that the future Palestinian state would not have territorial contiguity. This created bitterness and a feeling of helplessness on the Palestinian side. All later discussions on the remaining topics took place in the shadow of this map, which might have appeared to the Israelis as a far-reaching concession, but was perceived by the Palestinians as proof of their fears."

Similar to what Martin Indyk had suggested to me a few weeks earlier, Dahlan and Rashid thought that the key to the solution was Jerusalem. If it was solved, everything else would be solved. All the Arab neighborhoods must be transferred to the Palestinian state, and a "correct" solution must be found for the Temple Mount. "What is a 'correct' solution?" I asked. Rashid said that in his personal opinion, it was possible to reach agreement to give sovereignty over the Temple Mount and the Western Wall to the United Nations Security Council, granting the Palestinians administrative control over the Temple Mount and Israel administrative control of the Western Wall area. Dahlan said that a proposal of this sort had been made by President Mubarak but was rejected by Arafat.

And then the most surprising thing occurred, which turned out to be the reason the meeting had been called in the first place. Rashid asked to speak privately with me, and Gur and Dahlan left the room. "You may be surprised," Rashid told me, "but I have close ties with [far-right Knesset member] Avigdor Lieberman and [former Shas party leader] Aryeh Deri. I speak to them a lot, and believe me, both of them are prepared to reach a realistic political solution." I thought he was going to ask me to meet them for a political discussion, but he evidently understood that I would not do so. He said that if "the political future" of Deri—who had been convicted of fraud and bribery following his tenure as Interior Minister—was blocked, it would not be possible to retain the support of the members of Shas at this critical moment. He appealed to me not to block Deri's future, and to recommend, in my capacity as Justice Minister, that Deri be pardoned before entering prison the following month.

Wonderful are the ways of the Lord. If I had not been present at this talk, it is doubtful I would have believed such a thing could happen. I answered Rashid, with all the courtesy I could muster at that moment, that even if peace depended on Deri, he could not be pardoned. When I told Barak about this, he was puzzled at first, and he needed awhile to understand the connection. There was no follow-up to that bizarre meeting.

On August 10 I arrived in the United States on a visit, and in Washington I met officials from the White House and the State Department. Sandy Berger asked Bruce Reidel, the Director of Near Eastern and South Asian Affairs at the National Security Council, to join the meeting. They each presented a different perspective on what had happened at Camp David. Reidel said that Arafat behaved like the leader of a liberation movement who could not, or did not want to, take the required steps, and was now trying to garner support for the final decision. Berger suggested that Abu Mazen's role was critical and asked me to try to convince him to help Arafat make an affirmative decision. The common denominator between them was that both rated the chance of an agreement at forty-five percent.

We agreed that the end of September was the final date for an agreement: because the thirteenth was the agreed target date; because it was the end of the Knesset recess, and without a majority the government could fall; and because the American timetable corresponding to the end of Clinton's tenure drew closer. We discussed the solution to the Temple Mount at length. Berger said he had no doubt that this was the principal stumbling block in the way of an agreement. In his view there was a possible solution because it was more important to the Palestinians for Israel not to have sovereignty over the Temple Mount than it was for them to be granted it. In the estimation of the members of the National Security Council, who reiterated what Indyk had said, the second Camp David summit would last a day or two at most and it would not involve negotiations because nobody would be allowed to embarrass Clinton a second time. All the issues would be solved beforehand and then the parties would come to Camp David to sign.

My second meeting was with Madeleine Albright and the peace team of Dennis Ross and Aaron Miller. I thought I would find them dejected and pessimistic. To my surprise, their mood was not grim at all. In fact, they were optimistic about the next steps. Albright hinted that more experienced negotiators had been missed at Camp David. She said there had been considerable progress in the positions of the sides and pointed out, half in jest and half seriously, that some of this progress occurred when Clinton traveled to Okinawa, when she stayed on to hold formal talks with the two sides. Ross and Miller reckoned that in the Palestinian Authority there was insufficient understanding of the internal Israeli political situation, and emphasized that it was essential to hold substantial talks immediately with Arafat at the highest level. However, this is precisely what Barak did not want. At that stage, his interest was to freeze the situation that had been created at the end of the Camp David summit. Clinton's support, the positive assessment of Barak's efforts in Europe, and the support he was getting from the peace camp in Israel made him think that reopening the negotiations would expose him to new Palestinian ideas which he would be unable to accept and which would nullify his achievements at Camp David.

IN A DISCUSSION AFTER I RETURNED FROM WASHINGTON, I told Barak that we had to take advantage of the next few weeks to hold intensive talks with the Palestinians in order to overcome the problem of the Temple Mount and the Holy Basin and to solve the refugee problem by the time of the second summit. Barak told me he would not meet Arafat until Arafat gave his final answer to the Clinton proposals. If the answer was yes, it was possible to complete the negotiation and attend a summit; if the answer was no, Barak would form a national unity government with Sharon and examine the possibility of an interim settlement with Arafat. I thought that Barak was making a mistake, that pushing Arafat even further into a corner would only make him more extreme, and then the next two months would be lost. I believed these were two critical months in which we had to reach a solution, and that it was possible to do so. We did not see eye to eye.

The talks with the Palestinians continued at a lower level. Gilead Sher met with Saeb Erekat dozens of times, but the two months between the end of the summit and the permanent settlement deadline were not utilized effectively. On August 29, Clinton and Mubarak met in Cairo. It appeared that the United States was examining the possibility of a mini-summit at the beginning of September in New York at the United Nations Millennium Assembly, but this would depend on progress in the talks before then. Erekat came to see me the same day, to try to prevent this from happening. According to him, it would be a mistake to turn the Millennium Assembly into a political milestone and another summit just because Barak, Clinton, and Arafat were already scheduled to attend. One had to be careful, Erekat insisted, with artificial dates that raise expectations and create frustration. He suggested a trilateral courtesy meeting, after which working groups would seclude themselves near Washington for ten days to prepare for the mid-September summit.

There was no meeting at the United Nations, and no courtesy meeting ever took place. Barak continued to resist meeting Arafat, and when they bumped into one another, by chance, at an elevator at the United Nations, Arafat turned to Nava Barak, the Prime Minister's wife, and asked with a smile who the man was standing next to her. A journalist reported Arafat's rare moment of humor, but the picture revealed absolute estrangement.

On September 3, shortly before I left for New York, my friend Yair Hirschfeld sent a letter to Danny Yatom. It was ten days before the end of the extended interim settlement, and Hirschfeld suggested that if a settlement with the Palestinians could not be reached in the coming weeks, an attempt should be made to reach agreement on an alternative that would reduce the tension in the air. Reiterating some of the ideas we had raised on the eve of Camp David, Hirschfeld proposed recognizing a Palestinian state on areas already transferred to the Palestinian Authority and conducting negotiations with it until a final status agreement is reached. "The possibility of negotiations breaking down," Hirschfeld warned, "is liable to exacerbate relations and even lead to violence, as well as strengthen the 'Palestinian antagonists' who will enable Arafat to build a renewed rejectionist front under his leadership."

Barak thought it would be a mistake to make a move at that point. At a conference in Tel Aviv on September 1, he promised that if an agreement was signed at the meeting with Clinton and Arafat in New York, he would "build a Jerusalem stronger and greater than ever, with a Jewish majority, a Jerusalem that will gain recognition by the whole world as the capital of Israel. And if that happens, no struggle will be more exhilarating to wage, on the streets and at the junctions."

"Up till now we have seen no signs of Palestinian flexibility or openness that might indicate a renewal of negotiations," Barak said two days later, on the eve of his trip to New York. "The decision rests with Yasser Arafat, and for our part it would not be right to do anything but sit and wait."

The three main Camp David players arrived at the Millennium Assembly on September 6. Clinton met Barak and Arafat separately, but was unable to orchestrate a trilateral meeting. On Saturday Clinton surprised Barak by arriving at his hotel suite with Albright and Berger. An amiable, informal talk was held, which did not change the general feeling that the opportunity for peace was about to pass, and that around the corner the unknown awaited both sides. The New York weekend did not bring the chance of holding another summit—and signing what had been impossible to bridge at Camp David—any closer. As he accompanied the President on his way out of the hotel, Barak said to him, "I am prepared to make the peace of the brave, but not the peace of the ostrich."

Another American attempt to reconcile the positions of the two sides without direct negotiations was made on September 14. The Americans met Shlomo Ben-Ami, who had replaced David Levy as Foreign Minister, and Gilead Sher, who had in the meantime become the head of the Prime

Minister's office and had returned to playing a central role in the negotiations. Albright also met with Erekat and Dahlan. The two sides released pessimistic reports to the media citing time as a key factor. The next day Clinton told journalists at the White House, "We should all wait and see. Everybody is working hard . . . But I have nothing to report . . . You should be encouraged only by the fact that they are working. But there are no breakthroughs, no reason for hope, no reason for despair." At a meeting in Jerusalem with the President of Micronesia (a tiny island nation that receives royal treatment in Israel because of its unstinting support for us at the United Nations), Barak said, "One hopes that Arafat will recognize the magnitude of the opportunity for reaching peace, the intensity of the danger if we do not reach it, and the short amount of time at our disposal."

On the sixteenth of the month, *Newsweek* published a major article by Michael Hirsh, its Washington correspondent, in which he unfolded the story of the Beilin–Abu Mazen Understandings in detail. The article referred the interested reader to *Newsweek's* website, where the original document was published for the first time, word for word. In the article, Hirsh claimed that President Clinton saw the understandings as the core of his proposals at Camp David; in 1995, Clinton believed, both sides had seen exactly where the great difficulties would lie, and had apparently solved all the main problems.

The news traveled around the world. Many newspapers quoted the proposals that were revealed and concluded that the present crisis could be solved, particularly if both the Palestinians and the Israelis regarded the Beilin–Abu Mazen document as the basis for speedy negotiations, essential to avoid missing the opportunity. It was widely publicized in Israel, and the full document was translated into Hebrew and published in *Ha'aretz*. When Barak was asked why he chose not to use the paper as a basis for the negotiations at Camp David, he replied that the document had been presented to the Palestinians, who rejected it. But while some elements of the agreement may have been discussed and rejected, the document in its entirety had never been put forward as a starting point.

On September 19, Abu Mazen was asked in an appearance before the

Palestinian Legislative Council if he had indeed agreed five years earlier to postpone the decision on Jerusalem, to the annexation of the settlement blocs, and to the non-implementation of the right of return. He replied very angrily and stressed that these understandings were never signed, and that they had been published without the maps that were originally attached to them. He presented an adamant stance, in the spirit of his position since the crisis after the Wye talks, repudiating any shared sovereignty over the Temple Mount, insisting on the right of return—"It is unacceptable that Israel absorbs a million immigrants from Russia and negates the Palestinian right of return"—and demanding that the June 4, 1967 border was the only border that could be contemplated between Israel and the future state of Palestine.

According to the newspaper *Al-Hayyat Al-Jadida,* which reported on this meeting, Abu Mazen also rejected any appeal to diminishing time and a vanishing opportunity: "Neither the fall of Barak's government nor the end of Clinton's term of office interest us. What interests us is recognition of our national and legal rights. Barak is not less extreme or less stubborn than his predecessor on this matter. We are now standing at the water's edge. We cannot manage another step without getting swept away by it. It is they who have to advance in our direction." The Abu Mazen of the meeting with Sandy Berger, at the home of Ambassador Indyk, now found himself on the defensive before the Council and presented traditional Palestinian positions. I have no doubt that at the moment of truth, anyone who did not confront Abu Mazen with the document he had helped craft made things a lot easier for him.

That evening, in an incident characteristic of the tremendous tension between the sides during the fall of 2000, Barak announced the suspension of the talks taking place between the two delegations, only to retract this declaration two hours later after an emphatic negative reaction from the Palestinians and noisy reverberations in the Israeli and world press. Following a round of talks with Erekat and Dahlan the day before, Gilead Sher had told Barak, "There is no movement at all; the Palestinians are not even signaling any intention of compromising." Barak told Sher that if this was the case, it was better to stop the talks for a while. Danny Yatom appeared before the press and declared, "We have decided to take time out in order to summarize and evaluate the positions."

The Palestinian response was not long in coming. Erekat was in contact with Arafat and blamed Barak for changing his political agenda, claiming that he was attempting to forego the continuation of the peace negotiations. "We were amazed by the decision," the Palestinians announced. "We denounce the termination of the talks. In any event, we are still set on peace." For a moment the foreign offices of Egypt, Jordan, Europe, and the United States were terrified, demonstrating the extent to which they felt the entire process was hanging by a thread. The Prime Minister's office hastily tried to correct the impression that Israel had slammed the door on the Palestinians. "There was no special intent behind the Prime Minister's decision," Barak's office announced. "No negotiations have been conducted between Israel and the Palestinians since Camp David; there cannot therefore, be a cessation in negotiations that are not being held." Gilead Sher wanted to add his own clarification: "Since Camp David we have held about thirty meetings. Sadly, we have learned that we have actually not identified any substantial movement on the core issues indicating any acceptance of, or compliance with, the American ideas raised during the negotiations. Sometimes there are situations where, like other parties, we want to take time out and reassess the situation."

The French president, Jacques Chirac, was persuaded by Ben-Ami that this was a case of misunderstanding. White House spokesman Joe Lockhart said that the Israeli representatives "have not hinted at any sort of time-out," and Madeleine Albright added, "I am convinced that the sides cannot and will not want to retreat from the settlement path." However, even at that time, and notwithstanding the apprehension around the world, nothing was more important to Barak than to stress that all the contacts taking place between Israel and the Palestinians were not negotiations, but "contacts with the Palestinians and Americans, aimed at examining if there is a basis for renewing negotiations." In other words, Arafat still needed to reply to Clinton. Negotiating with Arafat before he gave final unequivocal answers would weaken Israel's stance. That being the case, it was *contacts* yes, but *talks* no.

Toward the end of September my friend Danny Abraham, Chairman of the Center for Middle East Peace and Economic Cooperation, arrived in Israel determined to get Barak and Arafat to meet. He simply decided that he was not going to leave the country before they did so. He had a long talk with Arafat and then spoke to Barak.

In retrospect the whole scene was surreal. It was only three days before Sharon would visit the Temple Mount, and it seemed that a critical meeting between Barak and Arafat might be called off because of a disagreement about location. Abraham, who had never acted as a mediator, went to Arafat's office and asked him whether he would agree to Barak's request to hold the meeting at the Prime Minister's private home in Kochav Ya'ir. Arafat insisted that the meeting should take place at the home of Abu Mazen in Ramallah. Abraham called Barak from Arafat's office and described Arafat's insistence. Barak did not give up. He said to Abraham: "Go up to Arafat, hug him, and say to him, 'This is a hug from Ehud Barak. You are living in the Middle East and must abide by its customs. For the last three meetings Barak visited the Palestinian Authority. He asks you to do him the honor and go to visit his house.'" Needless to say, the request was accepted immediately; the Middle East is the Middle East.

The meeting, on September 25, was particularly cordial. They were joined by a few other Israeli and Palestinian companions. President Clinton learned about the meeting from Danny Abraham, who was in attendance, and called Barak's house, speaking to both leaders, urging them to work together quickly so as not to forfeit what looked like the last opportunity. The atmosphere was good, and the Prime Minister's office reported that it was the most successful meeting between the two men. For an hour and a half they sat alone in the garden, with their entourages left behind in the guest room. After the talk, however, it was important to Barak to emphasize that no negotiation had been conducted during the meeting, and that its purpose had been enhancing contact and building trust.

The next day, talks between the negotiating teams were renewed in Washington. The aim was still only to examine the possibility of renewing negotiations, in anticipation of the second and final summit at which the framework agreement would be signed. A senior political source in

Jerusalem did not attach much importance to what was happening in the American capital, saying, "The teams have exhausted the negotiations. It will be left to the leaders to make the final decision."

In the meantime, the Temple Mount had become a central issue on the public agenda. There were increasing hints from the Palestinian side that eventually the Palestinians would be given sovereignty over the Temple Mount in return for relinquishing the right of return. On the Israeli side more and more people, including some from the peace camp, began voicing their distaste for any agreement that granted Palestinian sovereignty over the Temple Mount, even in return for peace. Various benevolent souls made all sorts of proposals to solve the problem either by postponement, by internationalization, or by dividing up sovereignty in a variety of ways.

In a discussion I had in Jerusalem with Faisal Husseini about the failure at Camp David, I asked him the significance of the Palestinian position on the Temple Mount. I was surprised by his reply, and no less by how quickly it came. This was his explanation: "Let us suppose that in seven or eight years' time there is an earthquake, and the two mosques collapse. If sovereignty remains with you, you will be able to build the temple there!" I said to him, "Are you joking? Who is going to build a temple on the Temple Mount? The secularists, who would not entertain the idea of doing something like that because they are not believers? Or the religious people, who believe that the temple will be built only when the messiah comes?" To this Husseini had an almost ready-made answer: "It is clear to me that if the Israeli government at that point is like the one presently in power, it will have no interest in building a temple, but the public will prevent it from rebuilding the mosques. According to your perception, we are talking about the holiest place in the world, where the first temple stood and where the second temple was built. Then, apparently, the Muslims arrived and built their mosques there. If the mosques collapsed in an earthquake and sovereignty was in Israel's hands as part of a peace agreement, will your public permit you to build the mosques there again? The majority will say that it was an act of nature and the place must be left in ruin. There will be some, the 'Temple faithful' and others, who will demonstrate and demand that the temple be built. They will tell you they know precisely how it has to be done, since there are people preparing to install themselves in various priesthoods in the temple, and are in a constant state of readiness. Only if sovereignty is not in your hands will you be able to explain that there is no other choice, and that the mosques are being rebuilt by the Palestinian state." Husseini did not smile when he finished talking.

When I told Barak about this, he had me summon, by virtue of my new position as the Minister of Religious Affairs, the two chief rabbis for a discussion. The Prime Minister explained the fundamental importance of the subject to the negotiations, told them about his deliberations, and asked whether Israeli sovereignty was essential in religious terms. Rabbi Bakshi Doron said that there was a total religious prohibition on visiting the Temple Mount. There was nothing to be gained from having a synagogue on the Temple Mount, since there would be a prohibition against praying in it. This prohibition did not only apply to Jews. Apparently, the purpose of Israeli political sovereignty was to implement this decree and to prevent any visitors from entering the precinct. However, when the Temple Mount was captured in the 1967 war, it was already administered by the Waqf; because it was such a sensitive area, the subsequent Israeli governments had no desire to institute changes there. Hence, non-Jews were allowed to pray there, and it now seemed to many of them that the holiest place in the world to Jews was a place the Jews did not want.

"If the Palestinians have sovereignty over the Temple Mount," Doron added, "they will do everything they can to wipe out the remains of the temple. They will dig, destroy, and erase the remnants of our roots. We need political sovereignty over this holy place in order to prevent them from doing this, but not to go up to the Mount ourselves."

This issue became the subject of discussions between the White House and the Egyptian administration after the Egyptians took it upon themselves to suggest a number of alternative solutions. On September 20, Egyptian Foreign Minister Amr Moussa put forth a proposal that the Temple Mount be placed under the custodianship of the United Nations Security Council. But the next day, Israeli Foreign Minister Ben-Ami announced that Israel had no intention of transferring the Temple Mount to the Security Council.

On the twenty-fifth, Yasser Abed Rabbo, the head of the Palestinian delegation to the final settlement negotiations, told *Le Monde:* "The Israelis say that the temple lies underneath the mosques on the Temple Mount. If we look at things from an archaeological perspective, I am convinced that there was never a temple on the Temple Mount. They have dug up tunnel after tunnel, with no results. Even if we suppose there was a temple there, can somebody today use three-thousand-year-old history to claim sovereignty?"

CHAPTER 8
THE GENIES COME OUT OF THE BOTTLE

W ITH THE COMPETING PROPOSALS for the Temple Mount under heated discussion, Ariel Sharon, as leader of the opposition, decided to visit the Mount with some fellow Likud Knesset members on September 28, 2000. He would later explain that he intended to actualize Israel's sovereignty over it. Many people—Palestinians, officials in the Israeli security apparatus, and politicians—sought to dissuade Sharon from making the visit, which apparently only reinforced his belief that it was necessary. The chairman of the Likud faction, Ruby Rivlin, organized the tour and announced in advance that his group would visit the Mount even if the police tried to stop them. "The police would not dare try that," said Rivlin, "but if they do, we will reject the request. Is it conceivable that a person living in Israel should be unable to go to any place that is under Israeli sovereignty?"

The Palestinians argued that this was a case of open provocation and announced that the visit would not go unchallenged, which in turn led the entire Likud faction to join Sharon on the Mount. A day before his visit, he said, "We are not visiting Judaism's holiest site with a message of provocation, but with a message of peace . . . The Temple Mount is the most sacred place, it is the basis of the existence of the Jewish people, and I am not afraid of riots by the Palestinians."

On the morning of the twenty-eighth, I was on my way to the airport, going to Rome. In the car I was interviewed on Israeli radio and I was asked if Sharon's visit was a provocation and whether it should be prevented. I said this was indeed a case of provocation, because the leader of the opposition planned to go to the most fiercely contested place at a delicate time in the negotiations, in order to say to the Palestinians, "There is no intention of compromising with you." However, it would be very difficult to prevent the visit of any Knesset member to the Mount, especially the leader of the opposition. For the government, his visit was a problem and preventing it was also a problem—the decision not to prevent it stemmed from democratic considerations.

These were the last moments of sanity for the region and for the peace process of that time. This was the calm before the storm, before the tyranny of insanity, hatred, revenge, and blindness, and before the descent into helplessness. The moment before things went out of control.

The round of talks in Washington ended, and it was reported that the atmosphere was good, though there had been no progress. One could still hope that at the next round there would be more substantial progress and that there might be a breakthrough. But very soon only one question remained: Can the conflagration be stopped?

I flew to Rome at the invitation of the Archbishop Toran, the Foreign Minister of the Vatican, and Minister Monsignor Cheli, to discuss informally how the Catholic Church might be affected by the permanent agreement. I was also set to meet the Pope, the Italian Foreign Minister, and the General Secretary of the leftist Democratic Party. I conducted the secular discussions on Thursday the twenty-eighth, together with my advisor, Daniel Levy. The subject on the agenda was, of course, the likelihood of reaching a permanent settlement while Clinton remained in office, and the role of Europe in assisting both sides to reach this settlement. We followed what was happening on the Temple Mount with concern, and I was relieved that nobody was killed during Sharon's visit.

Sharon's ascent to the Temple Mount—with most of the members of his faction and masses of police to protect him and his associates—had the distinctive flavor of his well-known aggressive excursions. Facing them were about a thousand Palestinian demonstrators and Israeli Arab members of the Knesset. The chants and cries against Sharon and his entourage were offensive, and the police reacted. Five Palestinians claimed they were hit by rubber bullets. Thirty policemen were lightly wounded, as were a number of Palestinians; the Israeli Arab Knesset member Ahmed Tibi broke his hand.

After the visit Sharon said, "It is the right of every Jew to visit the Temple Mount. It is unthinkable that a Jew should be unable to visit the Holy of Holies. I regret that people were wounded during the visit, but it had to be made." The police began to prepare for the next day, estimating that repercussions from the visit might explode at the end of Friday prayers. Twenty-two Arab states published a joint announcement through the Arab League denouncing Sharon's visit to the Temple Mount as "an attempt to destroy the peace efforts . . . Sharon killed hundreds of Palestinians at Sabra and Shatila," the announcement stated with predictable inaccuracy, "and today he is trying to strike at the places holy to Islam." Arafat added, "The visit was a dangerous step that strikes at sites holy to Islam. Israel's efforts to prove she has rights over the Temple Mount are a nightmare, a provocation, and an incitement."

Would the Intifada have broken out without Sharon's visit to the Temple Mount? It may have, or it may not have. Would the First World War have begun without the murder of the Archduke Ferdinand? It is hard to say. Certainly, great frustration had been simmering in the territories. The possibility of a violent outburst had been discussed at all the talks between us and the Palestinians. It is true that September 13 had passed without a permanent settlement and without a Palestinian state; that the economic situation was grim; that additional prisoners were not released and the third phase was not implemented. But all these factors would not necessarily have caused the eruption on Friday, September 29, if Sharon had not begun his march toward the premiership with an irresponsible act like this.

Another summit was still a very realistic possibility at that juncture; a permanent agreement was achievable, and if it was possible to reach either a full or a partial settlement, it would have been possible to avoid the nightmare that began with Sharon's visit to the Temple Mount. A pretext is a very grave matter if it causes a disaster, even if it is not the direct cause of it. Sharon, not by chance or unknowingly, created a pretext for the Palestinians. He could not have predicted the entire turn of events, but it was clear to him that he would cause great anger on the Palestinian side, and he thought that this anger would advance his political ends. There is no question here of criminal responsibility. His act was legal, and he did it with the government's approval, even if his associates announced in advance that they would not respect a negative decision by the police. The Mitchell Committee later absolved Sharon of responsibility for causing the Intifada, but it did place a question mark on the timing of his ascent to the Mount.

For Sharon, however, timing was everything. At that moment, when the Temple Mount was the focus of argument in the anticipation of an historic rapprochement between Israel and the Palestinians, the visit was like a bomb dropped on the negotiators. Sharon's admirers explicitly regard his journey from the Temple Mount to the premiership as a single narrative.

Sharon also benefited from the fact that Barak refused from the outset to blame him for provoking the Intifada, although it does not require any special intellectual effort to deduce that Sharon's visit on Thursday led to the Intifada on Friday. Barak refrained from doing so because a statement of this sort would supposedly absolve the Palestinians of their responsibility. Sharon's aggression in the name of Zionism cannot, of course, lift the heavy burden resting on the Palestinians' shoulders. The very use of force; the collaboration of the security forces in striking at Israelis; the failure to extinguish the fire immediately after it broke out; riding the wave of the Intifada to free themselves from international pressure; neglecting to grasp the opportunity to reach an agreement with Israel—for all this the Palestinians bear responsibility. And even if one or another explanation can be found, there is no way, at least for me, to justify it. However, the understandable wish to point to the severity of the Palestinians' acts cannot, historically, mitigate Sharon's deed.

IT WAS ONLY WHEN I ARRIVED AT THE VATICAN on the evening of Thursday, September 28, that I realized I had never been there at night. For a few minutes we traveled on completely empty roads with barren sidewalks, in library-like silence and in darkness. No large mass, no blessings by the Pope from his balcony, no American and Japanese tourists, and no souvenir stands. A ghost town. We arrived at an apartment building and went up in a tiny elevator to Cheli's apartment, where his other guests were already waiting. Cheli boasted about his culinary talents with some degree of justification, and our discussion took place over roast meat and rice. The apartment itself was very special—heavy with an abundance of books and extremely valuable works of art. A sort of combination of simplicity and rarity.

I got to know Cheli in 1992, when we were both deputy foreign ministers in charge of the negotiations between Israel and the Vatican. At the time, we conducted a difficult and very complex negotiation on sensitive symbolic issues, and on issues like education systems and assets. The accepted view was that the Vatican would not agree to establish diplomatic relations with Israel before a final agreement determined the status of Jerusalem. We surprised ourselves and the world when, at the end of that year, we managed to overcome all the obstacles: During the last days of December 1993, at the Vatican and in Jerusalem, we signed an historic agreement that led immediately to diplomatic relations and an exchange of ambassadors. For a long time I had maintained that negotiations with the Vatican were more difficult than with the Palestinians. Now I had to apologize with a smile, and admit to Monsignor Cheli that negotiating with him had been far easier.

My hosts presented their concerns to me and I told them that whatever happened, the principal feature of the permanent agreement, in religious terms, would be the status quo: All the various religions and denominations within each religion would retain their rights. They were concerned about the mosque set to be built in Nazareth opposite the Basilica of the Annunciation; this matter was indeed still unresolved and remained very vexing. We talked at length about the chances of peace and about the implications of Sharon's visit that morning. I expressed the hope that there would not be riots the next day on the Temple Mount. I was proved wrong only after my meeting with the Pope the next day.

To get to my meeting with the Pope I was led a long distance by uniformed people and aides. We passed visiting nuns, children in school uniforms, and a community of black priests. An antechamber led to his large room where the two of us sat alone and talked for twenty minutes. I bore the main burden of the discussion. I told him about impressions of his successful visit to Israel, about the intention to maintain the status quo among the religions in Jerusalem, and about the peace process. He wanted to hear about the new president, Moshe Katsav, and to find out why Peres had not been elected. He asked if there would also be a change of Prime Ministers, and I assured him that Barak was staying. He asked about the origins of my family and was happy when he realized that we were both from Poland. At the end of the conversation he expressed his appreciation for the negotiations conducted between Cheli and me that had led to the historic change in relations between the Church and Israel, and I thanked him for his part in them. When the discussion was over, an aide entered and brought me a gift—a medallion with the face of the Pope engraved on it. I gave the Pope a silver dove. When the photographer came in to take the official photograph, we shook hands and he expressed his wish that the Jewish new year, which was starting that night, would be a year of peace.

When I got back to the car I understood that this was now unlikely. Palestinians had been killed in the riots on the Temple Mount, and Major General Yair Yitzhaki, the Jerusalem police chief, was wounded, along with dozens of Palestinians and Israeli policemen. By the afternoon, it appeared that the situation was under control. On Saturday we traveled from Rome to Florence and were entranced by the Tuscany area, but telephone calls from Israel gave little cause for optimism. That night we returned to Rome, and the next day, the second day of Rosh Hashanah, I took the first plane to Israel. I returned to the heart of the crisis.

THE VIOLENCE WAS UPON US. We had not ceased discussing it, trying to prevent it, or preparing for it, but when it erupted, it struck us like a bolt of lightning. Priorities and perspectives changed, as did our routines. From then on we entered a chronic situation of inexorable, escalating violence: attacks followed by worse counter-attacks, demonstrators confronted by guns, terror against an army, innocents pitted against innocents. In the first few months, hundreds of Palestinians and dozens of Israelis were killed. Agreements were violated, each time more flagrantly. Personal tragedies abounded, hatred intensified, and trust dissolved. And inevitably, there was a return to old questions: Is there anybody to talk to? Is there anything to talk about?

Our hope was that the outburst would be limited, perhaps something along the lines of the Nakba Day riots that May, only longer. But the violence continued and even intensified after Rosh Hashanah, both in the occupied territories and within the Green Line. A tough battle was fought at Joseph's Tomb near Nablus. Violent confrontations broke out at the Netzarim junction in the Gaza Strip, in which ten Palestinians were killed. Visitors to the Netzarim settlement were evacuated by helicopter. Arab citizens of Israel were killed in Umm al-Fahm, near Lotam settlement in Sakhnin, and in Nazareth.

The world tried to calm things down. Miguel Moratinos, permanent envoy for the European Union, came to Israel and tried to talk to both sides. Albright visited Paris, put the blame on Sharon's visit to the Temple Mount, and called on the sides to control the situation. Clinton expressed shock at the killing of a young boy, Mohammed al-Dura, in Gaza. Television footage of this tragic incident immediately became the symbol of the Intifada. Clinton called on both sides to take action to end the violence and restore calm. The Pope and Jacques Chirac followed suit, while the Sheikh of Egypt's al-Azhar mosque, Mohammed Tantawi, called for the Palestinians to engage Israel in armed confrontation.

The first diplomatic attempt to stop the insanity was made in Paris, where Madeleine Albright invited Barak and Arafat to come and see her. Less than three months earlier the world had smiled with satisfaction at the sight of these two leaders on television, going out of their way to be polite by allowing each other to go first into the building Clinton had assigned them for a meeting. At the end of that clip, Barak employs a controlled measure of force to push Arafat inside, and Clinton bursts out laughing. Today that picture has the look of a delightful reverie—a remnant of a bygone age. In fact, a meeting between the two had now become a virtual impossibility.

At nine o'clock on the morning of Wednesday, October 4, Arafat landed in Paris, straight into the arms of President Chirac. Arafat set four conditions for meeting with Barak: an announcement by Barak of a ceasefire; the withdrawal of the heavy armaments from the junctions to Palestinian towns and villages; agreement to an international commission of inquiry to examine the use of violence; and the release of Palestinian political prisoners. Barak landed at ten o'clock. He too went to the Elysée Palace, where he found the French president disgruntled and hostile. This was the same president who only a few weeks earlier had been convinced that Barak had gone further than Arafat at Camp David. "Israel is to blame for the riots," Chirac insisted. "It began with Ariel Sharon's provocation, and it was clear to see that this provocation suited you. The IDF used excessive force. It was unreasonable . . . I served as a company commander in Algeria and did things like that. Today I know I made a mistake back then."

Barak announced that he would not agree to an international commission of inquiry, and repeatedly blamed Arafat and the Palestinian Authority for the outbreak of the riots. "The Palestinian leadership," he declared, "has to decide if it wants to move in the direction of a peace agreement—which is attainable, in our view—or leave the whole region in an impasse, the result of which is very likely to be deterioration, and perhaps even confrontation. We, of course, prefer the first option. Israel is prepared to put an end to the confrontation, and all that is needed now is for Arafat to give an unequivocal instruction to the Tanzim and to the Palestinian police to stop shooting. Then everything will calm down immediately."

Everybody seemed gripped by a not-unfamiliar state of nerves. Albright invited the sides to a meeting at the American embassy in Paris at quarter to two. Arafat refused to attend. Albright held a meeting with Barak alone at three o'clock. At four o'clock Arafat arrived for a meeting with the Secretary of State, on the condition that Barak did not participate. Barak waited in an adjoining room for an hour and a half until Albright managed to persuade the Palestinian leader to hold a trilateral meeting. It finally began at five-thirty in the evening, and Albright declared: "No cameras, no announcements to the press." With Barak were Amnon Lipkin-Shahak, Deputy Chief of Staff Moshe Ya'alon, and Yossi Ginosar, formerly Deputy

Chief of the Security Services and now a private businessman. Arafat repeated his demand for a United Nations commission of inquiry, only to encounter a united front of American-Israeli opposition. After dinner together, an agreement regarding a ceasefire began to emerge, but the lack of agreement on the commission of inquiry remained. At nine o'clock the two sides departed for separate consultations.

Two hours later, thunderous shouts were heard coming from the room of Arafat and his advisors. The door was forcefully flung open and the Israelis were astounded to find themselves watching Arafat screaming, "It's a humiliation, it's a humiliation! They don't respect me!" The Palestinian president ran in the direction of the exit. "We are leaving," he barked at his associates, who surrounded him on all sides, no less bewildered than the Americans and the Israelis. Ginosar, who in 1986 was the first Israeli to be sent to Arafat and had gained the particular trust of the Palestinian leader, tried to prevent his departure and began to run after him. Secretary of State Albright did not miss her cue in this surreal drama, and she too began to pursue the fugitives, shouting to the American security guards, "Close the gate! Don't let anybody leave the building!" And they, of course, carried out her order. At this point, Arafat's car reached the gate of America's ex-territorial sovereignty in Paris. It was locked and the gatekeeper refused to open it. Albright, out of breath, got to the blocked car and urged Arafat to return to the discussion. Moderate physical pressure was applied and Arafat acquiesced as if he was making a grand gesture.

The trilateral discussion restarted and the ceasefire began to take shape on the table. After midnight it emerged that Arafat was prepared to postpone the discussion of his demand for a commission of inquiry to a later date, and to stop the firing immediately. At two in the morning it was agreed that the next day they would all join in a ceremony to sign, in principle, the ceasefire agreement that had been formulated by Dennis Ross under the auspices of Mubarak in Sharm el-Sheikh. But at four in the morning, a bizarre meeting took place in the Elysée with Chirac, Kofi Annan, Albright, Arafat, and Barak, at which Arafat surprised everyone by returning to the issue of the commission of inquiry and, to the chagrin of the Secretary of State, got backing from Chirac.

The Israelis and the Americans made their way to the home of the American ambassador to sign the agreement, but Arafat returned to his hotel and insisted he would sign only in Sharm el-Sheikh. For Barak and Albright, this was beyond the pale, and at seven in the morning this grueling marathon ended for them when the Prime Minister's plane left for Israel. Arafat flew to Egypt and updated Mubarak. Months later, members of Arafat's entourage told us that he could not sign in Paris because of his special relationship with Mubarak. His intention had been to sign in Sharm el-Sheikh as a political gesture to the Egyptian president as well as to carry out what was agreed. But that was not the understanding of the Israeli delegation on that Parisian dawn. Barak and his associates felt that Arafat had decided at the last moment to beat a hasty retreat from the commitment he had nearly entered into. The Palestinians did not understand why the Americans and the Israelis refused to fly to Sharm el-Sheikh with them that morning. Barak feared a further slight, and Albright felt similarly. Either way, a momentous opportunity was missed in Paris, and the sides went back to a period of bloodshed.

Three IDF soldiers were kidnapped the following Friday in Har Dov, on the Lebanese border, and it seemed that the northern front would be added to those ablaze in the West Bank and Gaza. In Jerusalem, after prayers on the Temple Mount, a number of policemen were trapped in a burning police station at the Lion's Gate. Then, on Saturday, the IDF vacated Joseph's Tomb after it was attacked by Palestinians. The Palestinians announced that the number of casualties had reached 113 dead and 2,800 wounded. A resident of Rishon Letzion was killed by a stone thrown at his car while he was traveling on the Haifa–Tel Aviv highway near Jisr ez Zarqa. On Yom Kippur, October 9, there were violent clashes between Arabs and Jews in Nazareth, and two Arabs were killed.

The hope was that after this drastic deterioration in relations between the two communities, we had reached a nadir from which things could only begin to improve. But the situation got even worse. A special cabinet meeting was held at the Defense Ministry in Tel Aviv on the night following Yom Kippur. Barak had decided, even before the discussion, to present Arafat with an ultimatum for a ceasefire, saying: "We all want peace with the Palestinian people, but their leadership is not ready at this point to take courageous decisions, despite our far-reaching proposals. We have to insist on protecting our vital interests, and peace will arrive only when our neighbors recognize that each side has essential interests that it is unable to relinquish." The mood in the conference room was very grim. The Prime Minister was criticized for preparing this ultimatum without consulting the cabinet beforehand, and without making it clear what he intended to do if nothing happened within forty-eight hours. Later, he delayed the ultimatum and gave up on the idea.

One of the security guards came into the room in the middle of the meeting, after we had all heard some noises from outside. He asked us to remain in our places and not leave the room because there was an "incident" in the compound. The discussion continued as if nothing had happened, and the guard remained in the room. Half an hour later we were told that a man on a motorcycle, wrapped in an Israeli flag, had broken into the compound. His brother managed to break in after him, and the guards only succeeded in overpowering them right near the office of the Minister of Defense. It seems their intention had been to protest the severity of the situation, but the astonishing ease with which they broke into the secure compound worried the powers that be.

Hatred, the wish for revenge, and fury were the order of the day. In the Hatikvah neighborhood in Tel Aviv, Jews went on a rampage and torched apartments and cars belonging to Arabs. In Tiberias a mosque was attacked; in Carmiel some Arab passersby were assaulted. In Gaza there was a rare demonstration of unity: Representatives of Hamas participated in the discussions of the Palestinian leadership headed by Arafat.

"The world" began to arrive in an attempt to mediate. Kofi Annan came for a few days and shuffled to and fro between Arafat and Barak a number of times. We met at his hotel in Jerusalem and discussed a number of options for a summit either in the region or outside of it, at which the sides would commit themselves to a ceasefire, renew the talks, and assign an agreed commission the task of examining how events unfolded. Annan was disappointed and dejected, and promised to do all he could to get information on the kidnapped Israeli soldiers, but proved unable to do so. We discussed the possibility of establishing unofficial UN commissions of inquiry so that a summit could be convened. One of the ideas had Annan himself appointed to examine the events. He called my home late at night a few times, after returning from one of his trips. On one occasion he told me he had come to a decision not to leave the region until a meeting was held between the decision-makers.

One of the most horrific events of the Intifada took place on October 12: Vadim Norzitz and Yosef Avrahami, two reserve soldiers, lost their way and ended up in Ramallah, where they were lynched by a mob in the Palestinian police station. The pictures were terrifying; people were stunned. It seemed that each day another bridge between the sides was burned. In response, the Air Force bombed the police station in Ramallah and parts of Gaza as well. Morocco decided to recall its representative from Israel. Oman closed its Israeli office in the capital. Barak embarked on a marathon effort to establish an emergency government, and met, one after another, with the leaders of opposition parties.

In an effort to coordinate a summit meeting by Saturday, Kofi Annan had managed to meet with Arafat ten times and hold slightly fewer meetings with Barak. On Saturday, October 15, Clinton announced that a summit would be convened: "There must be no illusions. The good news is that the sides have agreed to meet and the situation looks calmer. But the road ahead of us is hard after the terrible events of recent days. The situation is still tense, but President Mubarak and I are convinced that we have to make every effort to break the cycle of violence."

The Sharm el-Sheikh summit began on Monday, October 17. The principal obstacle remained the Palestinian demand for an international commission of inquiry. Mubarak took on the task of persuading Arafat to drop the idea, while Clinton tried to convince Barak to compromise on the matter. During the course of the day, Clinton met Barak and Arafat separately three times. Barak also met with Annan, Mubarak, and King Abdullah. Clinton and Barak met for a fourth time at two in the morning, and they labored together until dawn on a draft security agreement. Barak asked Clinton not to mention the renewal of peace negotiations in his declaration, but to make do with a statement that the subject would be discussed in two weeks' time. By Tuesday morning the main issues on the agenda were agreed, after it seemed during the night that the talks had reached a deadlock and that the Paris affair was going to repeat itself. The hard times had left their mark—there was no direct talk between Barak and Arafat.

The rancor and mutual incrimination got worse. A handshake, which had become taken for granted in recent years between four consecutive Israeli Prime Ministers and Arafat, did not take place. Furthermore, no real summation was signed. Both sides authorized Clinton to sum up the meetings on their behalf and gave him a commitment to implement this.

In his speech, Clinton presented the three parts of the agreement achieved at the summit:

> First, both sides have agreed to issue public statements unequivocally calling for an end of violence. They also agreed to take immediate, concrete measures to end the current confrontation, eliminate points of friction, ensure an end to violence and incitement, maintain calm, and prevent recurrence of recent events . . .
>
> Second, the United States will develop with the Israelis and Palestinians, as well as in consultation with the United Nations Secretary-General, a committee of fact-finding on the events of the past several weeks and how to prevent their recurrence. The committee's report will be shared by the U.S. President with the UN Secretary-General and the parties prior to publication. A final report shall be submitted under the auspices of the U.S. President for publication.
>
> Third, if we are to address the underlying roots of the Israeli-Palestinian conflict, there must be a pathway back to negotiations and a resumption of efforts to reach a permanent status agreement based on the UN Security Council Resolutions 242 and 338 and subsequent understandings. Toward this end, the leaders have agreed that the United States would consult with the parties within the next two weeks about how to move forward . . .
>
> We have made important commitments here today against the backdrop of tragedy and crisis, and we should have no illusions about the difficulties ahead. If we are going to rebuild confidence and trust we must all do our part, avoiding recrimination and moving forward.

The President summed up what he had to say to the media: "I am sure it will be a disappointment to some of you, but one of the things that all the leaders agreed was that our statement should stand on its own, and we should begin by promoting reconciliation and avoiding conflict by foregoing questions today."

President Mubarak declared the summit adjourned. The participants remained somber. Throughout the proceedings, Barak and Arafat sat at either side of the hosts, and were careful not to interact, even at the time of departure. News from the ground was not particularly encouraging, but at Sharm el-Sheikh a fresh start had been made—or so we hoped. It very quickly became apparent that our optimism was premature.

The ability of the Palestinians to keep to a ceasefire would be tested in the coming days, the matter of setting up a fact-finding committee would be discussed, and there would be consultations on renewing negotiations. Forty-eight hours passed after the summit and calm did not prevail. On the contrary, the violence increased when dozens of settlers went for a hike on Mount Ebal in the West Bank and one was killed by Palestinian gunfire. The IDF retaliated, Palestinian violence increased, and the Palestinians had something between an excuse and a reason not to abide by the principal commitment to a ceasefire.

An emergency summit convened by Arab leaders in Cairo was adjourned on October 22. The decisions that resulted bore no spirit of conciliation. They included: a scathing condemnation of Israel over its responsibility for the killing of Palestinians; the demand for an international force to protect the Palestinians; a reiteration of the demand to set up an international commission of inquiry in the framework of the UN; a demand to charge Israeli leaders with crimes against humanity; a call to terminate diplomatic contacts between Israel and Arab states that do not maintain full, peaceful relations with her; a boycott of multilateral talks; the termination of all forms of regional collaboration; and so on and so forth.

Answering the call, Tunisia severed relations with Israel. Arafat returned to Gaza from the summit and arrogantly declared, "We will push on to Jerusalem, the capital of the independent Palestinian state. If Barak wants to, he'll accept it. If not, let him go to hell."

Barak, for his part, made a declaration that included the ill-advised phrase "time out from the peace process," and a few of us, his ministerial associates, criticized him for doing so. Saeb Erekat responded publicly: "This announcement of Barak's makes a total mockery of the peace process, despite the fact that at the summit, the Arab states decided that the peace process is a strategic objective."

Within a short time I arranged a conference of the peace camp in the Labor Party, the purpose of which was to express opposition to the "time out from the peace process" and to a national unity government in which Sharon would hold a veto over further negotiations. I also told Barak that if a government of this sort was formed, I would not serve in it, because I had no interest in being subject to the whim of Sharon. Barak asked me to postpone the meeting so that he could participate and speak. Many of the active Knesset members attended the conference and it was given wide media coverage. The atmosphere was tense, the debate stormy. We told the Prime Minister that a unity government meant a stop to the peace process and that it would be giving in too early. There was still somebody to talk to, Clinton was still President, and even if the elections were brought forward, it would be possible to conduct accelerated negotiations and present the results to the people for a final decision. Shimon Peres was agitated: "Precisely at this time, we must not give up!" he said. "Not for one moment! A great opportunity might be concealed in the worst crisis. We must not veer from the path; despite all the anger and the pain, we have to return to talking." It appeared to me that Barak did not reject our approach. He spoke at length, diminished the importance of his own "time out" statement, and called the criticism of it "much ado about nothing." He went on to promise, "We will not cover our ears, we will not close our eyes, and we will search for every opportunity to reach peace. The formation of an emergency government is a national necessity because a broad government, representing the majority, can—in a state of emergency—reflect the common wish of the people to reach peace."

However, a national unity government was not formed. The winter session of the Knesset began on October 30, and that evening an agreement was signed between me and the chairman of the Shas Knesset faction, Yair Peretz, assuring that Shas would give the government a "safety net," and would not vote in favor of a no-confidence measure for at least one month. Barak had asked me to do this because he believed that despite everything, during November, particularly after the elections in the United States, Clinton would be able help achieve peace, and that would be impossible were a government formed with Sharon. At the same time, he regarded the safety net as a sort of bridging loan for a few weeks. Since he viewed Clinton's tenure as the last chance, for the time being, to reach peace, he wanted a safety net for two months. At the end of the two-month period he would either bring a framework agreement for peace to a referendum or declare that, despite his readiness, he had not received a reciprocal response from the Palestinian side, and he was going to establish a national unity government.

The four weeks we got from Shas did in fact prevent the fall of the government and early elections, but we did not manage to take advantage of them to work intensively toward a settlement. The month got off on the wrong foot when a nighttime meeting between Peres and Arafat in Gaza on Wednesday, November 1 produced an agreement on a list of detailed steps that were not implemented. They were supposed to have led to public statements by the two sides with regard to halting the violence, ending the closures and encirclements by Israel, and the cessation of Palestinian violence. The next day there was an unrewarding, prolonged wait just to hear Arafat's public announcement, so that Barak could make his declaration. But Arafat found a unique way to fulfill his obligation. Miguel Moratinos, who was visiting him for the umpteenth time, spoke about the need to end the violence, and Arafat just stood next to him nodding his head. One day later, a car bomb exploded in Jerusalem's Mahaneh Yehuda market. Two people were killed, one of whom, Ayelet Hashahar Levy, was the daughter of former minister Yitzhak Levy, the leader of the National Religious Party.

I went with a heavy heart to visit Levy during the *shiva*—seven days of mourning—at his family home in Kfar Maimon. We sat outside in a mourners' enclosure, filled with people despite the relatively early hour of the morning. With tears in their eyes, Levy and his wife told me how Ayelet had moved to Jerusalem that very day, seeking to begin a new chapter in her life. I was reminded of an argument I had with Yitzhak Levy some months before, in the cabinet meeting approving the scale of the second phase of redeployment. He had said that he understood that the redeployment had to be carried out because it was an Israeli commitment according to the Wye Agreement, but that he would vote against it because he could not relinquish parts of the greater land of Israel. I had asked permission to speak, and expressed appreciation of his consistency, but I added, "What is the meaning of 'relinquish'? After all, there are places where no Israeli had set foot before they were transferred to the Palestinians, and only after their transfer to the Palestinians have Israelis started going there. Perhaps neither of us is happy about the casino in Jericho, but how many Israelis go there without any security precautions, and how many of them dared to visit the place when we controlled it? And how many Israelis go into restaurants in Ramallah? And how many buy furniture in Bidya village? Relinquishing the territory might actually make it a lot more accessible to Israelis!" That argument seemed very far away at the beginning of November 2000, but the question remained: How could a cruel murder like this have been prevented, and how could similar murders be prevented in the future? Could it be done through a stubborn policy which allowed no concessions at all, in the hope that the other side would weaken, surrender, and calm down—or by means of an historic agreement and acceptable compromises?

THE RESULTS OF THE ELECTIONS that took place in the United States on November 7 were inconclusive. For some weeks the most important democracy in the world was caught in an awkward situation: The whole apparatus of government was virtually paralyzed and the transition team which was meant to prepare the transfer of power was not even formed. Consequently, no new entity emerged in the United States with which to talk about the future, besides Clinton.

Leah Rabin died on the morning of Sunday, November 12, 2000. It was almost exactly five years since her husband's murder. These days of sadness were deepened by her death. Since Rabin's murder, she had dedicated herself to his memory and to encouraging the peace process. She was happy to collaborate with me on a list of initiatives, as on the Israeli-Palestinian framework for the protection of the environment that she led. We met often and spoke on the phone even more frequently. Over the years she had become one of the clearest voices for peace, and her voice had fallen silent just when we needed it most. I could only think of the Book of Job: *"While he was yet speaking, there came also another . . ."*

BARAK VISITED THE UNITED STATES and met Clinton on November 11, but they did not achieve any breakthrough. Four Israelis were killed in three separate shooting incidents two days later. In response, Barak instructed the army to encircle all the Palestinian towns. A senior source in the Prime Minister's delegation to the U.S. said, "Until the attacks today, it seemed we were moving in the right direction. If the quiet had been maintained for another few days, the peace process would have been renewed in its full intensity. Now the cards have been shuffled again." The extraordinary ease with which terror could undermine efforts to combat it was a recurrent and persistent phenomenon.

A very serious incident occurred on November 20, when an explosive device exploded next to a bus carrying children near an Israeli settlement in the Gaza strip. Two adults were killed, and eleven children were severely injured, some of whose limbs had to be amputated. That evening the IDF carried out an unprecedented attack on Gaza, employing helicopters, and then bisected the Strip. The Palestinians reported that eighty people were injured in the attacks; the electricity was cut off in large parts of the area, and the telephone network collapsed. The Palestinian Authority itself had become a target for Israeli responses, signaling a major upgrade in the confrontation.

The next day the papers publicized the fact that at the cabinet meeting, the decision to attack had not been made unanimously. Of the six cabinet members, only three supported the operation: Barak himself, Shlomo Ben-Ami, and Beiga Shochat; two abstained—Shimon Peres and Amnon Lipkin-Shahak; and one opposed it—Beilin.

IN THE ARAB WORLD THE RESPONSE WAS MILITANT, and the conflict began to take on dimensions reminiscent of war. Egypt decided to withdraw its veteran ambassador Mohammad Bassiouni for "consultations." Bassiouni, who had served in Israel for nearly twenty years as a deputy and as ambassador, had become part of the scene of the peace process. When he packed his bags he understood only too well that a dramatic shift in circumstances would be required before he could return to Israel. Jordan followed suit, and announced that it would not appoint a new ambassador to Israel after the present one completed his duties. We had regressed to a point it seemed we had long passed.

The four weeks of the Shas safety net ended on Tuesday, November 28. Because of the deterioration in the security situation, the leaders of Shas could not contemplate extending the arrangement. We tried to persuade them to join the framework of a new emergency government, but its leaders made it clear to us that it was impossible from their point of view. At the end of the four weeks a vote was held on a bill to dissolve the Knesset. After the debate and prior to the vote, Barak repeated what Netanyahu had done in 1998: From the moment he realized there would be a majority against him, he joined it. He announced that he was not opposed to bringing the elections forward. On the contrary, if that was what the majority in the Knesset wanted, he would support it too. Seventy-nine members voted in favor of early elections, only one member opposed the bill, and twenty-seven abstained. It was estimated that the elections would take place in May, two years after the elections in which Barak had won a large majority even while the Labor Party Knesset faction became smaller than it had ever been.

I WENT TO NEW YORK ON NOVEMBER 29 and met Kofi Annan. He had made great efforts in an attempt to find a formula that would calm the situation on the ground. He thought that the Mitchell Committee, which had been established by the Sharm el-Sheikh summit on October 17, could assist with solving the problem, and complained that Israel was not cooperating with the members of the committee and the experts acting on its behalf. We discussed the deployment of UNIFIL forces in southern Lebanon and the fact that the Lebanese army was not deployed there. He promised he would continue to investigate the matter of our soldiers held captive by

Hezbollah, while I agreed to convey to Barak his message about the Mitchell Committee.

The next day I went to the White House to meet with Sandy Berger. President Clinton was waiting for me at the door of his office, and suggested his personal assistance in the fifty days he had remaining in the White House. In our meeting, Berger reinforced my hope that the White House was prepared to make an enormous final effort to put an end to the Intifada and get an agreement signed. He also regarded the Mitchell Committee as the most promising instrument to work toward reducing the violence and to enable visits by high-ranking Americans to the region to bridge the gaps in the peace agreement. When I asked Berger what the chances were of getting the special aid package promised to Israel after the withdrawal from Lebanon, he told me that the package involved additional aid to Egypt, and rumor had it that AIPAC was trying to sabotage the Egyptian component, so the whole package might be scuttled. He asked, half-facetiously, if we had any sway over AIPAC.

My next meeting was at the State Department with Dennis Ross. Ross, a veteran of the peace battles, confronted the calamity of the Intifada like the rest of us, and was not prepared to give up. His message was similar to the one I had heard at the White House: It was still possible to do something over the next fifty days. After that, there would be a long wait until the new administration was ready to deal with the Middle East headache. I described to him the disappointment of the Israeli peace camp, as well as that of Jewish Americans, about which he of course knew more than I did. He said that if we reached an accord soon, public opinion would swing without much difficulty. It was unfortunate, he added, that the two sides had not managed to maintain secret channels for sustained periods. If they had done so, it might have facilitated a successful outcome at Camp David. The Intifada itself was exacting a price for the absence of genuine secret channels, he suggested. "Do you really believe it is still possible to do something?" I asked as we parted. He reckoned that Arafat's real target date throughout the whole of the recent period was January 1, 2001, because he is a person who believes in last-minute decisions. And this really was the last minute.

I peered at this familiar office, which had been a regular stop on dozens of trips to Washington in recent years—the desk piled high, walls covered with drawings by Dennis's children, and the sitting area where our meetings were always held. I knew this would be our last meeting here. Ross was not staying on to work in the next administration. Would the new people coming to fill these offices in the future be prepared to pay the price Ross and his associates had paid—the long hours, the criticism from Arabs that they were Jewish, and from Jews that they were leftists? I knew that the next time I was in Washington it would be a different city for me.

AT THE END OF MY VISIT TO NEW YORK and Washington, as a result of these talks and meetings with other people in the administration, I reached three main conclusions: First, the administration was genuinely willing to enter into a quick and intensive exercise in order to save the peace process before it got frozen for a few years, on the condition that both sides wanted this. Second, there was serious concern in the White House about AIPAC's efforts to prevent Egypt from receiving their part of the economic aid package. And third, both the UN and the administration were unable to understand Barak's unwillingness to maintain contact with the Mitchell Committee.

Once I got back to Israel I submitted my conclusions to Barak. He had no interest at all in preventing the Egyptians from receiving aid, and he promised to do something to change the attitude toward the Mitchell Committee and increase cooperation with its members. However, on the most important subject—American willingness to be involved in mediation, and Clinton's personal commitment—he told me he would only consider the possibility of American involvement once the bilateral approach had conclusively hit a dead end. I protested that Clinton's offer was too good to refuse with time running out.

At that stage, the whole struggle was directed toward January 20, Clinton's last day in office. This date marked the end of a fifty-day period in which it still seemed possible to reach a last-minute agreement. The right tried with all the force it could muster to prevent this from happening, whereas Barak believed that there was still a chance of achieving a settlement, and that turning the elections into a referendum would grant victory to the agreement and to him. On Saturday evening, December 9, Barak delivered a shock by calling a special press conference to announce that he had handed in his resignation. In his usual way, he waited until after the announcement to convene the Labor ministers. As a result, rather than general elections for the entire Knesset, a special vote for the premiership would be held within sixty days. Barak declared:

> As Prime Minister I bear supreme responsibility for the policies of my government. I see no point in dragging the whole country into an election campaign. Personally, as the Prime Minister elected by a large majority, I intend to request the people's permission to continue along the path on which we began. We will have elections within sixty days. That is the easiest and the quickest way in the existing situation, and the right one . . . Israel needs new special elections, so that we have a new government with a renewed mandate, and renewed trust in the person leading it, in order to contend with the challenges we face. I would have preferred an emergency government at this difficult time, but as that did not work out, I will work toward leading a new government after the elections. I hope it will be a broad government with a renewed mandate for action. This is the real referendum on the way to achieve peace and on Israel's path ahead.

It was a great gamble that failed. Barak thought that by doing it this way he would avoid subjecting the whole system to the arduous labor of primaries and elections, which would keep him from concentrating on the peace process until January 20. But even if the plan was to reach a framework agreement by the last day of Clinton's term of office, and then, two weeks later, to hold a referendum in the form of elections, precious time was wasted in which not enough was done to reach an agreement. More importantly, and this I could not understand, he did not appreciate the advantage of Clinton's great willingness to be much more involved.

After the news conference, but before the meeting of the Labor ministers at the Prime Minister's office in Jerusalem, Barak called me to say that he had been thinking about Matan Vilnai and me. We were the only two ministers who had acceded to his request to resign from the Knesset to make room for our colleagues at the end of the party list; if Barak lost the elections, we would find ourselves outside the government and without our otherwise safe Knesset seats. I told him that this was the last thing he should worry over, and that our principal concern from that moment on was to focus on victory in the elections, which would be a victory for the peace process. If we lost, God forbid, and if a national unity government headed by the Likud was established, I would not want to be part of it, and I would certainly have no interest in being a member of its Knesset coalition.

The next day, Barak's candidacy for premiership was proffered at the party's central committee and he was elected in an open ballot, which was denounced as a hijack by his adversaries. Constitutionally, there was no need for this process, because Barak had been elected as the Labor Party candidate for the full term of the Knesset, and this was only a special election in the middle of that term. Essentially, I thought it would be a mistake to begin an internal contest. On a personal level, there had been many disputes between us, but in three principal spheres he had fulfilled my expectations: He was genuinely committed to reaching a final settlement between Israel and the Palestinians and to paying its price. He had carried out the unilateral withdrawal from Lebanon courageously in the face of the army's vocal reservations. And with regard to another dream of mine— bringing every Jewish youngster on a visit to Israel at the expense of the Jewish people—he accepted the idea and agreed to budget tens of millions of dollars to it over five years. This was the "Birthright" project, which operated with great success. I thought it would be inequitable to dispense with Barak after a year and a half. I also estimated that he and Sharon had more or less equal chances of winning an election, and if we could reach a framework agreement during the next two months, Barak would win.

CHAPTER 9
AFTER THE CLINTON PLAN

A FTER BARAK'S ANNOUNCEMENT, I met with Shlomo Ben-Ami for an update on the informal talks on the permanent settlement, and he reported that progress had been made. He mentioned that Barak had established a consultative forum which included Amnon Lipkin-Shahak, Gilead Sher, Danny Yatom, and Ben-Ami himself, and that he had suggested to Barak that I join them. Barak agreed immediately, and also took on Yossi Sarid, who had resigned his post as minister six months earlier. Barak had considered the group a kind of kitchen cabinet since it first met on December 11, and in fact, during the last two months of his premiership, virtually no cabinet meetings would be held; instead, this "peace cabinet," which met at least once a week, took over. Leaks from it were rare and it suited Barak's decision-making approach. Later on, after Peres was thwarted in his attempt to run for the premiership, he was also added to the group, partly as a way of co-opting him. Peres contributed his tremendous experience and political wisdom, but the tension between Barak and him was always in the air, making the meetings a shade more formal.

I felt now that I had a greater ability to influence decisions than ever before; I had comfortable relationships with both the Foreign Minister and Prime Minister, and indeed, at a number of junctures, I had a significant impact on decisions. But at the same time, I was still disappointed by our ongoing refusal to consider Clinton's offer to intervene and help push toward a framework agreement. There was a foreboding sense those last few months that it was already too late, regardless of the influence I now had and my minor victories.

LATE AT NIGHT ON DECEMBER 14, Ben-Ami met Arafat at the Erez crossing to discuss the possibility of renewing political negotiations. Ben-Ami's impression was that Arafat believed it was possible to reach an agreement by the end of Clinton's tenure. For his part, Barak announced that he was willing to sign an agreement with the Palestinians, even if it cost him the elections. On December 19, the Israeli delegation headed by Ben-Ami and the Palestinian one headed by Erekat left for Washington, for discussions aimed at implementing the Sharm el-Sheikh understandings, and to examine the possibility of opening intensive political negotiations. Clinton told them that he was at their disposal until January 10. Thus, by his reckoning, twenty fateful days remained.

On the same day, the nineteenth, I paid a visit to Jordan, at Barak's request, to present King Abdullah with a picture of the situation as it appeared to the government of Israel, and to request his assistance in calming the situation down, ending the Intifada, and returning to the negotiating table. We had been introduced in Jordan and on his brief visit to Israel, but we had never met properly. Although I felt uncomfortable about starting a meeting with the King by talking to him about his parents, I was unable to avoid discussing his father, King Hussein, with him. We talked about the secret, somewhat magical meetings in a remote village in England and at Williams House in Eilat, and particularly about the moving and special meeting we had at the Mayo Clinic in August 1998. He knew about some of these meetings, and referred to the esteem in which his father held his Israeli interlocutors and Hussein's great hope to lead the region toward a much more promising future; a hope that had remained in the present king's heart, but was diminished slightly in light of recent events.

Abdullah came across as a young, forceful, well-informed, and very businesslike person, who shunned everything having to do with royal posturing. He was accompanied in the discussion by the Prime Minister, Ali Abul

Ragheb, and the Court Minister, Dr. Fayez Tarawneh, who was very involved in the negotiations with Israel as Jordan's ambassador to the United States and had served as my counterpart in multilateral talks, enabling us to have many long discussions throughout the '90s. The King did not talk like a casual observer seeking to improve things, but as a player in the crisis. He expressed great interest in stabilizing and calming the situation through Jordanian-Egyptian cooperation, and he spoke at length about the importance of economic efforts as the basis for genuine normalization in the region. He was convinced that in order to put an end to the Intifada, Arafat needed to be granted some sort of peg, some concrete achievement to display. And the most practical peg would be a force of United Nations observers: "It is you who say that the IDF responds to Palestinian violence, whereas the television cameras, by their very nature, will photograph precisely the response and not the cause. Hence, Israel should have an interest in acceding to this Palestinian demand to prove its claim to the world!"

Afterwards I held a one-on-one meeting with the Jordanian Foreign Minister, Abdul Ilah Khatib. I asked about the possibility of appointing a Jordanian ambassador to Israel, before the vacancy became an established fact, which would then be difficult to alter. I understood from what he said that the chances of changing the Jordanian decision were not great. The minister, a smart, professional diplomat, with whom I was acquainted through his role in negotiations with Israel since 1992, said that Jordan had a real interest in being more involved in the political process and in being updated more frequently. This was, of course, a diplomatic way of expressing dissatisfaction at the fact that Israel had tended to ignore its eastern neighbor since making peace with it. Jordan believed that it was not too late to achieve peace, and would be willing to make a great effort to save the whole region from decline.

A disturbing picture emerged from the talks I had with other acquaintances in Amman, one very different from what I had seen five years earlier, shortly before Rabin was killed. Amman then was gleaming and elegant, awaiting the opening of a regional economic conference, which hosted many Arab delegations alongside an Israeli group headed by Rabin, while a number of planning and economics ministers from the region, including myself, presented common projects on tourism, transportation, and infrastructure for the purpose of attracting investors. The great hope of those days had been supplanted by a profound sense of disappointment: Jordan was hit hard by the Intifada on the West Bank, particularly when it came to tourism, which had developed significantly in recent years. The accelerated economic growth evident until not long ago had ceased completely. For every funeral in the West Bank, a house of mourning opened in Jordan, as the same families were involved. There had also been a kind of communications revolution: During the first Intifada in the late '80s, the only television available in Jordan was the state network, and its broadcasts were tightly supervised. Now a new phenomenon had swept through the Arab world—satellite television—and all that was required to watch it was a small dish. There are now a number of these networks, the most prominent of which is Al-Jazeera. Their technical standard is high, their programming is interesting and without overtones of propaganda, they fearlessly criticize the Arab establishments, and they show images of events on the ground. I was told that at the time each day that Al-Jazeera broadcasts its main news bulletin, traffic dwindles visibly on the streets of Amman.

People were closely following the events in the territories, and the Jordanian Palestinians identified strongly with their brothers in the West Bank and Gaza; hundreds of demonstrations against Israel have been held in the country. The monarchy does not prevent the demonstrations, and the security forces behave very responsibly, taking care not to hurt people. But there is no doubt that the economic and political price that Jordan is paying as a result of the Intifada is great, exceeded only by that paid by the Israelis and the Palestinians themselves. Jordan, therefore, has a vital interest in putting an end to the present situation.

Jordan still desires some acknowledgment of its contribution to resolving the refugee problem: It is the only Arab state that has granted Palestinian refugees citizenship and work permits. It expects, as part of a permanent settlement, to be allocated a significant sum as payment for its absorption and rehabilitation of the refugees, which will enable it to dismantle the refugee camps inside its borders and build new homes for the camp population. But as the likelihood of a permanent settlement has decreased, Jordan's chances of receiving this reward have evaporated, only adding to the disenchantment in the streets.

The next day in Jerusalem, I met Abu Ala, who had also just returned from Jordan. I told him about my disturbing impression from the visit and the danger of undermining the responsible regimes in the Middle East. It was our first meeting since the outbreak of the Intifada and he seemed disappointed and circumspect, bearing no good tidings. In his view, it was important to reanalyze the events that preceded the Intifada in order to explain why the explosive potential had been so great. His principal argument was that in the Stockholm channel, during his secret negotiations with Shlomo Ben-Ami, real progress had occurred. But it had been exposed publicly and halted too early. It was his opinion that it would have been appropriate to continue those talks, or similar ones, for some time, and his view was shared by all the leading members of the Palestinian Authority. The sudden leap forced on them, from a faltering series of inconclusive negotiations to the moment of truth, the moment of historic resolution, was unrealistic. Furthermore, the Israeli decision, supported by the United States, to hold the Camp David summit at all costs was imprudent.

He refused to accept the characterization of his stance at Camp David as a negative one. He simply did not see the need to be particularly active, he told me, because he knew that nothing would come out of it. I reminded him of the law of self-fulfilling prophecies, and he smiled. According to Abu Ala, immediately after the failure of the summit he approached Israel and suggested taking steps on the ground to prevent an explosion. People were extremely frustrated by the failure to implement components of the interim agreement, its frequent delays, and the ongoing building on the settlements—all of which had combined to exacerbate the disappointment caused by the failure of the summit, and it had now exploded in all our faces.

I told him about my talks in Washington at the beginning of the month, and the Clinton administration's willingness to be involved intensively to facilitate a permanent settlement. Abu Ala looked at me with mirthless eyes and asked, "Do you really believe that a framework agreement can be reached before January 20?" I said that if we didn't try, we certainly would not succeed, and that the chances of reaching an agreement within a reasonable period of time after January 20, the day of the inauguration of the new president, were far smaller. Abu Ala said he did not believe there was a chance of reaching a permanent settlement before the end of Clinton's tenure, despite what was happening at that time in Washington, but promised that if the negotiating teams came to the Palestinian leadership with outlines for approval, he would support any agreement that was reached. "What we have to do now," he said, "is not to try to reach an overall agreement, which anyway would not be honored if Sharon wins the election." It was preferable, in his view, to operate in a framework of confidence-building measures: freezing settlement construction, freeing prisoners, an advance that would be deducted from the third-phase funding, and a reduction of the daily affront of the occupation. "And what would be the Palestinian side's contribution?" I asked. He replied that the Palestinian side would fulfill its part of the agreements—combating violence, terror, and incitement. I said in all seriousness that it would be easier for the two sides to reach a framework agreement than to take intermediate steps, for which the return would, necessarily, appear to be merely a partial achievement.

It appeared, however, that Abu Ala's stance was his alone. Rudolf Scharping, the German Defense Minister, who was visiting the region, talked to me three days later and gave me a contrasting impression, based on a prolonged discussion he had held with Arafat. Arafat remarked to him, as he had to Ben-Ami, that there was a realistic chance of signing a framework agreement with Israel by January 20. According to him, George W. Bush had granted Clinton the option of conducting negotiations up till the last moment of his tenure, and would honor their outcomes. But the moment Bush began his term of office, the process would cease.

On December 21 the central committee of Meretz decided not to present Shimon Peres as a competing candidate in the special election for Prime Minister. A public movement had begun calling for Peres to run, with the belief that his chances of winning the election were greater than Barak's, and that he could continue the peace process. I found myself in one of the strangest political predicaments of my life. I saw Peres, even at seventy-seven, as the greatest Israeli statesman, and thought he would be a better Prime Minister than Barak. I thought it would be a grave mistake, however, to lend any hand to tearing the Labor movement apart. In order for Peres to qualify, he needed at least ten Knesset members to endorse his candidacy. The left would then have two competing candidates, and the winner would advance to the second round against Sharon. Personally, I was not willing to harm Barak, and publicly, a devil's dance was liable to materialize in our midst. Peres thought that heading into the elections with Barak at the helm was like collective suicide. When I said to him that running separately would deal a fatal blow to the Labor Party, Peres told me that, sadly, there was no such party anymore. He could not understand why I did not support him, and I could not grasp why "Mr. Labor Party" was prepared to run against his own party. This was the darkest cloud to ever hang over our close relationship, which had lasted more than a quarter of a century, and even though we have largely overcome the strain that resulted, there is no doubt some lingering tension persists.

But after the date for announcing new candidates for Prime Minister passed, Barak gave a sigh of relief for two reasons: Shimon Peres could not contest the election, thus preventing an internal split that would have led to a second round; while from the right, Netanyahu, who was considered the most popular candidate, decided not to enter the election because it was only for the premiership and not for the Knesset. He believed—or at least said he did—that given the current situation in the Knesset, no Prime Minister could last long, and that any government would fall within a few months.

The two remaining candidates, Barak and Sharon, were the second choices within their respective camps. At the beginning of the race support for the two candidates was equal, but as the weeks passed it became clear that Sharon had the advantage, that many people did not intend to vote, and that if Peres were to run instead, there was a chance he could defeat Sharon. The only way to replace Barak was to convince him to resign at least three days before the election, and then to elect Peres as the representative of the Labor Party. Barak rejected this option outright, although a number of people suggested it to him in confidence. He was convinced that it was Peres's virtual candidacy that was affecting the polls, and that the moment the public realized that Peres could not be a candidate, three days before the election, their votes would be transferred to him. Fewer and fewer people were prepared to accept his theory, however. And now, something that months earlier would have been inconceivable—the victory of one of the Likud's rightmost members, one of the least popular politicians in Israel, Ariel Sharon, over Barak—was fast becoming a possibility.

I was put in charge of information in the Arab sector, and concluded quickly it was an impossible mission. The Arabs were determined to prove to themselves, and to the public at large, that they had the power to replace the Prime Minister. They were not prepared to support Barak, because they believed that after giving him tremendous support in 1999, he had ignored them: He did not appoint any Arab ministers, did not include any Arabs in the coalition, and he was indirectly responsible for the killing of thirteen Israeli Arabs in the October disturbances that marked the beginning of the Intifada. The bereaved families did everything they could to prevent Arab voters from reaching the polling stations, while the campaigns conducted by Hadash (a Jewish-Arab left-wing party) and the party headed by Arab MK Ahmad Tibi, proposing that voters cast a blank ballot, were regarded as very brave for even calling the public to get out and vote. A few weeks before the elections I gave Barak a clear message: This time, the Israeli Arabs would not be with him.

It was impossible to force Barak to resign. Either he really believed he was able to win despite the polls, or he felt the need to fight up till the last minute; he was a captain who was not going to abandon ship. Last-ditch attempts, including those by his own staff, to persuade him to retire from the race, were met by rage, and he did, in fact, stay until the end.

CLINTON'S FINAL OFFERING TO THE PEACE PROCESS was the Clinton Plan. It was not a new idea. For some time there had been talk that Clinton would at some stage throw the ultimate plan into the arena and force the sides to decide whether they were prepared to pay the price for it or not. Clinton's move had a critical advantage: Until that point, the proposals made by each side were inevitably seen as one-sided by the other, whereas the

American proposal was a sort of *deus ex machina*. It would be backed by the world's last superpower, which would be committed to the proposal, and to funding and assisting its implementation. At the same time, both sides had their reasons to be unenthusiastic about such a proposal. The Palestinians—who were convinced that American and Israeli aspirations were identical, and that any American proposal would be merely a reworked Israeli proposal—were afraid of an Israeli document being presented to them in the guise of an American package. Barak, on the other hand, was not keen on an American plan because he believed that in matters related to the substance of the solution, the traditional U.S. position was closer to that of the Palestinians than of the Israelis. He preferred that the Americans pass ideas between the sides, rather than initiate them.

Clinton, for his part, was about to complete his term of office with peace in the Middle East, particularly in the Israeli-Palestinian context, looking less and less likely. In spite of his willingness, he had not been invited to use his final days in office to reduce the gap between the positions of the two sides, and any progress achieved at Camp David and in other talks was liable to disappear without any achievements on the ground once his time at the White House ended. Despite the fact that previous American plans like the Rogers Plan and the Reagan Plan had not materialized either, Clinton decided to leave a legacy behind, although he did it in a unique way. While the previous plans had been official and public, his plan was not published, and it was never delivered to the parties. He read it out to the two delegations on Friday, December 22, and asked Barak and Arafat to inform him of their positions on his proposals by the following Wednesday. If one of the parties replied in the negative he would announce—so he promised Ben-Ami and Erekat—"the end of the process under my auspices"; he would give up and declare that all the ideas raised at Camp David and afterwards were null and void as far as he was concerned.

It seems that history will regard the Clinton Plan as a rumor. It was recorded only by people from the two sides who were not stenographers, and at the end of his tenure, Clinton announced that it no longer "existed." The plan had neither an introduction nor a conclusion, just the description of an outline of an agreement as Clinton saw it, based on his understanding of the two parties during and following the Camp David summit. Territorially, Clinton said, the Palestinian state would stretch over ninety-four to ninety-six percent of the West Bank. (The Gaza Strip was not mentioned because it was assumed that it would be transferred to the Palestinians without argument.) The Palestinians would be compensated for land annexed to Israel by an exchange of land from Israel, in addition to the areas specified in the permanent settlement, like the safe passages between Gaza and the West Bank, that cross through Israeli territory. It was also suggested that the sides consider additional exchanges of territory through leasing.

The map drawn was supposed to bring about a situation where approximately eighty percent of the settlers would remain in the settlement blocs, while most of the settlements would be removed. The Palestinian state would be guaranteed territorial contiguity, and the number of Palestinians who would be annexed to Israel as a result of the annexation of the settlement blocs would be minimal. With regard to security, the plan proposed an international presence whose duty would be to oversee the implementation of the agreement, and which could only be relieved of its duty with the consent of both parties. The IDF would remain in the Jordan Valley, under international supervision, for three years; Israel would retain three early-warning stations in the West Bank, which would have Palestinian liaison officers present. This arrangement would be reappraised ten years after it had been in operation. There would be arrangements for military deployment in case of a national threat, with the international force being informed in advance of any such action. The control of air space in the skies above the Palestinian state would be in the hands of the sovereign Palestinian state; however, arrangements would be made between the sides to meet Israeli training and operational requirements. The Palestinian state would be non-militarized, and an international force would defend its borders and serve as a deterrent.

The question of Jerusalem would be solved by making the Arab neighborhoods Palestinian and the Jewish neighborhoods Israeli. An effort would be made to have contiguity within the respective neighborhoods. With regard to the Temple Mount, the main point was respect for the various religions. Clinton put forth two alternatives, both under international monitoring. The first proposed Palestinian sovereignty over the Temple Mount, and Israeli sovereignty over the Western Wall and the Holy of Holies that is part of it. The two parties would be duty bound not to dig underneath the Temple Mount or behind the Wall. The second alternative proposed Palestinian sovereignty over the Temple Mount, Israeli sovereignty over the Western Wall, and combined functional sovereignty on excavation under the Temple Mount and behind the Wall, such that mutual agreement would be necessary in order to dig.

With regard to the refugees, Israel would acknowledge the mental and material suffering of the Palestinian refugees resulting from the 1948 war, and recognize the need to assist the international community in dealing with the problem. The refugees would be granted five absorption options: 1. in the Palestinian state; 2. in the areas that Israel would transfer to the Palestinian state in return for annexing parts of the West Bank; 3. in the states in which they currently live; 4. in various third states that were willing to absorb them; 5. in Israel, by consent. Preference would be given to refugees in Lebanon and the two sides would recognize that this was the fulfillment of the United Nations General Assembly Resolution 194. It would be made clear that the Palestinian right of return to Israel could not be exercised freely, and it would be stated that the Palestinians have the right of return to historic Palestine or to their "National Home." The agreement—according to Clinton—was intended to mark the end of the conflict, fulfill the implementation of United Nations Security Council Resolutions 242 and 338, and enable the release of Palestinian prisoners.

Ben-Ami and Sher returned to Israel on December 24, and that night we convened an urgent meeting of the peace cabinet. Barak was in the midst of the election campaign, appearing around the country; he was spending the night in Shlomi, a town in the north, so he flew all of us to an army base close by to hold the meeting. Ben-Ami read out to us what he had written down during Clinton's presentation. Peres, Lipkin-Shahak, Sarid, and I listened attentively and made some notes for ourselves.

Thirty-three years after the astounding victory in the Six-Day War, which brought upon us the curse of prolonged occupation and led to the settlement mania, an American president had, for the first time, presented the precise outline of a solution. If a suggestion like this had arisen a few years earlier, perhaps a lot of blood could have been spared. But the sides might have rejected it then, so maybe it was only now that the time was ripe. In any event, Clinton presented his ideas at the eleventh hour of his tenure, which turned out, in retrospect, to be the thirteenth.

No real argument developed at the peace cabinet. Essentially, it could be said that we spoke as one. No one suggested that we should not adopt the outline plan. It was decided that Israeli reservations would be prepared, and that the proposal should be presented for the endorsement of the full government without delay. On December 28, at a meeting of the government, the plan was endorsed in principle together with permission to send reservations that had not been presented to the government for endorsement. The following day it was announced in the media that two ministers, Roni Milo and Michael Melchior, opposed the decision and that two abstained, Matan Vilnai and Ra'anan Cohen. From that moment, the Clinton Plan embodied Israel's stance on the Israeli-Palestinian issue. Israel, which had said no to the Rogers Plan in 1969 and no to the Reagan Plan in 1982, said yes to the Clinton Plan in 2000.

Israel was prepared to accept the proposal within the time limit Clinton had set for it. But the Palestinians were not. They decided to postpone a decision, and instead sent a document to the Americans containing a series of reservations and a request for clarification before their final answer. Arafat added that "there are still many obstacles on the way to peace." When Barak found out about the Palestinian response, he announced that he could not, at this stage, consider the American proposal officially, or convey the final Israeli reply to the White House. The previous evening, in a telephone conversation with Arafat, the Prime Minister had agreed that the two of them would travel the following Thursday to Egypt to discuss, with Mubarak, giving a positive answer to Clinton. However, when it became apparent that the Palestinians were making do with an intermediate reply, Barak informed Mubarak that he would not be attending the meeting in Sharm el-Sheikh. Mubarak agreed, and said that only after meeting with Arafat could he recommend a summit of this sort.

Clinton was angry with the Palestinian response and informed Arafat by telephone that he would refuse to deal with the Palestinians' questions or to conduct a political dialogue with them until he received a clear reply to his proposal. Spelling it out, he said: "I want to hear 'Yes, but' or 'No', but on no account something in between." Clinton and Arafat finally met on January 2 in Washington. At the meeting, which included each man's entourage, the Palestinian side was unyielding, and it was a heated discussion. Clinton believed that it was still possible, within a few days, to reach an agreement on a document in the spirit of his plan, but Arafat had his doubts. Only after a further, more intimate meeting held between the two was Clinton prepared to interpret Arafat's reply as "Yes, but"—a readiness in principle to adopt the Clinton Plan, together with a number of reservations that did not turn it on its head.

THERE WERE STILL SOME DAYS OF HOPE: On January 7 at the Waldorf Astoria Hotel in New York, President Clinton delivered a speech to a group of Jewish peace advocates, the Israel Policy Forum, which was a summation of his years of involvement in the Middle East as well as a plan for the future. It was a moving speech, magnificently crafted, both personal and political. Clinton spoke with great admiration for Barak, his bravery in battle and his willingness to really examine the possibility of peace. The violence of the last three months, said Clinton, had raised questions in some people's minds about whether Palestinians and Israelis could ever really live and work together, and support each other's peace, prosperity, and security. "It's been a heartbreaking time for me, too," he said. "But we have done our best to work with the parties to restore calm, to end the bloodshed, and to get back to working on an agreement."

In the speech he laid out his guiding principles: A solution of the conflict has to deal with the religious and national sensitivities of the two sides; there is no military solution to the conflict; for an agreement to be stable, Israel has to be strong; it is essential to actually implement and monitor the agreements; if a solution is not found now, it will be found in the future, but the problems will not go away and the solution is liable to be more difficult then, after many more funerals and much more hatred.

Clinton reiterated his overwhelming impression that the negotiators at

Camp David knew one another well, even their families, and that they trusted each other. Given this sort of relationship, and knowing that there was no alternative to an agreement, the two parties had turned to him with a request to suggest parameters for such an agreement. He had, indeed, done this, based on his familiarity with the positions of the two sides over the last eight years. Barak and Arafat had accepted the proposal, both of them had adopted it with certain reservations, and the President was now making an effort to bridge the disparities.

Next he presented the components of his plan: a sovereign Palestinian state; settlement blocs annexed to Israel; exchanges of territory between Israel and the Palestinian state; a solution for the Palestinian refugee problem that will include their absorption into the Palestinian state, their absorption into various third states, including Israel, according to the decisions of the governments of those states; reparations for refugees within the framework of an international body that will deal with the matter. The solution would not upset the internal balance of Israel as a Jewish state; security arrangements would guarantee that the Palestinian state would be non-militarized and that there would be forces to monitor the implementation of the agreement; Jerusalem would be an open, united city, capital of the two states, with Jewish Jerusalem larger and more full of life than ever before; the agreement would put an end to the conflict and to the claims of the parties.

With a touch of humor, Clinton thanked God that he was not running for a third term in office on the basis of these ideas. He had been in the job for eight years and not raised them, only deciding to do so when the two sides requested his help because they felt they had reached the end of the road and they needed someone to extricate them from the dead end. The Palestinians have to cease being the ball in the game of Arab politics, Clinton said, and make decisions that will guarantee them their lives and honor, while Israel is closer than ever before to ending one hundred years of conflict. He hopes and prays, he said, that Israel will not relinquish the hope for peace.

Clinton was counting the days. He had another thirteen left in the job and he promised to do what he could in that time. He was working with

Egypt and the two sides to reduce the violence. That week he was sending Dennis Ross to the region to see how the process could be advanced in the coming days. "I think America will always be there for Israel's security," he concluded. "But Israel's lasting security rests in a just and lasting peace. I pray that the day will come sooner, rather than later, where all the people of the region will see that they can share the wisdom of God in their common humanity and give up their conflict." The audience gave him a standing ovation.

That speech was the Clinton legacy. His measured, considered words at the Waldorf Astoria were his final, coherent thesis on the subject of the Middle East. In the future, when people seek to understand his perception of the Middle East, it is here they will find its essentials.

CHAPTER 10
TABA: MOMENT OF HOPE

ONE WEEK LATER, ON JANUARY 20, Clinton's last day in office, the peace cabinet convened at Barak's home in Kochav Ya'ir. The Prime Minister said that it had been agreed with the Palestinians and the Egyptians to try to conduct political negotiations on the framework agreement. This would be a last-ditch effort to reach a solution before the elections, and though Barak was not too optimistic about the outcome, he was willing to give it a chance. The division of responsibilities was a bit vague—Ben-Ami would head the negotiating team, I would lead talks on the refugees, Amnon Lipkin-Shahak and Gilead Sher would deal with the other teams, and Yossi Sarid would attend the negotiations when he came down to Taba, while Barak and Peres would direct the proceedings from Jerusalem.

Over the years I had dealt with the refugee issue quite a lot, and I had read books and studies, but I was not prepared for a situation where I would be heading a team to continue the negotiations that had begun in Camp David only a few months earlier. I devoted many hours until the next day's government meeting to making a feverish search of my office and my home for material on the subject, piling it into a large briefcase that I borrowed from the office. I made a few hasty phone calls to the Attorney General, Eli Rubinstein, who had worked on the issue at Camp David, and to other people who had dealt with it, and when the government convened on Sunday, I knew where I stood.

At the meeting itself, the matter of the Taba talks was not taken for granted, although all the ministers were in the same camp. The concern that had been expressed in the peace cabinet, over legitimizing the talks so late, so close to the elections, and without parliamentary backing, had also percolated down into the ranks of Labor ministers. The next day, Haim Ramon was reported to have told the government that "it is improper, immoral, and irregular to hold talks now." That afternoon, we flew to Eilat, where we stayed at the Princess Hotel. From there we crossed the border to Taba, to get to the Hilton for the opening session of the talks. Our Egyptian hosts in Taba were nowhere to be seen. They had prepared a huge hall for the opening evening, though we preferred a much more modest room, as we were few in number. We passed through crowds of reporters and photographers who were waiting for us in the lobby, trying to catch a word from us, although we had nothing to report, and we finally arrived at the restricted meeting.

We were on borrowed time. The elation of the meeting was mixed with a sense that reaching an agreement at this point might be impossible. Pats on the back replaced strong embraces. Were the people across the table initiating terror, or working to prevent it? Had they fanned the flames of the Intifada, or had they attempted to scatter sand on them? Did they understand the significance of firing on Gilo [a Jewish neighborhood in East Jerusalem] night after night? Or of the lynching in Ramallah? In face-to-face talks with Arafat, did they challenge him or did they settle for executing his orders? Did they understand what was happening to the peace camp? Could they see the disappointment and despair among the believers? And what about all the strong statements only a few weeks earlier, when Yasser Abed Rabbo called Barak a war criminal and Mohammed Dahlan said that he would no longer negotiate with Israel? What did they think of the people sitting opposite them, whose votes had decided on the bombing of Gaza by helicopters? There was something new in the atmosphere among us. For a number of years we had viewed ourselves as a group of peacemakers standing against the world, against cynicism and extremism, constantly moving against the current, against the majority on every side, toward a joint truth and a common future. Now we were one against the other, polite, smiling, shaking hands.

The media entered the small, crowded room to photograph the first session. A round of TV cameras, a round of press photographers, and after that, one more photographer who had come late and was removed almost forcibly by one of the Egyptian or Palestinian security personnel. Eventually he was permitted to enter, but only for a moment, and again we were shaking hands and smiling professionally into the last camera lens.

Abu Ala and Shlomo Ben-Ami spoke about our attempt to complete what had been left open at Camp David: to put an end to the violence, the ongoing nightmare. There had been a great deal of progress in the past few months, more than ever before. There was the Clinton Plan; we were very close. It was possible to bridge the gap, there was no need for years to find a solution for everything, nor even months. We would try to do it in days. "We are not committed to the Clinton Plan," Abu Ala said, but Saeb Erekat corrected him: "We accepted the Clinton Plan as the basis, but we submitted reservations." Who could be sure?

Most of us rose to speak. It was a great hour, but time was short. There was a heavy burden on our shoulders, from our own high expectations and our commitment to what we had been preaching for so many years. And we knew that we had so little in our hands. A single extremist from either side taking someone's life would be enough to send us packing. Every moment that passed was like a near miracle. Every hour of sleep was a luxury.

The session dispersed and the next day negotiations would begin in the various committees—security arrangements, borders and Jerusalem, and refugees. "It is necessary to discuss water," Abu Ala said, and we had no water experts with us. Maybe we could call on someone tomorrow. In the meantime we separated for informal, individual talks at night. And in all the conversations, the same question and counter-question: we asked why the Intifada had started, they asked back, why did you not respond with more restraint at the beginning? Every interlocutor had his own answer. The consensus among the Israelis was that our opposites really believed that in the autumn of 2000 the talks that had begun at Camp David would continue until the American elections, and that a framework peace agreement would be signed in the White House before the end of Clinton's term. One of them said to me: "I have no good explanation for what happened, but our suffering is not only the large number of victims, it is also our daily life. My child has not been attending school since the Intifada began. If he comes home after school instead of throwing stones at your soldiers, his friends will scream at him, 'Traitor, traitor!' And if he throws stones, he might return home in a coffin. Ending the Intifada is in our interest. Every day in the occupied territories new suicide bombers are born to this desperate reality. Each day it is harder to make peace. In another few months it will be even harder. In a few years' time, hatred will make it impossible."

There was also criticism—hinted, subtle, between the lines—of Arafat. His unnecessary blustering, the waste of the first week at Camp David, his superfluous travel and badly managed negotiations. Never unequivocal. Never direct. Always finding justifications. His behavior lay heavy on his representatives.

The need to work constantly justified three formal meals a day, as if we were at a holiday resort. One needs, it turns out, to be very hungry or very disciplined in order to eat three full meals a day without substituting an occasional sandwich, or coffee and cake. But meal times were not wasted. We sat in small groups of Israelis and Palestinians, continuing the formal discussions or considering the lessons of the negotiations that had been unsuccessful in recent months. We were still attempting to analyze exactly what went wrong and how not to repeat mistakes that we had not yet identified.

The long hours had their effect, and the cloud that loomed over the opening night rose. It was still there, but receding. There was no substitute for such intensive effort, no replacement for the informal talks, the exchange of assessments, of personal experiences, political jokes, and our use of the common language of insiders: appendix seven, article twenty, the interim agreement, Wye, Sharm, Declaration of Principles, retreat, redeployment. There was a sense of ease, like the prisoners described in an old gag who have, over their long years in jail, memorized the jokes in a book by number; they tell each other the numbers instead of the jokes, but burst out laughing anyway.

"Why do you Israelis fear the right of return so much?" I was asked by one of the participants in an informal discussion.

"What do you mean?" I replied.

"If the right of return is exercised, and the majority of the refugees want to live in Israel, it will not be a Jewish state anymore, it will be the end of the Zionist dream and it will be no 'big deal' for Jews to live here. They can be a minority anywhere in the world."

"How many Jews are there in the United States—ten percent?" he asked.

"1.8 percent," I replied.

"You see," he said, as if this were the clinching argument, "with less than two percent you have practically made America into a Jewish country. Do you really think that if you don't have a numerical majority it will stop being a Jewish state?"

"I believe that without a doubt," I replied.

The difference between Jewish influence on a country where we constitute a minority and a country where there is a Jewish majority and it is the home, or at least the second home, for world Jewry, is all the difference in the world. Not only because the majority's culture is dominant, not only because without a Jewish majority there will be no Law of Return, but because the whole Zionist ideal arose from the desire to put an end to the situation whereby Jews are the minority wherever they live. The main advantage of living in Israel for a person like me is the fact that it is a country with a Jewish majority. If this advantage no longer exists, that removes the principal grounds for the state's existence.

FOR THE FIRST TIME IN A NUMBER OF YEARS we were talking to each other, and only to each other. With no Americans around. The message of the new president, George W. Bush, was "distance." The peace team had been dismantled. President Clinton had retired. Albright had returned to academe and Dennis Ross to the Washington Institute for Near East Policy. At first glance it was easy to say that wherever the Americans had been, nothing happened, while wherever they were not, agreements were reached. But that would be a very shallow and unfair statement. It was true that the talks held in Washington showed no progress, although they lasted many long months under the governments of both Shamir and Rabin. But without the Madrid Conference, which had been an outstanding United States initiative by George H. W. Bush and James Baker, his Secretary of State, there would have been no Washington talks in 1991 and 1992 and no Oslo Accord. It is true that on the Israeli-Syrian front we had not achieved an agreement, but it is also true that without American help this channel could never have existed, since the Syrians objected to direct talks with us. There is also no doubt that at Wye in 1996, and Shepherdstown in 2000, we achieved a great deal of progress and very nearly a real agreement with the Syrians. It is true that the Oslo talks were conducted, from their inception up to the signature of the agreement on the White House lawn, without any American involvement, with only partial and unofficial knowledge, and that the peace agreement with Jordan had also been signed with no American intervention. However, the economic aid furnished by the Americans themselves was vital to the realization of both agreements.

The American involvement fulfilled many functions. Very rarely was it the initiator, as with the most recent initiative, the Clinton Plan, which had come too late. Sometimes it was the host, laying the table without sitting down at it. That was the case at the Washington talks between Israel and the Jordanian-Palestinian delegation. On occasion it served as the bridge, as in 1999, ahead of the signature of the solitary agreement between Barak and Arafat—the Sharm el-Sheikh Memorandum. At times it was the broker, moving between two parties turning their backs on each other, which is what happened in 1991 with the Shamir government and the Palestinians headed by Faisal Husseini. There were times when America became an integral part of the negotiations, as at the Wye Plantation summit between Netanyahu and Arafat in 1998, and at the Camp David summit between Barak and Arafat in 2000. In almost every agreement, memorandum, or understanding, the United States became the judge before whom the two parties presented their complaints and demands. It was the "world" to which the parties referred, it was the authority before which the parties were willing to display their security programs in order to comply with agreements, which is what happened after the Wye Memorandum at the end of 1998 and the beginning of 1999. The United States closely monitored the performance of the Wye Agreement through the CIA personnel who have, in recent years, been participating in meetings with Israeli and Palestinian security forces.

Suddenly we were without the Americans, and this changed the rules of the game. When the United States participates in the negotiations, it becomes a part of them. The parties have an interest in appeasing the United States, each wanting to show that it is not to blame, that its hands are clean, that it has gone a long way without receiving any appropriate response from the other side. The parties are inclined to "deposit" their positions in the Americans' presence, and the brokers can explore one party's willingness to accept the other's position, or present it as their own proposal in the course of the negotiations. The third party has the option of raising trial balloons and withdrawing them from the table if they are unacceptable, while the parties themselves, when they do the same, cannot back down, since they have already exposed whatever it is they are willing to do.

But there is another side to the absence of an external factor. There is less room for maneuvering and games. Everything has to be done in real time, opposite your negotiating partner. There is no safety margin between you and the proposal. You do not have to guess whether the Americans have made the proposal themselves or whether they have presented the Palestinians' proposal, and vice versa. Whatever a party suggests, it is committed to. It is you who tests the temperature of the water, and you who enters the pool. You do nothing "for the Americans." You cannot decide in your heart to say no for the sake of the negotiations, and wait to be "persuaded" by the Americans. If you agree, you agree—and if you refuse, you refuse. Yes, you can always leave the room in anger, you can always ask for consultations with colleagues or leaders, but the moment of truth is much more tangible, and crucially, more exposed.

We were not really alone. The Egyptians were there at Taba, but only at the technical level, always ready to assist, never asking anything, and certainly not participating in the official or unofficial talks. The Americans dispatched to Taba monitors from the U.S. embassy, who did not disturb the negotiators. Miguel Moratinos, the permanent European emissary to the Middle East, who was the Spanish ambassador to Israel, and before that had participated on behalf of Spain during the multilateral talks, was the senior foreigner at Taba. He spoke a lot unofficially, both with us and the

Palestinians, went into details, and endeavored to help, in one instance listing possible places among the European Union countries where some Palestinian refugees could be taken in. But he also, of course, remained outside the negotiating room. We were, therefore, almost alone.

WE CONDUCTED THE NEGOTIATIONS on the refugees until the end of the week in Nabil Sha'ath's suite, which was constantly filled with coffee and sweetmeats, to prevent hunger between meals. A significant part of the talks were one-on-one. I had known Dr. Sha'ath since the Oslo Accords, but had heard about him many years before that. He was born in Safed, and his father, who was a teacher, had been transferred at the demand of the British. The family moved to Jaffa when Sha'ath was two years old. I grew up not far from there myself—our home on Kalisher Street in Tel Aviv was on the edge of Jaffa. When the Hassan Bek mosque was active we could hear the calls of the muezzin from our home. In the War of Independence, our house became a Haganah outpost in the front against Jaffa, and my family moved to the safer area north of Tel Aviv, where we lived with relatives on Mapu Street. I was born during the second lull, but our home was still at the front, and I was brought to Mapu Street. Only months later did we return to Kalisher Street.

Sha'ath was not exactly as I imagined the refugees of Jaffa in my childhood. He is one of the most prominent PLO spokesmen; his English is good and rich, and he has no fear of entering into long and complex conversations, as he is always able to get out of them comfortably. His accent does not give him away, and his patience is atypical of our region. An embarrassing incident occurred between us about two years before the Oslo Accord, when I came to Egypt with a delegation of Knesset members for a dialogue with senior Egyptians on the political process under the auspices of the International Peace Center. At a certain point, when I was told that Sha'ath was in the room, I simply left the meeting. Sha'ath remembered this well, and at one of the meetings between us reminded me of it with a smile. I explained to him that the Israeli law, which at that time prohibited meetings with the PLO, was a stupid one, that I did everything I could to repeal it and had been successful, but I could not have broken it before then. Even the Oslo talks could not begin before the law had been rescinded, and it is no coincidence that they commenced in the far north one day after the new law voiding the prohibition had been passed.

Since then Sha'ath and I have met many times: as members of delegations, at meetings with Arafat, at some of the Stockholm meetings which led to the Beilin–Abu Mazen Understandings, at appearances in the United States and elsewhere, at meetings when I served in a position parallel with his—Minister of Economy and Planning—and when, together, we prepared eight projects for regional cooperation which were presented jointly at the economic convention of the Middle East and North Africa held in Amman at the end of October 1995. Sha'ath's first wife was killed in a road accident, and in 1995 he remarried. My wife and I attended the wedding ceremony in East Jerusalem, and we found ourselves among quite a few Israelis who had become friends with Sha'ath during the '90s.

At the Taba talks, Sha'ath was accompanied by two young, impressive intellectuals, Ghaith Al-Omari, a young lawyer, and Dr. Diana Buttu, who was born in Canada and completed a doctorate at McGill University on compensation to the Palestinian refugees. On my side were Daniel Levy, my policy advisor, and Gidi Grinstein, Gilead Sher's advisor in the Prime Minister's office. They had come to these positions after a few years of work at ECF, and both had dealt with various aspects of the permanent and interim arrangements with the Palestinians. The face-to-face talks between Sha'ath and I mainly addressed the seriousness of the event in which we were participating. How serious was the other party, how real were its intentions to achieve an agreed document here and now, what mandate did it have, and how much detail could be resolved? The talks between the delegations dealt, at first, with a general presentation of the method of solving the refugee problem as both parties saw it, and ended up, within a short while, addressing the rehabilitation and compensation model. Sha'ath opened by presenting the refugees as the central issue of the PLO's ideology, and reviewed their situation in various parts of the Arab world and the possibilities for their rehabilitation, mentioning in particular the problem of refugees in Lebanon—two hundred thousand of them—whose situation was the worst, since they had neither citizenship nor the opportunity to work. He quoted with great erudition from the writings of the Israeli "new historians," and said that today, even Israeli professionals admit to what happened in 1948–49—the uprooting of hundreds of thousands of people from their land, the taking of their property, causing enormous damage to a whole people, in the course of what became the War of Independence for Israel and disaster for the Palestinians.

I told Sha'ath that the perpetual question in history is: When do you begin? The Palestinians begin history from a war in which they indeed paid a heavy price, while I begin history from November 29, 1947, when he was a ten-year-old child in Jaffa and I was in my mother's womb. Obviously, if the Palestinians had accepted the United Nations resolution on the partition of Palestine, which offered them forty-five percent of the land of Israel west of the Jordan, and granted the Jews bits and pieces of a state over all the rest, with a very small Jewish majority, there would have been no refugee problem. The Palestinians rejected everything offered to them—their own state in 1947; United Nations Resolution 194, which addressed, inter alia, the aspiration of Palestinians to return to their homes, and was adopted in December 1948; and Israel's willingness to absorb one hundred thousand refugees in the Lausanne talks in 1949. Now the Palestinians were putting Resolution 194 at the top of their list, though they were willing to settle for a state covering only twenty-three percent of the area. We could have both celebrated the fifteenth of May as the Independence Day of two small countries, side by side. Instead we have spent more than fifty years at war, in mutual slaughter; alongside Israel's Independence Day, the Palestinians commemorate al-Nakba, the Catastrophe. Who knows how many more days we will continue with this exhausting quarrel if we are not brave and wise enough to reach an agreement that may not fulfill all our dreams in their entirety, but responds to the real needs of both sides.

I removed from my briefcase one of the most moving documents from the days just before the establishment of the state, and I gave it to Sha'ath. This was the "Appeal from the Haifa Workers Council to the Arab Residents of Haifa, Workers and Officials." It was a short, one-page document, the right side written in Hebrew, the left in Arabic. It was dated April 28, 1948. Among other things, it stated:

Now we see the need to say to you openly: We are a peace-loving people! There is no basis for the fear cast on you. We have no animosity or bad intentions against peace-seeking residents, obligated, as we are, to work and creativity. Do not fear! Do not destroy your homes with your own hands. Do not block the source of your livelihood and do not bring disaster upon yourselves due to unnecessary evacuation and wanderings. Leaving will bring you only poverty and humiliation, while in the city of Haifa—both yours and ours—the gates are open before you for work, life, and peace, for yourselves and your families.

Honest and peace-loving residents! The Haifa Workers Council and the Histadrut advise you, for your own good, to remain in the city and to return to your regular jobs. We are prepared to come to your aid in returning life to its normal course, to make it easier for you to obtain food, to make jobs available to you. Workers! Our joint city, Haifa, calls you to participate in its construction, promotion, and development. Do not betray it and do not betray yourselves. Keep your eyes on your own interests and stay on the good and honest path!

Nabil Sha'ath took the document from my hands and read it carefully, then folded it and put it in his jacket pocket. "I read somewhere that there was such a thing," he said, "but I never saw the Appeal itself. There is no doubt that there were such cases; there is mercy and humanitarianism everywhere, just as there is cruelty and obtuseness. But the bottom line was disaster." I replied that if the two of us lapsed into an argument over the competing interpretations of the events that led to the refugee problem, we were certain to arrive at the same dead end as our predecessors. The most important thing was to understand the sensitivities and fears on each side, and the possibility of responding to real needs.

Past experience had taught us that one of the most efficient ways to get to the root of a matter—to understand it, and thereby to reach the bottom line—was to change roles. Each of us entered the shoes of the other for a short while, presenting his perception and positions as he understood them. We made side comments about the presentations, but it was clear to us both that no further words were required to explain the positions—the emerging picture enabled us to approach a solution.

According to the statistics of the UN High Commissioner for Refugees, there are presently about 3.7 million Palestinian refugees. About 1.5 million are in Jordan, about 1.4 million in the West Bank and Gaza, about 380,000 in Syria, and roughly the same number in Lebanon. The real numbers are much smaller, because many refugees who registered with the agency have left the camps and migrated to Europe, South America, and even North America.

The following is a synopsis of the understandings that Sha'ath and I, and our respective teams, were able to reach and the issues with which we were struggling: Since it is reasonable to assume that the refugees living on the West Bank and in Gaza will be rehabilitated and move to housing within the Palestinian state; since the refugees living in Jordan have been enjoying full citizenship for a whole generation; and since in Syria the refugees have the possibility of working and earning a living, the only remaining problem is Lebanon, where the real figure is no less than 180,000 but no more than 220,000. The refugees in Lebanon must be taken away from there, but the number of refugees that countries like Canada, the United States, and certain European countries are willing to accept is much higher than the number remaining in Lebanon, and any of them wanting to be absorbed into the Palestinian state when it is established will be able to do so.

Whoever wants to settle in the sovereign area of Israel before the Six-Day War can do so in housing built for them on the land that Israel will transfer to the Palestinian state in exchange for areas it annexes on the West Bank. Israel will continue to issue permits for family reunification and special humanitarian cases, and will also be able to deal with a very limited number of refugees which it will absorb in the course of the coming years. UNWRA, the United Nations Works and Relief Agency, which was established specifically to address the Palestinian refugee problem, will close down within five years.

The matter of compensation to the refugees is very complex, but it can be resolved, and herein lies the key to their rehabilitation. Tens of billions of dollars will be collected from various entities worldwide, mainly, but not solely, from the U.S. and Europe, as well as from Israel. The fund will be used for universal compensation to every refugee family, personal compensation for property presently in the possession of Israel, as well as compensation to be given to countries such as Jordan, which has absorbed refugees over the last few decades. The relationship between the international organization that will replace UNWRA—and deal with the rehabilitation of refugees—and the compensation fund; the relationship between these compensation funds and the compensation due to Jews who left the Arab countries, leaving their property behind; and the assessment of compensation for loss of property—all of this requires very detailed work toward the permanent agreement, on which we have established only guidelines in principle over the long hours.

What was left was to figure out how to address what the Palestinians call the right of return—UN Resolution 194 mentions the aspiration to return but not the right—and the question of the responsibility for creating the refugee problem. The agreement would include a concise history of events in the eyes of each party, recognition of the suffering and distress of the refugees, and separate interpretations of Resolution 194, while agreeing that Resolution 194 would be implemented commensurate with the Clinton Plan.

ON MONDAY MORNING THE NEWSPAPER HEADLINES described Ariel Sharon's *New Yorker* interview, in which he called Arafat a "murderer, liar, and bitter enemy." A few days earlier, Knesset member Avigdor Lieberman had said that the Sharon government would reoccupy Beit Jala, near Bethlehem. Sha'ath and I accelerated the talks with the aim of creating a very different picture to the one that seemed to be taking shape in the polls, which were no secret to anyone.

At noon on Tuesday we held a plenary meeting, with an interim summary of the work of the committees. This was definitely progress, which was commendable, but the positions were not yet identical. On the issue of borders, the Palestinians presented their own map in which, for the first time, Israel would annex 3.1 percent of the area of the West Bank and give back territory to the Palestinian state in other places. Israel presented a map in which it annexed six percent, leased another two percent, but transferred in exchange only three percent to the Palestinian state. The only remaining issues included permission for Israel to pass through the Palestinian state in emergencies on a number of routes, along with the question of communication during the period the IDF was to remain in the Jordan Valley, as well as matters related to air space.

On Jerusalem, however, there had been little progress. Neither side liked Clinton's suggestion, but neither could convince the other that their own solution was preferable.

There was a sense that time was running out and that it would be impossible to remain in Taba for much longer, although none of us had a target date to complete the talks. We had left behind us government offices and elections that were drawing to an end. The ability to ignore the outside agenda and maintain a "clear mind" was limited. We therefore proposed to the Palestinians that, in parallel with the work of the committees, we should start to prepare a draft of the entire agreement. In this way it would be possible to get all the clauses ready, and as soon as agreement was achieved on the various issues, we would be able to add passages to the prepared draft, instead of commencing work on the agreement only after completing all the committee talks.

Abu Ala hesitated. He admitted that the progress in the past few days was the greatest since the process began, with no comparison to the negotiations at Camp David. At the same time, he was afraid to commit to drafting just yet, because that would create, too early, the sense that we were almost finished. If it became known to the media, they would expect us to sign a peace agreement tomorrow or the next day, and we were not there yet. I told him that the chances that we would reach an overall and complete package that solved all the problems and could be signed were not great, but it was necessary to make a major effort to increase that possibility. Every passing moment was to our disadvantage. We would not be able to drag the negotiations on much longer, and any incidence of violence would terminate our work. If the desire to accomplish something at this late stage was mutual, it was important to start drafting immediately, and we would not publicize this. So, indeed, it was agreed, and Saeb Erekat and Gilead Sher met to begin preparing a paper, portions of which they had already drawn up at the dozens of meetings they had held since the Camp David summit.

THAT AFTERNOON WE HELD A MEETING of the Israeli team back at the Princess Hotel. The few guests there wished us success, and we felt that something had indeed moved. Each of us summarized his work and feelings, and most of us believed that it really was the Palestinians' intention to go forward. The consent to draft a document was a sign of their serious intentions and a gateway of hope.

Then one of our security officers came in with a note, which he handed to Shlomo Ben-Ami. We asked quickly if there had been a terror attack, and the look on his face made it obvious. By the time he said yes, we all already knew the answer.

Afterwards, the story became clear. Motti Dayan and Etgar Zeitouny, the owners of a restaurant called Yuppies, on Tel Aviv's trendy Sheinkin Street, had decided to go to Tulkarm to purchase flowerpots, despite the prohibition against Israelis entering the territories of the Palestinian Authority. They went with an Israeli Arab friend, Fuad Abu Hussein, and after they had bought what they wanted, they sat down to eat at a local restaurant. Their presence became known in town, and some masked men came in, took the two Jews away, and let the Arab go. They led the two outside the town and shot them in cold blood.

Hate and the desire for revenge had risen to new heights. At one time it was a lynching, at another it was a blood feud. Hate feeds hate and revenge always opens circles—it never closes them. And now, were we to be punished twice? Once, because innocent Israelis had been killed, and again, because we would be forced to cut short what was perhaps the last chance to put an end to this ongoing nightmare?

We interrupted the staff meeting and gathered as a smaller group—Ben-Ami, Lipkin-Shahak, Sher, and me—in Ben-Ami's suite, in order to discuss the issue among ourselves and to call the Prime Minister. Shlomo was a bit ashamed of the luxurious suite he had been given, which was reminiscent of the living quarters in a Maharajah's palace—lots of red, heavy wood, and dim lighting. The need to discontinue the talks following the cruel murder derived from the customary practice in such cases. But, we asked ourselves, is this the right thing to do? Stopping the talks now would be the greatest reward for those who wanted this cycle of blood to continue. And even if we paused for only a day, we would lose the great momentum we had achieved in the last two days, and to begin again would be difficult, there was no doubt about that.

Barak was on the line. We pressed the loudspeaker button, and his voice sounded tired. We told him about the progress, and the drafting. But he was not sufficiently impressed; he asked that we stop the talks and take the next plane home. Our persuasive ability was, apparently, limited. I felt that this decision had predetermined the fate of the talks even if they were to continue.

WE PACK OUR BAGS. Negotiators must be expert in this field as well. We say our goodbyes to our Palestinian partners by telephone. We ask them to stay in Taba, although we are not sure, at this moment, if we will be able to come back. The technical staff remains at the Princess Hotel in case the talks are resumed. We fly to Tel Aviv and return, after two days away, to the reality of Israel in January 2001—Intifada, elections, bewilderment, and anger.

Wednesday in Jerusalem. The funerals of the two victims are postponed till Thursday. At a meeting with the Prime Minister we report to him on the progress at Taba. He listens, and it is hard to interpret his reaction. He has not yet decided whether or not to continue the talks. I use this day in Jerusalem for urgent meetings at the Ministry of Justice, for updates on what is happening in the Ministry of Religious Affairs, of which I am also now in charge. I also meet with the elections staff for the Arab sector, at which all the participants repeat the same conclusion: Only an agreement with the Palestinians will lead the Israeli Arabs to vote for Barak. If there is no agreement, only replacing Barak will bring them out of their homes.

During the day, we call our negotiating partners, who have been sitting around at the Taba Hilton, not knowing what to do. Some of them are inclined to just get up and leave. The others, more experienced, attempt to calm them down. By nightfall, the anticipated decision is made—the talks will resume after the funerals, with the aim of completing them on Sunday or Monday. Barak asks us not to come north over the weekend but to stay for informal talks. A good sign.

The two funerals are held on Thursday morning. At noon we return to Eilat. Yossi Sarid joins us. We unpack. I prepare the materials I had collected a day earlier in my library on the refugee issue: updated figures, various proposals for solutions, booklets, some ten or fifteen years old, some new, addressing the origin of the problem and different rehabilitation options. We hold a plenary session and then disperse to committees.

Questions are raised when we address various models for establishing an international organization for rehabilitating refugees: Which countries should participate? Should each participant take part in financing the solutions? Can a decision be vetoed? Will there be political representatives in the organization or will it be solely a professional entity? To what extent will the new entity be controlled by the fund? After all, the fund will have enormous influence due to the vast amounts of capital flowing through it. The longer the discussion goes on, the more questions we discover that need to be answered in order to design an orderly model to resolve the problem of the refugees; and we attempt, together, to move from layer to layer, to outline the problems and what has to be done to resolve them.

At first glance, this part of the discussions begins in a healthy atmosphere, all of us heading down to the beach to wave to a boat filled with Peace Now activists, taking real encouragement from the high expectations placed on us by the peace camp. Nevertheless, something has snapped. The break was long, and it seems to have stopped the momentum that began a few days earlier. Our Palestinian partners express their shock at the murder of the two Israelis. But they find it difficult to understand why, in their view, we always play into the hands of those who want to sabotage the talks—a single shot by an extremist suddenly prevents the possibility of a cease-fire. If hope had been momentarily kindled on Tuesday, it was almost gone by the time we returned on Thursday.

There are no Jewish guests at the Taba Hilton. I take the elevator down with an Arab Israeli family from Majdal Khrum. They shake my hand warmly and express their hope that the talks will succeed. Between the third and the second floors, and before it is too late, I try to give them some election propaganda, and ask them to vote on February 6. "Only if there is peace," the woman says. "As it is, we will not give our vote to Barak. We can't."

Back in Eilat, the Princess Hotel begins to fill up with local tourists. Employee groups, young couples, families with small children. A representative sample. Those who want to encourage us give us the "thumbs up." The objectors hiss, "Don't sell out everything." The majority, though, are silent. This is the first election campaign that I wish would never end. Every passing day brings us closer to the inevitable close.

On the news we hear that the Supreme Court has decided that negotiations with the Palestinians may continue. A sigh of relief. But a short time later there is another attack. An Israeli, Akiva Pashkos, a forty-seven-year-old father of six, is murdered by gunfire in his car in the vicinity of Atarot, Jerusalem. Of course, we are boiling at the repeated cruelty. But we must ask ourselves, should the reward for the murder be both the death of the victim and the cessation of the talks? We convene again, the members of the Israeli team, in Ben-Ami's suite and talk with Barak. This time we all believe we should not return northwards and that if we stop the talks this time as well, it will be the end of them, for all intents and purposes. The Prime Minister agrees with us, and the talks continue.

UP UNTIL FRIDAY EVENING WE CONDUCTED TALKS in the various committees. In the committee on refugee issues the four young people went far beyond the level of detail we had hoped for in the framework agreement, but we did not prevent them from doing so. In this type of negotiation, the real issue for each side is its true interest. Often it is a purely economic question, similar to buying futures on the capital market. At Taba we had to ask certain questions: Is it preferable for Israel to announce in advance the sum it is willing to contribute as compensation for the refugees? Or would it be better not to indicate a specific amount, on the assumption that the evaluation formula will be balanced?

Although we were dealing with mathematical details at this stage, it was fascinating because each side had to now ask itself what it really wanted—

beyond the obvious fact that the Palestinian leadership wanted to announce to the world that every refugee had the right to return to his home, while the Israeli side wanted to announce that no Palestinian refugee would be allowed to enter the borders of Israel.

I was beginning to believe that the problem was much more easily resolved than had been imagined, and that on the majority of questions it was possible, immediately or in the near future, to come to terms. The stronger this sense became, the greater—for me, and perhaps the other Israelis—my anger at the Palestinian leadership. For so many years they had prevented a solution to the refugee problem, had perpetuated the camps, encouraged the countries of the world not to offer immigration quotas for refugees. A second and third generation of people had grown up in the Arab world, saying that they were from Jaffa or Haifa, when everyone knew that they had never actually been to either place; instead of decent living condtions, they dwelled in the harsh poverty and squalor of the refugee camps. It is the very fact that the refugee problem is so central to the Israeli-Palestinian dispute, and the fact that without a resolution there will be no end to the dispute, that enables us today to tackle it properly, responsibly, and morally, and to enable millions of people to live better lives.

As soon as Shabbat began on Friday night our activity was relocated to the Princess Hotel. A cold wind, almost a storm, kept us away from the balcony, and we continued our work inside our rooms. Our guests came to the evening Shabbat meal very elegantly dressed, and sat with us in a corner allocated for the negotiators in the hotel's dining room. We all wore *kippot*, someone recited Kiddush, the wine cup was passed among us all, the Challah bread was broken and the pieces distributed. Everyone was very serious during the short ceremonial moments. Later, in sight of many local tourists, a long conversation ensued about what Arafat had said to someone, and what Rabin had said to someone else, and what had transpired at Oslo.

After the meal, and until midnight, we continued the committee meetings. These were seemingly informal discussions but real progress was, in fact, being made in them, and when we renewed the talks on Shabbat morning, still in Eilat, we had already concluded a draft solution for the refugee problem as part of the framework agreement. With smiles we said that if we were left here until Monday, we would produce a full permanent agreement. With smiles, because we knew very well that quite a few months of hard work remained before that milestone.

At the conclusion of Shabbat we were called to a joint meeting of the heads of committees at the Taba Hilton, ahead of the press conference which would summarize and end the week of negotiations. Only when we convened at this stage was it possible to determine, for the first time, what had really been accomplished at Taba in four days of discussions under the direction of Shlomo Ben-Ami and Abu Ala. On the territorial issue, the principles of the Clinton Plan had been adopted. The Palestinians had proposed that Israel annex 3.1 percent but, they told us explicitly in side talks, eventually the annexation would consist of three settlement blocs, and it would be at least four percent. Israel had demanded to annex eight percent, but two of these on lease, so therefore the real argument concerned two percent, approximately 110 square kilometers. The solution was written on the wall. The principle of exchange of territory had also been agreed upon.

As for Jerusalem, here also the parties' willingness was emerging—to accept the Clinton Plan, to agree that the Israeli neighborhoods in East Jerusalem would be part of Jewish Jerusalem, that the Arab neighborhoods would be part of the Palestinian al-Quds, that the Temple Mount would remain under Palestinian control and the Western Wall would remain under Israeli control. The matter of sovereignty over the holy places remained open, lingering somewhere between the Clinton proposal and internationalization.

On security issues it was agreed that the parties would work together in the struggle against terrorism, and on regional and security cooperation. The Palestinians were willing to have an international presence in the Jordan Valley, a non-militarized Palestinian state, and the construction of three Israeli warning stations. The issues of deployment in emergencies and questions connected with air space were not finalized, and were left to be discussed by a team of security experts.

On the refugees issue—which was the only one on which drafts had been exchanged—consent was formulated on the development of events, and almost full agreement was reached with respect to principles for resolving the problem. The financial compensation by Israel was left for the permanent agreement stage, while reference to the number of refugees that Israel would be ready to accept remained symbolically to be assessed by the leaders.

The parties' joint announcement, which had been given to the journalists, radiated optimism without revealing anything about the content of the talks. It said, among other things, that there was no precedent to these talks, with their positive atmosphere and each side's mutual willingness to respond to the other's national, security, and local needs. Circumstances and the troubled times did not allow for an understanding on all issues, despite the significant progress achieved on many subjects.

"The sides," said the announcement, "declare that they have never been closer to reaching an agreement and it is thus our shared belief that the remaining gaps can be bridged with the resumption of negotiations following the Israeli elections." There was a commitment to implement the Sharm el-Sheikh understandings of October 2000, and reference to the Clinton Plan and the parties' comments about it as the basis for solutions presented on the four issues discussed—refugees, security, boundaries, and Jerusalem.

At the end of the announcement there was a reference to the impending elections, stating that this is what had prevented full agreement on all issues:

In light of the significant progress in narrowing their differences, the two sides are convinced that in a short period of time and given an intensive effort and the acknowledgment of the essential and urgent nature of reaching an agreement, it will be possible to bridge the remaining differences and attain a permanent settlement of peace between them . . . The two sides are confident that they can begin and move forward in this process at the earliest practical opportunity . . . We leave Taba in a spirit of hope and mutual achievement, acknowledging that the foundations have been laid both in reestablishing mutual confidence and in having progressed in a substantive engagement on all core issues.

But when Abu Ala was presenting to the heads of the committees his planned remarks for the beginning of the press conference, and came to the matter of the refugees, he suggested: "On the refugee issue it is better for me to state that we demanded the right of return and that you, the Israelis, refused." Nabil Sha'ath and I almost leaped from our seats, shouting: "Not true!" and asked him to report the enormous progress that had taken place, including a way to present the subject that would not be detrimental to either side. Abu Ala did not accept our position, and even added—as if he were an experienced politician speaking to a layman—"It is also good for you!" It was as if he was saying to me, "Why should you get embroiled right before the elections in an agreement with us on the refugee issue? It is better for each side to stick to its own position."

We could not dissuade him, and he did indeed emphasize this in his statement at the press conference held in the large hall on the ground floor of the hotel. The impression created among the reporters was that even here, in the best of talks, in which the parties had come close to each other and had resolved almost all the disputed issues, the Palestinians still claimed for themselves full implementation of what was in their eyes the right of return of the Palestinian refugees into sovereign Israel, a position which no Zionist could accept. It followed, of course, that a permanent agreement would therefore be impossible, whatever the solutions to all the other problems.

Thus, the issue on which there had been the greatest consensus became a symbol of the inability to reach a solution, even with Israel governed by a "dovish" administration. The press conference did not help public perceptions: An Israeli journalist quipped that, based on the conclusions, everything that had occurred at Taba was just *harta*, meaning nonsense— and Mohammed Dahlan, who was standing next to him, said with a smile that it was *harta barta*, double nonsense, which within seconds became the slogan of the week in the media. Dahlan managed to insert a clarification on a remote page of one of the newspapers, in which he said that Taba constituted the greatest progress since the commencement of the peace process, and that anyone trying to turn his lighthearted statement into his position regarding the talks was completely wrong. But it was a pathetic attempt to change the impression he had created.

The talks at Taba were stopped on Saturday night, January 27, because Shlomo Ben-Ami and Abu Ala agreed that it would be difficult to reach further breakthroughs at that juncture. It was resolved that the talks would continue in a more limited framework over the next two days, ahead of a possible summit meeting between Barak and Arafat in Sweden on the thirtieth, both in order to endeavor to adopt a number of resolutions attainable only at such a level, and in order to conclude how and when the talks would continue should Barak win the elections.

But a series of events prevented the summit. First of all, Clinton's absence was prominent. At this critical stage, he could have appeared in person, or—if he was worried about interfering in the Israeli election process—he could have sent Madeleine Albright. But he was no longer available. The Swedes themselves became hesitant about holding the summit. And then on Sunday, Shimon Peres and Yasser Arafat appeared before a large audience at Davos, and after Peres's speech, Arafat issued a poisonous attack on the Israeli government. He accused Israel of using nonconventional weapons and deliberate economic suffocation, in language reminiscent of the pre-Oslo Arafat. The surprised members of his entourage would later explain that his statements for the Davos conference had been prepared and filed away well in advance, while Gaza was under attack by IAF helicopters, a long time before the Clinton Plan and the Taba talks, and that nobody had taken the trouble to return to the file and update the speech. But whatever the explanation, the irreversible impression had been created that Arafat was not prepared for a reconciliatory summit meeting.

Barak was stunned by the speech and the tone with which it was presented. In an interview with Emanuel Rosen, a reporter from Israel's Channel 2, Arafat attempted to correct himself, and expressed his desire to reach an agreement, but this could not soften the harsh impression he had made. Barak said that he would not meet with Arafat in light of the Davos speech, but later decided not to close the door on the summit.

On Monday, Arye Hershkovitz, a resident of the Ofra settlement, was murdered on the road near Atarot. On Tuesday, there would be no summit, but perhaps it would take place on Thursday, February 1. I spoke on the phone with the late Swedish Foreign Minister, Anna Lindh. The Swedes were now concerned about interfering in the elections. They believed that perhaps there should be a Swedish invitation for a meeting in Egypt. By Thursday, no invitation to a summit had been received. On Thursday itself, two Israelis were killed: Lior Atiya, of Afula, was murdered close to Jenin, when he came to collect his car from the garage where he had left it to be repaired, while Dr. Shmuel Gillis, a physician at the Hadassah Hospital, was shot on the way to his home in Gush Etzion. Barak announced that there would be no summit meeting with Arafat. But even if he had not ruled it out, it was not likely to happen.

In retrospect, the Taba talks damaged the electoral campaign. This meeting in particular, which had succeeded in bridging so many gaps, was nevertheless perceived by the majority of the Jewish electorate as further proof, on the surface, that even great concessions couldn't lead to an agreement. The majority of the Arab voters, for their part, did not consider the conclusion of the talks as close enough to an agreement to justify voting. Many believed that if it had been possible to sign a framework agreement before the elections, the public would have given its consent, so the sense that the target had been missed was now exacerbated. There was also the perception that the last-minute talks had been illegitimate, only compounding the voters' great disappointment with Barak following the outbreak of the Intifada.

It was the chronicle of a defeat foretold. Nobody spoke seriously about our prospects of winning. On Monday night, at midnight, seven hours before the polling stations opened, Barak asked me to come to his residence in Jerusalem. We sat alone in his living room, and I could not avoid the sense that this would probably be our last meeting here. He was encouraging, even smiling. He did not ask me about the Arab vote. He already knew that this vote would not be his. He wanted to discuss the advantages and disadvantages of joining a national unity government headed by Sharon immediately after the elections, and he wanted me to forget, for a moment, my own objections to doing that.

I looked at this man, whose face revealed nothing about what he was well aware awaited him on the morrow. We had been close friends since 1984, when he was the youthful head of the Intelligence Branch and I was the government secretary. I had been among those who encouraged him to enter politics. We faced off against each other in 1997 for leadership of the Labor Party, and he won. Afterwards there was rivalry but also a renewed closeness, though it never quite returned to the way of our first years of friendship. He came to the office of Prime Minister with a broad coalition and the intention to bring peace within fifteen months. But after fifteen months he was left with no government and no peace, and was facing the Palestinian Intifada. He left Lebanon bravely, and people were angry that the exit from this superfluous eighteen-year occupation did not end in military marches. He made important political decisions, maintained his position in the economic field, and knew how to fight for peace with a "killer" instinct, as Yitzhak Ben-Aharon, the Labor Party elder statesman, said when he backed Barak to be Prime Minister. But now, on the night of the great battle, Barak was already drafting his letter conceding defeat.

It is not every day that a man like Ehud Barak is born. Although mature, he hid within himself a curious, lively small child. He is a complex person: breaking open locks, dismantling clocks, a book lover, a piano player, a charmer with a knowledge of mathematics, a great hero with tremendous ambition and a sense of humor, truly family- and friendship-oriented, a believer in utilitarianism and Zionism and a little hedonism, with a short fuse sometimes, and an amazing ability to absorb harsh criticism quietly, but without forgetting the critic. In him remained the former Kibbutznik: Suits always looked somewhat artificial on him; he was very direct—lacking in diplomacy and manners—but ready to embrace the most difficult tasks without fanfare. He was chronically late—this feature was stronger than him. Even the President of the United States had to wait for him. Barak did not usually apologize for this, as if everyone knew of his weakness and would forgive him for it. For the first time in history, no government meeting began on time. Some of the compulsively punctual ministers still came to the conference room every Sunday morning at 9:00 a.m., but everyone knew that Barak would not arrive before 9:20. Then he would march quickly to his seat and urge his colleagues with a statement like, "We have to start work, there are many issues on the agenda and only 128 hours until the Sabbath begins . . ."

He told me that the state of Israel was about to make a terrible mistake the next day, and that we should not give up by refusing to join the government. "Forget it," I said to him. "If Sharon sets up a government, it will be best to expose its futility as early as possible. It will never have a solution for peace, or for security. It is populism riding on the wave of violence. And if we are there with Sharon, we will turn this experiment from an episode into an ongoing phenomenon, and we will be unable to offer any alternative. The people love a national unity government, but we will hate ourselves for joining it. A national unity government can find itself responsible for the most dangerous and immoral decisions, because it has no brakes. We must not play the role of second driver."

AT NIGHT AFTER THE ELECTIONS, I appeared on television as they broadcast the exit polls. I had agreed to this in advance, in an attempt to immediately present a message opposing the unity government. In the end, Sharon won with a margin of 62.5 percent against 37.4 percent for Barak, with the lowest turnout since the establishment of the state—only 62 percent. From the Channel 2 studio I drove to Kibbutz Shefayim, where a party was being held for Barak in the events hall. I came into a place crowded with media representatives from all over the world, which looked at first glance like the winner's camp, save for the tears glinting here and there on the cheeks of young activists. The Labor Youth gave their rallying cry: *"Ho! Ha! Who goes there, the next Prime Minister,"* along with other optimistic chants. There were balloons and posters and banners proclaiming: *Ehud.*

I was standing next to the stage when Ehud Barak arrived. Defeat was not visible on his face, which looked exactly as it had the night before. He made his speech, expressing support for the establishment of a national unity government and announcing his resignation from the party leadership and the Knesset. Twenty stormy, fascinating, strange months ended on that night. I could not find the strength to push into the circle closing in to shake the hand of the outgoing Prime Minister.

CHAPTER 11
THE EIGHTH DAY OF TABA . . . IN GENEVA

AFTER THE TABA TALKS IN 2001, Yasser Abed Rabbo and I met in Atarot, near the northern edge of East Jerusalem, at the offices of *Al-Quds*, a Palestinian daily. We both felt strongly that an opportunity had been missed. Others who had participated in the talks—Israelis and Palestinians—believed that Taba was a kind of *fata morgana*, and that there had been no real chance of reaching an understanding. Abed Rabbo and I were sure that additional talks under the same intensive framework, for just a few more weeks, could have culminated in an agreement. We wanted to prove that it was possible, that there was both a partnership and a plan for peace, so we decided to continue together the work that had been halted at Taba.

Those days were exceptionally demoralizing. The violence persisted and grew even worse. After Ariel Sharon was elected Prime Minister, the Intifada entered a new and more violent phase, with the first suicide bombing since the start of the uprising.

To the Israeli public, electing Sharon was a way of punishing Arafat; it was obvious that the chances of returning to the political process, headed by Arafat, were now very slim. The Labor Party joined Sharon in a national unity government that included elements of the extreme right. I, however, refused to join the Sharon government.

Abed Rabbo is one of the most exceptional members of the Palestinian leadership. Born in Jaffa in 1945, he completed his studies at Cairo University. He has surprisingly fond memories of the Six-Day War: His final examinations at the university were held on June 5, 1967, and all students who sat their exams that day were automatically awarded degrees when the war broke out. He is a professional politician who has never been involved in the PLO's military operations. As a young and enthusiastic socialist and Palestinian nationalist, he worked with Dr. George Habash to establish the Popular Front for the Liberation of Palestine in late 1967. Less than two years later he left the organization, believing it to be insufficiently Marxist, and became second in command to Naif Hawatmeh in the Democratic Front for the Liberation of Palestine.

After 1973, he represented the Democratic Front on the PLO's Operations Committee and served as the Chairman of the PLO's Information Department. He built an independent status for himself with the PLO, developed connections within the Communist bloc, particularly in the U.S.S.R., and distanced himself from his partner, Hawatmeh, eventually leaving the Democratic Front to establish his own movement.

Abed Rabbo became known outside the PLO after heading a delegation at the December 1988 talks with Robert Pelletreau, the U.S. ambassador to Tunisia. The talks did not last long, but Abed Rabbo, who for decades had been involved with internal matters, had become the PLO's representative to the outside world and embarked upon a new career as a negotiator.

By the late 1980s, he had expressed unreserved support for a two-state solution, based on the 1967 borders and a demilitarized Palestinian state. When the Palestinian Authority was established, he moved with his family from Tunis to Ramallah and became the Palestinian Minister of Information and Culture. He has been involved in all the negotiations since the Oslo Agreement, and was even appointed Chairman of the Palestinian delegation in the talks on the permanent status agreement. Since Abed Rabbo is not a "Fatah" man (Arafat's Party), he is not considered to be a candidate for the leadership of the Palestinian Authority, and perhaps it is precisely for this reason that he has developed a good relationship with Arafat, even though Abed Rabbo is well-known for his willingness to criticize the man.

Shortly after we began to meet, Abed Rabbo brought Nabil Kassis and Ghaith Al-Omari along with him to the talks. Kassis, like Abed Rabbo, is not a Fatah man. Born in Ramallah, where he has lived for his entire life, he is a professor of nuclear physics. He studied in East Germany and speaks fluent German. A Christian, he served as the Vice President of Birzeit University and was appointed as head of the Bethlehem 2000 Project. At a later stage, he joined the government as Minister of Tourism, and subsequently became Minister of Planning. Unlike Abed Rabbo, Kassis is not a politician in any shape or form. He is considered a professional and a man of precision; he concentrates on the details, hates negligence, and rarely smiles. Ghaith Al-Omari, a young lawyer, served as a legal advisor to the Palestinian negotiators. He studied in England, and participated in the talks at Camp David and Taba. Since it looked as though he would not be particularly busy with official negotiations in the near future, he was pleased to join the Palestinian side in the talks with me. I was accompanied by Daniel Levy, my political advisor, who had come to live in Israel from Britain after completing his M.A. and serving as Chairman of the World Union of Jewish Students. During his military service in Israel, he was involved in negotiations following the Oslo talks, and after his discharge he joined the Economic Cooperation Foundation.

For a long period of time, this group worked intensively on the draft agreement. We were later joined by Dr. Samih Abed, PA Deputy Minister of Planning, and Colonel (Res.) Shaul Arieli; they worked to prepare the maps. Shaul Arieli was commander of the Northern Brigade in the Gaza Strip at the time that the IDF withdrew in 1993, and since then he has been closely monitoring all stages of the negotiations. During Ehud Barak's term as Prime Minister, he headed the Peace Administration, which coordinated the negotiations between Israel and the Palestinians. He remained in the army for some time after the Taba talks came to an end, but following his discharge he appeared at my office. He told me that he identified with my political views: He believed it was possible to reach a permanent status agreement and he was willing to help, if there was any need for him. When I told him about the talks underway, he joined forces with us.

At first we met in Ramallah. It was not yet illegal for Israelis to travel to

Area A—the zone under Palestinian control—and I would request approval from the army each time I wanted to enter the West Bank. But after a few months, following protests by right-wingers who petitioned the High Court of Justice, I was no longer given permission to enter. Before we could even begin to deal with the problems and challenges of the negotiations themselves, we were forced to contend with many such practical obstacles.

We met with Arafat on three occasions, and he expressed tremendous interest in our project and encouraged us to continue. At my last meeting with him, in New York in November 2001, we did not discuss the details of the talks, but he conveyed his awareness of the proceedings. Key figures in Israel, the United States, Russia, and the European Union were informed of our activities, and almost everyone encouraged us to complete our project and to present to the world a signed draft permanent status agreement, with appendices that would be completed after the signing.

In July 2001, we expanded our circle of support without exposing our project prematurely. A respectable group of Israelis and Palestinians, comprised of both politicians and intellectuals, assembled together at the border between Ramallah and Jerusalem to sign a document that established the principles for the permanent status agreement. The document had been prepared by Daniel Levy and Ghaith Al-Omari under the supervision of Abed Rabbo and myself, and it was more detailed than similar documents used in prior negotiations. We gained the support of many, both inside Israel and abroad, when a joint declaration was published in the Israeli and Palestinian press—though not a single word was mentioned about the simultaneous work on the detailed permanent status agreement.

Determined to breathe new life into the peace camp on both sides, and determined to prove to each side that a partner for peace still existed, Abed Rabbo and I established the Israeli-Palestinian Peace Coalition in January 2002. A forum that included public figures, politicians, and intellectuals who worked, both together and separately, to influence public opinion on both sides, the Peace Coalition held meetings, published joint notices, and arranged discussions with visitors from abroad. The Peace Coalition was, in those days, practically the only group that could show the world that Israelis and Palestinians were capable of working together, with a joint aim, and against the surrounding background of despair and violence. Our meetings and activities generated great interest around the world; in the summer of 2002, the Peace Coalition received the Friedrich Ebert Foundation Award from German Foreign Minister Joschka Fischer. Fischer, like Kofi Annan, Russian Foreign Minister Igor Ivanov, and Javier Solana, the European Union Foreign Policy Chief, knew that our key project was not just the joint lobby for peace, but the preparation of a comprehensive draft agreement.

THE INVITATION I RECEIVED in the summer of 2001 from Professor Pierre Alain of the University of Geneva seemed no different from the others that regularly arrive at my office. I was asked to present a comprehensive paper on "A Just Peace" at a large conference in Geneva in October, at which Edward Said would also be speaking. I deliberated over attending; the subject was interesting and important to me, but work on the paper and the trip itself were sure to cost valuable time. I could not have imagined then what would emerge as a result of this conference.

Some two thousand participants came to the large auditorium at the University of Geneva and many others watched the conference on closed-circuit TV. Edward Said, in his presentation, argued that there was no point in peace if it violated justice. I contended that while the quest for justice is infinite, the deferral of peace until justice can be achieved is the least just thing in the world, particularly for those forced to pay with their lives in the meantime.

I was introduced in Geneva to Dr. Alexis Keller, a tall young man with a Ph.D. in the Philosophy of Science, and I learned that he had been responsible for my invitation to the conference. Alexis had read my books and articles published in English, and decided he wanted to help me make peace. There was something naïve about his approach—it was simultaneously very fair and honest. He promised professional assistance and the provision of services to future negotiators, and he amazed me with his in-depth knowledge of the details of recent negotiations with the Palestinians. He also told me about his family, a family of Swiss bankers, and about his Jewish grandmother on his father's side and his Lebanese wife. We agreed to work together, and a few weeks later there was a trilateral meeting in Geneva between Alexis, Abed Rabbo, and myself.

We had lunch with Alexis's father, a former Swiss diplomat of the Swiss Foreign Ministry who had become a successful banker, and he expressed great interest in helping us complete a draft agreement. The Swiss assistance, which had fallen into our laps, was to be critical to the success of the project.

Over the next year, 2002, intensive work was put into the preparation of the draft. Ghaith Al-Omari and Daniel Levy spent a week at Keller's home in Geneva with Robert Malley, a member of the U.S. National Security Council staff and a former advisor to President Clinton on the Middle East peace process, and together they resolved many of the most significant difficulties. Later in the year, when meetings between Israelis and Palestinians became impossible with Operation Defensive Shield underway, Keller came to the region to shuttle messages from one side to the other. One of Keller's meetings with Abed Rabbo, at the latter's home in Ramallah, was conducted with the barrel of a tank aimed at his balcony. Shaul Arieli and Samih Abed worked on the maps, according to our instructions, and in May 2002 the agreement started to take shape.

We tried to take advantage of every time the Palestinians were given permission to leave the country to attend a conference outside the region—the Israelis would travel to the same destination and a meeting would be held. In this way, for example, we traveled to a conference at Weston Park, two hours away from London, hosted by *The Guardian*. Israelis and Palestinians took part in the conference together with Catholic and Protestant representatives from Northern Ireland, while simultaneously, Abed Rabbo and I, with the two draftsmen, completed additional sections of our agreement.

IT WAS TIME TO BEGIN BUILDING OUR COALITIONS. At the outset of our work, we had agreed on two principles: The talks would culminate with a signed document and the project would not be confined to a small group of negotiators, but instead would involve a large coalition on each side. I held conversations with dozens of people in 2002, aiming to secure their participation, and I was surprised to find nearly all of them willing to take part; I am convinced that many others, whom I did not reach, would also have been pleased to join. Retired senior figures in the security establishment began to recommend one another, and an encouraging picture emerged. Senior officers, many of whom had taken jobs in the private sector, held views on resolving the conflict very similar to my own; some even remarked they had "overtaken me a long time ago."

The Israeli side of the coalition grew to include Amnon Lipkin-Shahak, the former army Chief of Staff who had been my colleague in the government and at the Taba talks; Brigadier-General (Res.) Gideon Sheffer, former head of the Manpower Branch and former Deputy Air Force Commander; Shlomo Brom, who served in the Planning Branch as a Brigadier-General and is currently a Senior Research Associate at the Jaffee Center for Strategic Studies, Tel Aviv University; Brigadier-General (Res.) Giora Inbar, former Commander of the IDF Liaison Unit to Lebanon; Brigadier-General (Res.) Doron Kadmiel, former Chief Artillery Officer; David Kimche, former Director General of the Ministry of Foreign Affairs and previously deputy head of the Mossad; authors Zvia Greenfield, Amos Oz, and David Grossman; economists and businessmen Professor Aryeh Arnon, Avi Shaked, and Yoram Gabai, former head of the Public Income Department at the Ministry of Finance; Dr. Menachem Klein, Dr. Ron Pundak, and others.

During a visit to the United States back in October 2001, I had met with former President Jimmy Carter at his center in Georgia. We knew each other from several previous meetings, and I have always admired the major part he played in the Camp David Accords in 1978 and in the peace with Egypt the following year. When he asked me if I was involved in talks with the Palestinians, I told him the story of the "Eighth Day of Taba," our attempt to complete the talks that began in January 2001. He grabbed my hand with excitement and said, "I am with you. If you want my participation, you've got it, whenever you want. I have no doubt that the work can be completed."

We kept Carter informed of developments in the negotiations, and he provided encouragement when difficulties arose. And arise they did; above all, we were still hampered by trouble with establishing a regular location to meet. Most of our meetings were held at the offices of the World Bank, near the A-Ram checkpoint between Jerusalem and Ramallah. It was the northernmost point the Israelis could reach from Jerusalem, and the southernmost point the Palestinians—with permission—could travel from Ramallah. But as the coalition grew, more and more crossing permits were needed for the Palestinian side, and difficulty obtaining them led to the cancellation of many meetings. The deteriorating security situation—terrorist attacks and Israeli retaliations—made the granting of permits even rarer. It was hard not to feel that at precisely those times when a real breakthrough was imminent, terrorist attacks would occur, as if deliberately, to stall our progress. One day, under a torrential downpour, Abed Rabbo and I were forced to sit together in a car at the Qalandia checkpoint reviewing documents, because there was simply no other place to meet.

When the text was almost ready, I informed Carter, who asked to see the agreement. A few days later he was awarded the Nobel Peace Prize. Daniel Levy flew to Georgia to show him the document, and he complimented the solutions we had devised. Carter suggested that he announce our project at the prize ceremony in Oslo on December 11, 2002, and then come to Sweden the next day to participate in a grand ceremony to launch the agreement, under the auspices of the Swedish government. I discussed this idea with the late Swedish Foreign Minister Anna Lindh, and she promised me government support and a massive event on the day requested by Carter.

But this did not come to pass. On November 19, Haifa Mayor Amram Mitzna was elected leader of Israel's Labor Party and the party's candidate for Prime Minister in the upcoming January 2003 elections. Amnon Lipkin-Shahak suggested I meet with Mitzna to inform him of our plan, so that he would not be presented with a *fait accompli*. I had supported Mitzna in the elections, in which his opponents sometimes claimed he was no more than "Beilin with a beard." I had told him about the existence of the project months earlier, but he knew nothing about the contents of the agreement itself.

Amnon and I met with Mitzna two days after his election and we brought him the agreement, which was still in progress. We did not ask for his direct support, but we told him that if he felt our plan might damage his election campaign, we would defer the event. Even though his election as leader of the Labor Party greatly enhanced the party's status, it was not sufficient to bring about victory, and his loss in the general elections was already written on the wall. We thought that the announcement of our agreement could transform the positions of the peace camp into a more tangible proposition, and Mitzna agreed. He was enthusiastic about the idea, but he asked us to present the paper to some of his advisors. Almost all of them, unfortunately, recommended that he not become involved in such a far-reaching project. I was extremely disappointed: After two years of Intifada, of horrific bloodshed, with the peace camp wounded and withered, seemingly wall-to-wall support for Sharon, and a national consensus that there was "no one to talk to" on the other side, I believed it was imperative to present an alternative. We had to resume the public debate, to show that there was a partner for peace and to rekindle hope. But I informed Carter and the Palestinians that the elections had forced us to delay the event; I did not anticipate then that the delay would be nearly an entire year.

A short time after the Israeli elections, in February 2003, we convened the first large-scale meeting of both sides in Woking, about two hours outside of London. The meeting was held under Japanese sponsorship, with Alexis Keller and a representative of President Carter observing the discussions. The British government was aware of our meeting, though it was not represented; Abed Rabbo and I had visited 10 Downing Street to meet with Prime Minister Blair's advisors and inform them of our efforts.

The Palestinians had come to England to attend a conference on Palestinian Authority reforms, and the permits they had obtained allowed them to stay and meet with us as well. We were sure that it would be a long time before such a forum would again be available, and we took advantage of every single minute of the weekend. We divided into small groups to work on specific areas: the text, the maps, and the security arrangements. Progress was made on various issues in the text, and senior members of the security establishment were able to sit with a Palestinian group to work out aspects of the security arrangements that had remained unresolved. The most important decision made in Woking regarding the territorial issues was the annexation of the Alfe Menashe settlement to Israel in return for the concession of Efrat, which was not part of the historical Gush Etzion settlement bloc, and is situated east of Road 60.

At the end of the Woking meeting, very few issues remained: three minor territorial problems, the wording of the refugee issue, and the problem of Palestinian prisoners. At this point, unfortunately, the signing was delayed by complications in the Palestinian Authority: the government resigned; a new government was established with Abu Mazen at its head as the first Palestinian Prime Minister; before long, he resigned as well, and a second government was established, headed by Abu Ala; all of this against a backdrop of violence. The process dragged on for many more months.

We were, however, able to take advantage of the extra time to expand the coalitions. Several members of the Knesset joined the Israeli group: Yuli Tamir and Avraham Burg from Labor; Haim "Jumes" Oron from Meretz; Etti Livni from Shinui; and former MK Nehama Ronen from Likud. Amram Mitzna came to see me to express his wish to join as well, and within a short time he was devoting nearly all of his energy to the project, and became one of the key figures on the Israeli side. Key Fatah figures joined the Palestinian coalition, including Qadoura Fares and Mohammed Horani. Their involvement was welcome, but it was far from simple. They demanded that Israel give up the settlements of Ma'ale Adumim or Givat Ze'ev in order to create space for the development of East Jerusalem, and that additional territory be transferred to establish a large settlement for Palestinian refugees. We explained that although their involvement was very important to us, we would not be able to meet these demands.

We succeeded in holding small-scale meetings at the A-Ram checkpoint and at a nearby hotel. Two meetings were conducted by video conference at times when it was impossible to meet face-to-face. (These meetings by video conference, in which we had to speak one person at a time, were particularly odd for Israelis and Palestinians, accustomed to a more animated culture of speaking.) After the video conferences, the wording of the section on the refugee issue was resolved. But it was clear that in order to bridge the remaining gaps, a marathon session of two or three more days would be required.

THE MEETING AT THE MOVENPICK HOTEL in Jordan, on the eastern shore of the Dead Sea, from October 9 to 12, 2003, was our last—but we did not realize this until it was over. It was filled with severe crises, sleepless nights, arguments, and touching moments. About twenty-five people took part on each side, and since it was the Jewish festival of Sukkot, many of the participants came with their wives and children. Personal conversations developed and relationships formed, as they often do at such meetings. At the plenary session, many told their personal stories and shared the ideological evolutions that had led to their participation in this encounter.

As in Woking, we were not alone. In addition to Alexis Keller, we were joined by two representatives of the Swiss government. A few months earlier, Abed Rabbo and I had met with Swiss Foreign Minister Micheline Calmy-Rey, and we had agreed that this would be called the Geneva Agreement; a closed meeting would be held at the end of negotiations at which we would agree on the remaining details and sign a letter entrusting the agreement to Calmy-Rey. A group comprised of Palestinians and Israelis would then explain the results to the decision-makers in Israel and the Palestinian Authority, and following this stage, the agreement would be made public. The meeting at the Movenpick Hotel was also attended by a representative of the Japanese government; a representative of the Jordanian government; an advisor to Marc Otte, the European Union's Middle East envoy; a representative of the Canadian government; a representative of Norway; and an advisor to Jimmy Carter. Occasionally, during moments of dispute and crisis, they assisted us by conveying messages or making mediation proposals.

It was a marathon meeting that none of us will ever forget. We asked ourselves repeatedly, "What is the chance of signing an agreement?" and the consensus was always about 50-50. On the morning of Sunday, October 12, shortly before the Allenby Bridge was to close for *Chol Hamo'ed* (the intermediary days of the festival of Sukkot)—which would prevent our returning to Israel—Abed Rabbo, Kassis, Mitzna, and I held a crucial meeting during a fierce dispute over the border within Jerusalem. The difference itself was over such a minor matter that it is not worth detailing here, but at official talks, as I told Abed Rabbo, such a disagreement might have sent everyone packing. The tension and stress, the lack of sleep, and the anger that had been gradually accumulating all erupted over this low-key issue. We could not make the same mistakes, I said, that we had ourselves criticized at past talks. We could not get trapped by such small details, not at this stage of the game. Abed Rabbo stood up. We shook hands and prepared for the moment of the signing.

As always, external constraints determined the internal decisions. At Camp David, our time had been cut short by President Clinton's trip to Okinawa for the G-8 Summit. In Jordan now, we were forced to shorten the signing ceremony so that we Israelis could cross the Allenby before it closed. Until the very last moment, we were not sure that everyone would sign; some of the participants on each side had implied that their signature was still uncertain. But in the end, all the attendees signed the letter to the Swiss Foreign Minister, while moving words were delivered and tears shed. Each side had struggled for three long days to attain an agreement to its own advantage, but there was a sense that these two groups had been transformed at the signing into *one group*; soon, this new coalition would face many opponents and nonbelievers. We would have to explain, as one group, that this paper could be the saving grace of both peoples, after so many years of bloody conflict.

Before we had left Jordan, the Geneva Agreement was in the headlines, and we returned to Israel at the center of a public storm.

THE FORMAT OF THE GENEVA AGREEMENT is by now well-known and can be read in its entirety in this book's appendix. The innovation was in the serious commitment of the negotiators and our willingness to discuss *final* deals, as well as in the new formulae devised for dividing the territory, in the role proposed for an international entity to keep the peace, and in the preliminary statements. Here, for instance, the right of the Jewish people to a state is, for the first time in such a document, fully affirmed.

The heart of the agreement is the concession of sovereignty over the Temple Mount to the Palestinians in exchange for Israeli sovereign discretion over the number of refugees admitted to Israel, with the rest free to settle in the Palestinian state. For many years, both parties had been clinging to *virtual* rights: Israel has never actually exercised its right of sovereignty over the Temple Mount, which since 1967 has been under the control of the Waqf, the Islamic trust that administers the site; on the other side, the "right of return" of Palestinian refugees to Israel was a concept that even the Palestinian leaders knew could never be realized. If a large number of refugees did seek to return to Israel, the state would no longer possess a Jewish majority; this would be tantamount to the establishment of two Palestinian states side by side. The two parties traded these virtual rights in the Geneva Agreement, and this logic will undoubtedly be the basis for any future agreement as well.

It is possible, of course, that the Geneva Agreement will never be implemented, that it will become just another set of papers gathering dust in the archives. But by 2010, when there is a Palestinian majority between the Jordan River and the Mediterranean Sea, it will be too late to revert to this plan. Geneva is perhaps the last opportunity to realize the Zionist dream.

CHAPTER 12
ON THIN ICE

O N FEBRUARY 25, 2000, French Prime Minister Lionel Jospin came on a visit to Israel, during which he was asked about Hezbollah's attacks on Israel's northern settlements. In his reply, he strongly criticized Hezbollah's use of terror to achieve political objectives. A day later, he went to Ramallah to speak to students at Bir Zeit University. They were angry at his remarks about Hezbollah, but they did not settle for expressing this verbally—when he left the building they pelted him with stones, and his bodyguards rushed him to his armored car, which was also stoned. On Saturday night, television networks around the world showed the Prime Minister of France covering his head with an open briefcase, running toward his car with security personnel and other panicky escorts. As usually happens in this type of situation, it became the symbol of his entire visit.

At that time, an Israeli-Palestinian seminar was being held in the Ministry of Justice on the issue of intellectual property. This may sound somewhat abstract, but it is actually a very real and serious matter. Israel is still considered one of the countries in which brand-name goods, records, and books are forged on a large scale, and in this field there is very close cooperation between Palestinian and Israeli offenders. As part of the dialogue between Ministers of Justice which I resumed after a long break upon my entering office, Friekh Abu-Medein and I had agreed to hold this seminar to encourage cooperation between the legal systems of Israel and the Palestinian Authority, with the participation of Ministry of Justice personnel, lawyers, and judges from both sides. We decided that the first day of the seminar would take place in a guest house at Ma'aleh HaHamisha near Jerusalem, while the second day would be held at the Grand Park Hotel in Ramallah.

The first session was on a Thursday, while the second was scheduled for Sunday, one day after the rain of stones fell on Jospin. After a discussion with the security personnel, who attempted to persuade us not to visit that sensitive place less than a day later, we arrived at the hotel in pouring rain and gray skies. From which faculty were the stone-throwing students? I asked Abu-Medein. He did not know. He inquired, and came back to me with a bashful smile: It was the law faculty.

God knows, I said in my opening remarks, why the true statements by the Prime Minister of France on Hezbollah's violence should cause law students at Bir Zeit to throw stones at him. But the cause is really not important: It was simply another reminder of the thin ice on which we are walking. Even when it looks to us like a solid floor, it is important not to tread heavily on it. The water is very close. These students can complete their studies, become lawyers, judges, or law professors, and in a few years they will participate in seminars on intellectual property or taxes or human rights. They might also be stone-throwers, as their older brothers were, or their parents in 1987, and could lapse into aimless violence out of a sense of national self-realization, hate, and revenge, and sacrifice their future. However, the future is in our hands, to a large extent. Any meeting, seminar, closer ties, any extension of contacts, will thicken the layer of ice and will make it less hazardous. This is true before signing a peace agreement, and will continue to be true after such an agreement is signed.

THIS IS THE STORY OF THE THIN ICE. It was almost broken one hour before the signing of the Declaration of Principles on September 13, 1993, when Israel insisted on signing the agreement with the Palestinian delegation to Washington, and the Palestinians insisted it should be signed with the

PLO—until it was decided that it would be signed with both. It was almost broken by the massacre perpetrated by Baruch Goldstein at the Cave of Machpelah in Hebron on February 25, 1994; it was almost broken on May 4, 1994, when Arafat refused to sign the Cairo Agreement on Gaza and Jericho, but finally reconsidered; it was almost broken when Yitzhak Rabin was assassinated on November 4, 1995; when four consecutive terror attacks occurred in Israel at the beginning of 1996; when Netanyahu opened the Wall Tunnel and blood was spilled on both sides in September 1996; on Nakba Day, as the Palestinians call it, in May 2000.

The ice was finally broken on September 29, 2000, after Sharon's provocative visit to the Temple Mount—not because the visit was any worse than all the other events, but because the ice was still thin, and we had not managed, despite all our efforts, to thicken it. Thickening the ice is the job of the peacemakers and believers, and when the ice breaks it is necessary to do everything to save ourselves from drowning. And afterwards, we must continue thickening the ice.

There is nothing more understandable than the desire to "expose" the reason for the Intifada, but there is also no chance of finding it. A cause we have certainly found, and perhaps if Sharon had not entered the Temple Mount, and if the Taba talks had been held in September or October 2000, it might have been possible to reach a framework agreement even before the elections in the United States. Perhaps if Sharon had not entered the Temple Mount, another event would have provided the spark that led to the new Intifada. There is a great difference between cause and reason, though. Sometimes, the absence of a cause prevents disaster, but we were never so lucky.

The Intifada seemed to reinforce the arguments of the right. After all, Barak had come with the best of intentions, had offered the Palestinians an excellent deal, and they not only rejected it, but they took advantage of a violent incident on the Temple Mount to breach the agreements they had signed, and then used weapons received with Israel's approval in order to strike at Israelis. Barak, the right says, did us a favor by revealing the true face of the Palestinians, and proved how correct we were all these years when we insisted, "There is nobody to talk with, and nothing to talk about." And further, the right-wingers say, in the course of the Intifada it has become clear how correct we were when we said that there is no real difference between the PLO and Hamas and Islamic Jihad, that these are different faces of the same Palestinian goal: to put an end to the existence of Israel, whether by the "salami" method—taking over territory "slice by slice"—or by means of terror and defamation.

But this is only an appearance. Against all the proposals raised by the peace camp since the Six-Day War—territorial compromise, recognition of the Palestinian people's right to self-determination, approval of a Palestinian state, willingness to consider the PLO a partner—the right-wing's position has always been that there is nobody to talk to on the Palestinian side, that relinquishing the eastern part of the land of Israel (that is, Jordan) was sufficient, and that there was no need to compromise on the western part of the land of Israel as well. In their view, only forceful insistence on our rights would ensure our survival.

The Oslo process was designed to create a responsible addressee on the Palestinian side, to separate the pragmatic groups from the fundamentalists, to present principles for a permanent solution, and to implement, over a five-year period, an interim agreement in a format almost identical to that agreed on at Camp David in 1978 between Menachem Begin's Israel and Anwar al-Sadat's Egypt. In the correspondence between them, the parties decided to recognize each other and put an end to the violence. Self-rule was granted to the Palestinians at a stage earlier than that proposed by the Camp David accords, but territory was transferred gradually, while under the Camp David agreements it was to have been implemented all at once.

The strong police force under Palestinian self-rule was also set up pursuant to the Camp David agreements, which dealt explicitly with this issue. Israel approved the introduction of rifles into the Palestinian Authority, because without weapons it would have been impossible for the Palestinian Authority to function against the various opposition entities, particularly against Hamas, since over the years, despite our control there, the West Bank and Gaza had become veritable weapons depots. These rifles were also used by the Palestinian Authority to prevent terror activities which could have caused a great deal of damage to Israel. In any permanent arrangement, Israel would have no interest in leaving the Palestinian entity exposed to internal violence, with no means to maintain order. There is no doubt that as soon as the Palestinian police and security organizations took part in the Intifada, a pivotal principle of the Oslo Accord had been breached, but it would still be foolish to conclude that Israel should insist on an unarmed police force.

The contention that there has never been any difference between moderates and extremists in the Palestinian camp, and that this was exposed in the Intifada, is as false as the argument of Palestinian rejectionists that there is no difference between the peace camp and the extreme right in Israel, and that all Jews have the same goal. In this framework, whenever one side expresses itself moderately, the other has to claim that it is hypocrisy. The symmetry in this situation is fascinating, and is repeated in every single conflict of this type.

In fact, one of the most important steps in the Oslo process was the effort made to distinguish between the pragmatists and the extremists on the Palestinian side, between those who were willing to talk, and those for whom the very act of talking was considered a sin. Obviously, this process also led our side to sharp disagreement. So long as there was nobody to talk to, an interim arrangement, as had been originally proposed at Camp David in 1978, seemed far too abstract. But as soon as there was someone we could talk to, then of course there would be something to talk about. The Labor-Likud national unity government of the '80s could not have existed in the '90s for that reason, and the same was the case in the Palestinian camp—accepting the Oslo principles led to a rupture in the PLO, the secession of organizations, boycotts. The pragmatic camps on both sides came together against the extremists on both sides.

When this Intifada erupted, there was a movement back to the barricades. Israel saw Fatah and Hamas announcing brotherhood and cooperation, and the Palestinians saw Shimon Peres and Avigdor Lieberman sitting at the same government table headed by Ariel Sharon, who promised a struggle lasting generations and a decisive move away from the permanent agreement.

Does this prove that although both sides have separate pragmatic and extremist camps, they are now fused into one and the truth has finally been exposed? Of course not. The true distances remain. The believers in peace must make a supreme effort to return to the separation between these camps that existed during Oslo, because that is the only road to peace.

Another argument holds that Barak turned over every stone, that the Palestinians rejected him instead of agreeing to his proposals, and therefore it is impossible to reach an agreement with them. But this is a contention that has been refuted—in the 2003 Geneva Accord. Indeed, Barak did make very brave proposals, or, more accurately, Clinton made such proposals and Barak did not reject them. This was the most far-reaching position ever taken by an Israeli Prime Minister, not because Barak was the most moderate among them, but because he was the first Prime Minister prepared to enter talks on the *permanent* arrangement. He was the first who was forced to deal with real positions on borders, Jerusalem, solutions to the refugee problem, security arrangements, and the future of the settlements.

Since he did confront these issues, and surprised many with his courage to slaughter a few "sacred cows," he had to wait and see whether the Palestinians would accept or reject his offer. And if indeed it was rejected, their recalcitrance would be exposed to the world. But Ehud Barak did not turn over every stone, because a few months later, in January 2001, we went to Taba with directives based on the Clinton Plan, which were more ambitious than what had been proposed at Camp David. The Taba talks did not break down, and did not end in disagreement. They took place four months after the start of the Intifada, and after the talks, the elections in Israel were won by the extreme right, which had no serious intention of returning to the negotiating table. The argument that it was only after Israel had shown its willingness to make a fair compromise with the Palestinians that violence broke out, drastically violating the Oslo Accord and the subsequent agreements, is correct, and requires a Palestinian response that was never given and perhaps never will be. But anyone who infers, therefore, that every stone has indeed been turned and the arrangement with the Palestinians is over and done with—or that our partners in negotiations since the start of the process are no longer our partners—is wrong, and is misleading the public.

If there is anything that the second Intifada has proven most cruelly, it is the fallacy of claims about the PLO's "stage by stage" plan. This was one of Netanyahu's contentions: Israel had supposedly not given sufficient attention to a 1974 Palestine National Council decision, according to which the Palestinians would take every territory they could control with the intention of realizing their full dream at a later date. Instead of understanding this resolution as a victory by the pragmatic wing of the PLO (just as the pragmatic religious Jews say: We have a full religious right over all the land of Israel, but until the Messiah comes we have to live our lives and settle for less, so as not to endanger ourselves), the right-wing interpreted this as the "salami method," whereby the sophisticated Palestinians pose as moderates, looking to settle for what they can get, only to turn around and use it as the basis for an historic struggle in the course of which they will attempt to take everything.

If the "stages" or "salami" theory were correct, the right-wing should have expected Arafat to accept the proposals made at Camp David enthusiastically, to establish his state on the territory allotted to him, and to struggle from there with respect to all the rest. It is precisely the fact that the Intifada broke out when the Palestinians were close to achieving the majority of their political aims that negates the "salami" contention.

AND AS FOR EXPOSING THE TRUE FACE OF OUR OPPONENT? This kind of exposure is valuable only in rare cases. Considering Barak's own past, there is no doubt that the head of the Intelligence Branch must try to ascertain whether a particular agent constituting the source of his information is a double-agent. There is certainly nothing more important than exposing a spy. But what about exposing an opponent? What would we have exposed of Sadat, had we wanted to, in the negotiations with him? Sadat, the young officer, enchanted by certain European dictatorships? Nasserist Sadat, who did not display any difference between himself and the populist dictator who led his people to unnecessary wars? Sadat, who was willing to accept the compromise proposed by Gunnar Jaring in 1971, which was amazingly similar to the Camp David agreements? Sadat, who caused the Yom Kippur War, the death of 2,800 young people of my generation, and the wounding of tens of thousands more? Or Sadat, the man with the pipe and the deep voice, visiting us in November 1977 (after the statement by the security system that this was merely camouflage for the preparation of another war), immediately becoming the most popular man in Israel until his assassination in 1981?

And what about King Hussein? Which Hussein would we have exposed? The boy with the British smile in the '50s? The man, in his weakness, seduced by Nasser in 1967 into the hopeless war against Israel, losing the West Bank and embroiling us in the curse of occupation which we don't know how to end? The leader who was not willing to join Sadat at Camp David in 1978 in order to make peace with Israel? The pleasant King who met with us in secret in the '70s and the '80s, always demonstrating goodwill alongside serious weakness? The man who hosted Yasser Arafat and the PLO in the '60s, or the one who the Palestinians later called the "Butcher of Amman" when he fought them with all his strength in September 1970 in order to save his kingdom? The man who was ready to sign the London agreement with us in 1987 (which was torpedoed by Yitzhak Shamir), or the one who totally relinquished the West Bank in 1988? The King who refused adamantly to join the American coalition against Saddam Hussein, or the one who negotiated with us and gave his hand to the Israeli-Jordanian agreement on principles signed in Washington on September 14, 1993, one day after the signing of the Oslo Accord? Would it be the Hussein who signed the peace agreement with Rabin in Arava in October 1994, despite the assessment of the Intelligence Branch that there was no chance of such an agreement before the signature of a permanent agreement between Israel and the PLO?

Which Barak would be exposed if we wanted to do so? Barak the army Chief of Staff, or Barak the politician? The Barak who spoke at the Merkaz Harav Yeshiva, or the one who spoke at the Labor Party center? Barak announcing that the Golan Heights are of great strategic importance even in peace time, or Barak stating bravely before the inhabitants of the Golan Heights, over their shouts of derision, that he was willing to give up the

Heights for peace? Barak fighting against acceptance of a Palestinian state, or Barak taking it for granted three years later? Barak stating that unilateral withdrawal from Lebanon was an unequivocal danger to the northern settlements, or Barak withdrawing from Lebanon over the protests of the military? Barak declaring on Jerusalem Day that the city would never be divided, or Barak at Camp David, two months later, considering the transfer of the Arab neighborhoods to Palestinian sovereignty and speaking thereafter of the greater Jewish Jerusalem?

And Rabin? If anyone had wanted to expose Rabin, would it be the Prime Minister whose advisor on the war against terrorism was the extreme right-winger Rehavam Zeevi, and whose security advisor was Ariel Sharon? Would it be the man who rejected King Hussein's proposal before the Rabat Conference in 1974 to reach territorial agreement on the West Bank? Would it be the opposition member who recommended to Minister of Defense Ariel Sharon that the water be shut off for the inhabitants of towns in Lebanon in order to tighten the siege? Would it be the man who called the "doves" of his own party "PLO lovers"? Or would it be the peace hero who shook hands with Arafat, who was awarded the Nobel Peace Prize, who was murdered in 1995 with the words to the "Song of Peace" still in his jacket pocket, stained with his blood?

And Begin? And Peres? And Ben-Gurion? And Moshe Dayan? And many, many others who in the course of their lives showed many faces and made completely contradictory statements which they were passionately willing to defend?

Arafat is both leader and follower, initiating terror and concerned for the orphans of his fighters. He is the blustering speaker still using the language of the past, but also making speeches of peace and understanding. He wants it all and understands that he will only get a part. Arafat traveled to Amman in order to kiss Sheikh Ahmed Yassin after Netanyahu released him, and then put him under house arrest in Gaza. He called for jihad, and then explained that he meant the "great jihad," signifying internal challenge and devotion, not holy war. He stood behind operations that led to the murder of innocent Israelis, as well as operations by his own security organization that saved many Israelis, particularly after 1996—including one potentially terrible operation that was prevented in Tel Aviv in 1999, at the end of Netanyahu's term. He was awarded the Nobel Peace Prize and then promised a few years later to continue the Intifada until complete victory was achieved, but on the eve of the Passover festival he phoned Sharon to wish him a happy holiday. Is he the Arafat whom many Israelis call "a two-legged animal," or the one who is depicted as a likable, if bumbling puppet on *Hartzufim*, a satirical TV show in Israel?

Perhaps it is the duty of the head of an espionage service to expose double-agents and spies. But a statesman's job is not to expose the person standing in front of him, it is to protect the national interests of his people. The Oslo process was an effort to shape circumstances. Previously, the Palestinians had objected strenuously to a long interim arrangement without agreement in advance (as was the case in the Camp David discussions with Egypt in 1978) on the principles of the permanent arrangement. If we had settled for "exposure," we could have shown the Palestinians as having no desire for an interim arrangement—but we wanted to achieve an arrangement, not exposure, and after interminable, difficult talks and crises, we did.

Ehud Barak exposed nothing, although he thought he had, to the joy of the right-wing. Arafat remains a multifaceted leader who wears many masks, like most other world leaders. In certain circumstances or conditions, under agreed formulae, it was possible to reach agreements that committed him to internal rupture and severe struggles within his own house. Under other circumstances, he maintained his adamant refusal. He is neither a pacifist at all costs nor a terrorist at all costs. He is still the man who can move his people, more than anyone else in his camp, even when Prime Ministers like Abu Mazen or Abu Ala are appointed, and he can also make surprising and brave decisions. No honest person in Europe was impressed by Barak's "exposure" of Arafat, even if there were many who appreciated the Israeli leader's courage. Arafat remained as he had been—a problematic and difficult partner, wearing a military uniform and making provocative speeches, with whom, by means of sensitive management, it would be possible to reach not only interim agreements, but even a permanent agreement. The group around him, aged sixty, fifty, and forty, some of whom went to university in Israeli prisons, and some of whom completed academic studies in the United States and England and other countries around the world, consists of people interested in the establishment of a Palestinian state, living normal lives, and developing democracy and culture, professional bureaucracy, and a physical infrastructure alongside Israel. This is the group facing up to Islamic fanaticism, religious madness, and those sending suicide bombers. There is no need to occupy ourselves with exposure. The picture is well known to us all, even if the right-wing in Israel will try to argue that Dr. Nabil Sha'ath is the other face of Ahmed Yassin—just as the Palestinian extremists will argue that Yossi Sarid is the other face of Benny Elon, the Moledet MK and an open advocate of "transfer." Our future here depends, among other things, on our ability to maintain the alliance of the moderates, the pragmatists, the people who believe that we were born to live, not to sacrifice ourselves on the altar of false dreams.

THE RIGHT-WING DEPICTS THE OSLO PROCESS as the product of a group of naïve people cut off from the cruel reality of the Middle East. However, the naïveté belongs to the right-wing, since there is nothing more naïve than the belief that it is possible to continue living like this, at the same level of risk to our existence, without reaching an arrangement. The peacemakers were very realistic people. Some of them were even quite skeptical. Among us were fighters in many wars, some of whom had lost loved ones. People who had learned and taught generations of students the history and culture of this region, who had reached the conclusion that the persistence of the present situation, with its intermittent terror that shows no signs of stopping, is untenable. It is a situation liable to change drastically for the worse in light of two impending developments: nonconventional weapons in the hands of regional Islamic states, and an Arab majority west of the Jordan. If these two come to pass with no Israeli-Palestinian agreement in place, and no agreed border between the two countries, it could surely place question marks on the future of the Zionist ideal. If the present situation, with no Palestinian state and our control (direct or indirect) over the Palestinians, continues until there is an Arab majority here, this will lead to ongoing Israeli-Palestinian hell. The naïveté of the right-wing is in its unwillingness to open its eyes to these developments, and its lack of practical answers to the situation developing in the region, except for dreams of mass immigration from the United States to Israel or a "voluntary transfer" of the Arabs.

In Oslo we initiated a process designed to lead to two nation-states, with a border and peace between them, and this is a crucial condition for the realization of Zionism in the twenty-first century. We gave our hand to the pragmatic Palestinian camp, and it grew stronger at the expense of Hamas, for its own and our benefit, and for the benefit of regional stability. In Oslo, for the first time, we found a Palestinian addressee, after years of failure with King Hussein, the heads of the large *hamulot* (clans), and Sharon's "village leagues." Before giving up on the addressee, it is crucial to consider that there may be no better substitute, before the next interlocutors become preachers in the extremist mosques and armed young men trying to take control of villages and neighborhoods.

None of this means that Oslo and the process that came in the wake of the Declaration of Principles were without mistakes, some of them significant. The true interest of both parties, in my opinion, was to attain the permanent agreement as early as 1993, and to implement it within two to three years. Postponing the discussions on the permanent agreement created an incentive for the extremists on both sides to torpedo the process. The closure of the territories, the continued construction in the settlements, the ongoing incitement in the Palestinian media, and the failure to make preparations for peace all led to a serious deterioration in the situation. But these developments were not stopped, largely because of the sense that peace was just around the corner, and with it would come change.

There are some who saw in Oslo the dream of an interim arrangement in which Israelis and Palestinians would become friends and sign a permanent agreement within five years, as the natural result of the cooperation created during that time. Nothing was farther from the truth. The five years of interim arrangement were proposed in the Camp David agreements in 1978, and copied at the Madrid Conference in 1991. We built up

Oslo as the implementation of the two previous stages, and therefore we repeated the principle of the interim period. When I presented a proposal to reach a permanent arrangement immediately in Oslo, it was rejected by both Rabin and Peres, and by the Palestinians. When I brought the Beilin–Abu Mazen Understandings to Peres two years later, when he was Prime Minister, in order to achieve implementation of the permanent arrangement in 1996, he believed that it was still preferable to wait. I thought that was a serious mistake, because what could have been achieved in 1995 might not be so easy a few years later, and as time passes hate grows stronger, especially when the time is not being utilized to build up trust.

One of the most important "achievements" of the Oslo process was the exclusion of specific language freezing settlement construction in the period of the interim arrangement. The Palestinians did raise the issue, and Rabin asked us to explain to them that his government had made a far-reaching decision concerning the cessation of public construction in the settlements, and had even frozen contracts signed with contractors. It had done this not because the Palestinians had pressured him, but because he had committed, even before the elections, to alter priorities. He had no intention of changing the decision, and the construction in the settlements would be minimal. If one of the clauses in the agreement explicitly addressed the freezing of the settlements, it would be difficult for him—with the small coalition he had assembled—to obtain broad support for the agreement. It was not easy for the Palestinians to accept this. They questioned what would happen if the government were to fall, if the coalition were replaced, and so on and so forth, but they eventually accepted Rabin's position.

In retrospect, I have no doubt that it would have been in our interest to include such a clause in the agreement. In the six years between 1994 and 2000, the Jewish population in the territories increased by as much as it had during the twenty-six years between the Six-Day War and Oslo. Since there was no settlements clause (of which Rabin was proud), he was under growing pressure to build in the territories, and from time to time he gave in. As a result, Netanyahu was able to promise not to build any more than Rabin had; he then cancelled the suspension resolutions of the Rabin government and increased the number of residential units in the territories, arguing that there was no restriction in the Oslo Agreement. Barak, who personally saw no benefit in building in the territories, allowed the construction to continue due to his great desire for the National Religious Party to join his coalition. He even gave the housing portfolio to the party's leader, Yitzhak Levy, who could then justify his participation in Barak's dovish government by the fact that he was building in the territories. At a certain stage, Barak and Levy agreed that new construction tenders would be issued in the territories only with Barak's consent, but the bottom line was that the number of settlers in the territories grew during Barak's term by twelve percent, and that is a much more significant expansion than the natural growth rate there. If the Oslo Agreement had contained a clause restricting this, Barak would not have been under pressure to build, while right-wing governments would have been careful about it, because it would have become a very measurable breach of the agreement.

In the course of Barak's term as Prime Minister, there were hardly any internal struggles over the construction in the settlements, because the members of the peace camp kept telling ourselves that the permanent agreement was around the corner. To a great extent we were deceiving ourselves. The Palestinians considered the construction in the settlements to be the greatest blow to the possibility of establishing a contiguous state. Much of the construction that came under the guise of "natural growth" involved redefining the boundaries of given settlements to allow new construction—including entirely new "daughter" settlements like Beit El B and Talmon C ostensibly built within the lines of their "parents" but often kilometers away. So long as no agreement had been signed, the ongoing construction during the term of a "peace government" was an affront that the Palestinian public—even more than the leadership—could not digest. One of the costs of the lengthy interim arrangement was that we came to see ourselves as the custodians of a deposit which would shortly be returned to its owners, and we failed to properly assess the terrible evils that were created as a consequence.

On the Palestinian side the incitement continued. A joint Israeli-Palestinian committee was established, and reports were prepared describing what had been said on Palestinian television and radio and in the educational programs—but there was no real change. The Palestinians said that it was difficult to change things before there was peace, before the public could see with its own eyes an improved situation. We—and I include myself—did not struggle enough. We did not demand enough. We were inclined to believe that peace would heal the incitement as well. When we resume talks in the future, we must not give that up.

I have no doubt that the cumulative effect of the ongoing construction in the settlements and the incitement was a sure recipe for the outbreak of the Intifada. The ongoing expansion of settlements is now a solid fact, while peace is no longer around the corner.

THIS MATTER IS DEEPLY ENTWINED with the way each side views the other, the great difference in attitudes toward particular words and deeds. The long years of the interim arrangement did not create any real closeness or mutual understanding. The great efforts made to arrange meetings of youth and professionals, the joint seminars, and the trips abroad—all these were a drop in the ocean. A new neighborhood on expropriated Palestinian soil, or on what we call "state land," will not be seen by us as it is by the Palestinians, and a little girl in kindergarten promising to fight until Jerusalem becomes the Palestinian capital will not give them the shivers it gives us. We have not succeeded in communicating to each other our feelings on these matters.

We did not really understand the issue of the incarcerated prisoners when their former commanders were sitting with our leaders in hotels, discussing the future. We continued with our "bloody hands" slogans, but we did not boycott negotiating partners with blood on their hands, and we differentiated between various kinds of blood—we released murderers of Arabs who cooperated with us, while those who had murdered Jews were not released.

Most of the Palestinians never understood our political problems. They knew well all the political gossip, the principal players in each party, and even the internal power struggles, but they didn't fully grasp the formal legal-democratic framework. Eventually, somehow, they believed that the

Prime Minister could do whatever he wanted. The problem we encountered with the referendum—the question of the regular majority versus the supermajority—seemed to some of them a display of artificial difficulties that could be easily resolved, if only we really wanted to.

We were not sufficiently aware of the significance of the closure, the many barriers, the restrictions on the Palestinians' movement and daily lives, the sense of occupation, the Palestinians' humiliation and despair (when we imagined that they had their own government and there was no problem with us). And they were not sufficiently aware of the great importance of public opinion in Israel and the destructive effect on the support for peace created by their belligerent statements and their attacks.

We were not sufficiently aware of the economic difficulties on the Palestinian side. Between 1994 and 1999, the Palestinian per capita gross national product declined by about twenty percent, while life expectancy decreased by two years. All this was not due to the Oslo Agreement, of course, but to the closures and separation between Gaza and the West Bank following the terrorist activities at the beginning of the '90s. However, there is no doubt that the decision to continue these actions, to one extent or another, until the start of the second Intifada—at which point closures became even more severe—derived from a sense that the the permanent agreement was approaching and the Palestinians would be responsible for their own fate. Withholding payment of Value Added Tax (VAT) to the Palestinians for goods arriving at Israeli ports and designated for them was a serious and unnecessary blow, delivered both in the days of Netanyahu and later on. On the Palestinian side, the Oslo process was seen as the principal cause of the economic damage. Their low standard of living and high levels of unemployment were always fertile breeding grounds for various types of unrest. Preventing this requires a reservoir of hope, but igniting it only takes one match.

Barak's statement on the interpretation of the UN Security Council Resolution 242 in Paris was almost that match. It was particularly important from our point of view, before commencing negotiations on the permanent agreement, to state that since no recognized international border had ever passed through the West Bank, contrary to the situation with

Egypt, Syria, and Lebanon, we were not obligated to implement 242—that is, withdraw from all territories—in the agreement with the Palestinians. In Paris, this statement served no purpose whatsoever. The 1967 borders were the point of reference at Camp David, in the Clinton Plan and at Taba, and in Geneva; they are the basis for the future border between the two states, and 242 is recognized in the Oslo Accord as the basis for the solution to the dispute. But the Palestinians saw this statement by Barak as an attempt to evade the permanent agreement, and this increased their distrust before and during the Camp David talks.

We did not do enough to strengthen the Palestinian Authority. We were worried that we would appear patronizing and did not think that it was in our interest to do something about the repeated rumors of corruption. There were entities within the Authority who warned against developing too close a relationship with those participating in this corruption. We did not always heed these hints which were, in fact, cries for help by people concerned about the degeneration of this new system. Israelis thought that so long as they themselves were not affected by corruption, there was nothing bad in maintaining a relationship with those who were. Ultimately, one of the reasons for the Intifada was the harsh internal Palestinian criticism of the Authority and Israel's perceived complicity in these matters. The Palestinians did not devote sufficient efforts to set up democratic organs and to encourage civilian, non-governmental institutions.

There were additional developments on the Palestinian side to which we did not attribute proper importance: the strengthening of the Tanzim, which became a potentially extremist factor after the events of the Wall Tunnel in September 1996; the elections of Tanzim members to the Central Council and the Revolutionary Council of the Fatah after eleven years; the arming of the Tanzim; and Arafat's failed attempt to disarm it in 1998. The clash between the Tanzim and the Palestinian police force, and the reconciliation between Arafat and the organization following the violent events of Nakba Day—these were internal Palestinian developments which had a direct effect on the situation in the territories, the outbreak of the Intifada, and its persistence beyond the first few days. We were inclined to see our own reflection only on the other side—a political entity making decisions and handing down orders to the field. In reality, the relationship between us and Arafat and the members of his cabinet was only part of the picture, and we did not see the internal processes in the background—the struggles for the future leadership and the rivalries within Fatah and the PLO, and between these organizations and the religious movements. Israel's true interest lay in strengthening the Palestinian government and helping it to ensure that all these struggles would be political and not violent. The weaker the government, the more difficult it would be to prevent the growth of militias in the area.

Without understanding how crucial it was to nurture an addressee on the Palestinian side, we did not wait long before hitting back at the Palestinian Authority and related institutions immediately after the Intifada broke out. Instead of distinguishing between the Authority and other entities, we hurried to retaliate for anti-Israel violence. Neither before the Intifada broke out nor afterwards did we act as if it were in our own interest to preserve our partner.

GOOD PEOPLE ON THE LEFT, who were quick to give up on the prospects of achieving peace with the present Palestinian leadership, are now playing with an old idea, which was raised in the past when there were no settlements on the West Bank: unilateral withdrawal.

The great effort of the Zionist movement was to become part of the region and not to be perceived as a foreign body that had been planted where it did not belong. This is a struggle for acceptance, integration, legitimization. The peace agreements with Egypt and Jordan are real Zionist successes, because they remove us from our geographical enclosure, where our only exit is to the sea, and release us from our psychological enclosure. This was the result of our ability to persuade our neighbors that Israel is not a passing episode but is here to stay, that good relations could also bring them a great deal of benefit. This is the normalization that is the essence of the Zionist concept.

A unilateral decision on withdrawal would gain legitimization—worldwide and regional—only with full withdrawal to the 1967 borders. That is the implementation of UN Security Council Resolution 242 with an interpretation acceptable to the majority of countries of the world. The 1967 border can be altered only with Palestinian consent, with an exchange of territories. But if we forego the partner, it will be necessary to do on the West Bank what we did in Lebanon: reach a precise definition of the Green Line with the help of an international entity, cut through towns and villages, give up all settlements, and relinquish the territory in Jerusalem taken over in the Six-Day War.

This is a very difficult and very painful task. Leaving neighborhoods that have become an integral part of Jerusalem in the past thirty years, where hundreds of thousands of Israelis now live, and relinquishing blocs in which the majority of the settlers live, will be difficult not only from the human and political aspects, but also economically. An agreement with the Palestinians will require compensation for relocation of 100,000 Israelis; in the event of withdrawal without an agreement, we will have to compensate about 400,000!

Anyone who thinks the framework for a unilateral withdrawal can be made solely between Israelis is deceiving himself. The world will not recognize an arbitrary boundary, and the territory between the Green Line and the new border will become the focus of a serious dispute between us and the Palestinians, as well as the wider Arab world.

The Palestinians know that they will derive quite a few benefits from peace with Israel, not the least of which will be opening the gateway to the United States, resolving the refugee problem, and providing employment for hundreds of thousands of workers. Peace and close ties with Israel will make it easier for them to become, as a state, more prosperous and freer than the majority of Arab countries, within a few years. They are doing us no favor by making peace with us, just as we are doing them no such favor. It is a meeting of the interests of both sides, after many years in which the Palestinians have been waiting for the disappearance of the "Zionist entity," and Israel has been waiting for a partner that is not the PLO. Today, when both sides are talking to each other, notwithstanding the lack of trust and the deep disappointment, neither of us has any alternative preferable to an agreement.

Any unilateral withdrawal, however, would have to be implemented unconditionally. We would not be able to assure the demilitarization of the Palestinian state, nor that it would refrain from signing security agreements with our enemies. We would pay the full price, without receiving anything in exchange. A peace agreement will not be easy to achieve, but unilateral withdrawal will be even harder. If it were a partial withdrawal, it would be a recipe for violence; and if it were full, it would be a broad concession that would not assure peace. Unilateral withdrawal must be retained as an emergency solution, for a situation in which it is impossible to attain an agreed border prior to the reversal of the demographic balance west of the Jordan. Only then would this solution be preferable to a continuation of the existing one, and even then it would be a bad solution both for Israel and the Palestinians.

ONE PERSON WHO MADE A DECISIVE CONTRIBUTION to our departure from an agreement, and made the way back very difficult, is Benjamin Netanyahu. The most serious damage on the Israeli side to the political process was done in the three years he was in office. Netanyahu did this deliberately, based on his belief in a Palestinian "stage by stage" plan to destroy Israel. He considered the settlements important, did not believe in the need to divide the land west of the Jordan, and thought that limited autonomy for the Palestinians would prevent an apartheid-like situation even if an Arab majority grows under overall Israeli responsibility.

Netanyahu came to power with the intention of "killing" the Oslo Accord, despite paying it lip service before the elections, and built up his entire policy on "reciprocity"—not out of a legitimate desire to ensure that the other side would fulfill its part in the agreement, but out of the wish to take advantage of the other side's failure to implement clauses in the agreement as ongoing grounds for non-fulfillment on his part as well.

Netanyahu refused to withdraw on the dates he had promised to do so. He preferred to talk of a permanent agreement without presenting a practical route there that would be acceptable to the Palestinians, or even the United States. The Palestinians refused to start talks with him on the permanent status before he implemented what he had promised in the interim agreement. Eventually, all Netanyahu did was to take the IDF out of Hebron, and to implement the first part of the sub-stages of the second withdrawal, which were agreed upon toward the end of his term in October

1998. He released only a small number of the security prisoners, did not open the "safe passages" between Gaza and the West Bank, and held up the VAT funds to the Palestinians for an extended period. He continued, of course, the expansion of the settlements. The Palestinians, for their part, did not collect the illegal arms within their jurisdiction, increased the number of those serving on the police force beyond what had been agreed, did not stop the incitement, and failed to imprison suspects whom Israel had asked to be arrested.

During Netanyahu's three years, Israel was supposed to implement the first, second, and third redeployments and reach a permanent agreement with the Palestinians. Almost none of this happened. The frustration on the Palestinian side was strong and deep. The nationalist and religious extremists, who had opposed the Oslo Accord from the start, admonished the Authority and insisted that, in its gullibility, it had signed an agreement with one government and failed to see that its successor would not implement it. Israel had benefited economically and internationally from the Oslo Accord, the Palestinians were weakened economically, the situation in the territories had grown worse, the interim agreement was not being implemented, and the permanent agreement was further away than ever before.

The Fatah and Tanzim organizations, cultivated by Arafat as his control arm on the Palestinian street, were greatly weakened by the Palestinian refusal front and Hamas. The end of the five years of the interim arrangement passed without mention. The talk of the unilateral declaration of a Palestinian state was shown to be unreliable, and the only answer that the Palestinian Authority had was to hope for a change of government in Israel and the return of the signatories of the agreement to a position in which they would be able to implement it.

ONE OF BARAK'S MISTAKES was that he did not consider Netanyahu's tenure to have delivered such a severe blow to the Palestinians' trust in Israel. Barak behaved as if he had come to power in June 1996 and not in July 1999. After Rabin and Peres, it might have been possible to act as he did: failing to implement the Wye Agreement, adding a framework agreement before the permanent agreement, and postponing the third stage as long as possible. But after the Netanyahu years he should have, first of all, executed Israel's part in the interim agreement and commenced, in parallel, serious and comprehensive negotiations on the permanent agreement. His behavior reminded the Palestinians of Netanyahu, and they did not know what to make of it.

Barak's desire to work on the Syrian route even before an agreement had been reached with the Palestinians compounded his difficulties. In the course of two very important months, between September and November 1999, he did not manage to find anyone to head his peace administration to conduct negotiations with the Palestinians, thus giving the sense that he had time to spare. Barak wasted his chance to act in the first hundred days in a way that could have altered the appearance of the region: exiting from Lebanon without waiting for anyone, immediately implementing all parts of the interim agreement which had not yet been executed, along with a demand for corresponding Palestinian performance, initiating intensive negotiations on the permanent agreement with the Palestinians, and in parallel, talks with the Syrians. This was his great failure.

The credit available to him at the beginning of the road, with a broad coalition that did not include the Likud, was short-lived. He seemed to be working in slow motion at the beginning his term. From May 17 to July 6, he was very occupied with assembling the government, nearly exhausting the forty-five days granted to him by law. In this period he refrained from any political action, and even after the government had been formed he continued at a pace that was too slow. When one looks back at the twenty months he was in office, it is difficult not to agonize over the wasted time.

Barak's government included members with vast political experience and a unique network of contacts with the Palestinians, the Arab world, Europe, and the United States. He refrained from utilizing this experience, in the desire—quite understandable—to do things his own way. But the price paid for that was high, because the advisors with whom he surrounded himself were not sufficiently experienced, resulting in multiple errors.

Only after his resignation, in the course of the two months in which he was preparing for the election campaign, did he set up a peace cabinet, which bore the character of a real advisory forum. The "blue bird" had been very close to Barak, but he did not see it, or preferred not to see it—as in the famous play by Maurice Maeterlinck: The children know that the blue bird is very important to them. They search for it everywhere, and they finally find it at home; the lesson, of course, is that your real treasures are never so far away—just search for them close by and you will find them.

Barak did not understand the importance of personal relationships as an element of political negotiations. He said many times that the most important thing was the policy, not those executing it. Even if he truly believed that it caused a great deal of damage, which peaked at the Camp David summit, when Barak avoided meeting Arafat face-to-face, except for one morning meeting. The feeling in both delegations was that utilization of the fifteen days for open discussions between the two leaders could have changed the course of the talks. Whether or not this is true, it is clear that keeping his distance made real communication difficult. Barak was concerned that his every undertaking would immediately be "filed," while if the meetings were held at another level, he could recant what he did not like. His avoidance at Camp David and his failure to meet with Arafat during the United Nations Millennium Assembly, with the strange jostling at the elevator, were errors in personal behavior, which had a negative political effect.

I believe that Barak was mistaken in his reluctance to place the understandings between Abu Mazen and me on the table at Camp David. I cannot be objective on this point, but a comparison between the 1995 understandings and the Clinton Plan does not show the latter to be more advantageous to Israel. Barak was wrong to discuss percentages instead of areas vital for Israel, and he was certainly mistaken in rejecting the option of the safety net on his way out to Camp David. Without sufficient preparation and no alternatives, he began a journey at the end of which he tried to force the Palestinians into a "take it or leave it" decision, for which the Palestinians were not ready—while he was not prepared to continue negotiating with them.

Barak's principal problem at Camp David was not the nature of his proposals, but his approach to the negotiations: the "bazaar" method of bargaining, the lack of concern with personal chemistry, and the refusal to turn to a partial alternative. Another error was his dependence on Clinton, to such an extent that the Palestinians had no doubt that every proposal from Clinton was, in fact, an Israeli proposal. The American mediation lost its power, at a certain stage, due to too much identification between Israel and the United States.

At the end of his term, Barak sent a letter to the leaders of the countries concerned, notifying them that everything Israel had proposed at Camp David and Taba was null and void. I asked him whether he wanted to over-turn the government resolution that had adopted the Clinton Plan (with the reservations which had never been codified). He replied in the nega-tive. The resolution remained in place, and it continues to obligate Israel so long as it has not been voided by the government. But everything that transpired at Camp David and Taba were also part of history, and nobody can ignore these events in the future. Barak can be proud of two important political achievements: the exit from Lebanon and the Clinton Plan. The Clinton Plan outlines a new situation in the region, and it is the legitimate child of the talks between Barak and Arafat at Camp David. It is a good thing that the creator was unable to destroy his creation.

Barak—like Rabin and Peres before him—insisted on serving both as Prime Minister and Minister of Defense. He felt that without this double authority it would be difficult for him to leave Lebanon and make an agree-ment with the Palestinians. But Israel needs a full-time Minister of Defense. The military, in Barak's time, felt free to criticize, to give inter-views, and to do its own thing in the system. The army Chief of Staff, to a great extent, fulfilled the function of Minister of Defense, and the army's position on every issue received great publicity.

The military system must feel that it is heard, that it has free access to the Minister of Defense, to the Prime Minister, the cabinet, and the govern-ment, but it should not play a public game. Prima facie, it is the advisor to the ministerial level and executor of its decisions, but this model has become merely theoretical. Intelligence estimates often reach the media immediately and are perceived as the absolute truth, despite the multiplicity of fallacious assessments. The military's objection to withdrawal from Lebanon was vociferous and the Chief of Staff was careful up to the very last minute to say that we would leave Lebanon only under an agreement, even when he already understood that Barak might not wait for that agreement.

The cabinet's refusal of an operational proposal by the Chief of Staff was broadcast in the media within the hour. Intelligence assessments concerning the Palestinians, their aims in the negotiations, the possibility of an outbreak of violence, and so forth, were in the public domain, whether or not they had been presented to the government. They played a negative role in the Israeli-Palestinian relationship, because it seemed to be "Israel" that was constantly attributing negative intentions to the Palestinians, and not just the Intelligence Branch.

The military has legitimate organizational objectives. It is supposed to solve problems by military means and it presents worst case scenarios in order to cover itself. When Dan Shomron, as Chief of Staff, said in 1988 that there was no military solution to the first Intifada, he was never forgiven. Theoretically, there has to be a military solution for every situation (provided, of course, that the army is given the manpower, budget, equipment, and it is released from restrictions it considers superfluous). An army without a challenge, that does not conduct campaigns, loses its vitality, its rationale, and its prestige. Most officers will not easily pass up battle experience, even if they don't identify with the statements constantly being made by young soldiers in favor of encounters, "action," and "revenge." As Chief of Staff, Amnon Lipkin-Shahak pushed to execute Operation Grapes of Wrath in Lebanon; as a cabinet member, he would probably never have approved it.

A military organization without significant civilian control can compromise democracy without intending to. The calls heard in the course of the second Intifada—"Let the IDF win"—were the nadir of a phenomenon in which an elected government was separated from the army operating according to its directives. The notion that there could be a situation in which the government enables the army to make its own decisions, or that it approves every one of the army's demands, is the breakdown of a first-class democratic principle. A situation whereby ministers have to apologize to the media for having voted against a particular military action, or whereby they have to fear that their vote to reject this or that military proposal will cost them a political price, is intolerable. Obviously, I cannot give examples here, but I have no doubt that the relationship between the government and the military, and the army's exaggerated independence in this period, had a negative impact on our ability to reach an arrangement. The moment in which the state allows the IDF to "win" will be the moment of its own defeat.

Military reporters have a share in this process, perhaps without knowing it. They represent (although there are exceptions) the army's businesslike position against the politicians, who always have external interests. These reporters are much less critical of the military system, and its ongoing effort to defend itself, than political journalists, who see their role—and rightly so—as the politicians' critics.

THE PALESTINIANS FELT THAT THE PRINCIPAL concession on their part had been made in 1988, when they agreed to establish a Palestinian state, alongside Israel, within the 1967 borders. This meant a state on twenty-three percent of the land west of the Jordan, which is less than half the area offered to them in the 1947 partition proposal. The Palestinians viewed the Oslo process as if it had to lead to certain resolutions, even though the permanent status had not been discussed there. They were not prepared for Camp David, and in the course of the summit gave no backing to Arafat's concessions.

The internal struggles among them often had a great effect on the proceedings. The competition between leaders, the tension between the Tanzim and the Hamas for influence over the Palestinian street, and power struggles within the Fatah, produced a certain paralysis which took hold of the leaders just when they were required to make decisions. Add to that the behavior of the moderate Arab states—who promised backing for any decision made by Arafat, but adamantly refused the requests made by some of the Palestinian leadership to issue moderate announcements and to actively persuade the rest of the Arab world of the need to reach territorial compromise with Israel. They too were concerned about their own internal opposition. In telephone conversations with Arafat, many Arab leaders pushed him to compromise, but in public they were silent or belligerent.

One of the reasons for this dynamic is the revolution that has occurred in the Arab media. Satellite communication does not encourage moderation, and preparing the public for concessions might put leaders in a position of weakness in front of cameras and aggressive television broadcasters asking hard questions. Many leaders preferred to avoid such embarrassment, and to create an impression of unity in the Arab world.

The Palestinians came to Camp David because Arafat was unable to refuse Clinton. Arafat had never concealed his opinion that the summit was premature. He was worried about a confrontation with Clinton and Barak, and wanted to come to the summit after several more weeks of negotiations so that he would not have to negotiate himself. Clinton felt that only at a summit of leaders would it be possible to reach the moment of truth. Arafat went there under duress, his entourage grumbling that the Americans were attempting to maneuver between the older and younger generations among them.

The Camp David summit ended with the failure to reach an agreement. However, there had been no actual breakdown in the talks, and there was real progress toward another summit in the near future. In Palestinian public opinion, the summit ended with Barak demanding annexation of about nine percent of the West Bank, in exchange for only one percent of the sovereign territory of Israel, while demanding that the settlements stay in place and objecting to the transfer of the Temple Mount to Arafat. What was perceived in Israel as a generous move by Barak, and by Clinton as courage from a responsible leader, was seen by the Palestinians as rigidity and obstinance. We would draw our lessons from this in Geneva, where the territorial issue was the first on the agenda, the basis of which was the Green Line of 1967, and the compensation for the modifications was on a scale of 1:1.

Arafat, who was well aware of the progress that had been made at Camp David, made no effort to calm things down; quite the opposite—he encouraged discord, in order to justify his failure to sign an agreement with Israel. When the riots began in the territories after Sharon's visit to the Temple Mount, Arafat made no effort to stop them, but rode the tiger, believing that the developments would lead to an improvement in his status, both among the Arabs and internationally. The Tanzim, which had been cultivated by Arafat as a political organization that could encourage support for peace, became a leader of the violence, with the aim of securing its own sway on the Palestinian street against Hamas. Marwan Barghouti took this opportunity to reinforce his internal leadership position after having failed a few months earlier in the internal elections to the Fatah institutions. A generational struggle within the Palestinian leadership was visible as some of the young leaders "took over" the Intifada, leaving the traditional leaders behind. Instead of building a Palestinian peace coalition, an anti-Israel national unity front was very quickly established, and matched only a few months later by an Israeli national unity government, the two camps now clearly positioned against one another.

What seemed to Israel like a collapse of the Oslo process was viewed by the Palestinians as a temporary breakdown of diplomatic negotiations that would lead, under conditions more advantageous to them, to a continuation of the political process. We could not accept this, since one of the most important principles of the Oslo Accord had been the agreement to resolve the dispute by peaceful means. Even though eighteen months had passed since the time when the permanent agreement should have been reached, we did not understand how they could resort to violence at that particular time.

The writing was on the wall. For over a year, our Palestinian colleagues had been speaking to us a great deal about the danger of explosion, about frustration, bitterness, economic hardship, and the importance of implementing the interim arrangement. But, like many other writings on the wall, we saw it only after the eruption had occurred. Only then did we understand how real that warning had been.

CLINTON INVESTED VAST AMOUNTS of his time and energy in the Middle East, making great efforts to achieve peace agreements between Israel and all its neighbors. But mistakes were made even by the Americans. The Camp David summit had not been properly prepared, and was left, to a large extent, to improvisation. The American government did not attribute sufficient importance to the interim periods and believed that everything would sort itself out when there was peace. In the meantime, it closed its eyes to both the expansion of the settlements and to the incitement against Israel.

The fact that ultimately Clinton left a plan on the table was crucial to the success of the Taba talks, but it all took place too late. Perhaps Clinton should have placed that very plan on the table at a much earlier stage, even if the parties were not happy with it, so that they could conduct negotiations from that position. In any future negotiations between Israelis and Palestinians on the permanent status agreement, Clinton's plan will be the starting point, and that is certainly an important legacy left by the President.

As we agreed in Geneva, Israel will have no sovereignty over the Temple Mount and the Palestinians will have no right of return to sovereign Israel, but the central interests of both parties will be maintained. When this happens, the role played by President Clinton in making peace in our region will be ripe for reevaluation.

IT IS IN ISRAEL'S NATIONAL INTEREST to assure a high level of personal security for its citizens, and for those entering it as new immigrants or tourists, and to guarantee a stable Jewish majority for the foreseeable future. It is an important national interest to assure the legitimacy of the state of Israel in the region, with the world's recognition of an expanded Jerusalem as its capital. The more these objectives are realized, the more attractive Israel will be for both its citizens and the Jews of the world; it will attract more foreign investors, and it will be able to assure a higher economic standard for those living there.

It is in Israel's national interest to ensure the completion of an Israeli-Palestinian agreement before an Arab majority is created in the region west of the Jordan. Without an agreement the region will soon reach a boiling point. An Arab majority would not agree to be ruled by a Jewish minority, and a Jewish minority would not agree to relinquish the existence of a Jewish state. Those interested in preventing such a confrontation, both

Israelis and Palestinians, must make a supreme effort to draw up an agreed border and reach a political agreement.

It is in Israel's national interest to reach an arrangement with a partner representing the Palestinian people. For twenty-five years we looked for a negotiating partner, then found one in the PLO. This has been a problematic partnership, in the course of which there have been crises and successes. When the second Intifada began, there were many people in Israel who wanted to forego the partnership. But the alternatives to the PLO are extremist, nationalist, and religious entities who refuse to recognize or to negotiate with Israel. We have an interest in the existence of a strong partner, with a broad span of control, who can fulfill its commitments.

FOR MANY YEARS WE ASKED OURSELVES who would be the second Arab entity ready to reach a peace agreement with Israel. We knew well that Jordan and Lebanon would be happy to do so, but it was also clear that weakness prevented this. Egypt, the largest Arab country, paid a heavy price for its agreement with Israel—cessation of diplomatic ties with the Arab world and exclusion from the Arab League. The other Arab entities are weaker than Egypt, and would therefore have to give careful consideration before making any decision on the issue. In the end, it was the PLO who surprised us.

The signature of the Oslo Accord broke taboos in Israel, and was a very brave act on the part of Yitzhak Rabin, but it also broke a taboo in the PLO and was a very brave act on the part of Yasser Arafat. Arafat moved from an outlook of rejection, in which Israel's existence was regarded as a passing episode, to one of acceptance, or at least an understanding that Israel's presence was an enduring fact in the Middle East. Until the Oslo Accord, he may have continued to adhere to the PLO's positions of the 1960s and 1970s—calling for a secular democratic state on all of the land west of the Jordan and demanding that all Jews who had come to Israel after the Balfour Declaration (the 1917 British edict that enabled the eventual establishment of a Jewish state in Palestine) should return to their country of origin—but whatever the case, in the Oslo Accord, he agreed to accept not only the very fact of the existence of the Jewish state, but even its borders based on Security Council Resolution 242. A policy that licensed interaction and discussion only with anti-Zionist Israelis was replaced by one permitting contact and dialogue with all Israelis.

This was not just lip service. Arafat's signature on the Oslo Agreement enabled King Hussein to reach a peace agreement with Israel, and President Hafez Assad to announce that he too was ready to reach a new agreement.

Arafat came under great fire from many opponents and critics who believed that the Oslo Accord was an Israeli trap that would leave him as little more than Mayor of Gaza, and that kept him from achieving a state with reasonable borders, while granting Israel greater access to the Arab world and beyond. He understands well that implementation of the right of return for the Palestinian refugees to Israel would alter the demographic balance to such an extent that no Israeli government can agree to it, but he believes that Israel can give up the Temple Mount and settle for the Western Wall. He understands that without a permanent agreement, his opponents will be proven right. From his point of view, signing a permanent agreement would be his greatest achievement.

SOME FORESEE FOR ISRAEL another hundred years of living by the sword, believing that those with faith in peace are naïve and do not understand the region in which they live. They explain constantly that if we had a European neighbor, all would be well—their word is their bond, their promises can be relied upon, and their agreements are engraved in stone. But these doubters have short memories, and *they* are the naïve ones. First of all, anyone who prepares for another hundred years of war will find himself within a short time part of a Jewish minority ruling over an Arab majority. Anyone encouraging more generations of violence might just as well say to other Jews, "Do not come to Israel," and to young people, "Do not stay here." If the state of Israel, instead of being the safest place for Jews in the world, becomes the most dangerous place for them, the only people who will remain here will be those without the ability to leave. That is an absolute distortion of the Zionist ideal, and although it sounds very nationalistic and proud, it is in fact a kind of post-Zionist concept. As for the short memory—what was done to the Jewish people in Europe only sixty years ago has not been done to us anywhere else in the world. The constant complaint about the absence of a suitable partner merits not only the response, "Physician, heal thyself," and the recognition that it was Israel in Netanyahu's time who rejected an agreement, but also an historic reminder of the agreements that were indeed reached.

THE GENEVA AGREEMENT, which is set forth here in its entirety in Appendix 5, may be a glimmer of light for those who believe in peace. The agreement, reached by a significant group of Israelis and Palestinians, proves once again that there is someone to talk to and something to talk about. If we can muster the necessary courage, we can transform this agreement into reality.

APPENDIX 1
THE BEILIN–ABU MAZEN UNDERSTANDINGS
October 31, 1995

FRAMEWORK FOR THE CONCLUSION OF A FINAL STATUS AGREEMENT
BETWEEN ISRAEL AND THE PALESTINE LIBERATION ORGANIZATION

THE ATTAINMENT OF PEACE BETWEEN THE ISRAELI AND THE PALESTINIAN PEOPLES RESOLVES THE CORE PROBLEM AT THE HEART OF THE ISRAELI-ARAB CONFLICT AND COMMENCES AN ERA OF COMPREHENSIVE PEACE CONTRIBUTING THEREBY TO THE STABILITY, SECURITY, AND PROSPERITY OF THE ENTIRE MIDDLE EAST.

The Government of the State of Israel and the Palestine Liberation Organization (hereafter "the PLO"), the representative of the Palestinian people;

WITHIN the framework of the Middle East peace process initiated at Madrid in October 1991;

AIMING at the achievement of a just, lasting and comprehensive peace in the Middle East based on the implementation of UN Security Council Resolutions 242 and 338 in all their aspects;

REAFFIRMING their adherence to the commitments expressed in the Declaration of Principles (hereinafter "the DOP") signed in Washington D.C. on September 13th 1993, the Cairo Agreement of May 4th 1994, and the Interim Agreement of September 28th, 1995;

REAFFIRMING their determination to live in peaceful coexistence, mutual dignity and security;

DECLARING as null and void any agreement, declaration, document or statement which contradicts this Framework Agreement;

DESIROUS of reaching a full agreement on all outstanding final status issues as soon as possible, not later than May 5, 1999, as stipulated in the DOP;

HEREBY AGREE on the following Framework for a Final Status Agreement.

ARTICLE I: THE ESTABLISHMENT OF THE PALESTINIAN STATE AND ITS RELATIONS WITH THE STATE OF ISRAEL

1. As an integral part of this Framework Agreement and the full Final Status Agreement:

a. The Government of Israel shall extend its recognition to the independent State of Palestine within agreed and secure borders with its capital al-Quds upon its coming into being not later than May 5, 1999.

b. Simultaneously, the State of Palestine shall extend its recognition to the State of Israel within agreed and secure borders with its capital Yerushalayim.

c. Both sides continue to look favorably at the possibility of establishing a Jordanian-Palestinian confederation, to be agreed upon by the State of Palestine and the Hashemite Kingdom of Jordan.

2. The State of Israel and the State of Palestine (hereinafter: "the Parties") will thereby extend mutual recognition of their right to live in peace and security within mutually agreed borders as defined in Article II of this agreement and in the Final Status Agreement. In particular, the Parties shall:

a. Recognize and respect each other's sovereignty, territorial integrity and political and economic independence.

b. Renounce the use of force, and the threat of force as an instrument of policy and commit themselves to a peaceful resolution of all disputes between them.

c. Refrain from organizing, instigating, inciting, assisting or participating in acts of violence, subversion or terrorism against the other party.

d. Take effective measures to ensure that acts of or threats of violence do not originate from or through their respective territories, including their airspace and territorial waters, and take appropriate measures against those who perpetrate such acts.

e. Undertake not to join, assist, or cooperate with any military or security coalition, organization, or alliance hostile to either party.

f. Exchange and ratify the instruments of peace between them as shall be defined in the full Final Status Agreement.

ARTICLE II: THE DELINEATION OF SECURE AND RECOGNIZED BORDERS

1. The secure and recognized borders between the State of Israel and the future State of Palestine are described in the attached Maps and in Annex One of the Final Status Agreement. The Parties recognize that these borders, including their respective subsoil, airspace and territorial waters shall be inviolable.

2. The Parties shall define the route and mode of implementation of, as well as the extent of, territory to be yielded by Israel for the agreed extraterritorial passage between the Gaza Strip and the West Bank (as described in Annex One of the Final Status Agreement).

3. The border in the Jerusalem area is to be delineated in accordance with the provisions of Article VI of this Framework Agreement.

4. The Parties shall recognize the final borders between the two states as permanent and irrevocable.

ARTICLE III: THE CREATION OF NORMAL AND STABLE INTERSTATE RELATIONS

1. Upon the exchange of the instruments of ratification of the peace treaty, the Parties agree to establish full diplomatic and consular relations between them and to promote economic and cultural relations including the free movement of people, goods, capital and services across their borders.

2. The Parties shall continue to cooperate in all areas of mutual interest and will seek to promote jointly and separately similar regional cooperation with other states in the area and the international community.

3. The Parties shall seek to promote mutual cultural relations and will encourage mutual programs for the dissemination of their respective national customs, folklore and traditions between them.

4. The Parties shall secure freedom of access to places of religious, and historical significance on a non-discriminatory basis. Access to, worship in, and protection of all holy places and sites shall be guaranteed by both Parties.

ARTICLE IV: SCHEDULE OF ISRAELI MILITARY WITHDRAWAL AND SECURITY ARRANGEMENTS

1. In implementing UN Security Council Resolutions 242 and 338, the Parties agree that the withdrawal of Israeli Military and Security Forces shall be carried out in three stages:

   a. Withdrawal from the Central areas of the West Bank and the entire Gaza Strip (as defined in Annex Two to the Final Status Agreement and attached map/s), to commence not later than May 5, 1999 and be completed not later than September 4, 1999;

   b. Withdrawal from the Eastern areas of the West Bank (as defined in Annex Two to the Final Status Agreement), to commence not later than September 5, 1999 and be completed not later than January 4, 2000;

   c. Withdrawal from the Western areas of the West Bank (as defined in Annex Two to the Final Status Agreement) to commence not later than January 5, 2000 and be completed not later than May 4, 2000.

2. Thereafter Israel shall maintain a minimal residual force within agreed military compounds and in specified locations. This residual force will comprise:

   a. Three reinforced battalions, two existing Military Emergency Stores, and integral logistical forces (their location and terms of lease, duration, mode of deployment, function and numerical strength, are detailed in Annex Two to the Final Status Agreement).

   b. Three Early Warning stations and three Air Defense Units as defined and agreed in Annex Two to the Final Status Agreement will be maintained until May 5, 2007 or until peace agreements and bilateral security arrangements between Israel and the relevant Arab parties are attained, whichever comes last.

3. The Parties agree to the formation of an Israeli-Palestinian Coordinating Security Commission (hereinafter "the CSC") to oversee the implementation of Israel's military withdrawal, to establish the modalities governing its residual military presence, and to coordinate all other security matters (its structure and

authorities are detailed in Annex Two to the Final Status Agreement). The CSC shall also implement an agreed schedule for the introduction of Palestinian Security Forces (hereinafter "PSF") into Palestinian territories commensurate with and parallel to the withdrawal of Israeli forces. The Parties agree that the CSC shall commence its deliberations not later than May 5, 1998 (see Annex Two to the Final Status Agreement).

4. Joint Israeli-Palestinian patrols will be held along the Jordan River as well as along both sides of the Israeli-Palestinian border, in order to deter, prevent and combat the infiltration or organization of cross-border terrorism and other forms of violent activities. The mandate and duration of these patrols shall be determined by the CSC, as detailed in Annex Two to the Final Status Agreement.

5. The Parties agree that the State of Palestine shall be demilitarized. The PSF shall remain subject to agreed limitations as defined in Annex Two to the Final Status Agreement. By mutual agreement, and not before May 5, 2007, Palestinian self-defense capabilities shall be negotiated by the Parties.

6. The Parties agree that the cosponsors and other parties agreed upon, shall be invited to guarantee the arrangements for Israel's military withdrawal and other bilateral security agreements as stipulated in this Framework Agreement. In their capacity as guarantors, the said third parties shall also be invited to participate in observation, verification and other technical duties to be agreed in the CSC. The said third parties shall accordingly be requested to establish and finance a permanent International Observer Force (hereafter the IOF) whose mandate and functions are described in Annex Two of the Final Status Agreement.

ARTICLE V: ISRAELI SETTLEMENTS

1. Subsequent to the establishment of the Independent State of Palestine and its recognition by the State of Israel as described in Articles I and III of this agreement:

a. There will be no exclusive civilian residential areas for Israelis in the State of Palestine.

b. Individual Israelis remaining within the borders of the Palestinian State shall be subject to Palestinian sovereignty and Palestinian rule of law.

c. Individual Israelis who have their permanent domicile within the Palestinian State as of May 5, 1999, shall be offered Palestinian citizenship or choose to remain as alien residents, all without prejudice to their Israeli citizenship.

d. Within the agreed schedule for the withdrawal of Israeli forces from Palestinian territories as described in Article IV and Annex Two to the Final Status Agreement, the Israeli Government and its security forces shall maintain responsibility for the safety and security of Israeli settlements outside the areas of Palestinian security jurisdiction, pending the transfer of said areas to full Palestinian rule.

e. The CSC shall establish the mechanism for dealing with security issues relating to Israeli citizens in Palestine and Palestinian citizens in Israel.

ARTICLE VI: JERUSALEM

1. Jerusalem shall remain an open and undivided city with free and unimpeded access for people of all faiths and nationalities.

2. The Parties further agree that a reform of the current Jerusalem Municipal System and its boundaries shall be introduced not later than May 5, 1999, and shall not be subject to further change by law or otherwise, unless by mutual consent, prior to the fulfillment of the provisions of paragraph 9 below. This reform shall expand the present municipal boundaries of Jerusalem and shall define the city limits of the "City of Jerusalem", to include: Abu Dis, Azariyeh, A-Ram, Az-zaim, Ma'ale Adumim, Givat Ze'ev, Givon, and adjacent areas in the attached map/s.

3. Within the "City of Jerusalem," neighborhoods inhabited by Palestinians will be defined as "Palestinian boroughs." The exact borders of the "City of Jerusalem" and of the Israeli and Palestinian boroughs are delineated and described in Annex Three to the Final Status Agreement and attached map/s. The number of Israeli boroughs and of Palestinian boroughs will reflect the present demographic balance of 2:1. This proportion will be updated in accordance with the modalities, criteria and schedule as described in Annex Three to this Final Status Agreement.

4. The Parties agree to maintain one Municipality for the "City of Jerusalem" in the form of a Joint Higher Municipal Council, formed by representatives of the boroughs. These representatives will elect the Mayor of the "City of Jerusalem." In all matters related to the areas of the "City of Jerusalem" under Palestinian sovereignty, the Joint Higher Municipal Council shall seek the consent of the Government of Palestine. In all matters related to the areas of the "City of Jerusalem" under Israeli sovereignty, the Joint Higher Municipal Council shall seek the consent of the Government of Israel.

5. The "City of Jerusalem" shall consist of the Joint Higher Municipal Council, two sub-municipalities—an Israeli sub-municipality, elected by the inhabitants of the Israeli boroughs, and a Palestinian sub-municipality, elected by the inhabitants of the Palestinian boroughs—as well as a Joint Parity Committee for the Old City Area as described in paragraph 12 below.

6. The Parties further agree that the municipality of the "City of Jerusalem" shall:

a. Delegate strong local powers to the sub-municipalities including the right to local taxation, local services, an independent education system, separate religious authorities, and housing planning and zoning, as detailed in Annex Three to the Final Status Agreement;

b. Develop a twenty-five year Master Plan for the "City of Jerusalem" with agreed modalities for its balanced implementation, including safeguards for the interests of both communities.

c. Provide for Israeli and Palestinian citizens resident within the jurisdiction of the City of Jerusalem Municipality and sub-municipalities to vote and seek election for all elected posts as shall be specified in the Jerusalem Municipal bylaws.

7. Within the "City of Jerusalem" both parties recognize the Western part of the city to be "Yerushalayim" and the Arab Eastern part of the city, under Palestinian sovereignty, to be "al-Quds" (see attached map/s).

8. Upon the exchange of the instruments of ratification of the peace treaty between them:

a. The Government of the State of Palestine shall recognize Yerushalayim, as defined under Article VI, paragraph 7 and Annex Three to the Final Status Agreement, as the sovereign Capital of the State of Israel.

b. The Government of the State of Israel shall recognize al-Quds, as defined under Article VI, paragraph 7 and Annex Three to the Final Status Agreement, as the sovereign Capital of the State of Palestine.

9. The ultimate sovereignty of the area outside Yerushalayim and al-Quds, but inside the present municipal boundaries of Jerusalem, shall be determined by the parties as soon as possible. Each party maintains its position regarding the sovereign status of this area. A joint Israeli-Palestinian committee for determining the final status of this area shall be established not later than May 5, 1999 and shall

commence its deliberations immediately thereafter. Without prejudice to the determination of the final status of this area:

a. Palestinian citizenship shall be extended to Palestinian residents of this area.

b. In certain matters Palestinian citizens residing in this area shall resort to Palestinian law (as detailed in Annex Three to the Final Status Agreement).

c. The Parties will enjoy free access to and use of the Qalandia Airport in this area. A new designated Palestinian terminal shall be constructed, to commence operation concurrent with the signing of the Treaty of Peace (for the modalities of operation, see Annex Three to the Final Status Agreement).

10. The Parties acknowledge Jerusalem's unique spiritual and religious role for all three great monotheistic religions. Wishing to promote interfaith relations and harmony among the three great religions, the Parties accordingly agree to guarantee freedom of worship and access to all Holy Sites for members of all faiths and religions without impediment or restriction.

11. In recognition of the special status and significance of the Old City Area (see map/s) for members of the Christian, Jewish, and Muslim faiths, the parties agree to grant this area a special status.

12. The Parties further agree that:

a. The Palestinian sub-municipality shall be responsible for the municipal concerns of the Palestinian citizens residing in the Old City Area and their local property.

b. The Israeli sub-municipalies shall be responsible for the municipal concerns of the Israeli citizens residing in the Old City Area and their local property.

c. The two sub-municipalities shall appoint a Joint Parity Committee to manage all matters related to the preservation of the unique character of the Old City Area (its structureand modalities are detailed in Annex Three to the Final Status Agreement).

d. In case of a dispute between the two sub-municipalities on matters related to the Old City Area, the issue shall be referred for a decision to the Joint Parity Committee.

13. The State of Palestine shall be granted extraterritorial sovereignty over the

Haram al-Sharif under the administration of the al-Quds Waqf. The present status quo regarding the right of access and prayer for all, will be secured.

14. The Church of the Holy Sepulchre shall be managed by the Palestinian sub-municipality. The Joint Parity Committee, shall examine the possibility of assigning extraterritorial status to the Church of the Holy Sepulchre.

15. Supervision of persons and goods transiting through the "City of Jerusalem" shall take place at the exit points. Other security matters related to persons, vehicles and goods suspected of involvement in hostile activity are dealt with in Annex Two to the Final Status Agreement.

ARTICLE VII: PALESTINIAN REFUGEES

1. Whereas the Palestinian side considers that the right of the Palestinian refugees to return to their homes is enshrined in international law and natural justice, it recognizes that the prerequisites of the new era of peace and coexistence, as well as the realities that have been created on the ground since 1948, have rendered the implementation of this right impracticable. The Palestinian side, thus, declares its readiness to accept and implement policies and measures that will ensure, insofar as this is possible, the welfare and well-being of these refugees.

2. Whereas the Israeli side acknowledges the moral and material suffering caused to the Palestinian people as a result of the war of 1947–1949, it further acknowledges the Palestinian refugees' right of return to the Palestinian state and their right to compensation and rehabilitation for moral and material losses.

3. The Parties agree on the establishment of an International Commisssion for Palestinian Refugees (hereinafter "the ICPR") for the final settlement of all aspects of the refugee issue as follows:

   a. The Parties extend invitations to donor countries to join them in the formation of the ICPR.

   b. The Parties welcome the intention of the Government of Sweden to lead the ICPR and to contribute financially to its activities.

   c. The Government of Israel shall establish a fund for its contribution, along with others, to the activities of the ICPR.

   d. The ICPR shall conduct all fundraising activities and coordinate donors' involvement in the program.

e. The ICPR shall define the criteria for compensation accounting for:

(1) moral loss;

(2) immovable property;

(3) financial and economic support enabling resettlement and rehabilitation of Palestinians residing in refugee camps.

f. The ICPR shall further:

(1) adjudicate claims for material loss;

(2) prepare and develop rehabilitation and absorption programs;

(3) establish the mechanisms and venues for disbursing payments
and compensation;

(4) oversee rehabilitation programs;

(5) explore the intentions of Palestinian refugees on the one hand
and of Arab and other countries on the other, concerning wishes for
emigration and the possibilities thereof;

(6) explore with Arab governments hosting refugee populations, as
well as with these refugees, venues for absorption in these countries
whenever mutually desired.

g. The ICPR shall implement all the above according to the agreed schedule
defined in Annex Four to the Final Status Agreement.

4. The ICPR shall be guided by the following principles in dealing with the
"refugees of 1948" and their descendants as defined in Annex Four to the Final
Status Agreement:

a. Each refugee family shall be entitled to compensation for moral loss to a
sum of money to be agreed upon by the ICPR.

b. Each claimant with proven immovable property shall be compensated as
per the adjudication of the ICPR.

c. The ICPR shall provide financial and economic support, enabling the
resettlement and rehabilitation of Palestinians residing in refugee camps.

d. The refugees shall be entitled to financial and economic support from the
ICPR for resettlement and rehabilitation.

5. The State of Israel undertakes to participate actively in implementing the program for the resolution of the refugee problem. Israel will continue to enable family reunification and will absorb Palestinian refugees in special defined cases, to be agreed upon with the ICPR.

6. The Palestinian side undertakes to participate actively in implementing the program for the resolution of the refugee problem. The Palestinian side shall enact a program to encourage the rehabilitation and resettlement of Palestinian refugees presently resident in the West Bank and Gaza Strip, within these areas.

7. The PLO considers the implementation of the above a full and final settlement of the refugee issue in all its dimensions. It further undertakes that no additional claims or demands arising from this issue will be made upon the full implementation of this Framework Agreement.

ARTICLE VIII: ISRAELI-PALESTINIAN STANDING COMMITTEE

1. The Parties shall establish an Israeli-Palestinian Standing Committee (hereafter: "IPSC"), which will commence activities upon the signing of this Framework Agreement.

2. This IPSC shall be authorized to deal with all matters related to the smooth transition between the Interim Agreement and Final Status Agreement.

3. The IPSC shall also coordinate activities related to the implementation of the Final Status Agreement.

ARTICLE IX: WATER RESOURCES

1. The Parties agree that they possess the same natural water resources essential for each nation's livelihood and survival.

2. Water rights and issues are laid out in Annex Five to the Final Status Agreement.

3. With a view to achieving a comprehensive and lasting settlement of all water problems between them, the Parties jointly undertake to ensure that the management and development of their water resources should not in any way harm or imperil the water resources of the other.

4. The Parties further agree to the following:

   a. The development of existing and new water resources to increase availability and minimize wastage.

b. The prevention of contamination of water resources.

c. The transfer of information and joint research and the review of the potential for water enhancement.

5. The Parties agree to prepare as soon as possible, but not later than May 5, 1999, an agreed upon coordinated separate and joint water management plan for the joint aquifers that will guarantee optimal use and development of water resources for the benefit of the Israeli and Palestinian nations.

6. The Parties agree to seek to extend their joint cooperation to the Hashemite Kingdom of Jordan, in particular with regard to the waters of the Jordan River and the Dead Sea and to seek to promote wider regional understanding on the exploitation and management of water resources in the Middle East.

ARTICLE X: TIME FRAME AND IMPLEMENTATION

A. *The Preparatory Period: May 5, 1996 to May 4, 1999*

1. With the signing of this Framework Agreement and its entry into force not later than May 5, 1996, the Preparatory Period for Final Status shall commence. Immediately thereafter, the Parties shall:

a. Establish the IPSC (Israeli-Palestinian Standing Committee) along the lines laid down in Article VIII.

b. Extend invitations to donor countries to join the Government of Sweden and themselves in formation of the ICPR (International Commission for Palestinian Refugees).

The Preparatory Period shall end not later than May 4, 1999.

2. During this period it is agreed that the following shall be implemented:

a. The Final Status Agreement with all Annexes will be prepared, based on the agreements and principles laid down in this Framework Agreement.

b. Consequently, and based on the mechanisms for border delineation set out in Annex One to the Final Status Agreement, the joint delineation of borders and official extraterritorial and other passages shall be finalized.

c. The Israeli-Palestinian Coordinating Security Commission (CSC) shall be established and commence its deliberation, not later than May 5, 1998. The CSC shall establish the mechanism for dealing with security issues relating to Israeli citizens in the State of Palestine, and Palestinian citizens in the State of Israel.

d. The Parties shall invite the cosponsors to the Peace Process and other agreed upon third parties, to establish an International Observer Force (IOF) as agreed upon in Annex Two to the Final Status Agreement.

e. The Government of Israel shall establish a program to encourage Israeli settlers to resettle within Israel's sovereign territory. Settlers wishing to take part in this program shall be compensated by the Israeli government before January 1, 1999, according to guidelines to be announced within three months of the entry into force of this Framework Agreement.

f. The agreed upon reformed Jerusalem Municipal System shall be inaugurated not later than May 5, 1999.

g. Both sides shall prepare and agree on a Jerusalem Master Plan as described in Article VI.

h. In accordance with Article VII of this Framework Agreement, the PLO shall establish a program to encourage the rehabilitation and resettlement of Palestinian refugees presently residing in the West Bank and Gaza Strip, within these areas.

i. The Parties shall promote the work of the ICPR as stipulated in Article VII to this Agreement.

j. The Parties shall prepare an agreed upon coordinated, separate and joint water management plan for the joint aquifers.

k. As soon as possible, but not later than May 4, 1999, the interim period shall come to an end and a full Final Status Agreement shall be signed and a Peace Treaty shall be initiated.

B. *The Implementation Period: May 5, 1999 to May 4, 2000*

1. With the signing and entry into force of the Israeli-Palestinian Final Status Agreement, the implementation of the Final Status settlement will commence. The creation of the Independent State of Palestine within secure and recognized borders shall be promulgated by the PLO and its relevant agencies. Immediately thereafter, but not later than within two months, the Peace Treaty shall be signed.

2. The Government of the State of Israel shall extend immediate and full diplo-

matic recognition to the State of Palestine and to al-Quds as its capital, as described in Article VI and Annex Three to the Final Status Agreement.

3. The Government of the State of Palestine shall extend immediate and full diplomatic recognition to the State of Israel and to Yerushalayim as its capital, as described in Article VI and Annex Three to the Final Status Agreement.

4. Provisions relating to the normalization of Israeli-Palestinian relations shall be implemented as described in Article III.

5. Upon entry into force of the Israeli-Palestinian Final Status Agreement, the withdrawal of Israeli Military and Security Forces shall commence and the agreed security provisions shall be implemented according to the schedule described in Article II and Annex Two to the Final Status Agreement.

6. Within the "City of Jerusalem" elections for the two sub-municipalities will be held. The two sub-municipalities shall appoint a Joint Parity Committee for the Old City Area (as outlined in Article VI paragraph 12 to this agreement), and a proportional (2:1) Joint Higher Municipal Council which will elect the Mayor of the "City of Jerusalem."

7. The parties agree to continue to work jointly and separately within the framework of the multilateral working groups and other relevant fora towards:

   a. The establishment of a Middle East free from hostile coalitions and alliances.

   b. The creation of a Middle East free from weapons of mass destruction both conventional and non-conventional within the context of a comprehensive, lasting and stable settlement.

C. *The Post-Implementation Period: May 5, 2000 to May 4, 2007*

1. Israeli residual forces shall remain on Palestinian territory. The CSC shall continue to coordinate Israeli and Palestinian security needs.

2. Responsibility for the security of Israeli citizens residents in the State of Palestine, shall remain with the CSC.

D. *The Post–November 5, 2007 Period*

Remaining Israeli residual forces shall withdraw from the Palestinian State contingent on the attainment of peace treaties and security arrangements between Israel and the relevant Arab parties.

APPENDIX 2
THE BEILIN–EITAN AGREEMENT
January 22, 1997

NATIONAL AGREEMENT REGARDING THE NEGOTIATIONS ON THE PERMANENT SETTLEMENT WITH THE PALESTINIANS

The central objective of the Zionist movement, from the day of its founding, was the establishment of a sovereign state in the Land of Israel. The Jewish state was established in 1948, but it was not until 1977 that the first Arab state, Egypt, recognized and later signed a peace treaty with the State of Israel.

The Camp David Agreements, the Oslo Accords, the Mutual Recognition between the Israeli Government and the PLO and the projects of the settlements in the territories under Israeli control since 1967 have created a reality from which none of the involved parties can escape.

Both danger and opportunity are concealed in the dialogue between the Israeli and Palestinian leaderships. The last two Israeli governments made the strategic decision to take on calculated risks with the goal of pursuing every possible chance for attaining peace and good neighborly relations between Jews and Arabs in the Land of Israel.

Against the backdrop of a readiness to find a means of historic compromise between Jews and Arabs, a bitter controversy has developed within the Jewish nation: giving up parts of the homeland. In addition to the prevalent ideological controversy, there are bitter differences of opinion about the degree of security risk that it is acceptable to assume given the risks and threats from the Arab side.

There are those who are suspicious that a secure peace is nothing but an illusion, a deceptive vision that will lead Israel into a trap that will, in the end, exact a heavy price of blood. Opposing them are those who claim fervently that the process has potential and that a lasting peace is essential to ensure the security of the State of Israel for generations.

This grave political polarization reached its climax towards the end of 1995. In September the Israeli government signed Oslo II, which was understood to be a step towards the transfer of the territories of the West Bank to the Palestinians. Protest demonstrations intensified and many saw the signing of the accord as fundamental heresy. This climate of intense polarization led to the political assassination, several weeks later, of Yitzhak Rabin.

Despite the fact that the murder and the murderer were condemned unequivocally by the high-ranking leadership in Israel, there were more than a few who identified with the nefarious act and in their identification made clear that a real risk of civil war existed. It was as if we had not learned the historical lesson of what was bound to happen in the aftermath of the use of terror as a means of settling an internal political disagreement between Jews and other Jews, not least when an "enemy [is] besieging the city."

Members of Knesset from the Likud Gesher Tzomet faction and from the Labor faction came together with the common objective of clarifying the areas of agreement and disagreement between them regarding the future negotiations with the Palestinians on a permanent settlement. Following a series of discussions and clarifications they have arrived at the conclusion that it is necessary to reach a national consensus on the basis of the following three principles:

1st. It is necessary to continue the dialogue with the Palestinian representatives and to pursue exhaustively every opportunity to achieve a permanent agreement with them. In the framework of such an agreement it is necessary to permit the establishment of a Palestinian entity whose status will be determined in negotiations between the parties and the limits on the sovereignty of which will be discussed in the following sections.

2nd. Under conditions of peace and following the achievement of an agreement on the issue of the permanent settlement, the State of Israel must preserve its ability to prevent every attack or risk of an attack on its territorial integrity, the safety of its citizens and their property and in its vital interests in Israel and in the world.

3rd. No agreement signed by the Israeli government can include a commitment to uproot Jewish settlements west of the Jordan River nor will any agreement compromise the rights of the residents to keep their Israeli citizenship and their ties as individuals and as a community with the State of Israel.

A. BORDERS

The position of Israel on every issue relating to the question of borders will be based on the following principles:

1. There will be no return to the 1967 borders.

2. The majority of settlers will live on their settlement under Israeli sovereignty, in order to preserve territorial continuity between the settlements and the State of Israel.

3. The residents of the Israeli settlements that will exist outside of the area that will be annexed by the State of Israel will receive special, agreed upon, arrangements within the framework of which their Israeli citizenship and their ties with the State of Israel, as individuals and as a community, will be preserved. Thus their right of free and safe passage to the territories under full Israeli sovereignty will be preserved.

4. The Jordan Valley will be a special security zone and Israeli army forces will be posted along the Jordan River. The residents of the area will be permitted to remain where they are, according to point 3, above. Another version insists upon an Israeli sovereignty over the Jordan valley.

B. SECURITY COMPONENTS

1. The Palestinian entity will be demilitarized and it will have no army.

2. The Jordan River will be the security border of Israel. Secure crossing conditions will be regulated by IDF forces in proportion to need and to the changing conditions within the Palestinian entity, and IDF deployment on the borders.

3. The Palestinian entity will establish a strong police force to meet the needs of internal security.

4. No foreign army may be stationed within the boundaries of the Palestinian entity.

5. The security forces of Israel and the Palestinian entity will work to deter and foil acts of terrorism aimed against Jews and Arabs.

6. The Palestinian entity will not sign any military agreement or any other agreement that includes a threat to the territorial integrity of the State of Israel, the security of its citizens or the integrity of their property. It will not sign any agreement regarding boycott or any other illegal steps against the Israeli economy nor any agreement involving negative propaganda against the State of Israel or against the Jewish people.

7. The commitment of the two parties to the agreement regarding the permanent settlements will be strengthened by the fulfillment of all of their other commitments.

8. Any basic violation of the commitments presented in this section will allow the violated party to regard the whole agreement as annulled and will grant the assailed the right to act freely to right the violations and to prevent further violations.

C. STATUS OF THE PALESTINIAN ENTITY AND LIMITS ON ITS SOVEREIGNTY

Subject to the limits presented in this document, the right of the Palestinian entity to self-determination will be recognized. According to an alternative opinion it will be regarded as an enlarged autonomy, and according to another opinion, as a state.

D. JERUSALEM

1. Jerusalem, the capital of Israel, with its existing municipal borders, will be a single unified city within sovereign Israel.

2. The Palestinians will recognize Jerusalem as the capital of Israel and Israel will recognize the governing center of the Palestinian entity which will be within the borders of the entity and outside the existing municipal borders of Jerusalem.

3. Muslim and Christian holy places in Jerusalem will be granted special status.

4. Within the framework of the municipal government the Palestinian residents of Arab neighborhoods in Jerusalem will receive a status that will allow them to share in the responsibility of the administration of their lives in the city.

E. REFUGEES

1. The right of the State of Israel to prevent the entry of Palestinian refugees into its sovereign territory will be recognized.

2. The administration of the entrance of refugees into the Palestinian entity and the limits to that entry will be decided upon during the negotiations of the permanent settlement, within the larger discussion of Israel's security issues.

3. An international organization will be founded, in which Israel will play an important role, with the goal of financing and carrying out projects for compensation and rehabilitation of the refugees in their places. The organization will also address Israeli claims for reparations for Jewish refugees from Arab countries.

4. Israel and the Palestinian entity, each within its own boundaries, will rehabilitate the refugees on the basis of the disengagement of the UNRWA, the repealing of the refugee status and the arrangement of housing and employment with international aid. (For Israel this refers to the Shuafat and Qalandia refugee camps in Jerusalem.)

5. Israel will continue its policy of family reunification on the basis of existing criteria.

F. WATER

The agreement on the issue of water usage, as it was signed in the framework of the interim agreement, will remain in effect. The water authorities of Israel and the Palestinians will establish shared control over its usage.

Any future change of anything related to the issue of division of water, modes of production or means of protection of water purity must be made with the agreement of both parties. In the absence of such an agreement the status quo will remain.

Israel and the Palestinian entity will act together in regards to everything pertaining to desalination and regional water enterprises.

G. ECONOMY AND TRADE

The economic sphere is one of the cornerstones in the relationship between Israel and the Palestinian entity, with the goal of strengthening their interests in achieving a just, lasting and comprehensive peace. The two parties will cooperate in this arena in order to create a solid economic basis for these relations, which will be grounded in the different economic spheres on the values of mutual respect of each party for the economic interests of the other, mutuality, justice and protection. The parties will invite the Kingdom of Jordan to participate in this economic cooperation.

H. EDUCATION, CULTURE AND GOOD NEIGHBORS

The Israeli leadership and the Palestinian leadership must create a fitting environment for the development of peaceful relations between Jews and Palestinians. It is necessary to encourage educational initiatives, cultural connections and to foster models of Jewish-Arab cooperation as a basis for good neighborly relations. A true peace between Jews and Arabs in the Land of Israel will be attained when each population accepts the existence of its counterpart on a basis of mutuality and equality.

I. THE INTERIM AGREEMENT AND THE PERMANENT SETTLEMENT

1. There will be a special effort to conclude the talks of the issue of the permanent settlement and especially to finalize the borders between Israel and the Palestinian entity before the intended date for further redeployment.

2. If the borders are not finalized before the third redeployment Israel will redeploy so that up to fifty percent of the West Bank will be designated as territories A and B.

APPENDIX 3
THE BERLIN DECLARATION
March 25, 1999

The Heads of State and Government of the European Union reaffirm their support for a negotiated settlement in the Middle East, to reflect the principles of land for peace and ensure the security both collective and individual of the Israeli and Palestinian peoples. In this context, the European Union welcomes the decision by the Palestinian National Union and associated bodies to reaffirm the nullification of the provisions in the Palestinian National Charter which called for the destruction of Israel and to reaffirm their commitment to recognize and live in peace with Israel. However, the European Union remains concerned at the current deadlock in the peace process and calls upon the parties to implement fully and immediately the Wye River Memorandum.

The European Union also calls upon the parties to reaffirm their commitments to the basic principles established within the framework of Madrid, Oslo and subsequent agreements, in accordance with UNSC Resolutions 242 and 338. It urges the parties to agree on an extension of the transitional period established by the Oslo agreements.

The European Union calls in particular for an early resumption of final status negotiations in the coming months on an accelerated basis, and for these to be brought to a prompt conclusion and not prolonged indefinitely.

The European Union believes that it should be possible to conclude the negotiations within a target period of one year. It expresses its readiness to work to facilitate an early conclusion to the negotiations.

The European Union urges both parties to refrain from activities which prejudge the outcome of those final status negotiations and from any activity contrary to international law, including all settlement activity, and to fight incitement and violence.

The European Union reaffirms the continuing and unqualified Palestinian right to self-determination including the option of a state and looks forward to the early fulfillment of this right. It appeals to the parties to strive in good faith for a negotiated solution on the basis of the existing agreements, without prejudice to this right, which is not subject to any veto. The European Union is convinced that the creation of a democratic, viable and peaceful sovereign Palestinian State on the basis of existing agreements and through negotiations would be the best guarantee of Israel's security and Israel's acceptance as an equal partner in the region. The European Union declares its readiness to consider the recognition of a Palestinian State in due course in accordance with the basic principles referred to above.

The European Union also calls for an early resumption of negotiations on the Syrian and Lebanese tracks of the Middle East Peace Process, leading to the implementation of UNSCRs 242, 338, and 425.

APPENDIX 4
THE CLINTON PLAN
December 23, 2000

TERRITORY:

• Based on what I heard, I believe that the solution should be in the mid-ninety percents, between 94–96 percent of the West Bank territory of the Palestinian State.

• The land annexed by Israel should be compensated by a land swap of one to three percent in addition to territorial arrangements such as a permanent safe passage.

The Parties also should consider the swap of leased land to meet their respective needs. There are creative ways of doing this that should address Palestinian and Israeli needs and concerns.

• The Parties should develop a map consistent with the following criteria:

   * Eighty percent of settlers in blocs.

   * Contiguity.

   * Minimize annexed areas.

   * Minimize the number of Palestinians affected.

SECURITY:

• The key lies in an international presence that can only be withdrawn by mutual consent. This presence will also monitor the implementation of the agreement between both sides.

• My best judgment is that the Israeli presence would remain in fixed locations in the Jordan Valley under the authority of the International force for another thirty-six months.

• This period could be reduced in the event of favorable regional developments that diminish the threats to Israel.

• On early-warning stations, Israel should maintain three facilities in the West Bank with a Palestinian liaison presence. The stations will be subject to review every ten years with any changes in the status to be mutually agreed.

• Regarding emergency developments, I understand that you will still have to develop a map of the relevant areas and routes. But in defining what is an emergency, I propose the following definition:

• Imminent and demonstrable threat to Israel's national security of a military nature that requires the activation of a national state emergency. Of course, the international forces will need to be notified of any such determination.

• On airspace, I suggest that the state of Palestine will have sovereignty over its airspace but that two sides should work out special arrangements for Israeli training and operational needs.

• I understand that the Israeli position is that Palestine should be defined as a "demilitarized state" while the Palestinian side proposes "a state with limited arms." As a compromise, I suggest calling it a "non-militarized state." This will be consistent with the fact that in addition to strong Palestinian security forces, Palestine will have an international force for border security and deterrent purposes.

JERUSALEM:

• The general principle is that Arab areas are Palestinian and Jewish ones are Israeli. This would apply to the Old City as well.

• I urge the two sides to work on maps to create maximum contiguity for both sides.

• Regarding the Haram/Temple Mount, I believe that the gaps are not related to practical administration but to the symbolic issues of sovereignty and to finding a way to accord respect to the religious beliefs of both sides.

• I know you have been discussing a number of formulations, and you can agree to one of these. I add to these two additional formulations guaranteeing Palestinian effective control over the Haram while respecting the conviction of the Jewish people. Regarding either one of these two formulations will be international monitoring to provide mutual confidence.

1. Palestinian sovereignty over the Haram, and Israeli sovereignty over

a) the Western Wall and the space sacred to Judaism of which it is a part; b) the Western Wall and the Holy of Holies of which it is a part. There will be a fine commitment by both not to excavate beneath the Haram or behind the Wall.

2. Palestinian sovereignty over the Haram and Israeli sovereignty over the Western Wall and shared functional sovereignty over the issue of excavation under the Haram and behind the Wall such that mutual consent would be requested before any excavation can take place.

REFUGEES:

• I sense that the differences are more relating to formulations and less to what will happen on a practical level.

• I believe that Israel is prepared to acknowledge the moral and material suffering caused to the Palestinian people as a result of the 1948 war and the need to assist the international community in addressing the problem.

• An international commission should be established to implement all the aspects that flow from your agreement: compensation, resettlement, rehabilitation, etc. The U.S. is prepared to lead an international effort to help the refugees.

• The fundamental gap is on how to handle the concept of the right of return. I know the history of the issue and how hard it will be for the Palestinian leadership to appear to be abandoning this principle.

• The Israeli side could not accept any reference to a right of return that would imply a right to immigrate to Israel in defiance of Israel's sovereign policies and admission or that would threaten the Jewish character of the state.

• Any solution must address both needs. The solution will have to be consistent with the two-state approach that both sides have accepted as a way to end the Palestinian-Israeli conflict: the state of Palestine as the homeland of the Palestinian people and the state of Israel as the homeland of the Jewish people.

• Under the two-state solution, the guiding principle should be that the Palestinian state would be the focal point for Palestinians who choose to return to the area without ruling out that Israel will accept some of these refugees.

• I believe that we need to adopt a formulation on the right of return that will make clear that there is no specific right of return to Israel itself but that does not negate the aspiration of the Palestinian people to return to the area.

• In light of the above, I propose two alternatives:

1. Both sides recognize the right of Palestinian refugees to return to historic Palestine, or,
2. Both sides recognize the right of Palestinian refugees to return to their homeland.

• The agreement will define the implementation of this general right in a way that is consistent with the two-state solution. It would list the five possible homes for the refugees:

1. The state of Palestine.
2. Areas in Israel being transferred to Palestine in the land swap.
3. Rehabilitation in a host country.
4. Resettlement in a third country.
5. Admission to Israel.

• In listing these options, the agreement will make clear that the return to the West Bank, Gaza Strip, and areas acquired in the land swap would be the right of all Palestinian refugees, while rehabilitation in host countries, resettlement in third countries and absorption into Israel will depend upon the policies of those countries.

• Israel could indicate in the agreement that it intends to establish a policy so that some of the refugees would be absorbed into Israel consistent with Israel's sovereign decision.

• I believe that priority should be given to the refugee population in Lebanon.

• The parties would agree that this implements resolution 194.

THE END OF CONFLICT:

• I propose that the agreement clearly mark the end of the conflict and its implementation put an end to all claims. This could be implemented through a UN

Security Council Resolution that notes that Resolutions 242 and 338 have been implemented and through the release of Palestinian prisoners.

CONCLUDING REMARKS:

• I believe that this is the outline of a fair and lasting agreement. It gives the Palestinian people the ability to determine their future on their own land, a sovereign and viable state recognized by the international community, al-Quds as its capital, sovereignty over the Haram, and new lives for the refugees.

• It gives the people of Israel a genuine end to the conflict, real security, the preservation of sacred religious ties, the incorporation of eighty percent of the settlers into Israel, and the largest Jewish Jerusalem in history recognized by all as its capital.

This is the best that I can do. Brief your leaders and tell me if they are prepared to come for discussions based on these ideas. If so, I would meet them next week separately. If not, I have taken this as far as I can. These are my ideas. If they are not accepted, they are not just off the table, they also go with me when I leave office.

APPENDIX 5
THE GENEVA ACCORD

COVER LETTER

We, the undersigned, a group of Palestinians and Israelis, endorse, on this day, October 12, 2003, a model draft framework final status agreement between the two peoples. At this point in time, after the Palestinian government and the Israeli government have accepted the Road Map, which includes reaching a final status settlement by 2005, based on a two-state solution, we consider it to be of the utmost importance to present to the two peoples and the entire world an example of what such a final status agreement could include. This is proof that despite all the pain entailed in concessions, it is possible to reach an historical compromise which meets the vital national interests of each side. We present this model agreement as a package—which stands together as an integral whole.

In the near future we will launch a campaign whose goal is to convince both sides of the value of such an historical compromise in the spirit of this model framework agreement, designed to put an end to the protracted conflict.

We see this as an educational endeavor, as people who believe in peace, who believe in advancing our respective national interests and who believe that a peace agreement is attainable. It is against our interests to indefinitely postpone such an agreement. In addition, we consider it as a service to the decision-makers.

Past experience has proven how difficult it is for official entities to prepare themselves for the negotiations on the final status settlement, due to fears that any detailed, technical work is proof of a concession. To this end we will also be involved in the preparation of the supplements and appendices which will specify the solutions at the highest level of detail, and will be available to the decision-makers at the time of their talks on the final status settlement.

Among the participants, on both sides, there are people, who have held official positions in the past, and people who continue to do so today, yet, in this document, none of us represents their respective peoples in any binding sense. We believe that our approach represents vast sections of public opinion on both sides. We were supported in this process from the beginning by a private Swiss Foundation and the Department of Foreign Affairs of Switzerland.

The decision to complete and later present this model draft agreement was not easy for any of us, however, we have decided to pursue this path since we believe that action of this type can serve as a source of hope after a long period of suffering, killing and mutual accusations, that it can help build trust and facilitate the removal of the walls between our nations. In the context of the Road Map process, this draft agreement signifies a mutually acceptable and realizable endgame—to be reached by 2005, and as an answer to the skeptics and supporters of endless interim agreements. This agreement will bring about the creation of a sovereign Palestinian State alongside Israel, put an end to the occupation, terminate conflict and bloodshed, and end all mutual claims.

We are today depositing this model framework agreement with the Swiss Foreign Minister.

We have decided to meet in the very near future in Geneva, after completing our preparations, for a public signing and launching of this initiative.

GENEVA ACCORD
A Draft Permanent Status Agreement
October 2003

Preamble

The State of Israel (hereinafter "Israel") and the Palestine Liberation Organization (hereinafter "PLO"), the representative of the Palestinian people (hereinafter the "Parties"):

REAFFIRMING their determination to put an end to decades of confrontation and conflict, and to live in peaceful coexistence, mutual dignity and security based on a just, lasting, and comprehensive peace and achieving historic reconciliation;

RECOGNIZING that peace requires the transition from the logic of war and confrontation to the logic of peace and cooperation, and that acts and words characteristic of the state of war are neither appropriate nor acceptable in the era of peace;

AFFIRMING their deep belief that the logic of peace requires compromise, and that the only viable solution is a two-state solution based on UNSC Resolution 242 and 338;

AFFIRMING that this agreement marks the recognition of the right of the Jewish people to statehood and the recognition of the right of the Palestinian people to statehood, without prejudice to the equal rights of the Parties' respective citizens;

RECOGNIZING that after years of living in mutual fear and insecurity, both peoples need to enter an era of peace, security and stability, entailing all necessary actions by the parties to guarantee the realization of this era;

RECOGNIZING each other's right to peaceful and secure existence within secure and recognized boundaries free from threats or acts of force;

DETERMINED to establish relations based on cooperation and the commitment to live side by side as good neighbors aiming both separately and jointly to contribute to the well-being of their peoples;

REAFFIRMING their obligation to conduct themselves in conformity with the norms of international law and the Charter of the United Nations;

CONFIRMING that this Agreement is concluded within the framework of the Middle East peace process initiated in Madrid in October 1991, the Declaration of Principles of September 13, 1993, the subsequent agreements including the Interim Agreement of September 1995, the Wye River Memorandum of October 1998, and the Sharm el-Sheikh Memorandum of September 4, 1999, and the permanent status negotiations including the Camp David Summit of July 2000, the Clinton Plan of December 2000, and the Taba Negotiations of January 2001;

REITERATING their commitment to United Nations Security Council Resolutions 242, 338 and 1397 and confirming their understanding that this Agreement is based on, will lead to, and—by its fulfillment—will constitute the full implementation of these resolutions and to the settlement of the Israeli-Palestinian conflict in all its aspects;

DECLARING that this Agreement constitutes the realization of the permanent status peace component envisaged in President Bush's speech of June 24, 2002 and in the Quartet Road Map process.

DECLARING that this Agreement marks the historic reconciliation between the Palestinians and Israelis, and paves the way to reconciliation between the Arab World and Israel and the establishment of normal, peaceful relations between the Arab states and Israel in accordance with the relevant clauses of the Beirut Arab League Resolution of March 28, 2002; and

RESOLVED to pursue the goal of attaining a comprehensive regional peace, thus contributing to stability, security, development and prosperity throughout the region;

Have agreed on the following:

ARTICLE I: PURPOSE OF THE PERMANENT STATUS AGREEMENT

1. The Permanent Status Agreement (hereinafter "this Agreement") ends the era of conflict and ushers in a new era based on peace, cooperation, and good neighborly relations between the Parties.

2. The implementation of this Agreement will settle all the claims of the Parties arising from events occurring prior to its signature. No further claims related to events prior to this Agreement may be raised by either Party.

ARTICLE II: RELATIONS BETWEEN THE PARTIES

1. The state of Israel shall recognize the state of Palestine (hereinafter "Palestine") upon its establishment. The state of Palestine shall immediately recognize the state of Israel.

2. The state of Palestine shall be the successor to the PLO with all its rights and obligations.

3. Israel and Palestine shall immediately establish full diplomatic and consular relations with each other and will exchange resident Ambassadors, within one month of their mutual recognition.

4. The Parties recognize Palestine and Israel as the homelands of their respective peoples. The Parties are committed not to interfere in each other's internal affairs.

5. This Agreement supercedes all prior agreements between the Parties.

6. Without prejudice to the commitments undertaken by them in this Agreement, relations between Israel and Palestine shall be based upon the provisions of the Charter of the United Nations.

7. With a view to the advancement of the relations between the two States and peoples, Palestine and Israel shall cooperate in areas of common interest. These shall include, but are not limited to, dialogue between their legislatures and state institutions, cooperation between their appropriate local authorities, promotion of non-governmental civil society cooperation, and joint programs and exchange in the areas of culture, media, youth, science, education, environment, health, agriculture, tourism, and crime prevention. The Israeli-Palestinian Cooperation Committee will oversee this cooperation in accordance with Article 8.

8. The Parties shall cooperate in areas of joint economic interest, to best realize the human potential of their respective peoples. In this regard, they will work bilaterally, regionally, and with the international community to maximize the benefit of peace to the broadest cross-section of their respective populations. Relevant standing bodies shall be established by the Parties to this effect.

9. The Parties shall establish robust modalities for security cooperation, and engage in a comprehensive and uninterrupted effort to end terrorism and violence directed against each others persons, property, institutions or territory. This effort shall continue at all times, and shall be insulated from any possible crises and other aspects of the Parties' relations.

10. Israel and Palestine shall work together and separately with other parties in the region to enhance and promote regional cooperation and coordination in spheres of common interest.

11. The Parties shall establish a ministerial-level Palestinian-Israeli High Steering Committee to guide, monitor, and facilitate the process of implementation of this Agreement, both bilaterally and in accordance with the mechanisms in Article 3 hereunder.

ARTICLE III: IMPLEMENTATION AND VERIFICATION GROUP

1. Establishment and Composition

i. An Implementation and Verification Group (IVG) shall hereby be established to facilitate, assist in, guarantee, monitor, and resolve disputes relating to the implementation of this Agreement.

ii. The IVG shall include the U.S., the Russian Federation, the EU, the UN, and other parties, both regional and international, to be agreed on by the Parties.

iii. The IVG shall work in coordination with the Palestinian-Israeli High Steering Committee established in Article 2/11 above and subsequent to that with the Israeli-Palestinian Cooperation Committee (IPCC) established in Article 8 hereunder.

iv. The structure, procedures, and modalities of the IVG are set forth below and detailed in Annex X.

2. Structure

i. A senior political-level contact group (Contact Group), composed of all the IVG members, shall be the highest authority in the IVG.

ii. The Contact Group shall appoint, in consultation with the Parties, a Special Representative who will be the principal executive of the IVG on the ground. The Special Representative shall manage the work of the IVG and maintain constant contact with the Parties, the Palestinian-Israeli High Steering Committee, and the Contact Group.

iii. The IVG permanent headquarters and secretariat shall be based in an agreed upon location in Jerusalem.

iv. The IVG shall establish its bodies referred to in this Agreement and additional bodies as it deems necessary. These bodies shall be an integral part of and under the authority of the IVG.

v. The Multinational Force (MF) established under Article 5 shall be an integral part of the IVG. The Special Representative shall, subject to the approval of the Parties, appoint the Commander of the MF who shall be responsible for the daily command of the MF. Details relating to the Special Representative and MF Force Commander are set forth in Annex X.

vi. The IVG shall establish a dispute settlement mechanism, in accordance with Article 16.

3. Coordination with the Parties

A Trilateral Committee composed of the Special Representative and the Palestinian-Israeli High Steering Committee shall be established and shall meet on at least a monthly basis to review the implementation of this Agreement. The Trilateral Committee will convene within 48 hours upon the request of any of the three parties represented.

4. Functions

In addition to the functions specified elsewhere in this Agreement, the IVG shall:

i. Take appropriate measures based on the reports it receives from the MF.

ii. Assist the Parties in implementing the Agreement and preempt and promptly mediate disputes on the ground.

5. Termination

In accordance with the progress in the implementation of this Agreement, and with the fulfillment of the specific mandated functions, the IVG shall terminate its activities in the said spheres. The IVG shall continue to exist unless otherwise agreed by the Parties.

ARTICLE IV: TERRITORY

1. The International Borders between the States of Palestine and Israel

i. In accordance with UNSC Resolution 242 and 338, the border between the states of Palestine and Israel shall be based on the June 4, 1967 lines with reciprocal modifications on a 1:1 basis as set forth in attached Map 1.

ii. The Parties recognize the border, as set out in attached Map 1, as the permanent, secure and recognized international boundary between them.

2. Sovereignty and Inviolability

i. The Parties recognize and respect each other's sovereignty, territorial integrity, and political independence, as well as the inviolability of each others territory, including territorial waters and airspace. They shall respect this inviolability in accordance with this Agreement, the UN Charter, and other rules of international law.

ii. The Parties recognize each other's rights in their exclusive economic zones in accordance with international law.

3. Israeli Withdrawal

i. Israel shall withdraw in accordance with Article 5.

ii. Palestine shall assume responsibility for the areas from which Israel withdraws.

iii. The transfer of authority from Israel to Palestine shall be in accordance with Annex X.

iv. The IVG shall monitor, verify, and facilitate the implementation of this Article.

4. Demarcation

i. A Joint Technical Border Commission (Commission) composed of the two Parties shall be established to conduct the technical demarcation of the border in accordance with this Article. The procedures governing the work of this Commission are set forth in Annex X.

ii. Any disagreement in the Commission shall be referred to the IVG in accordance with Annex X.

iii. The physical demarcation of the international borders shall be completed by the Commission not later than nine months from the date of the entry into force of this Agreement.

5. Settlements

i. The state of Israel shall be responsible for resettling the Israelis residing in Palestinian sovereign territory outside this territory.

ii. The resettlement shall be completed according to the schedule stipulated in Article 5.

iii. Existing arrangements in the West Bank and Gaza Strip regarding Israeli settlers and settlements, including security, shall remain in force in each of the settlements until the date prescribed in the timetable for the completion of the evacuation of the relevant settlement.

iv. Modalities for the assumption of authority over settlements by Palestine are set forth in Annex X. The IVG shall resolve any disputes that may arise during its implementation.

v. Israel shall keep intact the immovable property, infrastructure and facilities in Israeli settlements to be transferred to Palestinian sovereignty. An agreed inventory shall be drawn up by the Parties with the IVG in advance of the completion of the evacuation and in accordance with Annex X.

vi. The state of Palestine shall have exclusive title to all land and any buildings, facilities, infrastructure or other property remaining in any of the settlements on the date prescribed in the timetable for the completion of the evacuation of this settlement.

6. Corridor

i. The states of Palestine and Israel shall establish a corridor linking the West Bank and Gaza Strip. This corridor shall:

a. Be under Israeli sovereignty.

b. Be permanently open.

c. Be under Palestinian administration in accordance with Annex X of this Agreement. Palestinian law shall apply to persons using and procedures appertaining to the corridor.

d. Not disrupt Israeli transportation and other infrastructural networks, or endanger the environment, public safety or public health. Where necessary, engineering solutions will be sought to avoid such disruptions.

e. Allow for the establishment of the necessary infrastructural facilities linking the West Bank and the Gaza Strip. Infrastructural facilities shall be understood to include, inter alia, pipelines, electrical and communications cables, and associated equipment as detailed in Annex X.

f. Not be used in contravention of this Agreement.

ii. Defensive barriers shall be established along the corridor and Palestinians shall not enter Israel from this corridor, nor shall Israelis enter Palestine from the corridor.

iii. The Parties shall seek the assistance of the international community in securing the financing for the corridor.

iv. The IVG shall guarantee the implementation of this Article in accordance with Annex X.

v. Any disputes arising between the Parties from the operation of the corridor shall be resolved in accordance with Article 16.

vi. The arrangements set forth in this clause may only be terminated or revised by agreement of both Parties.

ARTICLE V: SECURITY

1. General Security Provisions

i. The Parties acknowledge that mutual understanding and cooperation in security-related matters will form a significant part of their bilateral relations and will further enhance regional security. Palestine and Israel shall base their security relations on cooperation, mutual trust, good neighborly relations, and the protection of their joint interests.

ii. Palestine and Israel each shall:

a. Recognize and respect the other's right to live in peace within secure and recognized boundaries free from the threat or acts of war, terrorism and violence.

b. refrain from the threat or use of force against the territorial integrity or political independence of the other and shall settle all disputes between them by peaceful means.

c. refrain from joining, assisting, promoting or cooperating with any coalition, organization or alliance of a military or security character, the objectives or activities of which include launching aggression or other acts of hostility against the other.

d. refrain from organizing, encouraging, or allowing the formation of irregular forces or armed bands, including mercenaries and militias within their respective territory and prevent their establishment. In this respect, any existing irregular forces or armed bands shall be disbanded and prevented from reforming at any future date.

e. refrain from organizing, assisting, allowing, or participating in acts of violence in or against the other or acquiescing in activities directed toward the commission of such acts.

iii. To further security cooperation, the Parties shall establish a high level Joint Security Committee that shall meet on at least a monthly basis. The Joint Security Committee shall have a permanent joint office, and may establish such subcommittees as it deems necessary, including subcommittees to immediately resolve localized tensions.

2. Regional Security

i. Israel and Palestine shall work together with their neighbors and the international community to build a secure and stable Middle East, free from weapons of mass destruction, both conventional and non-conventional, in the context of a comprehensive, lasting, and stable peace, characterized by reconciliation, goodwill, and the renunciation of the use of force.

ii. To this end, the Parties shall work together to establish a regional security regime.

3. Defense Characteristics of the Palestinian State

i. No armed forces, other than as specified in this Agreement, will be deployed or stationed in Palestine.

ii. Palestine shall be a non-militarized state, with a strong security force. Accordingly, the limitations on the weapons that may be purchased, owned, or used by the Palestinian Security Force (PSF) or manufactured in Palestine shall be specified in Annex X. Any proposed changes to Annex X shall be considered by a trilateral committee composed of the two Parties and the MF. If no agreement is reached in the trilateral committee, the IVG may make its own recommendations.

> a. No individuals or organizations in Palestine other than the PSF and the organs of the IVG, including the MF, may purchase, possess, carry or use weapons except as provided by law.

iii. The PSF shall:

> a. Maintain border control;
>
> b. Maintain law-and-order and perform police functions;
>
> c. Perform intelligence and security functions;
>
> d. Prevent terrorism;
>
> e. Conduct rescue and emergency missions; and
>
> f. Supplement essential community services when necessary.

iv. The MF shall monitor and verify compliance with this clause.

4. Terrorism

i. The Parties reject and condemn terrorism and violence in all its forms and shall pursue public policies accordingly. In addition, the Parties shall refrain from actions and policies that are liable to nurture extremism and create conditions conducive to terrorism on either side.

ii. The Parties shall take joint and, in their respective territories, unilateral comprehensive and continuous efforts against all aspects of violence and terrorism. These efforts shall include the prevention and preemption of such acts, and the prosecution of their perpetrators.

iii. To that end, the Parties shall maintain ongoing consultation, cooperation, and exchange of information between their respective security forces.

iv. A Trilateral Security Committee composed of the two Parties and the United States shall be formed to ensure the implementation of this Article. The Trilateral Security Committee shall develop comprehensive policies and guidelines to fight terrorism and violence.

5. Incitement

i. Without prejudice to freedom of expression and other internationally recognized human rights, Israel and Palestine shall promulgate laws to prevent incitement to irredentism, racism, terrorism and violence and vigorously enforce them.

ii. The IVG shall assist the Parties in establishing guidelines for the implementation of this clause, and shall monitor the Parties' adherence thereto.

6. Multinational Force

i. A Multinational Force (MF) shall be established to provide security guarantees to the Parties, act as a deterrent, and oversee the implementation of the relevant provisions of this Agreement.

ii. The composition, structure and size of the MF are set forth in Annex X.

iii. To perform the functions specified in this Agreement, the MF shall be deployed in the state of Palestine. The MF shall enter into the appropriate Status of Forces Agreement (SOFA) with the state of Palestine.

iv. In accordance with this Agreement, and as detailed in Annex X, the MF shall:

a. In light of the non-militarized nature of the Palestinian state, protect the territorial integrity of the state of Palestine.

b. Serve as a deterrent against external attacks that could threaten either of the Parties.

c. Deploy observers to areas adjacent to the lines of the Israeli withdrawal during the phases of this withdrawal, in accordance with Annex X.

d. Deploy observers to monitor the territorial and maritime borders of the state of Palestine, as specified in clause 5/13.

e. Perform the functions on the Palestinian international border crossings specified in clause 5/12.

f. Perform the functions relating to the early warning stations as specified in clause 5/8.

g. Perform the functions specified in clause 5/3.

h. Perform the functions specified in clause 5/7.

i. Perform the functions specified in Article 10.

j. Help in the enforcement of anti-terrorism measures.

k. Help in the training of the PSF.

v. In relation to the above, the MF shall report to and update the IVG in accordance with Annex X.

vi. The MF shall only be withdrawn or have its mandate changed by agreement of the Parties.

7. Evacuation

i. Israel shall withdraw all its military and security personnel and equipment, including landmines, and all persons employed to support them, and all military installations from the territory of the state of Palestine, except as otherwise agreed in Annex X, in stages.

ii. The staged withdrawals shall commence immediately upon entry into force of this Agreement and shall be made in accordance with the timetable and modalities set forth in Annex X.

iii. The stages shall be designed subject to the following principles:

a. The need to create immediate clear contiguity and facilitate the early implementation of Palestinian development plans.

b. Israel's capacity to relocate, house and absorb settlers. While costs and inconveniences are inherent in such a process, these shall not be unduly disruptive.

c. The need to construct and operationalize the border between the two states.

d. The introduction and effective functioning of the MF, in particular on the eastern border of the state of Palestine.

iv. Accordingly, the withdrawal shall be implemented in the following stages:

a. The first stage shall include the areas of the state of Palestine, as defined in Map X, and shall be completed within 9 months.

b. The second and third stages shall include the remainder of the territory of the state of Palestine and shall be completed within 21 months of the end of the first stage.

v. Israel shall complete its withdrawal from the territory of the state of Palestine within 30 months of the entry into force of this Agreement, and in accordance with this Agreement.

vi. Israel will maintain a small military presence in the Jordan Valley under the authority of the MF and subject to the MF SOFA as detailed in Annex X for an additional 36 months. The stipulated period may be reviewed by the Parties in the event of relevant regional developments, and may be altered by the Parties' consent.

vii. In accordance with Annex X, the MF shall monitor and verify compliance with this clause.

8. Early-Warning Stations

i. Israel may maintain two EWS in the northern, and central West Bank at the locations set forth in Annex X.

ii. The EWS shall be staffed by the minimal required number of Israeli personnel and shall occupy the minimal amount of land necessary for their operation as set forth in Annex X.

iii. Access to the EWS will be guaranteed and escorted by the MF.

iv. Internal security of the EWS shall be the responsibility of Israel. The perimeter security of the EWS shall be the responsibility of the MF.

v. The MF and the PSF shall maintain a liaison presence in the EWS. The MF shall monitor and verify that the EWS is being used for purposes recognized by this Agreement as detailed in Annex X.

vi. The arrangements set forth in this Article shall be subject to review in ten years, with any changes to be mutually agreed. Thereafter, there will be five-yearly reviews whereby the arrangements set forth in this Article may be extended by mutual consent.

vii. If at any point during the period specified above a regional security regime is established, then the IVG may request that the Parties review whether to continue or revise operational uses for the EWS in light of these developments. Any such change will require the mutual consent of the Parties.

9. Airspace

i. Civil Aviation

a. The Parties recognize as applicable to each other the rights, privileges and obligations provided for by the multilateral aviation agreements to which they are both party, particularly by the 1944 Convention on International Civil Aviation (The Chicago Convention) and the 1944 International Air Services Transit Agreement.

b. In addition, the Parties shall, upon entry into force of this Agreement, establish a trilateral committee composed of the two Parties and the IVG to design the most efficient management system for civil aviation, including those relevant aspects of the air traffic control system. In the absence of consensus the IVG may make its own recommendations.

ii. Training

a. The Israeli Air Force shall be entitled to use the Palestinian sovereign airspace for training purposes in accordance with Annex X, which shall be based on rules pertaining to IAF use of Israeli airspace.

b. The IVG shall monitor and verify compliance with this clause. Either Party may submit a complaint to the IVG whose decision shall be conclusive.

c. The arrangements set forth in this clause shall be subject to review every ten years, and may be altered or terminated by the agreement of both Parties.

10. Electromagnetic Sphere

i. Neither Party's use of the electromagnetic sphere may interfere with the other Party's use.

ii. Annex X shall detail arrangements relating to the use of the electromagnetic sphere.

iii. The IVG shall monitor and verify the implementation of this clause and Annex X.

iv. Any Party may submit a complaint to the IVG whose decision shall be conclusive.

11. Law Enforcement

The Israeli and Palestinian law enforcement agencies shall cooperate in combating illicit drug trafficking, illegal trafficking in archaeological artifacts and objects of arts, cross-border crime, including theft and fraud, organized crime, trafficking in women and minors, counterfeiting, pirate TV and radio stations, and other illegal activity.

12. International Border Crossings

i. The following arrangements shall apply to border crossings between the state of Palestine and Jordan, the state of Palestine and Egypt, as well as airport and seaport entry points to the state of Palestine.

ii. All border crossings shall be monitored by joint teams composed of members of the PSF and the MF. These teams shall prevent the entry into Palestine of any weapons, materials or equipment that are in contravention of the provisions of this Agreement.

iii. The MF representatives and the PSF will have, jointly and separately, the authority to block the entry into Palestine of any such items. If at any time a disagreement regarding the entrance of goods or materials arises between the PSF and the MF representatives, the PSF may bring the matter to the IVG, whose binding conclusions shall be rendered within twenty-four hours.

iv. This arrangement shall be reviewed by the IVG after five years to determine its continuation, modification or termination. Thereafter, the Palestinian party may request such a review on an annual basis.

v. In passenger terminals, for thirty months, Israel may maintain an unseen presence in a designated on-site facility, to be staffed by members of the MF and Israelis, utilizing appropriate technology. The Israeli side may request that the MF-PSF conduct further inspections and take appropriate action.

vi. For the following two years, these arrangements will continue in a specially designated facility in Israel, utilizing appropriate technology. This shall not cause delays beyond the procedures outlined in this clause.

vii. In cargo terminals, for thirty months, Israel may maintain an unseen presence in a designated on-site facility, to be staffed by members of the MF and Israelis, utilizing appropriate technology. The Israeli side may request that the MF-PSF conduct further inspections and take appropriate action. If the Israeli side is not satisfied by the MF-PSF action, it may demand that the cargo be detained pending a decision by an MF inspector. The MF inspector's decision shall be binding and final, and shall be rendered within twelve hours of the Israeli complaint.

viii. For the following three years, these arrangements will continue from a specially designated facility in Israel, utilizing appropriate technology. This shall not cause delays beyond the timelines outlined in this clause.

ix. A high level trilateral committee composed of representatives of Palestine, Israel, and the IVG shall meet regularly to monitor the application of these procedures and correct any irregularities, and may be convened on request.

x. The details of the above are set forth in Annex X.

13. Border Control

i. The PSF shall maintain border control as detailed in Annex X.

ii. The MF shall monitor and verify the maintenance of border control by the PSF.

ARTICLE VI: JERUSALEM

1. Religious and Cultural Significance

i. The Parties recognize the universal historic, religious, spiritual, and cultural significance of Jerusalem and its holiness enshrined in Judaism, Christianity, and Islam. In recognition of this status, the Parties reaffirm their commitment to safeguard the character, holiness, and freedom of worship in the city and to respect the existing division of administrative functions and traditional practices between different denominations.

ii. The Parties shall establish an interfaith body consisting of representatives of the three monotheistic faiths, to act as a consultative body to the Parties on matters related to the city's religious significance and to promote interreligious understanding and dialogue. The composition, procedures, and modalities for this body are set forth in Annex X.

2. Capital of Two States

The Parties shall have their mutually recognized capitals in the areas of Jerusalem under their respective sovereignty.

3. Sovereignty

Sovereignty in Jerusalem shall be in accordance with attached Map 2. This shall not prejudice nor be prejudiced by the arrangements set forth below.

4. Border Regime

The border regime shall be designed according to the provisions of Article 11, and taking into account the specific needs of Jerusalem (e.g., movement of tourists and intensity of border crossing use including provisions for Jerusalemites) and the provisions of this Article.

5. Haram al-Sharif/ Temple Mount (Compound)

i. International Group

a. An International Group, composed of the IVG and other parties to be agreed upon by the Parties, including members of the Organization of the Islamic Conference (OIC), shall hereby be established to monitor, verify, and assist in the implementation of this clause.

b. For this purpose, the International Group shall establish a Multinational Presence on the Compound, the composition, structure, mandate and functions of which are set forth in Annex X.

c. The Multinational Presence shall have specialized detachments dealing with security and conservation. The Multinational Presence shall make periodic conservation and security reports to the International Group. These reports shall be made public.

d. The Multinational Presence shall strive to immediately resolve any problems arising and may refer any unresolved disputes to the International Group that will function in accordance with Article 16.

e. The Parties may at any time request clarifications or submit complaints to the International Group which shall be promptly investigated and acted upon.

f. The International Group shall draw up rules and regulations to maintain security on and conservation of the Compound. These shall include lists of the weapons and equipment permitted on the site.

ii. Regulations Regarding the Compound

a. In view of the sanctity of the Compound, and in light of the unique religious and cultural significance of the site to the Jewish people, there shall be no digging, excavation, or construction on the Compound, unless approved by the two Parties. Procedures for regular maintenance and emergency repairs on the Compound shall be established by the IG after consultation with the Parties.

b. The state of Palestine shall be responsible for maintaining the security of the Compound and for ensuring that it will not be used for any hostile acts against Israelis or Israeli areas. The only arms permitted on the Compound shall be those carried by the Palestinian security personnel and the security detachment of the Multinational Presence.

c. In light of the universal significance of the Compound, and subject to security considerations and to the need not to disrupt religious worship or decorum on the site as determined by the Waqf, visitors shall be allowed access to the site. This shall be without any discrimination and generally be in accordance with past practice.

iii. Transfer of Authority

a. At the end of the withdrawal period stipulated in Article 5/7, the state of Palestine shall assert sovereignty over the Compound.

b. The International Group and its subsidiary organs shall continue to exist and fulfill all the functions stipulated in this Article unless otherwise agreed by the two Parties.

6. The Wailing Wall

The Wailing Wall shall be under Israeli sovereignty.

7. The Old City

i. Significance of the Old City

a. The Parties view the Old City as one whole enjoying a unique character. The Parties agree that the preservation of this unique character together with safeguarding and promoting the welfare of the inhabitants should guide the administration of the Old City.

b. The Parties shall act in accordance with the UNESCO World Cultural Heritage List regulations, in which the Old City is a registered site.

ii. IVG Role in the Old City

a. Cultural Heritage

1. The IVG shall monitor and verify the preservation of cultural heritage in the Old City in accordance with the UNESCO World Cultural Heritage List rules. For this purpose, the IVG shall have free and unimpeded access to sites, documents, and information related to the performance of this function.

2. The IVG shall work in close coordination with the Old City Committee of the Jerusalem Coordination and Development Committee (JCDC), including in devising a restoration and preservation plan for the Old City.

b. Policing

1. The IVG shall establish an Old City Policing Unit (PU) to liaise with, coordinate between, and assist the Palestinian and Israeli police forces in the Old City, to defuse localized tensions and help resolve disputes, and to perform policing duties in locations specified in and according to operational procedures detailed in Annex X.

2. The PU shall periodically report to the IVG.

c. Either Party may submit complaints in relation to this clause to the IVG, which shall promptly act upon them in accordance with Article 16.

iii. Free Movement within the Old City

Movement within the Old City shall be free and unimpeded subject to the provisions of this article and rules and regulations pertaining to the various holy sites.

iv. Entry into and Exit from the Old City

a. Entry and exit points into and from the Old City will be staffed by the authorities of the state under whose sovereignty the point falls, with the presence of PU members, unless otherwise specified.

b. With a view to facilitating movement into the Old City, each Party shall take such measures at the entry points in its territory as to ensure the preservation of security in the Old City. The PU shall monitor the operation of the entry points.

c. Citizens of either Party may not exit the Old City into the territory of the other Party unless they are in possession of the relevant documentation that entitles them to. Tourists may only exit the Old City into the territory of the Party which they posses valid authorization to enter.

v. Suspension, Termination, and Expansion

a. Either Party may suspend the arrangements set forth in Article 6.7.iii in cases of emergency for one week. The extension of such suspension for longer than a week shall be pursuant to consultation with the other Party and the IVG at the Trilateral Committee established in Article 3/3.

b. This clause shall not apply to the arrangements set forth in Article 6/7/vi.

c. Three years after the transfer of authority over the Old City, the Parties shall review these arrangements. These arrangements may only be terminated by agreement of the Parties.

d. The Parties shall examine the possibility of expanding these arrangements beyond the Old City and may agree to such an expansion.

vi. Special Arrangements

a. Along the way outlined in Map X (from the Jaffa Gate to the Zion Gate) there will be permanent and guaranteed arrangements for Israelis regarding access, freedom of movement, and security, as set forth in Annex X.

1. The IVG shall be responsible for the implementation of these arrangements.

b. Without prejudice to Palestinian sovereignty, Israeli administration of the Citadel will be as outlined in Annex X.

vii. Color-Coding of the Old City

A visible color-coding scheme shall be used in the Old City to denote the sovereign areas of the respective Parties.

viii. Policing

a. An agreed number of Israeli police shall constitute the Israeli Old City police detachment and shall exercise responsibility for maintaining order and day-to-day policing functions in the area under Israeli sovereignty.

b. An agreed number of Palestinian police shall constitute the Palestinian Old City police detachment and shall exercise responsibility for maintaining order and day-to-day policing functions in the area under Palestinian sovereignty.

c. All members of the respective Israeli and Palestinian Old City police detachments shall undergo special training, including joint training exercises, to be administered by the PU.

d. A special Joint Situation Room, under the direction of the PU and incorporating members of the Israeli and Palestinian Old City police detachments, shall facilitate liaison on all relevant matters of policing and security in the Old City.

ix. Arms

No person shall be allowed to carry or possess arms in the Old City, with the exception of the Police Forces provided for in this agreement. In addition, each Party may grant special written permission to carry or possess arms in areas under its sovereignty.

x. Intelligence and Security

a. The Parties shall establish intensive intelligence cooperation regarding the Old City, including the immediate sharing of threat information.

b. A trilateral committee composed of the two Parties and representatives of the United States shall be established to facilitate this cooperation.

8. Mount of Olives Cemetery

i. The area outlined in Map X (the Jewish Cemetery on the Mount of Olives) shall be under Israeli administration; Israeli law shall apply to persons using and procedures appertaining to this area in accordance with Annex X.

a. There shall be a designated road to provide free, unlimited, and unimpeded access to the Cemetery.

b. The IVG shall monitor the implementation of this clause.

c. This arrangement may only be terminated by the agreement of both Parties.

9. Special Cemetery Arrangements

Arrangements shall be established in the two cemeteries designated in Map X

(Mount Zion Cemetery and the German Colony Cemetery), to facilitate and ensure the continuation of the current burial and visitation practices, including the facilitation of access.

10. The Western Wall Tunnel

i. The Western Wall Tunnel designated in Map X shall be under Israeli administration, including:

a. Unrestricted Israeli access and right to worship and conduct religious practices.

b. Responsibility for the preservation and maintenance of the site in accordance with this Agreement and without damaging structures above, under IVG supervision.

c. Israeli policing.

d. IVG monitoring

e. The Northern Exit of the Tunnel shall only be used for exit and may only be closed in case of emergency as stipulated in Article 6/7.

ii. This arrangement may only be terminated by the agreement of both Parties.

11. Municipal Coordination

i. The two Jerusalem municipalities shall form a Jerusalem Coordination and Development Committee ("JCDC") to oversee the cooperation and coordination between the Palestinian Jerusalem municipality and the Israeli Jerusalem municipality. The JCDC and its subcommittees shall be composed of an equal number of representatives from Palestine and Israel. Each side will appoint members of the JCDC and its subcommittees in accordance with its own modalities.

ii. The JCDC shall ensure that the coordination of infrastructure and services best serves the residents of Jerusalem, and shall promote the economic development of the city to the benefit of all. The JCDC will act to encourage cross-community dialogue and reconciliation.

iii. The JCDC shall have the following subcommittees:

a. A Planning and Zoning Committee: to ensure agreed planning and zoning regulations in areas designated in Annex X.

b. A Hydro Infrastructure Committee: to handle matters relating to drinking water delivery, drainage, and wastewater collection and treatment.

c. A Transport Committee: to coordinate relevant connectedness and compatibility of the two road systems and other issues pertaining to transport.

d. An Environmental Committee: to deal with environmental issues affecting the quality of life in the city, including solid waste management.

e. An Economic and Development Committee: to formulate plans for economic development in areas of joint interest, including in the areas of transportation, seam line commercial cooperation, and tourism,

f. A Police and Emergency Services Committee: to coordinate measures for the maintenance of public order and crime prevention and the provision of emergency services;

g. An Old City Committee: to plan and closely coordinate the joint provision of the relevant municipal services, and other functions stipulated in Article 6/7.

h. Other Committees as agreed in the JCDC.

12. Israeli Residency of Palestinian Jerusalemites

Palestinian Jerusalemites who currently are permanent residents of Israel shall lose this status upon the transfer of authority to Palestine of those areas in which they reside.

13. Transfer of Authority

The Parties will apply in certain socioeconomic spheres interim measures to ensure the agreed, expeditious, and orderly transfer of powers and obligations from Israel to Palestine. This shall be done in a manner that preserves the accumulated socioeconomic rights of the residents of East Jerusalem.

ARTICLE VII: REFUGEES

1. Significance of the Refugee Problem

i. The Parties recognize that, in the context of two independent states, Palestine and Israel, living side by side in peace, an agreed resolution of the refugee problem is necessary for achieving a just, comprehensive and lasting peace between them.

ii. Such a resolution will also be central to stability building and development in the region.

2. UNGAR 194, UNSC Resolution 242, and the Arab Peace Initiative

i. The Parties recognize that UNGAR 194, UNSC Resolution 242, and the Arab Peace Initiative (Article 2ii) concerning the rights of the Palestinian refugees represent the basis for resolving the refugee issue, and agree that these rights are fulfilled according to Article 7 of this Agreement.

3. Compensation

i. Refugees shall be entitled to compensation for their refugeehood and for loss of property. This shall not prejudice or be prejudiced by the refugee's permanent place of residence.

ii. The Parties recognize the right of states that have hosted Palestinian refugees to remuneration.

4. Choice of Permanent Place of Residence (PPR)

The solution to the PPR aspect of the refugee problem shall entail an act of informed choice on the part of the refugee to be exercised in accordance with the options and modalities set forth in this agreement. PPR options from which the refugees may choose shall be as follows;

i. The state of Palestine, in accordance with clause a below.

ii. Areas in Israel being transferred to Palestine in the land swap, following assumption of Palestinian sovereignty, in accordance with clause a below.

iii. Third Countries, in accordance with clause b below.

iv. The state of Israel, in accordance with clause c below.

v. Present Host countries, in accordance with clause d below.

    a. PPR options i and ii shall be the right of all Palestinian refugees and shall be in accordance with the laws of the State of Palestine.

b. Option iii shall be at the sovereign discretion of third countries and shall be in accordance with numbers that each third country will submit to the International Commission. These numbers shall represent the total number of Palestinian refugees that each third country shall accept.

c. Option iv shall be at the sovereign discretion of Israel and will be in accordance with a number that Israel will submit to the International Commission. This number shall represent the total number of Palestinian refugees that Israel shall accept. As a basis, Israel will consider the average of the total numbers submitted by the different third countries to the International Commission.

d. Option v shall be in accordance with the sovereign discretion of present host countries. Where exercised this shall be in the context of prompt and extensive development and rehabilitation programs for the refugee communities

Priority in all the above shall be accorded to the Palestinian refugee population in Lebanon.

5. Free and Informed Choice

The process by which Palestinian refugees shall express their PPR choice shall be on the basis of a free and informed decision. The Parties themselves are committed and will encourage third parties to facilitate the refugees' free choice in expressing their preferences, and to countering any attempts at interference or organized pressure on the process of choice. This will not prejudice the recognition of Palestine as the realization of Palestinian self-determination and statehood.

6. End of Refugee Status

Palestinian refugee status shall be terminated upon the realization of an individual refugee's permanent place of residence (PPR) as determined by the International Commission.

7. End of Claims

This agreement provides for the permanent and complete resolution of the Palestinian refugee problem. No claims may be raised except for those related to the implementation of this agreement.

8. International Role

The Parties call upon the international community to participate fully in the comprehensive resolution of the refugee problem in accordance with this Agreement, including, inter alia, the establishment of an International Commission and an International Fund.

9. Property Compensation

i. Refugees shall be compensated for the loss of property resulting from their displacement.

ii. The aggregate sum of property compensation shall be calculated as follows:

a. The Parties shall request the International Commission to appoint a Panel of Experts to estimate the value of Palestinians' property at the time of displacement.

b. The Panel of Experts shall base its assessment on the UNCCP records, the records of the Custodian for Absentee Property, and any other records it deems relevant. The Parties shall make these records available to the Panel.

c. The Parties shall appoint experts to advise and assist the Panel in its work.

d. Within 6 months, the Panel shall submit its estimates to the Parties.

e. The Parties shall agree on an economic multiplier, to be applied to the estimates, to reach a fair aggregate value of the property.

iii. The aggregate value agreed to by the Parties shall constitute the Israeli "lump sum" contribution to the International Fund. No other financial claims arising from the Palestinian refugee problem may be raised against Israel.

iv. Israel's contribution shall be made in installments in accordance with Schedule X.

v. The value of the Israeli fixed assets that shall remain intact in former settlements and transferred to the state of Palestine will be deducted from Israel's contribution to the International Fund. An estimation of this value shall be made by the International Fund, taking into account assessment of damage caused by the settlements.

10. Compensation for Refugeehood

i. A "Refugeehood Fund" shall be established in recognition of each individual's refugeehood. The Fund, to which Israel shall be a contributing party, shall be overseen by the International Commission. The structure and financing of the Fund is set forth in Annex X.

ii. Funds will be disbursed to refugee communities in the former areas of UNRWA operation, and will be at their disposal for communal development and commemoration of the refugee experience. Appropriate mechanisms will be devised by the International Commission whereby the beneficiary refugee communities are empowered to determine and administer the use of this Fund.

11. The International Commission (Commission)

i. Mandate and Composition

> a. An International Commission shall be established and shall have full and exclusive responsibility for implementing all aspects of this Agreement pertaining to refugees.

> b. In addition to themselves, the Parties call upon the United Nations, the United States, UNRWA, the Arab host countries, the EU, Switzerland, Canada, Norway, Japan, the World Bank, the Russian Federation, and others to be the members of the Commission.

> c. The Commission shall:

> > 1. Oversee and manage the process whereby the status and PPR of Palestinian refugees is determined and realized.

> > 2. Oversee and manage, in close cooperation with the host states, the rehabilitation and development programs.

> > 3. Raise and disburse funds as appropriate.

> d. The Parties shall make available to the Commission all relevant documentary records and archival materials in their possession that it deems necessary for the functioning of the Commission and its organs. The Commission may request such materials from all other relevant parties and bodies, including, inter alia, UNCCP and UNRWA.

ii. Structure

a. The Commission shall be governed by an Executive Board (Board) composed of representatives of its members.

b. The Board shall be the highest authority in the Commission and shall make the relevant policy decisions in accordance with this Agreement.

c. The Board shall draw up the procedures governing the work of the Commission in accordance with this Agreement.

d. The Board shall oversee the conduct of the various Committees of the Commission. The said Committees shall periodically report to the Board in accordance with procedures set forth thereby.

e. The Board shall create a Secretariat and appoint a Chair thereof. The Chair and the Secretariat shall conduct the day-to-day operation of the Commission.

iii. Specific Committees

a. The Commission shall establish the Technical Committees specified below.

b. Unless otherwise specified in this Agreement, the Board shall determine the structure and procedures of the Committees.

c. The Parties may make submissions to the Committees as deemed necessary.

d. The Committees shall establish mechanisms for resolution of disputes arising from the interpretation or implementation of the provisions of this Agreement relating to refugees.

e. The Committees shall function in accordance with this Agreement, and shall render binding decisions accordingly.

f. Refugees shall have the right to appeal decisions affecting them according to mechanisms established by this Agreement and detailed in Annex X.

iv. Status-determination Committee :

a. The Status-determination Committee shall be responsible for verifying refugee status.

b. UNRWA registration shall be considered as rebuttable presumption (prima facie proof) of refugee status.

v. Compensation Committee :

a. The Compensation Committee shall be responsible for administering the implementation of the compensation provisions.

b. The Committee shall disburse compensation for individual property pursuant to the following modalities:

1. Either a fixed per capita award for property claims below a specified value. This will require the claimant to only prove title, and shall be processed according to a fast-track procedure, or

2. A claims-based award for property claims exceeding a specified value for immovables and other assets. This will require the claimant to prove both title and the value of the losses.

c. Annex X shall elaborate the details of the above including, but not limited to, evidentiary issues and the use of UNCCP, "Custodian for Absentees' Property", and UNRWA records, along with any other relevant records.

vi. Host State Remuneration Committee:

There shall be remuneration for host states.

vii. Permanent Place of Residence Committee (PPR Committee):

The PPR Committee shall,

a. Develop with all the relevant parties detailed programs regarding the implementation of the PPR options pursuant to Article 7/4 above.

b. Assist the applicants in making an informed choice regarding PPR options.

c. Receive applications from refugees regarding PPR. The applicants must indicate a number of preferences in accordance with article 7/4 above. The applications shall be received no later than two years after the start of the International Commission's operations. Refugees who do not submit such applications within the two-year period shall lose their refugee status.

d. Determine, in accordance with sub-Article (a) above, the PPR of the applicants, taking into account individual preferences and maintenance of family unity. Applicants who do not avail themselves of the Committee's PPR determination shall lose their refugee status.

e. Provide the applicants with the appropriate technical and legal assistance.

f. The PPR of Palestinian refugees shall be realized within 5 years of the start of the International Commission's operations.

viii. Refugeehood Fund Committee

The Refugeehood Fund Committee shall implement Article 7/10 as detailed in Annex X.

ix. Rehabilitation and Development Committee

In accordance with the aims of this Agreement and noting the above PPR programs, the Rehabilitation and Development Committee shall work closely with Palestine, Host Countries and other relevant third countries and parties in pursuing the goal of refugee rehabilitation and community development. This shall include devising programs and plans to provide the former refugees with opportunities for personal and communal development, housing, education, healthcare, retraining and other needs. This shall be integrated in the general development plans for the region.

12. The International Fund

i. An International Fund (the Fund) shall be established to receive contributions outlined in this Article and additional contributions from the international community. The Fund shall disburse monies to the Commission to enable it to carry out its functions. The Fund shall audit the Commission's work.

ii. The structure, composition and operation of the Fund are set forth in Annex X.

13. UNRWA

i. UNRWA should be phased out in each country in which it operates, based on the end of refugee status in that country.

ii. UNRWA should cease to exist five years after the start of the Commission's operations. The Commission shall draw up a plan for the phasing out of UNRWA and shall facilitate the transfer of UNRWA functions to host states.

14. Reconciliation Programs

i. The Parties will encourage and promote the development of cooperation between their relevant institutions and civil societies in creating forums for exchanging historical narratives and enhancing mutual understanding regarding the past.

ii. The Parties shall encourage and facilitate exchanges in order to disseminate a richer appreciation of these respective narratives, in the fields of formal and informal education, by providing conditions for direct contacts between schools, educational institutions and civil society.

iii. The Parties may consider cross-community cultural programs in order to promote the goals of conciliation in relation to their respective histories.

iv. These programs may include developing appropriate ways of commemorating those villages and communities that existed prior to 1949.

ARTICLE VIII: ISRAELI-PALESTINIAN COOPERATION COMMITTEE (IPCC)

1. The Parties shall establish an Israeli-Palestinian Cooperation Committee immediately upon the entry into force of this agreement. The IPCC shall be a ministerial-level body with ministerial-level Co-Chairs.

2. The IPCC shall develop and assist in the implementation of policies for cooperation in areas of common interest including, but not limited to, infrastructure needs, sustainable development and environmental issues, cross-border municipal cooperation, border area industrial parks, exchange programs, human resource development, sports and youth, science, agriculture and culture.

3. The IPCC shall strive to broaden the spheres and scope of cooperation between the Parties.

ARTICLE IX: DESIGNATED ROAD USE ARRANGEMENTS

1. The following arrangements for Israeli civilian use will apply to the designated roads in Palestine as detailed in Map X (Road 443, Jerusalem to Tiberias via Jordan Valley, and Jerusalem—Ein Gedi).

2. These arrangements shall not prejudice Palestinian jurisdiction over these

roads, including PSF patrols.

3. The procedures for designated road use arrangements will be further detailed in Annex X.

4. Israelis may be granted permits for use of designated roads. Proof of authorization may be presented at entry points to the designated roads. The sides will review options for establishing a road use system based on smart card technology.

5. The designated roads will be patrolled by the MF at all times. The MF will establish with the states of Israel and Palestine agreed arrangements for cooperation in emergency medical evacuation of Israelis.

6. In the event of any incidents involving Israeli citizens and requiring criminal or legal proceedings, there will be full cooperation between the Israeli and Palestinian authorities according to arrangements to be agreed upon as part of the legal cooperation between the two states. The Parties may call on the IVG to assist in this respect.

7. Israelis shall not use the designated roads as a means of entering Palestine without the relevant documentation and authorization.

8. In the event of regional peace, arrangements for Palestinian civilian use of designated roads in Israel shall be agreed and come into effect.

ARTICLE X: SITES OF RELIGIOUS SIGNIFICANCE

1. The Parties shall establish special arrangements to guarantee access to agreed sites of religious significance, as will be detailed in Annex X. These arrangements will apply, inter alia, to the Tomb of the Patriarchs in Hebron and Rachel's Tomb in Bethlehem, and Nabi Samuel.

2. Access to and from the sites will be by way of designated shuttle facilities from the relevant border crossing to the sites.

3. The Parties shall agree on requirements and procedures for granting licenses to authorized private shuttle operators.

4. The shuttles and passengers will be subject to MF inspection.

5. The shuttles will be escorted on their route between the border crossing and the sites by the MF.

6. The shuttles shall be under the traffic regulations and jurisdiction of the Party in whose territory they are traveling.

7. Arrangements for access to the sites on special days and holidays are detailed in Annex X.

8. The Palestinian Tourist Police and the MF will be present at these sites.

9. The Parties shall establish a joint body for the religious administration of these sites.

10. In the event of any incidents involving Israeli citizens and requiring criminal or legal proceedings, there will be full cooperation between the Israeli and Palestinian authorities according to arrangements to be agreed upon. The Parties may call on the IVG to assist in this respect.

11. Israelis shall not use the shuttles as a means of entering Palestine without the relevant documentation and authorization.

12. The Parties shall protect and preserve the sites of religious significance listed in Annex X and shall facilitate visitation to the cemeteries listed in Annex X.

ARTICLE XI: BORDER REGIME

1. There shall be a border regime between the two states, with movement between them subject to the domestic legal requirements of each and to the provisions of this Agreement as detailed in Annex X.

2. Movement across the border shall only be through designated border crossings.

3. Procedures in border crossings shall be designed to facilitate strong trade and economic ties, including labor movement between the Parties.

4. Each Party shall each, in its respective territory, take the measures it deems necessary to ensure that no persons, vehicles, or goods enter the territory of the other illegally.

5. Special border arrangements in Jerusalem shall be in accordance with Article 6 above.

ARTICLE XII: WATER

ARTICLE XIII: ECONOMIC RELATIONS

ARTICLE XIV: LEGAL COOPERATION

ARTICLE XV: PALESTINIAN PRISONERS AND DETAINEES

1. In the context of this Permanent Status Agreement between Israel and Palestine, the end of conflict, cessation of all violence, and the robust security

arrangements set forth in this Agreement, all the Palestinian and Arab prisoners detained in the framework of the Israeli-Palestinian conflict prior to the date of signature of this Agreement, DD/MM/2003, shall be released in accordance with the categories set forth below and detailed in Annex X.

i. Category A: all persons imprisoned prior to the start of the implementation of the Declaration of Principles on May 4, 1994, administrative detainees, and minors, as well as women, and prisoners in ill health shall be released immediately upon the entry into force of this Agreement.

ii. Category B: all persons imprisoned after May 4, 1994 and prior to the signature of this Agreement shall be released no later than eighteen months from the entry into force of this Agreement, except those specified in Category C.

iii. Category C: Exceptional cases—persons whose names are set forth in Annex X—shall be released in thirty months at the end of the full implementation of the territorial aspects of this Agreement set forth in Article 5/7/v.

ARTICLE XVI: DISPUTE SETTLEMENT MECHANISM

1. Disputes related to the interpretation or application of this Agreement shall be resolved by negotiations within a bilateral framework to be convened by the High Steering Committee.

2. If a dispute is not settled promptly by the above, either Party may submit it to mediation and conciliation by the IVG mechanism in accordance with Article 3.

3. Disputes which cannot be settled by bilateral negotiation and/or the IVG mechanism shall be settled by a mechanism of conciliation to be agreed upon by the Parties.

4. Disputes which have not been resolved by the above may be submitted by either Party to an arbitration panel. Each Party shall nominate one member of the three-member arbitration panel. The Parties shall select a third arbiter from the agreed list of arbiters set forth in Annex X either by consensus or, in the case of disagreement, by rotation.

ARTICLE XVII: FINAL CLAUSES

Including a final clause providing for a UNSCR/UNGAR resolution endorsing the agreement and superceding the previous UN resolutions.

The English version of this text will be considered authoritative.

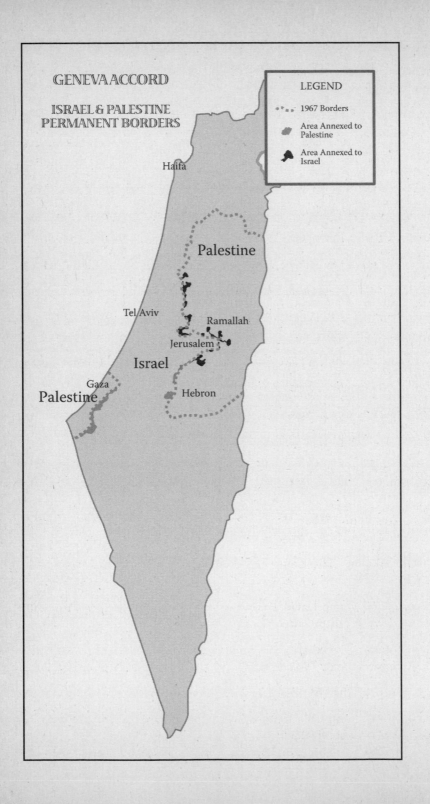

SELECT BIBLIOGRAPHY

Aburish, Said K., *Arafat: From Defendant to Dictator*, Britain, Bloomsbury Publishing, 1998.

Arzt, Donna E., *Refugees into Citizens*, U.S.A., Council on Foreign Relation Press, 1997.

Bavli, Dan, *Dreams and Opportunities Missed, 1967–1973*, Jerusalem, Carmel Publications, 2002.

Bechor, Guy, *PLO Lexicon*, Israel, Ministry of Defense, 1995.

Beilin, Yossi, *Touching Peace*, London, Weidenfeld & Nicolson, 1999.

Enderlin, Charles, *Paix ou Guerres*, Paris, Bussiere Camedan Imprimeries Stock, 1997.

Hirschfeld, Yair, *Oslo: A Formula for Peace*, Israel, Am Oved, 2000 (Hebrew).

Klein, Menachem, *Jerusalem: The Contested City*, New York University Press, 2001.

Morris, Benny, *The Birth of the Palestinian Refugee Problem, 1947–1949*, Cambridge University Press, 1987.

Netanyahu, Benjamin, *A Place Among the Nations*, New York, Bantam Books, 1993.

Netanyahu, Benjamin, *Fighting Terrorism*, U.S.A., Noonday Press, 1997.

Savir, Uri, *The Process*, New York, Random House, 1998.

Watson, Geoffrey R., *The Oslo Accords*, U.S.A., Oxford University Press, 2000.

ARTICLES

Baskin, Gershon, "What Went Wrong: Oslo, The PLO (PA), Israel, Some Additional Facts," http://www.ipcri.org.

Haniyeh, Akram, "The Camp-David Papers," http://www.nad-plo.org/eye/cdpapers.pdf.

Horowitz, Uri, "Camp David 2 and President Clinton's Bridging Proposals—The Palestinian View," http://www.tau.ac.il/jcss/sa/v3n4p5.html.

Meital, Yoram, "The Khartoum Conference and Egyptian Policy After the 1967 War: A Reexamination," *Middle East Journal*, Vol 54, No. 1 Winter 2000, pp 64–82.

Ma'oz, Moshe, "The Oslo Peace Process: From Breakthrough to Breakdown."

Pundak, Ron, "From Oslo to Taba: What Went Wrong," http://www.peres-center.org/downloads/survival.pdf.

INDEX